Press comments on
THE ROUGH GUIDE TO THE INTERNET

"Über-hip. Smarter than *Dummies*. Now even idiots
can become Internet savants"
*Newsweek*

"Anyone who isn't ordering and selling this by the
lorry-load shouldn't be running a bookshop"
*The Bookseller*

"A seriously good book. The best, in fact"
*Sun Herald, Sydney*

"If knowledge is power, this is a pocket-sized
battering ram"
*Kansas Morning Star*

"Cuts through the hype and makes all others look
like nerdy textbooks"
*The Australian*

"Best little guide to the Internet I've ever seen"
*British Computer Society Bulletin*

"A boon. Simply written, painless practical advice"
*Business Traveller*

# THE ROUGH GUIDE TO

# The Internet

There are more than 150 Rough Guide travel,
phrasebook, and music titles, covering
destinations from Amsterdam to Zimbabwe,
languages from Czech to Vietnamese, and musics
from World to Opera and Jazz.

To find out more about Rough Guides,
and to check out our coverage of more than
10,000 destinations, get connected to the Internet
with this guide and find us on the Web at:

www.roughguides.com/

This book is dedicated to the memory of my mother

# Acknowledgements

There are many I should thank for the staggering success of this book, particularly at Rough Guides and Penguin, as well as those who helped research, edit and shape the text in this edition: namely Jason Smith, David Pitchford, Johan Ingles-le Nobel, Ian Howie, Orla Duane and Henry Iles.

But this year I'd like to break tradition and use this short space to acknowledge my mother, who died of a brain tumor last November. Although I was able to return home and help my father nurse her through the last months, I feel I've never really thanked her formally. It's hard to look at yourself objectively and attribute so much of what's you to a parent when you've spent most of your life trying to prove you're an individual. I guess this means I'm finally giving in. I admit what little sense I'm running with was at least partly bashed in by my mother. And what a bashing it was.

For instance, she would never answer my questions, but instead make me work things out myself. She made me recite infuriating phrases like "good, better, best, never let it rest", "a place for everything and everything in its place", and inevitably "temper never helps". Stuff I didn't want to know, stuff I didn't want to do, stuff that simply made me cranky. That was her specialty. But somehow it all sunk home, and this book is just one of the many byproducts. And you know what? As much as she was the bane of my life, if we had our time all over again, I wouldn't change a thing about her.

# THE ROUGH GUIDE TO

# The Internet

## by Angus J. Kennedy

ROUGH
GUIDES

## Rough Guide to the Internet Credits

**Text editor**: Orla Duane
**Series Editor**: Mark Ellingham
**Production**: Julia Bovis, Michelle Draycott, Helen Ostick,
Katie Pringle
**Design and layout**: Henry Iles
**Proofreading**: Elaine Pollard

## Publishing Information

This sixth edition published October 2000 by
Rough Guides Ltd, 62–70 Shorts Gardens, London WC2H 9AH
375 Hudson Street, New York 10014
Email: *mail@roughguides.co.uk*

## Distributed by the Penguin Group

Penguin Books Ltd, 27 Wrights Lane, London W8 5TZ,
Penguin Putnam USA Inc., 375 Hudson Street, New York
10014, Penguin Books Canada Ltd, 10 Alcorn Avenue,
Toronto, Ontario MV4 1E4, Penguin Books Australia Ltd,
PO Box 257, Ringwood, Victoria 3134,
Penguin Books (NZ) Ltd, 182–190 Wairau Road, Auckland 10

Printed in the United Kingdom by Omnia Books Ltd.

© Angus J. Kennedy, 2000
528 pages; includes index

A catalogue record for this book is available
from the British Library
ISBN 1-85828-551-8

# Contents

# Read Me

## WHAT THIS BOOK'S ABOUT

Everyone I meet tells me the Internet is moving too fast to keep up. And not just beginners either. Even the propeller heads are struggling. So if you're new to the Net, you must find the whole thing pretty daunting. The simple truth is you don't need to know that much to find your way around. You don't even need to buy any software. But you could certainly use a helping hand to get started. It's important to be set up properly in the first place and to allow yourself to be steered in the right direction. On top of that you'll need to know what works and what doesn't. Otherwise you'll waste a lot of time.

What you don't need is to be patronized or misled. You'll get nowhere online by thinking of yourself as a "dummy" or an "idiot". If that's the way you regard yourself, then the Internet is not for you. Nor is this guide. No matter what your age, the Internet will become a cornerstone of your education. It will make you smarter. It will force you to think. It will fundamentally change your life for the better. But best of all it will be fun.

I have very little patience for bad business practices, flaky software and technology for technology's sake. This guide doesn't attempt to mince words, nor does it set out to waste your time. I write short sentences that are short on jargon. I own no stocks. I have no vested interests. I even list Rough Guides' competitors in the travel section of the Web guide. So while I might be fitting you out with everything from Microsoft this year, that's only because it's what's best right now. Next year might be a different story. But if you want next year's story, you'll have to buy next year's guide. Quite a lot will have changed by then. It always does.

Start by skimming the Basics (the first half). It's crammed with step-by-step instructions on everything you'll need to know from choosing an Internet provider to building your own Web site. You won't need to read every word, but it wouldn't hurt to come back and read it properly later when your demands are higher. The second part contains the Web guide, which is like a condensed directory listing of the Web sites you should visit first. Of course, it's only the tip of the iceberg, but it's capable of leading you to everything else.

If you only read one chapter, make it "Finding It". Know that back to front and you'll have the Net around your little finger. You'll be surprised at how quickly you become an expert.

The fact that I find myself flipping through this guide from time to time suggests to me that it's as much a desktop reference for old timers as a beginner's guide. If I've done my job properly, I'm hoping you'll buy it again, and maybe even keep a dog-eared copy by your computer for many years to come.

Best wishes and bon voyage!

Angus Kennedy
angus@easynet.co.uk

# 1

# FAQs

## FREQUENTLY ASKED QUESTIONS

**B**efore we get into the nitty-gritty of what you can do on the Internet – and what it can do for you – let's answer a few of the most Frequently Asked Questions (or FAQs, as acronym-loving Netizens call them).

## Big-picture questions

### Okay, what's this Internet good for?

**The Internet**, or the **Net** as it's more often called, is a real bag of tricks. You can seek, and usually find, answers to every question you've ever had, send messages or documents across the world in a flash, shop in another continent, sample new music, dabble in the stock market, visit art galleries, read books, play games, chat, catch the latest news from back home, make new friends with similar interests, grab free software, manage your bank account or just fritter hours away surfing across waves of visual bubble-gum.

That's not to say the Internet is merely something to play on when you get home from work. Far from it. The Net is also a serious business communications tool for everyday correspondence, marketing products, financial transactions, customer support, publishing, and much more. In fact, it's become as indispensable as the fax and telephone.

## Sounds like fun, but what is it exactly?

Strictly speaking, the Internet is an **international network of computers** linked up to exchange information. The word Internet is a contraction of **inter**national and **net**work.

The core of this international network consists of computers permanently joined through high-speed connections. To get on the Net, you simply connect your computer to any of these networked computers via an **Internet Service Provider**. Once you're **online** (connected to the Net) your computer can talk to any other computer on the Internet whether it's down the street or on the other side of the world.

That's plain enough, but if you want a more picky definition you have to consider what it's used for as well. Mostly, that's the transfer of **electronic mail** (**email**) and digital publishing on the **World Wide Web**. So when people say they found something on the "Internet", they didn't find it by randomly zipping around the wires hooking up the computers, they either retrieved it from where it was stored on a computer connected to this international network, or someone sent it to them by electronic mail.

Most importantly, the Net is not about computers or the fancy phone lines that string them together. **It's about people,**

**communication, and sharing knowledge**. It's about over-coming physical boundaries so like minds can meet. And that's why you want it.

## So, is this "the Information Superhighway"?

The Information Superhighway is a term so out of fashion, indeed almost cringe-worthy, that it's almost due to come back in. Whatever you want to call it, Al Gore's vision, as talked up by software magnate Bill Gates and pals, is still some way beyond the horizon. The Net has huge capabilities for cheap, global, and immediate communication; it may grow to dominate areas of **publishing**, **news,** and **education**; it is already providing an alternative **shopping mall**; and it will almost certainly make major inroads into **banking** and **customer support**. But, to get big-screen fingertip action, like video on demand, we'll need a much faster network than today's Internet.

The Net's main arteries are already straining under the pressure of new users, and some fear it may suffer a seizure before it gets better. Until the **Internet backbone** can withstand the added demands from **high-speed alternatives** such as ADSL, cable, and direct satellite feeds, the real digital "revolution" is still on hold.

## The Internet & the Web are the same thing, right?

No, but don't be embarrassed. Not too many reporters seem to know the difference either. The **World Wide Web** (or Web) is the popular face of the Internet. It provides a simple way to navigate the vast troves of information stored online. In practice it works a bit like flicking through a huge magazine by clicking on links with your mouse. But, the Internet is much more than just the Web. See p.73.

## What's the difference between the Internet, AOL and CompuServe?

CompuServe and AOL are classed as **Online Services**. They plug in to the Internet, and thus form part of the Internet, but each also has exclusive services and content available only to their members and not to the general Internet public. See p.41.

## Is it another state of the USA?

If you're reading this from the relative comfort of one of the 50 United States of America, you've every reason to feel smug. The Net is about as chock-full of US content as your average bottle of diet cherry soda. If not, you might find it a touch frustrating at times that you can, say, get everything down to the local traffic conditions and grasshopper counts in

Note:
Alaska & Hawaii
Not to scale
www.50states.com

some Midwest burb, but next to nothing about your bustling tropical metropolis. You needn't worry too much as the rest of the world's rapidly catching up – though the US will probably continue to lead the way in many areas. Of course, if you feel entrepreneurial you can always plagiarize a few smart ideas from abroad and apply them locally. Or better, start a world first on your home turf!

## What is "new media"?

Advertising suits and recruitment agencies use the term **new media** mainly to differentiate between the **old** media world of print, radio, and television and the **new** media world of audio, video, print, and software publishing on the Internet and other digital formats such as CD-ROM.

## Can I shop online?

You bet, and we've dedicated a whole chapter to it (p.201).

## Can I make money out of the Internet?

Yes, no, maybe – perhaps it's better to ask, "Can I continue to make money without the Internet?" The last few years have seen a gold rush in the computer hardware, software, training,

[ 7 ]

and publishing industries. Some who got in early, made a killing getting businesses on the Web – the Net's "commercial zone". Today, it's settled down somewhat. Web page designers are commonplace, and can no longer charge extortionate rates unless they're tied in with a major agency. However, those with serious technical and programming skills are always in big demand.

If you're wondering whether to throw a Web site into your existing **marketing mix** to help boost sales, the answer's probably yes. But rather than use it to try to attract customers, it's better to think of the Net as a place to post in-depth product literature, provide customer support, and canvass feedback. Not too many firms are making big money from **direct sales** – though that's improving, particularly for hard-to-get products, or deep-catalog items such as CDs, books, and computer parts.

Another way to profit is to charge others to **advertise on your Web page**. You'll either need to run a very popular site or attract a certain type of customer, and you are usually paid according to the number of times visitors pursue links from your site to your sponsor's. Alternatively, if your site generates heavy traffic and looks promising, someone may want to buy you outright.

Advertising on the World Wide Web is perfectly acceptable but emailing protocols are more delicate. **Never, ever, ever, send bulk email** other than to people you know or who've requested information. And never post an advertisement in Usenet or to a mailing list. **Junk email is called "spam", and those who send it (spammers) are universally detested.** Try it and you'll be flooded with hate mail, and kicked offline. On the other hand, email is by far the most efficient direct response device you'll find. For instance, you could set up an **autoresponder** to send out product details upon receipt of a blank message. No dictating over the phone, no data entry from a coupon. It's instant and informal. Plus, you'll have their email address on record to follow up later. So next time you put your phone number on an ad, put on your email address, too, and compare response rates.

## Is there a lot of really weird stuff on the Net?

Yes, lots. Just like in real life, except it's easier to find. See our Web guide, "Weird" (p.432).

## Which is better: the Net or an encyclopedia?

They don't really compare. You can look something up in an encyclopedia and get a concise answer instantly. Encyclopedias are generally well researched and reliable, and the answer is probably correct. They're also expensive, bulky, date quickly, parochial, conservative, and might not provide enough, or any, information. The Net, on the other hand, isn't edited by a single publisher. So you can find a diverse range of factoids and opinions on even the most obscure subjects. That means you're more likely to get a rounded view, but the process might take longer. Of course, the Net has the best of both worlds as most of the major encyclopedias have their very latest editions online. And what's more, they're free!

## So who's in charge?

Well, technically no-one, though a number of powerful commercial players such as **CompuServe**, **AOL**, **Microsoft**, **Cisco**, **MCI**, **Worldcom**, and **Netscape** have played major roles in putting the framework in place, and there are various bodies concerned with the Net's administration. Foremost among the latter are **ICANN** which co-ordinates domain names; the **Internet Society** which, amongst other things, acts as a clearing house for technical standards; and the World Wide Web Consortium (**W3C**), which mulls over the Web's future. See: http://www.astalavista.com/en/resources.asp

No-one, however, actually "runs" the Internet. As the Internet is, in effect, a network of networks, most responsibilities are contained within each local network. Say you have connection problems, you would call your connection supplier. If you object to material located on a server in another country, you'd have to complain to the administrator of that local server.

While it certainly promotes freedom of speech, **the Internet is not so anarchic** as some sections of the media would have you believe. If you break the laws of your country while using the Net, and you're caught, you're liable to prosecution, irrespective of whether you're accessing something that's legal, or overlooked, at the source. So just because you can download a copy of Photoshop from the public domain of a Russian Web server it doesn't make you immune to copyright laws at home. And conversely, while you might have the freedom to express your views about the leader of a foreign oppression, nationals of that state may not be so free to read it.

## But isn't it run by the Pentagon and the CIA?

When the Internet was first conceived thirty-odd years ago, as a network for the American Defense Department, its purpose was to act as a nuclear-attack-resistant method of exchanging scientific information and intelligence. But that was then. In the 1970s and 1980s several other networks, such as the **National Science Foundation Network** (NSFNET), joined, linking the Internet to research agencies and universities. It was probably no coincidence that as the Cold War petered out, the Internet became more publicly accessible and the nature of the beast changed totally and irreversibly. **Intelligence agencies** have the same access to the Internet as everyone else, but whether they use it to monitor insurgence and crime is simply a matter for speculation.

## So is the Net basically a geek hangout?

It's about as geek as you want it to be, which can vary between twin hip-slung logic probes with a matching pocket protector, to not in the slightest. They say if you're bored with the Net, you're bored with life itself.

## But isn't it yet another male-dominated bastion?

No, those days are well behind us. Recent studies reckon the online population in the USA to be reaching 50:50, with women now driving the growth of the Internet. Meanwhile at AOL, **women actually outnumber men**.

## Will I make friends on the Internet?

It's easy to meet people with common interests by joining in **Usenet (newsgroup) or mailing list discussions**. And being able to discuss sensitive issues with strangers while retaining a comfortable degree of anonymity often makes for startlingly intimate communication.

Translating email pen pals into the real world of human contact, or even romance, is another matter.

# More technical questions

## What's electronic mail, again?

Electronic mail or **email** is a way of sending messages from one computer to another. A letter can cross the world in seconds.

## What's an Intranet?

The mechanism that passes information between computers on the Internet can be used in exactly the same way over a local network such as in an office. When this is not publicly accessible, it's called an **Intranet**. Many companies use Intranets to distribute internal documents – in effect publishing Web pages for their own private use.

## What are newsgroups, mailing lists, and chat?

**Usenet** – the Net's prime discussion area – comprises over 85,000 **newsgroups**, each dedicated to a specific topic. So if you have a question, this is the place to raise it. Usenet messages are stored online for a matter of days or weeks, a bit like an online notice board.

**Mailing lists** perform a similar function, though the messages aren't stored online. The discussions are carried out by email. Each list has a central email address. Everything sent to that address goes to everyone on the list.

**Chat**, on the other hand, is instant, like a conversation. It's typically more of a social medium than an information tool. For more on Usenet, see p.129; Mailing lists, see p.124; and Chat, see p.188.

## What's a portal?

The tools for searching the Net have improved exponentially over the last few years, but the methodologies have barely changed. Despite that, they now cluster under a variety of new names courtesy of those very smart people with MBAs. And you can bet those names will continue morphing into even more marketing-friendly nonsense.

You'll almost certainly come across the term **portal**. A site can be classed as a portal if you go there to be directed elsewhere. All search engines and directories (see p.163) are portals. If it concentrates on a specific subject, it's classed as a **vortal** (vertical portal). A site is a **hub** if you would go there regularly for news or information contained within the site. But if they make a concerted effort to attract repeat visitors by setting up bulletin boards, discussion lists, chat forums, or free Web space for members, they might prefer to call themselves a **community**.

## How can I get my own Web page?

Putting a page on the Web is a two-step process. First, you have to prepare it in **HTML**, the Web's mark-up language. Even a word processor can do a basic job by saving a document as HTML. To prepare something more elaborate, you need to use a dedicated HTML editing tool, or to learn HTML code – which isn't too hard for a computer language. Once you have an HTML document ready to go, you need to transfer it to your own special reserved **Web space**. For more on this, flip to "Creating Your Own Web Page" (p.239).

## Can I rely on email?

In general Internet **email** is considerably more reliable than the postal service. If a message doesn't get through, it should bounce back to you telling you what went wrong. Occasionally, though, mail does go astray. During 1997, AOL and Microsoft Network – to name just the big players – had severe mail outages resulting in the delay, and in some cases loss, of email. And many corporate mail servers have had growing pains, experiencing holdups and the odd deletion, especially over weekends. But on the whole you can confidently assume that email will arrive. If you don't get a reply within a few days, of course, you can always send your message again. At worst, it will act as a reminder. If you find your mail regularly takes more than a few minutes to arrive, you should seriously consider switching providers.

## Who pays for the international calls?

The Internet is barely affected by political boundaries and distance. For example, suppose you're in Boston, and you want to buzz someone in Bangkok. Provided you both have Net access, it's as quick, easy, and cheap as sending a message across the street. You compose your message, connect to your local Internet Service Provider, upload your mail and then disconnect.

Your **mail server** examines the message's address to determine where it has to go, and then passes it on to its appropriate neighbor, which will do the same. This usually entails routing it toward the **backbone** – the chain of high-speed links that carry the bulk of the Net's long-haul traffic. Each subsequent link will ensure that the message heads towards Bangkok rather than Bogotá or Brisbane. The whole process should take no more than a few seconds.

Apart from your Internet access subscription, **you pay only for the local phone call**. Your data will scuttle through many different networks, each with its own methods of recouping the communication costs – but adding to your phone bill isn't one of them.

## Then how does the pricing model work?

Once you're on the Net, most of what's there is free. But unless you have free access through work or study, you'll probably need to pay for the privilege of being connected. That means paying an **Internet Service Provider** (ISP) to allow you to hook into its network. Depending on where you live, that could be a set price per month or year, an hourly rate or a tariff based on how much you download. Then on top of that, you'll have some sort of **telephone, ISDN or cable charge**. It's possible – indeed probable – that none of this money will ever go to the people who supply the content you'll be viewing. It simply goes toward maintaining the network. This imbalance is unlikely to continue. In the future you'd expect many publications (or sites) might charge a subscription. As yet, that's still rare, other than for technical and financial publications, so enjoy it while it lasts.

## What about free Internet access – is it really free?

Internet access is a costly business to run, so revenue has to come from somewhere. In the UK, where free ISPs have been flourishing to the point of becoming the norm, they survive by getting a slice of your phone bill, both while you're online and through premium rate support lines. This situation exists only because of the UK's extortionate timed local call charges. Still, if you don't use support, a free ISP is cheaper than one that charges. There's no guarantee that either would provide better service.

Elsewhere, where local calls are unmetered or free, such as the US and Australia, access is subsidized by bombarding customers with advertising, tracking their movements, or by locking them within their sponsor's sites. As yet, these aren't wildly successful or attractive.

## What are hosts, servers, and clients?

In Net-speak, any computer that's open to external online access is known as a **server** or **host**. The software you use to perform online operations such as transfer files, read mail, surf the Web, or post articles to Usenet, is called a **client**.

A Web client is more commonly called a **Web browser** – a field dominated by **Netscape** and **Microsoft (Internet Explorer)**. A **Web server** is a machine where Web pages are stored and made available for outside access.

## How do I read an email address?

Internet email addresses might look odd at first glance but they're really quite logical. They all take the form someone@somewhere. As soon as you read that aloud, it should begin to make sense. For example, take the email address angus@roughguides.com The "@" sign says it's an email address and means "at", so the address reads "angus at Rough Guides dot com". From that alone you could deduce that the sender's name is "Angus" and he's somehow associated with "Rough Guides". It's not always that obvious but the format never changes.

The somewhere part is the **domain name** of the Internet **host** that handles someone's mail – often their Internet Service Provider or workplace. Anyone who uses someone's provider or works with them could also share the same **domain name** in their email address, but they wouldn't be called someone. That's because the someone part identifies who, or what, they are at that host address. It's usually a name or nickname they choose themselves, or, with companies, a function like "help" or "info".

## What's a domain name?

A **domain name** identifies and locates a host computer or service on the Internet. It often relates to the name of a business, organization, or service and must be registered in much the same way as a company name. It breaks down further into the subdomain, domain type, and country code. Look at: sophie@thehub.com.au The subdomain is **thehub** (an Internet Service Provider), its domain type **com** suggests it's a company or commercial site, and the country code **au** indicates it's in Australia.

Every country has its own distinct code, even if it's not always used. These include:

| | |
|---|---|
| **au** | Australia |
| **ca** | Canada |
| **cc** | Cocos Islands |
| **de** | Germany |
| **es** | Spain |
| **fr** | France |
| **jp** | Japan |
| **nl** | Netherlands |
| **no** | Norway |
| **uk** | United Kingdom |

If an address doesn't specify a country code, it's more than likely, but not necessarily, in the USA. At present, domain types are usually one of the following; however, the range will expand dramatically as recent changes to the domain registration system filter through:

| | |
|---|---|
| ac | Academic (UK) |
| com | Company or commercial organization |
| co | Company or commercial organization (UK, NZ) |
| edu | Educational institution |
| gov | Government |
| mil | Military |
| net | Internet gateway or administrative host* |
| org | Non-profit organization |

For more on the way domains work, see:
http://www.internic.net/faq.html

*Because of the domain name shortage, it's now become acceptable for commercial sites to use .net

## What's an IP address?

Every computer on the Net has its unique numerical IP (Internet Protocol) address. A typical address is four numbers separated by dots and looks like: 149.174.211.5 This is its official location on the Internet.

Your computer will be assigned an IP address when you log on. If it's **dynamically**, or **server**, **allocated**, the last few digits could vary each time you connect.

Internet traffic control relies on these numbers. For example, a router might send all addresses beginning with 213 in one direction, and the rest in another. Eventually, through a process of elimination, everything ends up in the right place.

Thankfully, you don't have to use these numbers. Humans are numerically dim so we use domain names instead, by matching up the names and numbers in a table. Isn't it easier to remember "roughguides" than 204.52.130.112?

Not all IP addresses have attached domain names, but a domain name will not become active until it's matched to an IP address. The table is co-ordinated across a network of **Domain Name Servers** (DNS). Before you can send a message to someone@somewhere.com, your mail program has to ask your Domain Name Server to convert somewhere.com into an IP address. This process is called a **DNS lookup**.

## What's bandwidth and broadband?

**Bandwidth**, which is expressed in bits per second (bps), describes Internet connection capacity. It measures the speed at which you can download material from the Net. Modems are only capable of achieving a relatively **low bandwidth** connection. **Cable**, **satellite**, and **ADSL** fall into the so-called **broadband** category, meaning that they're much faster than modems. Strictly speaking, though, the bits and bytes don't move any faster as they're limited by the speed of light. A faster connection simply means you can move more of those bits and bytes across the wires at a time.

## I have a fast connection so why are some sites still slow?

The speed at which you connect to your ISP can make a huge difference to the speed at which you can cruise the Web, listen to audio, and download files, but it's not the final word. Once you start accessing material stored outside your ISP's server – often everything except your mail – you're at the mercy of the bandwidth of all the links in between you and the external server. It's not unlike driving across town. At peak hours, when there are lots of other cars on the road, it's going to take longer. So if a site is painfully slow, try again later and hopefully the traffic will have subsided.

# What if?

## What if I'm harassed online?

It's not easy to harass someone seriously via the Net and get away with it. After all, it generates evidence in writing. There have already been convictions for relatively mild threats posted to Usenet newsgroups. Apart from the nature of the harassment, whether you have a case for action will depend on where you're both based. Across US State lines it becomes an FBI matter, while internationally you might have no recourse other than to appeal to their ISP.

If you're being harassed by email; in a newsgroup, mailing list or chat channel; or on a Web page, you needn't put up with it. Though, to start with maybe you should. If you simply ignore them they'll probably go away. Most of the time, this is the best defense. If you don't put up a fight, then you're no fun. And if you're being harassed unfairly in a public forum, others will usually come to your aid. But if it persists, or the harassment becomes serious you may have to react.

Your first action should be to contact them personally and politely ask them to desist. If that doesn't work, you'll have to decide whether reporting them to their ISP, and getting them booted offline will start an ongoing vendetta. Whether you have their email address or not, you can find out their ISP by tracing their IP address. That's where a Traceroute/WHOIS tool such as **NeoTrace** (http://www.neoworks.com) comes in handy. Even if they've forged their email address, you should be able to figure out where it's come from by picking through the headers for the originating IP address. Once you have the domain responsible, try an email to: abuse@ that domain. If this sounds too technical, call your ISP support for help, or turn the matter entirely over to them. For more, see: http://www.cyberangels.org and http://www.getnetwise.org

## Can I cancel an email I've sent?

No. So, you'd better think before you click "send".

## What if my children discover pornography or drugs?

If you're at all prudish, you'll get a nasty shock when you hit the Web. You only need type **the merest hint of innuendo** into a search engine to come face to face with a porno advert. In fact, what once wasn't much more than schoolboys trading Big & Busty scans has become the Net's prime cash cow. Most perfectly normal kids will search on a swearword the first chance they get – after all, children are pretty childish. Consequently, if they're the slightest bit curious about sex, it won't be long before they end up at a porno merchant. That's the truth, if you can handle it.

To be blunt, the Net isn't meant for kids, and furthermore, it's not a babysitter. If your children are at a sensitive age, and you leave them online unsupervised, you are a bad parent. While there are plenty of online activities that are perfectly suitable for all ages, risky material is never more than a few clicks away.

What can you do about it? Well, that depends whether you'd rather shield them from such things or prepare them for it. There are **censoring programs** that attempt to filter out questionable material, either by letting only known sites through, banning certain sites, or withholding pages containing shady words. Internet Explorer and Netscape, for example, can restrict access according to a rating system. Bear in mind that a smart kid – and no doubt that's what you're trying to raise – might be able to find a way to veto these filters. Whatever the case, if you're worried about your kids, the Net, and sex, then talk to them about it.

As for **drugs**, there's no way to get them from the Net. In fact, they're likely to find out the dangers of abusing them. So when they come across them in real life they'll be informed. And that has to be a good thing.

If you'd like to spy on their online activities, simply click on their browser's History (p.80) button. Should they be smart enough to work out how to cover their tracks, they're probably smart enough to know how to handle what they find.

## What about bomb plans?

 While the thought of your teenage son locked in his bedroom stacking his hard drive with porn might make you feel a bit uneasy, at least you know it's not going to kill him. Unfortunately, the same can't be said of the advice contained in the **Anarchist's Cookbook** and similar titles. Again, like porn, it's mostly a boy thing, and you'll have to assume he'll find it. Not that you can get mad at him for being interested. Things that go bang have been the focus of teenage fascination long before the Internet arrived.

As fun as they might make it all sound, it's vital for him to know he can't trust their recipes. These guides are ill researched, entirely irresponsible and downright dangerous. And, of course, about as against the law as it gets. The sooner you discuss the subject the better.

## Will being on the Internet put me at risk?

Unless you go out of your way to invite trouble, the Internet should impose no added risk on your **personal safety**. However, you should still take a few precautions:

Don't put your home address or phone number in; your email or Usenet signature; your mail program's address book; an online email address register; or your chat profile. And, it goes without saying to bring a friend along if you decide to meet up with someone from a chat room.

On the other hand, **going online suddenly exposes your computer to all sorts of new risks**, particularly with Windows 95/98. The first thing to do once you're online is follow the instructions in our **Software Roundup** chapter (p.439) and update your browser with the latest security patches; install a firewall; and bring your virus protection software up to date. Once you've done that, you'll be close to invulnerable from external attacks on your machine, whether random or intentional. However, you'll still have to watch out for programs that might contain hidden nasties, especially ones that arrive by email.

## What are viruses, Trojans, and worms?

A **virus** is a program that infects other program files, or floppy disk boot sectors, so that it can spread from machine to machine. In order to catch a virus you must either run an infected program, or boot your machine with an infected floppy disk inserted fully into the drive. There are thousands of strains, most of which are no more than a nuisance, but potentially they're capable of setting off a time bomb that could destroy the contents of your hard drive. A **macro virus** spreads by infecting Microsoft Word or Excel documents.

**Worms**, like viruses, are designed to spread. But rather than wait for a human being to transfer the infected file or disk, they actively replicate themselves over a network such as the Internet. For example, they might send themselves to all the contacts in your email address book. That means worms can spread much faster than viruses. The **"email viruses"** that made world news recently were strictly speaking, worms, not viruses.

A **Trojan** (horse) is a program with a hidden agenda. When you run the program it will do something unexpected, usually without your knowledge. While viruses are designed to spread, Trojans are usually (though not always) designed to deliver a once-off pay packet. There are dozens of known Trojans circulating the Net, most with the express purpose of opening a back door to your computer to allow hackers into your system while you're online. A custom-built Trojan can be bound to any program, so that when you install it, the Trojan will also install in the background. For a sobering insight into the power they can hand over to even the most inexperienced hackers, see: http://subseven.slak.org

## How can I stop them?

As mentioned tirelessly throughout this guide, if you're running Windows, the first thing you should do once you get online is **update your browser and pick up any security patches on offer**. This is extremely important, as the earlier versions of Outlook Express are susceptible to worms embedded in **ActiveX controls**. If you're unprotected, merely highlighting the message could infect you. If you receive a message telling you it contains an ActiveX control, tell the sender to update their system and then run a virus scan. Scanning and cleaning isn't enough, as they could easily reinfect themselves.

Next, get your virus and Trojan detection gear in order. Check our **Software Roundup** (p.439) for advice in that area. To protect yourself against hacking, including through backdoors opened by Trojans, install a **firewall program**.

The final, and most important, part is to **NEVER** run any program – a file ending in **.REG**, **.INF**, **.EXE**, **.COM**, **.VBS**, **.BAT**, or **.SHS** - that is sent to you by email, or through chat, no matter who sent it. Instead ask the sender to direct you to its source. Only download from the software publisher or through a reputable file repository, such as those listed in the software guides section of our Web guide (p.291). Treat the **gag programs** and **animated cards** that tend to circulate around the festive season, with utmost caution. These are some of the favorite vehicles of Trojan distributors.

Additionally, never accept to run a **macro** in any Microsoft Word or Excel document unless the sender assures you they've put it in for a good reason. If you use **Microsoft Office**, read the security advice at: http://officeupdate.microsoft.com

Finally, before you click on that attachment that appears to be a safe music, movie, image or document file, **check the icon** that comes with it. Is it the right one for that type of file? If not, you might find spaces have been inserted between the fake extension and the real one.

Some ISPs automatically scan your mail attachments for viruses. It's another factor to consider when shopping around for a provider. To see what's presently top of the virus pops, check the scanning stats at: http://www.star.net.uk

You'll find everything you need to know about viruses at:
http://antivirus.about.com
http://www.faqs.org/faqs/computer-virus/
http://www.symantec.com/avcenter/
http://www.cai.com/virusinfo/

## Should I forward virus warning emails?

Except for the odd petition, any email that insists you **forward it on to everyone you know** is almost certainly a **hoax**, or at best a **chain letter**. While the hysterical virus warnings might seem vaguely credible there is absolutely no excuse to fall for any email that suggests you might be **rewarded in some way** for forwarding it. If you get such a message, do not forward it to everyone you know. Instead flaunt your superiority by directing the forwarding peabrain to:

http://www.vmyths.com
http://www.chainletters.org/gallery.shtml
http://urbanlegends.about.com/culture/urbanlegends/

# Getting online

## What's full Internet access?

You can access the Internet – and send email – through several channels. But not all methods will let you do everything. The **World Wide Web**, **IRC**, **FTP**, and **Telnet** – key areas of the Net, which we'll deal with later in this book – require "full Internet access".

You can get full Internet access through any **Internet Service Provider** (**ISP**). You'll encounter a range of accounts, which may include standard **modem dial-up**, **ISDN**, **ADSL** and **cable.** There might also be a selection of pricing plans and added extras. Regardless of what type of full Internet access you choose, you'll be able to do the same things, though perhaps at different speeds.

## What do I need to get started?

You can get to the Net aboard an increasing number of devices from mobile phones to televisions, but the most popular and flexible route is via a home **PC**, hooked to an Internet Service Provider through a **modem**. So if you have a PC, a modem, and a telephone line, all you need next is an account with an ISP, and possibly some extra software to get rolling. This is covered in detail in the following chapters.

## Where can I get an email address?

You should get at least one email address thrown in by your Internet Provider with your **access account**. Many providers supply five or more addresses – enough for the whole family. The only problem with these addresses is that they tie you to that provider. If you want to switch providers, you either have to negotiate a mail-only account or obtain an address you can take on the road with you (see p.260). It's a hassle, either way, so choose your provider carefully.

If you already have an email address, say at work or college, but want a **more personal or funky-sounding address**, you can ask any ISP for a POP3 mail-only account, try a mail specialist such as MailBank (http://www.mailbank.com) or sign up with a Webmail or redirection service. That way you can choose an address and use it over any connection. To get yourself a free email address, see p.118.

## How can I find someone's email address?

See: "Finding It" (p.178).

## Will I need to learn any computer languages?

No. If you can work a word processor or spreadsheet, you'll have no difficulty tackling the Internet. You just have to get familiar with your Internet software, which in most cases isn't too difficult. The hardest part is **setting up for the first time**, but even that's becoming less of an issue as most ISPs supply startup packs or almost foolproof instructions.

Once online, most people access the Net through **graphical menu-based software**, with a similar feel to most Windows and Macintosh programs. And on the World Wide Web – the most popular part of the Net – **you hardly even need to type**: almost everything is accessible by a click on your mouse.

The one time you might need to use **UNIX commands** – the Internet's traditional computer "language" – would be when using Telnet to log on remotely to a UNIX computer and that's something most of us can avoid.

## Can I use the Internet if I can't use a computer?

As mentioned above, even if you can't type, you can still use the World Wide Web – all you have to do is **point your mouse and click**. That's about as far as you'll get though. If you've never had any contact with computers, consider the Internet a real opportunity. Don't think of computers as a daunting modern technology; they're only a means to an end. The best way to learn how to use a computer is to grab one and switch it on.

## So, how do I get connected?

Good question, and worth a whole chapter. **Read on.**

# 2

# Getting
# Connected

## GETTING ONLINE

**B**y now you should have come across a Net-connected terminal somewhere, perhaps through work, study or
friends. No matter where you live there should be somewhere nearby where you can rent Internet time by the hour
or even get online free, say at your local library. If you're not
in that position or you'd like to set it up at home, you
needn't wait. It's possible to get everything you need to be
up and running in a day or two. The good news is it's not
unreasonably expensive or complicated, and it's becoming
cheaper and easier by the day.

## You don't need to be a computer expert

Perhaps you're not already hooked up because you find the whole computing world a bit off-putting. Well, this is the perfect opportunity to get over it. The rewards of being online far outweigh the effort involved in learning to use a computer.

Although there's ample information in this guide to get you started on the Net, if you're entirely new to computers ask someone computer literate to baby-sit you through a session or two. If you don't know anyone suitable, drop into a **cybercafé** or **Internet center** (see "On the Road": p.266) and ask an attendant to kickstart you onto the World Wide Web. That's their business; they won't laugh at you, so there's no shame in admitting you're green. You should be able to figure out how to surf the Web within a matter of minutes. Finding your way around is another matter, but you're at an advantage – you have this guide.

If you strike problems remember that the **online community** – other folks on the Net – is always on tap for help as long as you direct your queries to the right area. Just wait and see; before long you'll be sharing your newfound expertise with others.

## What you'll need

Before you can get connected, you'll need three things: a **computer** with enough grunt to handle the software, an account with an **Internet Service Provider**, and a device – usually the fastest **modem** you can afford – to connect your computer to the Internet. How you connect can make the difference between pleasure and frustration. You don't necessarily need state-of-the-art computer gadgetry, but no matter what you have, you'll find a way to push it to the limit.

## Computer firepower

While it's possible to access the Net with almost any machine you could call a computer, if you can't run your Web browsing and mail software together without a lot of chugging noises coming from your hard drive, you'll get frustrated fast.

If you have an old **486 IBM-compatible PC** or **Macintosh 68030** series, equipped with at least **8MB RAM**, it's possible to get online in a fairly limited way by sticking to old software. You'll get further by adding more RAM, but it'll still be a struggle. For help with old Windows boxes, see: http://come.to/386/

While you can also connect to the Net with a slew of mobile phones, and portable devices such as the **Palm Pilot**, they're only meant for basic email, simple data retrieval, and bulletins on the run. Don't expect to browse the Net on a matchbox-sized screen.

For the full range of hardware that can connect you to the Net, see: http://www.allnetdevices.com

## PC, Mac or Linux?

If you're in the market for a new computer, you'll need to decide between a **PC** (running Microsoft Windows, typically) and a **Mac**. This can be an incredibly confusing question to answer. There's something of a holy war between supporters of the two platforms, as well as a rebellious undercurrent pushing the free **Linux** operating system. Unless you intend to make computing your life, you can safely overlook Linux for the time being. It's still too eggy for everyday use.

To be frank, **you won't get a straight answer from anyone** on this subject, particularly from the Mac minority, whose members can become **pathologically brand loyal**. Ignore anyone who tries to convince you that either option is without flaw or would deride you for choosing either. And for heaven's sake **don't bring the subject up at a dinner party!**

In other words, if you ask a Mac user for advice, they'll rarely steer you towards anything but a Mac. In some situations that might be good advice, but it will limit your options more than buying a PC. The Internet is overwhelmingly geared towards PCs. You might find yourself on the sidelines, (or entirely unaware), of the latest action, if that bothers you.

However, if you intend to work with **print standard color**, such as in publishing, get a Mac. Although PCs can now do the same job, Macs are so ingrained within the industry that it's not worth your while to go against the flow. You'll find it much easier to trade files with peers and turn to them for help. By all means check out the much-hyped **iMac**, but if you want to do anything serious, veer towards the more **expandable G4** range, with at the very least a 17" monitor.

While Apple's G4 processors are now comparable, and sometimes superior, to what's offered by Intel and AMD, you'll get more bangs per buck by going down the more popular Windows track. PCs have considerably **more (and newer) software**, **games**, and **peripheral options**, and are usually **a bit cheaper** for similar specifications. And since some **95 percent of computers run Windows** you won't feel like the entire industry is plotting against you. You'll soon find this out when you call your first ISP and ask if they support Macs.

With PCs, brand names mean less than **after-sales service**. PC components often come from several different manufacturers. The crunch comes when something goes wrong. Find out how long you'd be without your computer if it needs repair. Your corner shop might be able to do it on the spot, or help you set up your software. Name brands often offer a range of service agreements ranging from same-day replacement to potentially leaving you stranded for weeks. Don't undervalue a generous guarantee. And consider buying the same set-up as a friend so you have someone to lean on when things go haywire.

Whatever you buy, the Net is a full multimedia experience, so pack it with as much **memory** or **RAM** (64+ MB) as you can afford, a roomy **hard drive** (6+ Gig), a fast **CD-ROM or DVD drive** (for loading software and playing movies), a **decent monitor** (17") and check out the advanced options in **sound and video**.

## Do your own research

It's well beyond the scope of this book to unpick the entire Mac vs PC squabble. If you'd like to research further, scratch through this lot and decide for yourself. Caveat emptor!

### Comparisons

http://www.ihateapple.com/compare/
http://www.osopinion.com
http://www.people.cornell.edu/pages/jcs33/compare.html

### Pro PC:

http://geraldholmes.freeyellow.com
http://www.ihateapple.com
http://www.geocities.com/SiliconValley/Platform/2985/
http://www.geocities.com/SiliconValley/Sector/9295/

### Pro Mac:

http://www.macaddict.com
http://www.mackido.com
http://www.ihatewindows98.com

### Pro Linux:

http://www.slashdot.org

## Connecting your computer to the Net

A powerful computer won't make up for a slow link to the Internet. Get the fastest connection you can afford.

Unless you're hooked up through a network, you'll need a device to connect your computer to the telephone line or cable. There'll be a similar device at your ISP's end. This device will depend on the type of Internet account. The two main types are **Leased Line** and **dial-up**. Leased Lines are expensive and aimed at businesses that need to be permanently connected. Dial-up suits the casual user. Investigate the Net through a dial-up account before contemplating a Leased Line.

**Note:** If you're on a network at work or college, don't attempt to connect to the Net without your systems manager's supervision. Networked PCs and Macs can use the same software listed later in this book, but may connect to the Net differently.

## Buying a modem

 The cheapest, most popular, but slowest, way to connect is by installing a **modem** and dialing up through the standard telephone network. Modems come in three flavors: internal, external, and PCMCIA. Each has its advantages and disadvantages.

**Internal modems** are the cheapest option. They plug into a slot inside your computer called a bus. Installation is not difficult, but you do have to take the back off your computer and follow the instructions carefully (or get your computer store to do it). Because they're hidden inside your computer, internal modems don't take up desk space, clutter the back of your computer with extra cables, or require an external power source. On the downside, they lack the little lights to tell you how your call is going, and you can't swap them between computers without removing the case. If your PC

isn't cutting edge, avoid Soft Modems (eg. Winmodems).
These cut costs by using your PC's processor to do some of
their work. If your PC is not up to it, you can experience all
sorts of problems. Best to spend a little more to be safe.

An **external modem** is easier to install. Depending on the
model, it will simply plug straight in to your computer's serial
or USB (preferable) port, making it easily interchangeable
between machines (and simple to upgrade). External modems
require a separate power source, maybe even a battery. And
they usually give a visual indication of the call's progress
through a bank of flashing lights (LEDs).

The credit-card-sized **PCMCIA** modems are a mixture of
the two. They fit internally into the PC card slots common in
most modern notebooks and remove easily to free the slot for
something else. Being small makes them portable, which is of
supreme importance when you're traveling. They don't
require an external power source, but are expensive and you
can't use them with a desktop. You can, however, use any
external modem with a notebook simply by plugging it into
an available serial or USB port.

## All the way with 56K

Whichever type of modem you choose, the major issue is
speed. Data transfer speed is expressed in bits (not bytes!) per
second or **bps**. It can take up to ten bits to transfer a character. So a modem operating at 2400 bps (2.4 Kbps) would
transfer roughly 240 characters per second. That's about a
page of text every eight seconds. At 28.8 Kbps, you could
send the same page of text in two-thirds of a second.

A 14.4 Kbps (V.32) modem can browse the World Wide
Web, but only just. A faster modem might cost a little more,
but it will reduce your online charges, and give you more for
your money. The modem standard has now reached **56K**
(**V.90**)**,** which can theoretically download at up to 56 Kbps,

and upload at up to 33.6 Kbps. **Don't waste your money on anything less.**

Unfortunately, though, because of phone line dynamics, **you will never actually connect at 56K**, but you should still be able to get well above 33.6 Kbps, the previous speed barrier. If you have an **X2** or **K56flex** modem, upgrade to V.90, if possible. (See: http://www.56k.com)

Finally, **make sure whatever you buy will work with your computer**. And if you need help, see: http://www.modemhelp.com

# Broadband is better

What's good about modems is that they are the right-here right-now accepted standard worldwide and work over the regular telephone system without any excess charges. But once you try the Net at full steam over a **broadband** connection, you'll find it hard to go back. If you're fortunate enough to live somewhere where broadband is available and reasonably priced, you should definitely check it out. However, if you already have a modem, and you're new to the Net, you should get online first and get to know your demands. Most importantly, don't put money down for a year's subscription if you don't know what you're getting into. **One thing is guaranteed. Over the next couple of years: speeds will go up and prices will come down.**

## Doubling up modems

It's possible to bind two or more modems together using multiple telephone lines in parallel. In theory, this should give you a bandwidth equal to the sum of the combined modems, which often works out cheaper than ISDN. It's simple to set up in Windows 95 or later versions: just right-click on your provider's Dial-up Networking entry, choose "Properties", and add another device under **Multilink**.

If you don't see a Multilink option, install the latest Dial-up Networking and Winsock upgrades from: http://www.microsoft.com/windows95/downloads/ or, simply install Internet Explorer 5.x (http://www.microsoft.com/ie/).

The hardest part is finding a provider that supports it.

## ISDN

We should've all been using ISDN's superior line handling and speed for the last five-odd years, but overpricing by telcos put it **out of most home users' reach**. And now, with much faster alternatives available, it's not so appealing. It provides three channels (1x16 Kbps and 2x64 Kbps) that can be used and charged for in various ways. ISDN Internet accounts don't usually cost more but, depending on where you live, the line connection, rental and calls can cost anywhere from slightly to outrageously more than standard telephone charges.

To connect, you'll need a more expensive device called a **Terminal Adapter**. One bonus is that instantaneous connections mean you'll only be charged while you're transferring data. For details on how to upgrade Windows 95 to support ISDN see: http://www.microsoft.com/windows/getisdn/

## Cable

Chances are, if you can get cable TV, you can also get cable Internet. Cable access offers mega-speed rates (up to 10 Mbps, though more likely considerably less than 1 Mbps) without call charges, but suffers from having to share bandwidth with your neighbors. It's already available as a cable TV sideline in many cities in North America, Holland and Australia, and should become widespread within Europe and Asia soon. So, if you have cable in your street, ask if it's available. Check the fine print carefully, and beware of **download limits** (caps). If you're charged by the megabyte, once you go

over your limit, you could get a nasty shock on your first bill.
Unless you're a light user, if it's not all you can eat, it's probably worth avoiding.

For more on cable access, see:
http://www.cable-modem.net
http://www.cablemodemhelp.com
http://www.cable-modems.org

## DSL

If you haven't already heard of **DSL**, or its most common
form **ADSL** (Asymmetric Digital Subscriber Line), you soon
will. Although it's been commercially available across much of
the USA (eg http://www.megaspeed.com) for a couple of years,
the rest of the world has had to wait for their telcos to wake
up. ADSL is potentially capable of download speeds up to 6
Mbps, and uploads up to 640 Kbps via the normal telephone
system without interfering with your voice service. That
means you can surf the Net and talk on the phone at the
same time over one line. Unlike cable, you don't have to
share the line, so your download speeds will be unaffected by
your neighbors, though like any Internet service, you're still
at the mercy of your ISP's incoming bandwidth. However,
like cable services, providers will offer it at much lower rates
than its capability, and sometimes with draconian capping
plans. By the time you read this, if things go to schedule, the
UK should be in an ADSL price war, with several ISPs offering fast access throughout the major cities. Australians probably won't see it until well into the year 2001, possibly later.

For ADSL news, see:
http://www.adsl.com and http://www.dsllife.com

## Satellite and microwave cable

The catch with cable and ADSL is that you need the right
wire coming into your house. Although ADSL runs over the
normal telephone system, the exchanges need to be refitted

with special hardware, and then it's only good for a few miles. If you live outside a metro area, you have Buckley's chance of seeing either cable or ADSL in a hurry, if ever.

The good news is you can get zippy delivery almost everywhere right now, and at a reasonable price, via satellite or microwave cable link. You receive through a small dish or antenna, and send through a standard dial-up or leased line account with a regular ISP. So you can in theory browse the Web at up to 6 Mbps, but only send email or upload material at a standard modem rate. Again, the commercial speeds will be much lower, and capping might apply. Don't forget to factor in the price of the ISP uplink if it's not in the deal.

For availability and pricing, compare:

| | |
|---|---|
| **Chello** | http://www.chello.com |
| **DirecPC** | http://www.direcpc.com |
| **Telstra** (AUS only) | http://www.bigpond.com/advance/ |

## Wireless access

There's little doubt that the future of broadband Internet access is **wireless**. We already have the technology, but as yet, it's not quite ready for home consumption. Though mark our words; it's on its way…

## Broadband installation

As cable, ADSL and satellite (downfeed) services are "always on" you won't have to dial, but you'll still need a special modem-like device to connect between your computer and the line. Depending on the service provider this might work like a cable TV contract, where they rent you the box, and charge you some kind of once-off installation fee. As these speeds are in excess of serial card capacity, you'll either need to hook in through a network card, USB port, or their own special card. Whichever way, it shouldn't be a drama if you have a recent PC, but Mac support is relatively thin on the ground.

## Computer, check. Modem, check. Now what?

To connect to the Internet, you'll need someone to allow you to connect into their computer, which in turn is connected to another computer, which in turn . . . that's how the Internet works. But unless you have a working relationship with whoever controls access to the computer that gets you online, you'll have to pay for the privilege.

### ISPs

Companies in the business of providing Internet access are known as **ISPs (Internet Service Providers)**. The industry has matured steadily over the last few years to the point that most established ISPs deliver reasonable performance and service. However, all providers aren't equal, and it's difficult to tell a good one from a bad one, until you've used them over time. Try a few before settling, as poor access will jade your online experience. Some, for example, try to squeeze too many folk online, resulting in frequent busy tones when you dial, and slow transfer rates once you're online.

Ask around for personal recommendations, or check local **Internet and computer magazines** (who are forever doing comparative tests of speed, service, and so forth). An added bonus with the computer press is that they often carry cover-mounted disks with all the Net software you'll need to get started.

To help with your quest, there's an ISP listing at the end of this book (p.485), along with a **checklist of questions** – some of which will be important to you, others not, depending on circumstances.

## Online services

**CompuServe** and its new parent, **AOL**, are the last major players standing in the special class known as Online Services. What sets them apart from normal ISPs is that they value their exclusive online offerings more than their Internet access. They are, to a certain extent, a relic of the past. The Internet now offers far more than any Online Service could ever hope to produce in-house. Indeed, much of the content within them is either replicated from the Net or directs you to material located on the Net.

**AOL** is more of a family orientated service with the emphasis squarely on entertainment, whereas **CompuServe** fancies itself as a content provider for young professionals without kids. The one thing they have in common is that their access software is very much **dumbed down** for the new user. While you might find this an appealing prospect, it will soon become a shackle that will hinder your progress online.

But if you travel abroad regularly, a CompuServe account can get you connected in some 150 countries. The only catch is it will attract a premium charge over your regular access bill. Call for rates and access details before you set off, otherwise you could be up for a nasty credit card shock on your return.

If you feel like giving them a whirl, you'll find their disks on the cover of every second computer magazine, and probably in your mailbox once in a while. By all means try the free trials, but if you're not absolutely delighted, be sure to cancel your account. Otherwise you'll be billed a minimum monthly charge whether or not you use the service. And be sure to **completely uninstall their software once you've finished with them**, as it's known to cause problems.

Before committing yourself to either, compare their network speed, software standards (particularly email), pricing, line availability, and telephone support with a regular ISP.

# What's it cost?

Ever shopped for a mobile phone? Well, that was easy compared to trying to get the best deal on Internet access. And the range of pricing plans and types of provision will get even more confusing as broadband access hits the mainstream market.

## Internet access plans

The simplest, and most ideal, access plan is an "all you can eat" account that allows you to stay online for as long as you like for a set fee per month. This commonly goes for about $20 per month in the US with no hidden charges. As local calls are usually free in the US, that's all you should have to pay.

In **Australia**, where access rates vary as wildly as quality of the networks, untimed accounts are rare and tend to come with download limits, or be shunted off on inferior networks. Apart from the telco Dingo Blue, which offers genuinely unlimited access to its customers for $25 per month, most accounts work out at between $1–2 per hour.

At the time of writing, the UK remains the most complex market thanks to the ongoing **tyranny of timed local phone calls**. The most popular providers presently offer "free" access. But it's **not really free**. They can afford to give it away because they get to divvy up the spoils of your monstrous phone bill with British Telecom. On top of this, they often **charge extortionate rates for support through a tolled number**. Alternatively, some providers still offer full access with free support for about £7-12 per month, but of course, you still have to pay your phone charges on top.

There is **hope on the UK horizon**, and it should be in full swing by the time you read this. Watch out for a fiercely competitive range of unmetered access plans that include telephone charges. Expect a lump sum paid in advance, either per month, or year. Again, if the cost is substantial, be cautious of committing more than a few months in advance. For the latest rates and news, see:

http://www.internet-magazine.com/resource/isp/
http://www.theregister.co.uk

**Broadband access** should be somewhat more expensive everywhere, but that's not a rule. Sometimes **cable**, for example, can be just as cheap if you subtract the phone costs. For instance, the US Internet cable provider, **@Home** (http://www.home.com), charges between $40-50 flat per month depending on the cable reseller. In Australia, they offer unmetered cable access with no download limits through the Optus (http://www.optushome.com.au) network, for $60-70 per month. Which forced **Telstra** to drop its prices and offer a similar deal through Foxtel.

**DSL** (**ADSL**) is generally tiered into speed levels, and offered around the same price as cable. **Earthlink** (http://www.earthlink.com), for example, charges about $50 for unlimited access across the USA. Pricing in the UK, though not yet announced, is likely to be around £30-50 per month.

Most ISPs also charge a **once-off setup fee**. This might include a startup software kit, but if you have Windows 98, or a Web browser, you're much better off asking for instructions to set it up manually. Broadband setup fees are much higher, as they usually include hardware rental and a physical installation, as with cable TV.

Other providers, especially the Online Services, might offer a **free trial period**, but if you check their pricing for an average year it mightn't work out cheaper overall.

## Watch your phone bill

If you plan to connect through a telephone line, make sure you choose a provider with a **local dial-up number**. And, if you travel, favor an ISP with national access numbers, otherwise you might run up some serious phone bills.

These dial-up numbers are called **Points Of Presence** (**POPs**). In the US, if you need to call your provider from interstate, it may offer a free 1–800 number that could carry a surcharge of up to $10 per hour. If you have free local call access, then make sure your provider has a POP in your local zone.

Local calls in Australia are flat rate, which means it's cheaper to stay online all day than to dial up for a few minutes each hour to pick up mail. Check if you'd save money by switching to a telco with cheaper local calls.

The UK is due for the greatest upheaval with the impending death of timed Internet calls. Check out the deals that bundle access and phone calls for a fixed fee. Unless your demands are low, they're likely to work out cheaper.

Some telcos offer a discount to your choice of frequently called "**Friends and Family**" numbers. Put your provider on this list, as it's sure to become your most called number. Also ask about the possibility of capped monthly charges to certain numbers. This is sometimes offered with timed ISDN.

## Help

For more on choosing an ISP, see p.485.

# 3

# Connection Software

## DIALERS, TCP/IP
## AND ALL THAT JAZZ

It's standard practice for Internet Service Providers to supply
the basic connection software – usually for free. However,
because the Internet is constantly evolving, no matter what
you get, you'll soon want to replace or add components. It's
not crucial to start out with what's state of the art, because
once you're online, you can download the latest versions of
everything – again, usually for free. Or you can get it in disc
form as a cover-mount from one of the many Internet and
computer magazine titles: just browse the racks to see who's
offering the month's best package.

## The connection essentials

What you stand to get from a provider could be anything from a list of configuration settings to a full Internet tool kit.

First, you have to make sure your computer is **TCP/IP** enabled, so it can talk to the Net. In Windows, the core of the TCP/IP software is called the **Winsock** or **Windows Socket**. Once your TCP/IP software is in place, you'll need to enter a few details, either manually, or by running an installation routine. If this part is not set up properly, your Internet programs won't work.

Once the TCP/IP is correctly configured for your provider, you can pick and choose whatever components you see fit.

### Windows 95/98/NT/2000, or Mac?

If you're running **Windows 95/98/2000** or Macintosh **OS 8.0 or later**, you already have all the TCP/IP software you need to get started.

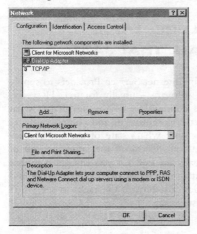

In **Windows 95/98**, right-click on the desktop Network Neighborhood icon and check you've installed the **Client for Microsoft Networks**, **TCP/IP protocol** and **Dial-up Adapter**. If not, click "**Add**" and install each in turn. Microsoft is the manufacturer in all cases. Then choose Client for Microsoft Networks as your

**Primary Network Logon**. Do not enable **File or Printer sharing** unless you want to let outsiders from the Net into your computer.

Your provider will either supply you with an installation program or give you written instructions on how to set up the finer details. Failing that, have someone talk you through it over the phone. Once that's done the rest is easy.

### Earlier systems

If you are running an **earlier version of Windows**, or a **pre-System 8.0 Mac**, you'll need either to **upgrade your operating system** or obtain a TCP/IP program. Be warned though, that although you can get online, you won't be able to run the latest browsers and programs, which will **lock you out of many of the best sites**.

The most popular **TCP/IP program** for **Windows 3.x** is **Trumpet Winsock**. It's freely available on the Internet and used as the core of many ISPs' Windows 3.x bundles. Its dial-up scripting takes a while to figure out, but once you have it going it's rock solid and works with everything. A better choice, if offered, is the version of **Internet Explorer 3.03 for Windows 3.x** that includes its own Winsock. Setting it up is as simple as following the prompts. It's free, if you can get someone to download it for you. It's no longer on Microsoft's site, but you'll find copies of the various versions at: http://browsers.evolt.org

Macintosh users need look no further than **MacTCP**, or its successor **Open Transport**, which can be obtained separately from most Access Providers or from your Apple dealer as part of the **Apple Internet Connection Kit**. Open Transport is superior, but will not run on 6800 or 68020 systems. Open Transport has been replaced by **Remote Access** in MacOS 8.0 and later. The best idea is to ask your Apple dealer for advice.

## Getting it to dial

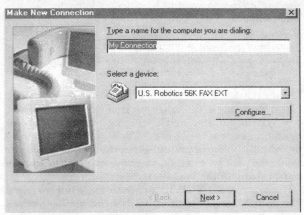

Unless you're connecting via a Local Area Network (LAN) you'll need to configure a **dialer** to automate the dial-up and log-in procedure. You can generally configure this in the same process as **TCP/IP**. This means if you're setting up through a step-by-step wizard, you'll usually enter your TCP/IP configuration, user details, password, provider's telephone number, and then attach a dial-up script (if used), all in one go. Depending on the set-up program you might also be able to configure your mail and news programs in the same process. After it's all configured, you should only need to click on "Connect", or something similar, to instruct your modem to dial. You shouldn't need to enter your dial-up (or mail, if it was included) password again.

### Windows dialing

If you're running **Windows 98**, you'll be able to set your dialing up in a jiffy either through the Internet Connection

Wizard, or by "making a new connection" under Dial-up Networking.

Windows 95 is another matter. If you have the **first release**, you might need to install a dialing component, as this was originally a Plus pack extra called the "Dial-up Scripting Tool". Installing Internet Explorer 4 or later will add everything you need.

Once online, update your system by **downloading the latest version of Internet Explorer** (see p.63), and then check **Windows Update** for the latest releases. Alternatively you can patch it up in pieces from:
http://www.microsoft.com/downloads/

### Mac dialing

**Older Macs** need a separate program to enable dialing. The most popular choices are: **FreePPP**, from http://www.rockstar.com; **ConfigPPP/MacPPP**, part of the Apple Internet Connection Kit; and **OT-PPP** for Open Transport, also from Apple. If you don't already have one of these, your provider or Apple dealer should be able to oblige. If you're running a PowerPC consider upgrading to the latest MacOS. Macs are user-friendly in most areas but Internet connectivity wasn't one of the MacOS strong points up until recently. Again, **don't think too hard about it, just ask your Apple dealer for advice**. They'll know it all back to front.

Once you're online visit http://til.info.apple.com for system upgrades and support. Articles 18238 and 24138 in the Tech Info Library explain how to obtain and configure Open Transport.

## Dialing different providers

Once your dial-up connection is set up you should be able to forget about it, unless you have to **dial a different provider**.

It's simple to set up **Windows 95/98/NT** to handle multiple providers, or switch to a new one. Just start a new account under Dial-up Networking and then set the TCP/IP under "Properties", or do it all in one go with the Internet Connection Wizard. To dial an ISP, simply click on its entry in Dial-up Networking.

The same goes for Mac users with **FreePPP**, **MacPPP**, and **OT-PPP**. Just look for the option "New" to start a new account. In the iMac and on MacOS 8.0+, simply open the **Apple Internet Setup Assistant** and follow the prompts.

There's no need in any case to install new software. You just have to change the TCP/IP and dial-up settings. That should take only a few minutes.

### Did you get all that TCP/IP stuff?

If you didn't understand a bar of the last few pages on getting connected, don't worry! Internet connection and TCP/IP configuration is your Internet Service Provider's specialty. It's in their interest to get you up and running, so if things go haywire, or you're confused, do things the easy way – give them a call. After all, if you can't get connected, they're not going to get paid. For a surprisingly entertaining explanation of how networks, routers, switches and firewalls work, download this movie:

http://www.warriorsofthe.net

# Setting the settings . . .

There are so many routes onto the Internet, it's difficult to draw up a set of generic step-by-step instructions. That's why we suggest you follow whatever directions you're given on your first sign-up. However, if you have to enter the settings yourself, these are the main ones you'll strike.

## TCP/IP SETTINGS

**Windows 95/98** – Open Dial-up Networking under My Computer, and click on "Make New Connection" or right-click and choose "Properties" of an existing connection.

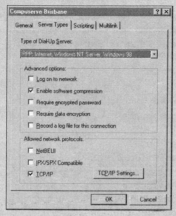

**iMac** – Go to the Apple menu, open the Internet Access folder and click on "Internet Setup Assistant".

**IP address:** Your location on the Internet. It's likely your ISP's server will allocate this afresh each time you log in. If so, you won't be given a numerical address, you'll be told to choose "server assigned" or "dynamically allocated".

**Two DNS server addresses:** The servers that convert friendly domain names into numerical Internet addresses. Sometimes these are also dynamically allocated, so you mightn't have to touch any settings. If not, they'll be numerical, in the form 123.345.123.12

**Domain or Search Domain:** This will look something like: provider.net It's not used in Windows 95/98.

CONNECTION SOFTWARE

## SERVER TYPES (Windows 95/98)

**Type of Dial-Up Server:** Unless instructed otherwise set this to PPP.

**Advanced Options:** Unless instructed otherwise, enable software compression and disable "Log on to network" and "Require encrypted password".

**Allowed Network Protocols:** Enable TCP/IP only.

## DIALER SETTINGS

**User name:** Your account name with the ISP.

**Dial-up password:** Your secret access code.

**Dial-up access number:** The number your modem dials to access the ISP.

## MAIL & NEWS SETTINGS

**Outlook Express** – Under "Accounts" in Tools menu.

**Netscape Messenger** – Open Mail & Newsgroups under "Preferences" in the Edit menu.

**Email address:** The address where you'll receive your mail. Will be in the form `someone@somewhere` where the `somewhere` part is a domain name.

**Mail login:** The name you choose as the `someone` part of your email address.

**Mail password:** The secret code you use to pick up your mail.

**Outgoing mail server (SMTP):** The server that will handle all mail you send. It will be a domain name.

**Incoming mail server (POP/IMAP):** Where your mail is stored. It will also be a domain name.

**News server address (NNTP):** Most ISPs maintain a Usenet server. Enter its domain name into your newsreader's preferences (see p.134).

**OTHER SETTINGS**

**Proxy settings:** Some providers use a gateway between you and the Internet to manage traffic. These settings go into your Web browser preferences (options) and **any other programs that are affected by the proxy such as FTP and Web search agents**. Proxies sometimes play up. Try surfing with and without and see which you prefer. (See p.95)

**IRC server:** Not all providers support chat locally, but they should be able to recommend a server to start you off. Enter this into your chat software preferences. For more see p.188.

**FTP server:** Where to transfer files to and from your ISP's local storage space. This isn't something you configure. You type it into your File Transfer program. (See p.149)

If you need further instructions on tinkering with your TCP/IP settings once you're online, check your provider's home page on the Web. Most ISPs maintain a set of pictorial instructions of what to fill in where for various operating systems. The best thing about these instructions is that they'll be tailored for your situation. If yours isn't so helpful, try another provider:

http://www.dial.pipex.com/support/connect/
http://help.mindspring.com/support/
http://www.dingoblue.com.au/Support_Guide.asp

# Right – is that it, or do I still need more software?

The **TCP/IP** and dialer (Dial-up Networking) combination is enough to get you connected to the Net. But you'll need more software to actually use it. If you have Windows 98, an iMac, or any Mac running MacOS 8.5 onwards you have all you need – at least for the time being. Ask your provider how to configure your Dial-Up Networking (TCP/IP), mail, news and browser rather than install any superfluous software over the top. **Don't believe any provider that insists you need to install their software. Consider switching providers if you get this line. Using what comes with Windows 98 or MacOS 8.0+, along with the latest updates downloaded from the Net is always superior.**

If you're running an earlier version of Windows or Mac, your ISP should supply some start-up software on a disk, or alternatively instruct you to download it off a local server using a Terminal program such as Hyper-Terminal. If they can't provide the software, they may not be such a great choice in your situation. Still, if you have no other option, you should be able to get it from a computer magazine cover CD.

The one program you'll definitely need is a **Web browser**. In fact, the latest Web browsers (including what comes with Windows 98, iMac and MacOS 8.5+) are so complete you might not feel the need to get any other Internet software. You certainly won't need a **mail** program as the ones that come bundled with browsers are as good as they come – and free. Most people these days also use their browsers (or the programs which come with them) to download other software (see p.149) and read newsgroups (see p.129).

In any case, once you have a browser you can surf around for new programs at will, enabling you to chat, play games and whatever else you desire. Don't worry, they're not hard to find with the whole Internet at your disposal – and they needn't cost a penny. For more on how to choose the right browser, and what it can do for you, read on.

# 4

# The Web Browser

## BROWSING THE NET

**A** Web browser is the most important piece of Internet software you'll ever install. It will serve as the window through which you look at the Net and act as a springboard to almost everything you do online. A couple of years back, the browser was basically a tool for viewing sites on the World Wide Web but today's generation of programs – essentially a choice between Microsoft's Internet Explorer and Netscape – come integrated with a whole show bag of Internet goodies that handle such tasks as email, news, Internet telephony, chat, home page editing, and multimedia playing. That makes your choice of browser pretty crucial.

## Choosing a browser

You may not get to choose your own browser initially if you decide to install your ISP's startup kit. If you do, it's likely to be **Internet Explorer**, as most providers and Online Services adopted it during the period when it was free and Netscape wasn't. Now that Netscape is also free, you might have a choice of either. And if you're using Microsoft Windows 98, you will find Internet Explorer seamlessly bundled into the operating system – the controversial move that resulted in anti-trust action in the US courts – for more on which, see our history of the Net (p.449). Internet Explorer is also on the desktop of every iMac, and Apple running MacOS 8.5+. If you'd prefer Netscape, you'll find it on the install disks.

If you don't have Netscape, it's not exactly hard to obtain – you can download it from the Net (see p.63 – "How to get the latest versions"), or load it onto your system from one of the myriad free disks mounted on computer or Internet magazines.

There's nothing to stop you from having more than one browser on your system. So, if you're curious try out both browsers side by side and make your own decision.

## Unraveling the numbers

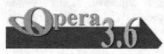

Both Microsoft Internet Explorer and Netscape Communicator come in various flavors, catering to Windows 95/98, Windows NT, Windows 3.1, Power Mac, Mac 68k, Unix, and in Netscape's case, OS/2. Microsoft also supports Windows' runt sibling, Windows CE.

You can tell the **latest release of a program** by its number. For example, in Netscape Communicator, version 4.73 is newer than 4.7. The first number is the series: these are both

"4.x" series browsers (as you'd expect, the "4.x" series came after the "3.x" series). The second number, after the decimal point, tells you if it is the **original release** (.0) or an **interim upgrade** (0.1, 0.2, etc) within the series. Such upgrades generally fix problems and add on a few minor features. In doing so, the previous release in that series becomes obsolete, and in the case of betas (test programs), expires.

A **new series release** – which at present happens about once a year – heralds major changes, new features and bug fixes, and usually adds extra system demands. Thus, if your computer resources are low, you may find an earlier series more suitable.

To make matters just a bit more confusing, developers sometimes release **a new build** of the same program. So you and a friend can both have IE5.5 but if you downloaded it later, you might have a later build that's fixed a few minor bugs. To see a program's build number, choose **About** from the **Help menu**.

## System requirements

Browsers consume a lot of **disk space**, especially the full installations of Internet Explorer with all the added accessories.

### PC requirements

**PC users** will need at least a 486 DX66 PC, with **16 MB of RAM** to get either **Internet Explorer or Netscape** to function under Windows 95/98/3.x, and 24-32 MB to run other programs at the same time. Windows NT versions demand at least 32 MB of RAM: depending on which optional components you install, Netscape 4.x requires between 18 and 30 MB of hard disk space, and Internet Explorer 4.x and 5.x, between 40 and 80 MB. **Windows 2000** (which includes Internet Explorer 5) demands at least a Pentium 133, with 64 MB of RAM.

They're the official minimum specifications as supplied by Microsoft and Netscape, but frankly if you're running anything **less than a Pentium 200 with 64 MB of RAM, it's going to hurt.**

New releases normally write over the old files. So if you're simply upgrading to a newer version, for example, installing IE5.x over Windows 98, then the increase in disk space might only be marginal. Netscape 6 bucks the trend by being somewhat smaller than past releases. However, if you accept all the add-on junk, you certainly won't free up any disk space.

## Mac requirements

You'll need a **PowerPC processor** to run Internet Explorer 4.5, Netscape Communicator 4.7x, and later versions of both. Internet Explorer 4.5 and 5.x will run on **MacOS 7.5.3 or later**, and 12 MB of RAM. Netscape 4.7x requires 16 MB of RAM if running MacOS 7.6.1, and 24 MB of RAM, for **MacOS 8.0** or greater. The requirements of any later releases by the time you read this should be no higher.

Again, while these are the official specs, realistically you'll be happier with a faster machine and more RAM. If you have an earlier **iMac with only 32 MB of RAM**, you should chock it up to at least 64 MB, so you can browse and read mail with a modicum of dignity.

Both also have earlier 4.0 series browsers that will run on **68K machines**. Whatever the machine, browser or version number, they'll all work best with Virtual Memory switched on.

## Humble PCs

The best choice for older machines running Windows 3.1 is **Internet Explorer 3.03**. It can get by (just about) on 4 MB of RAM and as little as 7 MB of disk space for a browser-only installation, plus it also includes the TCP/IP dialing software that Windows 3.1 omits. The Mac equivalent also requires somewhat less RAM and disk space than its successor. If that's still too heavy, **Netscape 2.0x** is better than no browser at all.

Alternatively, if you don't mind coughing up (after a free trial period), investigate the less-known but distinctly impressive **Opera** (http://www.opera.com). This packs a browser, mail sender, and newsreader into only a couple of MB – and it's even slightly quicker than the 4.0x series browsers.

You'll find every browser ever released across all platforms, including **Amiga** and **BeOS**, for free download at: http://browsers.evolt.org

## Explorer v. Netscape: what's on offer?

Okay, let's assume your computer is up to running the latest versions of Netscape Communicator and Internet Explorer. What's on offer?

### Microsoft Internet Explorer 5.x (IE5. x)

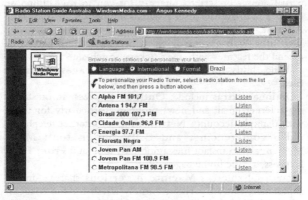

If you're running **Windows 98/2000**, you won't have to decide whether to download Internet Explorer. You already

have it as part of the operating system. Microsoft's policy has been to integrate the browsing experience into the desktop, so **Windows Explorer and Internet Explorer share the same interface** – whether you're surfing the Web or ferreting through your hard drive. Installing Internet Explorer over Windows 95 achieves almost the same effect.

Setting up is also a breeze, guided by the built-in **Internet Connection Wizard**, which can also refer you to a local ISP, if you haven't already signed up.

IE5.x's notable features include: **IntelliSense**, which can automate various tasks such as correcting address typos, filling in forms, remembering passwords, installing upgrades and completing addresses; **Windows Radio Toolbar**, which puts a host of Net radio stations on your toolbar for quick reference; **Media Player**, which supports most multimedia formats including Microsoft's new **streaming audio** standards; **Offline Browsing**, which can download whole or partial sites at prescribed intervals for you to read offline or enable you to go back over previous sessions offline; **Content Advisor**, which provides a way to bar kids from unsavory Web sites; **Web Accessories**, which allow third parties to extend the features with news tickers, search aids and the like; and the ability to **save complete Web pages as single files**.

**Optional extras** include: **Outlook Express**, an outstanding Internet email and news program, particularly for those with multiple accounts; **Netmeeting**, an Internet telephony, video conferencing, and collaboration tool; **MSN Messenger,** an instant messaging chat tool; and **Front Page Express**, a basic home page editor.

Internet Explorer's **Macintosh versions** share a similar appearance, but are written entirely afresh for the MacOS. Their developments and features had tended to lag behind the Windows equivalent until the release of IE4.5, which diverged somewhat and introduced a few new tricks of its own. By **IE5.0** it's starting to look and feel like a completely different browser with more unique features such as: a **download manager that supports resume downloads** (p.154); an **auction manager**; **custom skins**, to change its appearance; and a **Internet Scrapbook**, for taking snapshots of Web pages. It has also received accolades for conforming to the W3C's Web standards, unlike its Windows equivalent. While most commentators agree it's the Mac browser of the moment, few believe Microsoft is giving it away out of altruism. Should it succeed in elbowing Netscape off the Mac, Microsoft could control the Apple desktop – and ultimately, the fate of Apple.

### Netscape Communicator 4.7x

**Netscape's Communicator 4.7x** is based around a browser called **Navigator** that is also available as a **standalone** (in case you'd rather use another mail program). It's available in three editions. If you start with the simplest, you can always patch up to the full kit.

**Communicator Base Install** contains: the **Navigator** browser; **Messenger**, a fully-featured HTML email program and newsreader; **Composer**, a basic home page editor; and **AOL Instant Messenger**, a skeletal chat tool that alerts you when your buddies are online.

**Complete** adds **Real Player,** for streaming audio and video; and **Multimedia support** for other formats. There's also an edition with the **Enterprise Calendar**, a basic scheduling program. You'll also be incessantly pestered to download a wide selection of other utilities and multimedia programs created by Netscape's business partners when you go to **Smart Update**. Choose not to install any until you find your feet. You're better off finding your own software independently.

Communicator can also be set to block access to objectionable Web content via **NetWatch**, which works similarly to Internet Explorer's offering except you have to go online to set it up.

Netscape browsers are **notoriously buggy**, particularly the earlier releases. If you find your system crashing frequently, uninstall Netscape and see if Internet Explorer is any better.

### Netscape 6.0

 When Netscape threw in the towel and sold up to AOL, it handed over its browser's source code to the general programming public at **Mozilla.org** (http://www.mozilla.org). For a while it looked like the completely rewritten Netscape would never see the light of day. More than two years later, when all seemed lost, AOL suddenly announced **Netscape 6.0 pp1** (forget about 5.0), the **preview release** of the next generation browser. Reactions have varied, but it's universally agreed that the preview is way too unstable and slow for everyday use. At this stage, we can't really include it for consideration. For more, see:
http://www.gerbilbox.com/newzilla/

### Okay – so which one, then?

**Netscape is in such a mess** it's very hard to recommend even trying the browser, let alone basing your Internet existence around it. Its 4.7 series are slower, less stable and technologically behind Microsoft's 5 series on both the PC and Mac. The installation and upgrade process has become so crassly commercial you almost expect to be asked whether you'd like **Coke and fries with that**. And the sneak preview of its successor leaves you feeling **positively violated** with its wall-to-wall trapdoors into the **AOL abyss**.

In the opposite corner we have the decidedly staid, but functional, flagship of one of the **least loved companies of the 21st century**. In fact, it's the very program that landed Microsoft in court. What hasn't been said is that Internet Explorer is about the best thing Windows 98 has going for it. Even if Microsoft took it out, you'd want to put it back in. For all its bad points, and there are many, it's presently as good as it gets.

Frankly, there's no point wasting your time on software that will make your life harder. If you're running Windows, update your system to the latest version of Internet Explorer and be done with it. On the Mac, too, Internet Explorer seems the least painful option. And if you don't know which browser to install, you shouldn't be running **Linux.**

Nonetheless, if the preview of Netscape 6 showed anything it's that the browser war is not yet over. The **Gecko engine** being assembled by the unsung heroes of Mozilla.org may yet find its way into a stream of **Net devices beyond the PC world**. It may even spawn an AOL/Netscape badged browser that's worthy of your patience. So keep an eye out for reviews of the upcoming betas, and hopefully one day, the official release of Netscape, the next generation. But unless you see some serious fanfare, sit tight.

If you feel inclined to try them both, be prepared for some wrestling in your system settings. Both browsers will ask whether you'd like them to be the default, and whether you'd like them to keep asking the question. Take your time in deciding.

## How to get the latest versions

If you already have a browser, you can download the latest Netscape release from: http://www.netscape.com and Internet Explorer from: http://www.microsoft.com/ie/

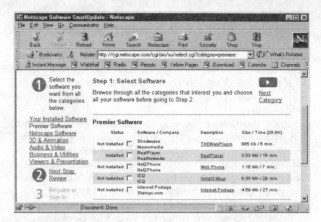

As Internet Explorer is part of Windows 98/2000, you can also update it to the latest version through **Windows Update** (on the Start menu or under the Tools menu in IE5.x). Or choose **"Product Updates"** from the Help menu in IE3 or IE4.

To update Netscape, go online and **choose Software Updates** from the Help menu.

In all cases, the server will automatically interrogate your system to determine which components you need to bring yourself up to date. Then it's just a matter of picking what you want.

Before you start, bear in mind that the entire kits weigh in between 6 and 30 MB. This means **the download could take an hour or more** – depending on which options you pick, how busy the sites are, and at what speed you connect. Count on about 6 MB per hour with a 28.8 Kbps modem. So, if you're paying by the minute to be connected, you might find it cheaper and more convenient to buy a computer magazine with the browsers (and more) on a CD cover disk. Plus you'll have a backup copy handy if you need to re-install.

**Preferably, though, get it from the source**, as some third parties like ISPs personalize the browsers with their own details. You can do without that.

## Want more information?

For the latest on browsers, reviews, tests, comparisons of new versions on release, tips, and downloads for a wide range of brands and platforms see:
**Browsers.com** (http://www.browsers.com) and
**Browser News** (http://www.upsdell.com/BrowserNews/).

For discussion of the latest beta releases, see:
**BetaNews** (http://www.betanews.com).

## More Net software . . .

Once you've installed your browser, you can surf the Web looking for other software. We've selected a few of the best programs from each category in the "Software Roundup" (see p.439). But that's only a smidgen of what you'll find in some of the software guides recommended in our Web directory (see p.291).

# 5

# Connecting

## FOR THE VERY FIRST TIME

If you've configured your TCP/IP, dialing, and mail software to your provider's specification, you should be ready to hit the Net. Hopefully, you also have a Web browser installed, as the ideal exercise for your very first connection would be to get straight onto the World Wide Web.

### Connect that modem . . .

Once you're set up, and browser-ready, **connect your modem** to the phone line, and **instruct your dialer to call**.

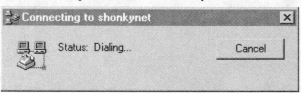

What you click on will depend on the way you're set up. If you've done it yourself in Windows 95/98, drag a shortcut from the connection in the Dial-Up Networking folder (under My Computer) onto your Desktop or your Quick Launch Toolbar. That way it's easy to get to in future.

The process is similar on the Mac but differs between system versions. It won't take you long to work it out. Look under the Apple menu. In the iMac, for example, you can connect through **Remote Access** or by clicking on "**Connect To**" within the **Internet Access Folder**.

If your modem speaker volume is turned up (look under your modem Properties), it will make all kinds of mating noises while connecting, like a fax machine. These sounds will cease once the connection's negotiated. At this point your provider's server will need to identify you as a customer, so if you haven't already entered your **user name and password**, you'll have to now. Once that's done, **click the box that says "Save Password"** otherwise you'll have to enter it every time you log in. Make sure you keep this password private – anyone could use it to rack up your bill or, perhaps worse, read your mail (although you should be issued with a separate password to retrieve mail).

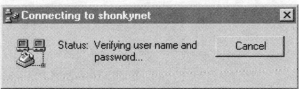

Now **start your Web browser** and try accessing a few of the addresses from our Web guide (p.277). You'll find instructions on how to browse the Web in the next chapter. If you can access the Web, it's close to plain sailing from now on. If not, you'll need to find out what's wrong. **Read on** . . .

## Troubleshooting

To access all the **connection settings** in **Windows 95/98** (modem, scripting, TCP/IP, phone, and dialer), open Dial-Up Networking (under My Computer), right-click on the connection, and choose **Properties**. To change the log-in settings, simply left-click as if dialing.

If you are using a **Mac with Free PPP** (or equivalent), you can access the settings by opening the **Free PPP** window and clicking on "General", "Accounts", or "Locations". You may also need to adjust the settings in your **TCP/IP file**, which you access through the Control Panel under the Apple symbol (top left-hand corner of the screen). **In the iMac**, look under **Remote Access**, **TCP/IP,** and **Modem** under the Apple menu Control Panel folder.

### If you didn't get through

If you **didn't succeed in connecting to your provider**, there's probably something wrong with your dialer or modem configuration. The most common errors are:

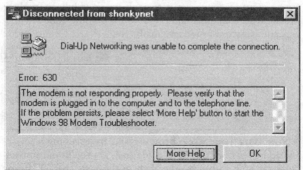

**No modem detected:** Is your modem installed, plugged into the right port, and switched on? To install or diagnose a modem in Windows 95/98, click on the Modem applet in the Control Panel.

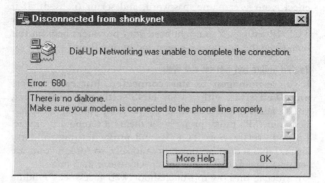

**Dial tone not detected:** Is your phone line plugged in? If this isn't the problem, try disabling Dial Tone Detect or Wait for Dial Tone under the modem settings. If the option's grayed out in Windows 95/98, you'll either need to re-install the modem with its correct driver (preferable) or manually enter the initialization string X1 into Extra Settings under the modem's Advanced Connection Settings.

**No answer:** Do you have the right phone number? You can verify your modem's working by dialing a friend's phone. If the phone rings you know your dialer and modem are talking to each other properly.

**Busy/engaged:** Access providers' lines can be occupied at peak hours such as the end of the working day. Keep trying until you get in: even though you dial a single number, there are several modems at the other end. If it happens often, complain, or get a new provider with a **lower user to modem ratio**.

## You got through but were refused entry

If you **succeeded in connecting** but were **refused entry**, check your user name, password, and script (if used). If it **failed to negotiate network protocols**, verify your TCP/IP settings. You might need your provider's help on this one. Keep the settings on screen and phone them.

## You're online but not on the Web

If you've **managed to stay connected, but can't access any Web sites**, either your DNS settings are incorrect, you've failed to establish an IP connection, you haven't specified your ISP's proxy properly, or there's a temporary outage. Log off, verify your TCP/IP and proxy settings, and try again. DNS servers go down occasionally, so (unless yours are server-assigned) make sure you specify more than one.

For details on how to troubleshoot Web access see "Finding It" (p.183).

## You're on the Web but another program won't work

If your browser's working, but your chat, search agent, newsreader, or FTP client won't connect to any sites, check the individual program's proxy settings. Ask your ISP for the address and port number if you're unsure.

## Your connection keeps going down

If everything works fine but **your connection often drops out,** you'll need to check each link in the chain between you and your provider. Unfortunately, there are a lot of links, so it's down to a matter of elimination.

**Does it happen only after an extended period of inactivity?** Then it could be an automatic defense mechanism in your dialer or at your provider's end.

**Do you have telephone Call Waiting?** If it's enabled, and you're called while online, those little beeps will knock out your connection.

**Pick up your phone. Does it sound clear?** Crackling sounds indicate a poor connection somewhere. Modems like a nice clean line.

**Do you share a line?** Picking up an extension will drop your connection.

**Do you have the latest modem driver and firmware revision?** Check your modem manufacturer's home page.

As a **last resort** try a different ISP, phone line, and modem.

For more troubleshooting advice, contact your ISP or see: http://php.iupui.edu/~aamjohns/

## Okay, it works – but it's very slow

When the **Net gets overloaded**, transfer rates slow down: it can happen to the whole Internet backbone at peak usage times, particularly with transoceanic routes. If transfers are slow from everywhere, however, it usually means the problem lies closer to home. It could be that your **provider or office network** has too many users competing online, or too much traffic accessing its Web area from outside. In this case your provider or office needs to increase its bandwidth to the Net.

**ISPs** tend to go through cycles of difficult traffic periods. If they have the resources and the foresight to cope with demand, you won't notice. But as it's such a low-margin business, they're more likely to stretch things. Always call your provider when you have complaints with its service. If you're not treated with respect, no matter how trivial your inquiry, take your money elsewhere. There's a prevailing arrogance within the computer industry. Don't tolerate it. You're the customer; they're not doing you a favor.

### Finding the bottleneck

If you'd really like to know what's slowing things down, you can arm yourself with some network diagnostic tools from the Net. The staples are: **Ping**, which works like a radar to measure how long it takes a data packet to reach a server and return; and **TraceRoute**, which pings each router along the path to see which one's causing the holdup.

**Windows users** have plenty of choices for obtaining these programs. **NetScan Tools** (http://www.nwpsw.com) has Ping, TraceRoute and loads more. **NetMedic** (http://www.vitalsigns.com) can tell you exactly where it's breaking down, whether your provider is falling short, monitor trends, and send off a complaint report. **NeoTrace** (http://www.neoworx.com) adds another level to TraceRoute by identifying who owns the routers, and then maps it all out in Hollywood style.

**For Macs**, try **WhatRoute** (http://crash.ihug.co.nz/~bryanc/) for tracing routers, and **CyberGauge** (http://www.neon.com) to monitor bandwidth.

## The single best piece of advice

If you know someone who's a bit of an Internet whiz, coax them over to help you hook up for the first time. Throw in enough pizza, beer, and compliments about their technical prowess, and you'll have an auxiliary support unit for life.

# 6

# Surfing
# the Web

## WWW.COME.AND.GET.ME

**W**hen you see www.come.and.get.me or such on an advert,
business card, or news story, you're being invited to visit
an address on the World Wide Web (the Web), the biggest
development in communications since TV. You'll have no
trouble finding such addresses online, as the Web is genuinely
the user-friendly face of the Internet.

In fact, you'll find all sorts of interesting stuff once you get
started. The Web is such a cheap and nifty platform for
expression that it has sparked off more publishing, both professional and DIY, than at any time in history.

Although getting about the Web is undeniably simple, you'll still need a little help to get off the ground. As preparation, we've dedicated this chapter to explaining **how to set up your Web browser** and point it in the right direction; there's another chapter on **how to find things** once you're there (see p.163); and most of Part Two of this book (see p.277) consists of reviews of **interesting and useful sites**.

## What to expect

The Web is the Internet's glossy, glamorous, point-and-click front door: a colorful assault of shopping, investment services, music, magazines, art, books, museums, travel, games, job agencies, movie previews, radio broadcasts, self-promotion, and much, much more. It has information on more than ten million companies and is accessed by more than three hundred million users in every corner of the globe from Antarctica to Iceland. It will bring the world to the keyboard of your computer. It's better than the best encyclopedia, and for the most part, it's free. **There's no doubt, if you're not on the World Wide Web, you're missing out**.

## How it works

When you enter a **Web address** into your browser it will retrieve the corresponding page from wherever it's stored on the Internet and display it on your screen. The page is likely to contain a mixture of text and images, laid out like a magazine. But what makes a Web page special is that it can contain **links**. When you **click on a link, something happens**. Generally, it brings up another page, but it might do something else like launch a Net radio broadcast, or start a file download.

## Clicking on links

You rarely have to enter addresses to get around the Web, because most of the time you'll simply be **clicking on links**. Web pages are written in **HTML** (HyperText Markup Language), which lets documents **link** to other documents. Clicking on such a link effectively turns the page. This creates a sort of third dimension. If you've used Help in Windows or on the Mac, you'll be familiar with the concept.

Depending on how you've configured your browser, **text that contains links** to other documents (or another part of the same document) is usually highlighted in another color and/or underlined. When you pass over a link (which can be an image as well as text) **your mouse cursor will change from an arrow to a pointing hand** and the target address will appear in a bar at the bottom of your browser.

To pursue the link, simply **click on the highlighted text or image**. A link is only a **one-way connection**, like a signpost. So when you get to the new page, there won't necessarily be a link back. You might imagine that once you've been clicking for a while you could easily get lost. You won't, because there are some simple ways to trace your steps, as we'll explain soon.

## Home pages and Web sites

On the World Wide Web, **home page** has two meanings. One refers to the page that appears when you start your browser and acts as your home base for exploring the Web. Whenever you get lost or want to return to somewhere familiar, just click on your **"Home"** button and back you go. The other usage refers to the front door to a set of documents that represents someone or something on the Web. This set of interconnected documents is called a **Web site**.

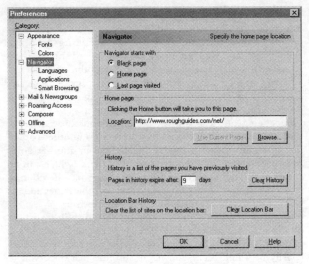

For instance, Rough Guides' "**official**" home page – found at: http://www.roughguides.com – acts as the publishing company's site index. You can access every page in the Rough Guides site by following links from the home page. Play your cards right and you'll end up at this book's home page.

If a site hasn't been endorsed by whom it represents it's called an "**unofficial**" home page. This is typical of the celebrity worship sites erected by doting fans. Some film and pop stars have so many they're linked into "Webrings" (http://www.webring.org).

## How to read a Web address

In tech-speak **a Web address is also called a URL** (Uniform Resource Locator). Every Web page has a unique URL that can be broken into three parts. Reading from left to right they are: the **protocol** (such as http:// ftp:// or news:); the **host name** (everything before the first single forward slash); and the **file path** (everything after and including the first single forward slash). Consider the address: http://www.star.com.hk/~Chow/Yun/fat.html The http:// tells us it's a HyperText file located on the World Wide Web, the domain www.star.com.hk tells us it's in Hong Kong, and the file path indicates that the file fat.html is located in the directory /~Chow/Yun/

Anyone who's serious about their presence on the Web has their own domain name. Typically, a company will choose an address that relates to its business name or activity. It's also common, but certainly not a rule, for such addresses to start with http://www. For example, you'll find: Apple computers at http://www.apple.com; the BBC at http://www.bbc.co.uk; and assorted spells and potions at: http://www.sorcerers-shop.com

## What to do with Web (http) addresses

**To visit a Web site**, you have to submit its address to your browser, either keying it in, or by clicking on a link. The **Address Bar** runs horizontally above the browser pane. In Netscape, when it's blank, it says **Go to** beside it, and when it retrieves a page the wording changes to **Location** or **Netsite** (for sites housed on Netscape servers). In Internet Explorer it says **Address**. You can bring up an alternative box by choosing **Open** or **Open Page** under the File menu. Key the address you're looking for into either box, **hit your enter (or return) key, and wait**.

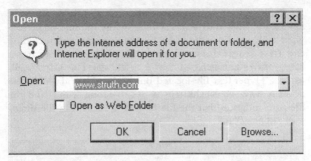

Your browser will examine the address and work out what to do next. If you've submitted a legitimate Web address it will contact your DNS server to convert the host name into an IP address. You'll see this process happening in the lower left corner of your screen. Once it's converted, the browser will contact the Web site's server and request the page.

It rarely takes more than a minute or two to locate and load Web pages. Over a 56 K modem, the average time is around 30 seconds, but if you've a broadband connection, it can be almost instant. If all works well, your browser will retrieve the page and display it on your screen. If you receive an error message, try again. If that fails, follow the instructions in "Finding the right Web address" (see p.183).

## Take care with capitals

Note that URL path names are **case sensitive**. So key them carefully, taking note of capitals as well as their bizarre punctuation. Host names are almost always written in lower case, but are actually case insensitive. **Don't bother keying the http:// part as your browser will automatically add it on if you omit it.**

## Other addresses (non http)

You can also access **FTP** (see p.149), **Telnet**, and **Usenet** (see p.129) from the helm of your Web browser.

To **use FTP**, you just add ftp:// to the file's location. So, to retrieve duck.txt located in the directory /yellow/fluffy from the anonymous FTP site ftp.quack.com you should enter: ftp://ftp.quack.com/yellow/fluffy/duck.txt (In fact, with recent browsers you can omit the ftp:// part as they know that any domain starting with ftp. is an FTP site.)

**Telnet** works in exactly the same way. So does **Usenet**, except that it omits the // part. Thus, to access the news-group alt.ducks key: news: alt.ducks

Addresses starting with file:/// are located on your own hard drive. You can browse your own computer by entering a drive letter followed by a colon (eg, c:).

## Getting around

All the main **navigation buttons** are located on the toolbar above the main browser window. Displaying them is optional, but they're hard to live without. Once you get to know them, choose to display them **small and without text**. It will free up some screen real estate.

You'll use the **Back** and **Forward** buttons most. To **go back to a page** you previously visited, click the Back button until you find it. To **return to where you were**, keep pressing Forward. And to go back to your start-up page hit **Home**.

You can go back and forward through pages pretty much instantly once you've visited them during a session, as your computer stores the document in its memory. How much material you can click through in this fashion, however, depends on the amount of storage space that's been allocated to **cache** or **temporary Internet files** in your settings. We explain cache later under "Browse Offline" (see p.88).

Two other important buttons are **Stop** and **Reload**. To **cancel a page request**, because it's taking too long to load a site, or you've made a mistake, just hit the Stop button. Occasionally you might have to hit Stop before Back will work. Alternatively, if a page doesn't load properly, you can hit **Refresh** or **Reload** to load it again. You'd also do this if a page changes regularly, and you want to load a new version rather than one that's stored in your session "cache".

## Use your mouse

The next most important navigation controls are in your **mouse button** (the right button on PCs). Just hold it down and try them all out. The menu will change depending upon what you click. For instance, if you click on a link, you'll have the option of opening the target page in a new window or saving it to disk. The latter is sometimes handy if you want to save time loading a large page or image. The saving process goes into the background while you continue in the foreground.

## Browse your History

During a session browsing the Web, you can **return to recently visited sites** through the drop-down menus found by either holding down the Back and Forward buttons or clicking on the adjacent down arrows. And you can return to the sites you visit most by scrolling through the drop-down menu where you enter addresses.

These, however, are but a pale imitation of the **History file**. You'll find the main History file under the Communicator menu in Netscape under Tools, or on a toolbar button or under the File menu in Internet Explorer. Think of it as a collection of signposts. You can use it to return to a visited page, rather than clicking the Forward and Back buttons. We'll discuss another use for the History file ahead in "Browse Offline" (p.88).

## Address and form tricks

Browsers are getting smarter with every release. Now, not only do you not have to key http:// but you can sometimes get away with **just putting in a company's name** if its URL starts with www. and ends in .com So to reach Yahoo in Netscape or Internet Explorer, simply key in yahoo and hit enter. Internet Explorer will also **autoscan** the other common root domains (.edu and .org, with and without www.) and then give you the option of looking it up in a search engine (see p.163). If that sounds like it might save you time, just try it. You probably won't bother again.

On a more useful level, Netscape will also attempt to **guess which URL you're entering** by looking at your History file and **autofilling** in the gaps. If it guesses correctly, you can stop typing and hit enter.

IE5.x takes this way further with its **IntelliSense** technology. It will present a drop-down list of all the sites from both your History and Favorites that so far match your keystrokes as you type. You can either complete the address or click on one of the selections.

It can also **remember your form entries** (such as search engine terms, user names and passwords) if you choose to enable **AutoComplete**. You'll find various settings, and the option to delete the current data, by clicking the AutoComplete button under the General tab in Options. To remove an individual entry, select it and hit the delete key.

If you're bored, you might like to experiment with the **Autosearch** and **"What's related"** features in Internet Explorer and Netscape. Both offer myriad ways to configure automatic searches. For instance, if you **key in a phrase instead of a URL**, they're smart enough to direct the query to a search engine rather than a DNS lookup. They can also offer you a list of related sites courtesy of **Alexa** (http://www.alexa.com). Click on **Show Related Links** under Tools in IE5.x, and **What's Related** on the Address toolbar in Netscape 4.5x. It looks impressive at first, but power users will get better value by going straight to the search engines and directories (p.163).

## How to find a page later

Whenever you find a page that's worth another visit, file it away for later reference. In Internet Explorer it's called adding to **"Favorites"**. Netscape calls it **adding** it to your "Bookmarks".

**Internet Explorer** stores each address as an individual **"Internet Shortcut"** in the same way it makes shortcuts to programs in Windows. To **arrange your Favorites** into logical folders, choose **Organize Favorites** from the Favorites menu. You can do the same in Netscape by opening **Edit Bookmarks** in the Communicator menu under Bookmarks or under Bookmarks on the Location toolbar.

When you add an address to your Favorites in IE5.x, it will ask if you'd like to **make it available offline**. If you agree, it will check the page at whatever intervals you specify to see if it's changed. At the same time, it can also download the page, and others linked to it, so that you can browse the site offline later (see "Browse Offline" – p.88). Netscape can't do that, but you can see which sites have changed by choosing Update Bookmarks from under the View menu in Edit Bookmarks.

You can also **save an address as a shortcut or alias** on your desktop. In Netscape, just drag the icon on the toolbar to the left of where it says **Location** or **Netsite** and plonk it down wherever you like. In Internet Explorer drag and drop the page icon to the left of the address or choose **Send Shortcut to Desktop** from under the File menu.

## Copy and paste

To copy text from Web pages, highlight the section, choose **Copy** from the Edit or mouse menu (or use the usual short-cut keys), then switch to your word processor, text editor, or mail program and choose **Paste**.

## Send addresses to a friend

One of the first things you'll want to do online is **share your discoveries** with friends. The simplest way is to copy the site's address into a mail message, along with a note, or perhaps a section copied and pasted from the page as described above. Alternatively, you can send a link or **whole page**, by choosing **Send** from under the **File menu** in Internet Explorer and Netscape. However, if you send a whole page to someone who uses a kludgy mail system that doesn't understand HTML mail (eg Lotus Notes), it will come through as mumbo jumbo.

That's straightforward but what if you want to **send a whole list**? Both browsers file addresses into folders for later retrieval, but approach the task from very different angles. Netscape stores them in an HTML file – it's actually a Web page in itself which means you can **put it on the Web**, specify it as your home page, or **attach it to mail** as a single file. Internet Explorer saves each address individually as a shortcut, which makes them less convenient to transfer. To send in bulk, **export** a single folder or the whole list as a Netscape Bookmark file with the **Import/Export Wizard** under the File menu in IE5.x. Then drag and drop the result into an email message like any other attachment. (See p.111)

## Save a page

To save a page, choose **Save as** from under the File menu in any browser. You can usually choose between saving in text or HTML. If you **Save as HTML**, you'll be able to view it only in a browser. Save it as text and you can read or edit it in any text viewer or word processor.

The problem with this method (your only choice in Netscape) is that you'll save only the text, but not the images. So, if you want the images you'll have to save them separately.

IE5.x offers the option of saving the **complete Web page** or a **Web archive**. The first option automatically saves the images into a separate folder. The latter combines all the elements into a single, transportable file that can be viewed only by IE5.x or later.

## Print a page

To print a page, simply choose **Print** from under the File menu. Note the various layout selections on the pop-up print window. IE5.x also gives you the option to print the contents of individual frames, something that causes Netscape problems. To alter the margins, headers and footers, and other details select **Page Setup**. To view how it will look on a page, select **Print Preview**.

## Download files

Almost, if not all, your **file downloads** and **software upgrades** can be initiated by a link from a Web page. When you click on that link both Netscape and Internet Explorer will start an **FTP operation** in the background, and let you carry on surfing.

Depending on your settings, once the file is found, you'll be asked where you'd like to save it. If it can log in but can't find the file, or you'd like to browse the FTP site, copy the address using the mouse menu, paste it to the Address bar, and delete the file name from the address. Then you can log into the FTP server and browse it like a Web site. If it's a big file, it might be wiser to pass the job over to a dedicated **download manager** that supports **Resumes Transfers**. Otherwise, if you lose your connection during the download you'll have to start again from scratch.

For more on file transfer, see p.149.

## Save an image, movie, or sound file

Web pages often display reduced images. In Web art galleries especially, such images often have links to another with higher resolution. To save an image, select it and then choose **Save as** or **Save Image as** from the File, or mouse button, menu. Windows 95/98 browsers can also save images as **desktop wallpaper.** To save a movie or sound clip, click on the link to it and choose **Save Target as**, or **Save Link as**, from the mouse menu.

Mass Downloader (http://www.massdownloader) integrates into your browser's mouse menu giving you the option of sending files its way instead. Which is handy for large files as it's faster and can resume broken downloads. It can also scan a page and download all links of your chosen type – handy if you come across a movie archive.

## Uncover the source

The smartest way to **learn Web design** is to peek at the raw HTML coding on pages you like. Choose **Source** from the View or mouse button menu. For more on Web page design, see p.239.

# Change the settings

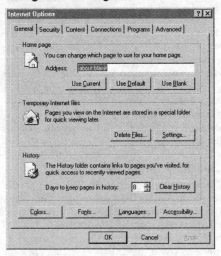

You can reconfigure Internet Explorer by either choosing "Internet Options" under either the View or Tools menu, "Internet" in the Windows 95/98 Control Panel, or by right-clicking the desktop Internet icon and selecting "Properties". In Netscape, the option is under "Preferences" in the Edit menu. The following are a few things you might change.

### Choose your own home page

Browsers come preconfigured with a **default page** – their own, or that of whoever supplied it to you. It will come up every time you start your browser, or whenever you hit **"Home"**. **This is the first thing you should change** in Options (Preferences). You can specify any page you like, even one located on your own hard drive such as your Bookmark file. **It's almost always better to start with a blank page.** That way you don't have to wait for anything to load before you start a Web session and it won't cause problems when you open your browser whilst offline.

### How to tell where you've been

An **unvisited link** is like a signpost to a new page. You click
on the link to go there. After you've been, nothing changes
on the page, but your browser records your visit by storing
the URL in a **History file**. It's then called a **visited link**.
See p.88 for how to use the History file to find all the pages
you've visited in the last few days (or weeks).

You can customize links by displaying them as **underlined**
and/or in a **special color**. The default is usually underlined
blue for unvisited links and either black, purple or red for visited links. See how this works for yourself. Look at any page.
Links you haven't followed should appear blue and underlined.
Now click one and load the page. Next, click "Back" and
return to the previous page. The link will have changed color.

What's more, **visited links will appear in the new color
wherever they crop up**, even on a completely different
page that you are visiting for the first time. This can be useful
if you're viewing directories and lists, as you can instantly see
what you have previously visited.

Visited links eventually expire and revert to their old color.
You can set the **expiration** period under Internet Options
(Preferences). It's wise to keep the expiry short (no more than
20 days). A big **History file** can dramatically slow things
down, especially if you surf a lot. After a month or so, click
on **Clear History** in your settings and see if it speeds things
up. If it does, reduce your expiry period.

## Send email from a Web page

You'll often come across an invitation to **email someone
from a Web page**. It mightn't look like an email address – it
might be just a name that contains a link. Whatever, it will be
obvious from the context that if you want to contact that person
you should click on the link. If you pass your mouse over this
link it will read something like: **mailto: someone@somewhere.com**.

And then when you click on it, it will call up your mail program, addressing a new message to someone@somewhere.com Just type your message and send it. Any replies will arrive through the normal channels.

If it doesn't work, your **browser/mail combination** isn't set up properly. Before you can send email, you have to complete your email details. Generally this is automated in your setup process. If not, you'll have to open your browser and email settings and enter it yourself. You can use any mail program with Internet Explorer. Just choose it from the list under Programs in Internet Options. Netscape forces you to use Messenger. For instructions on setting up mail, see p.102.

## Join a newsgroup from the Web

A Web page might **refer you to a newsgroup** for more information. When you click on the link, Netscape or Internet Explorer will open a newsreader in a separate window. You can continue surfing the Web in your browser while you wait for the newsgroup subjects to arrive.

Again you'll need to have your **newsreader set up** to get the link to work. With Internet Explorer, if you're using any Usenet program other than Outlook Express or Internet Mail & News, you'll have to specify it in Internet Explorer under Programs. Again, Netscape doesn't offer the option.

For more on newsgroups, see p.129.

## Browse offline

If time online is costing you money, consider spending it **gathering pages** rather than reading. Allow each page you want to read to load fully and it will cache for reading offline later. Then you can run back through your session, after you hang up, by choosing **Work Offline** under the File menu in Netscape Navigator or by toggling the plug icon in the bottom left-hand corner. IE5.x automatically detects whether you're online.

Once in this mode, you can **call up sites** either by typing in their addresses or following links as if you were online, or by clicking on sites in your History file. This works by retrieving files stored temporarily in a folder called **cache** in Netscape and **Temporary Internet Files** in Internet Explorer. Their primary purpose is to speed up browsing. When you return to a page, your browser will check the cache first rather than download its components again from the Net.

IE5.x is way ahead of Netscape at offline browsing. Clicking IE5.x's History button will toggle a window on the left-hand side. You can sort the sites by date, name, order of visits, or number of visits. This makes it very easy to backtrack your session. But even better, you can **search the contents of the pages stored in cache**. It's like having your own search engine.

Mind you, these pages won't sit on your hard drive forever – they're governed by your **Cache or Temporary Internet Files settings** and they'll also be overwritten next time you visit that same address. If you wish to archive a page permanently then save it as described earlier (see p.84).

## Clearing your cache

You'll find your Temporary Internet Files (cache) settings under Internet Options (Preferences). That's the place to change how much disk space to allocate, where it's kept, and when to check for newer versions. It's also the proper place to delete all the stored pages. If you try to do it manually it will cause problems.

It's best to select the **option to check for newer versions** just once per session. Then if you suspect the document's changed during a session revisit, just hit Refresh/Reload. Unless you plan to read offline, it's wise to **delete these files every week or two** as, like the History file, if it gets too big, it can slow things right down.

If your **browser is playing up** and not loading pages properly, try clearing your cache. It's often an instant fix.

## Download entire sites while you sleep

If you'd like to read an online newspaper offline – for example on the train to work – you can set up Internet Explorer to go online while you sleep and download as much of the site as you want. (Handy if your access or phone charges are less late at night and you'd like to browse a large site during working hours). Just save the site to **Favorites**, choose **make available offline**, and then click on "Customize" to set how many pages to download and when to grab them. To edit or delete your deliveries, choose **Synchronize** from under the Tools menu.

# Make the most of your session

Nothing happens instantly on the Net, so **make sure you're always doing at least three things at once**. You might as well download news, mail, and the latest software releases while you browse several sites at once. If you're reading with nothing happening in the background, you're wasting time online.

It's simple to open multiple sites. While you wait for one page to load, open a **New Window** or **New Browser**, and look elsewhere while you wait. For instance, when reading an online newspaper, scan for interesting stories, and then quickly fire them all open in separate windows. Just click each link in turn while **holding down the Shift key** or by selecting **Open in a New Window** from your **mouse menu**. Then you can read it all instantly, perhaps even offline.

Bear in mind, however, that each process is competing for **computer resources** and bandwidth, so the more you attempt, the higher the likelihood that each will take longer – and that your machine might crash. Mac users will need to allocate extra memory to the browser otherwise it won't be able to open more than three or four windows.

**Opera** (http://www.operasoftware.com) is the only browser specifically designed to encourage this practice. It can easily open forty or more site windows within the main window, at a fraction of the resources needed in Netscape and IE. The only catch is you'll have thirty windows open, and Opera will crash, losing the lot. So, it's best to experiment first and see how much your setup can take.

## Turn off your multimedia

The drawback of the Web's sights and sounds is the time it takes to download them. If your connection is very slow, there is an option of **not showing images and** in Internet Explorer's case, other **multimedia**. It's in the Advanced section of your browser settings.

While declining images might load pages faster, some pages contain nothing but images with links behind them. If you strike such a page, select the broken image, and choose **Show Image** from your mouse menu on Explorer, or **Show Images** from Netscape's View menu, or change your settings and refresh the page.

Installing IE5.x's **Web Accessories pack** will lob an **image toggle switch** on your toolbar. Clicking it will turn images on or off.

## Plug-ins and ActiveX

Although your browser can recognize a mind-boggling array of multimedia and other file formats, you'll occasionally come across something it can't deal with. Generally, there'll be an icon nearby suggesting you grab a **plug-in** or an **ActiveX control.** If not, you'll see a broken image which when clicked on will tell you what you need and where to get it.

A **plug-in** is an auxiliary program that works alongside your browser. You download this program, install it, and your browser will call on it when need be. To **see what plug-ins are already installed** in Netscape, choose **About Plug-ins** from the Help menu. Then follow the link to see what else you can try. Remember, plug-ins consume hard disk and memory, and you can do without most of them, so choose carefully.

**ActiveX controls** work similarly, but their scope is far greater. When you arrive at a site that relies on an ActiveX control, it checks to see if you already have it, and if not, installs it automatically after you approve the publisher's certificate. As a rule, don't accept certificates unless you're satisfied the publisher is reputable. ActiveX currently only works in Internet Explorer for Windows.

## Java and JavaScript

When **Java** – Sun Microsystems'
vision of a platform-independent
programming language – arrived,
it was instantly pounced upon by
the Web community. What once
was a static environment quickly
sprang to life with all sorts of
"animated" applications thanks to
its simple HTML adjunct,
**JavaScript**. The main difference

between Java and JavaScript is that Java involves downloading
and running a small program (called an applet) whereas
JavaScript is interpreted by your browser.

Designers can create some cool effects using Java and
JavaScript, but if it's not implemented properly it might work
inconsistently or even crash your browser. Script that works
fine with Netscape can cause Internet Explorer to crash, and
vice versa. It's even more pronounced if you're running an
old version. If it's causing you too many problems, update
your browser version or disable Java in your Internet settings.

## Shockwave and RealAudio

There are two plug-in/ActiveX controls you'll definitely need:
the **RealPlayer** (which includes **RealAudio** and **RealVideo**)
for Internet music and video broadcasts; and the **Shockwave
and Flash Players** for multimedia effects. Whether or not
they came with your browser download the latest versions
from: http://www.real.com and http://www.shockwave.com

**Shockwave Flash** appears to have replaced Java as the
defacto standard for producing high impact sites. When it's
used properly it's welcome, but mostly it gets in the way, particularly when you strike it on a site's front page. If you're not
interested in viewing a pompous animated billboard, hit the

"skip intro" link. With a bit of luck you'll get to the next page without crashing your browser.

Once you have RealAudio you can **sample CDs** before you buy at online music stores, listen to Internet concerts, and tune into live and archived radio broadcasts from all over the world. Although Internet Explorer's **Media Player** is capable of playing Real media, it supports only the older standards. So, when you install the **RealPlayer**, make sure it takes over as your default viewer for all Real media. You'll find the option under the RealPlayer's Preferences.

The reason for this is that Microsoft is pushing its own streaming media standard, which is starting to gain ground. For a taster, if you right-click on IE5.x's toolbar and tick **Radio**, a tuner will appear on a new bar. You'll find a bevy of live stations to listen to while you're online. Media Player also supports the much-publicized **MP3 audio standard**.

For an introduction to online Music and live Internet broadcasts, see: p.218 and p.391.

## Proxy settings

Most Access Providers have a server that caches copies of popular Web sites. If you specify this machine's address as your **proxy server,** it should make browsing faster. In some cases, you can't access the Net directly, so specifying it is a must. Ask your provider for its address and enter it into your settings under the **Connection tab** in Internet Explorer's Options (in IE 5.x, select the connection and click on the settings button), or **Advanced** in Netscape's Preferences. Experiment with or without the proxy to see which is faster and more reliable. Sometimes proxies get in the road more than they're worth.

## Cookies

A **cookie** is a small file, placed on your computer by a Web server, as a sort of ID card. Then, next time you drop by, it will know you. Actually, it doesn't quite know it's "you", it only recognizes your individual browser. If you were to visit on another machine or with a different browser on the same machine, it would see you as a different visitor. Or conversely, if someone else were to use your browser, it couldn't tell the difference.

Most Web sites routinely **log your visit**. They can tell a few harmless things like what browser you're using, which pages you've requested and the last site you've seen. This is recorded against your IP address. However, because most dial-up users are issued a different IP address each time they log on, this information isn't useful for building individual profiles. If analysts can log this data against a cookie ID instead, they have a better chance of recognizing repeat visitors. Amongst other things, this makes their lives easier when it comes to looking for sponsorship, which means the site has a better chance of staying afloat.

On the next level, if you **voluntarily submit further details**, they can store it in a database against your cookie, and use it to do things like tailor the site to your preferences, or save you entering the same data each time you check in. This won't be stored on your computer, so other sites can't access it. And most importantly, they won't know anything personal about you – not even your email address – unless you tell them. So unless you have a good reason for hiding your visit to that site, go ahead – accept the cookie. And if your browser is set up to warn you every time you receive a cookie, go into your options and turn it off. It will end up driving you nuts otherwise. See: http://www.cookiecentral.com

# Censor Web material from kids

It's possible to **bar access to certain sites** that might be on the wrong side of educational. Both Internet Explorer and Netscape employ the **PICS** (Platform for Internet Content Selection) system. You can set ratings for language,

nudity, sex, and violence. Look under the **Content Advisor** settings, within the Content tab in Internet Explorer's Preferences. In Netscape 4.7x, go online and select **Netwatch** from under the Help menu. AOL also gives you similar control.

There are several third-party programs such as Surf-Watch, ImageCensor, Cybersitter, and NetNanny, which can impose all sorts of restrictions. None, however, is foolproof or particularly satisfactory. See:

http://www.peacefire.org
http://www.censorware.org
http://www.rsac.org

If you're really concerned about what your children are viewing on the Web, you might do better spending a few hours each week surfing the Web with them. After all, banning something will only make them want it more.

## Help

If you need step-by-step help using or configuring your browser, refer to your Help menu. Microsoft provides excellent help, including all manner of troubleshooting wizards. Netscape's is adequate for basic instructions. If you strike serious problems with Internet Explorer, search **Microsoft's Knowledge Base** at: http://support.microsoft.com and the **Internet Explorer FAQ** at: http://www.activewin.com/faq/

But the best place to find help is on **Microsoft's support newsgroups** (http://support.microsoft.com/support/news/) located on the public server at: msnews.microsoft.com

For Netscape problems check out:
http://help.netscape.com/nuggies/ and http://www.ufaq.org

# 7

# Email

## PROGRAMS, ATTACHED FILES AND FINDING ADDRESSES

If you only need one good reason to justify getting online, email should do. Once you get used to emailing people, don't be surprised if it becomes your preferred way to get in touch. You'll write more and respond faster – which means you might become more productive. But watch out, because email is as time-consuming as it is addictive. At first you might rediscover the joy of old-fashioned letter-writing, but because it's so easy to copy (cc) a message to everyone in your address book you might invite more mail than you can handle.

# Why email will change your life

Email is such an improvement on the postal system it will revolutionize the way and the amount you communicate. You can send a message to anyone with an email address anywhere in the world – instantaneously. In fact, it's so quick that it's possible they could receive your message sooner than you could print it.

All you need to do is **type an address**, or choose it from your **email address book**, write a brief note, and click **Send**. No letterheads, layout, printing, envelopes, stamps, or visiting the post office. And once you're online your mail program can automatically check in at whatever interval you like. You needn't wait for the postie to arrive. Email is delivered 24 hrs a day, seven days a week, every day of the year.

Email is also better than faxing. It's always **a local call to anywhere, at any time**. No busy signals, paper jams, or failed attempts. Plus you receive the actual text and not a photocopy, or an actual image file and not a scan. So that means you can send **high-resolution color** and **long documents**. As a matter of fact, each edition of this book has been submitted and edited via email.

Email even **beats the phone** at times. You can send a message to a part of the world that's asleep and have a reply first thing in the morning. No need to synchronize phone calls, be put on hold, speak to voicemail, or tell some busybody who's calling. With email, you take the red carpet route straight through to the top. And you don't have to make small talk, unless that's the purpose of the message.

Replacing the post and fax is not email's only strength. You can also **attach any computer file to a message**. That means you can forward things like advertising layout, scanned images, spreadsheets, assignments, tracks from your latest CD, links to Web pages, or even programs. And your accompanying message need only be as brief as a Post-it note or compliments slip.

What's more, with email **everything you send and receive can be filed** in a relatively small amount of disk space. No filing cabinets, no taped phone calls, and no yellowing fax paper. All in writing, and instantly searchable for later reference. Though it doesn't hurt to back up occasionally in case someone steals your computer!

## Brief and intimate

Out with stuffy business letters, and in with email. As email messages are (for the most part) simply text files, there's no need to worry about fonts, letterheads, logos, typesetting, justification, signatures, print resolution, or fancy paper. It distills correspondence down to its essence – words.

And what's more it's encouraging people to be brief and efficient. Which means you'll be able to punch out more letters, and deal with more people than ever before.

Conversely, email is also putting personal correspondence back into letters rather than phone calls. Most new users remark on this – and the fact that email often seems to spark off a **surprising intimacy**.

# What you'll need

To get started, you'll need a connection to the Net, a **mail program** and an **email address**.

You'll automatically **get an email address** when you sign up with an ISP. If you access through work or someone else's account, you could shop around your local providers for a mailbox-only account or try one of the free email address services on the Net (see p.118).

You should get an **email program** with your Internet access account, most likely whatever comes with your Web browser, but if it's not up to scratch, it's easy to scrap it for another.

# Choosing an email program

As your **email program** will become the workhorse of your Net kit, you should choose it as carefully as your browser. Still, that need only be one decision, because Internet Explorer's **Outlook Express** and Netscape's **Messenger** are the two best programs around. They're reliable, user-friendly, cutting edge, and free. But neither is perfect. Outlook Express acts like an independent mail program whereas Messenger clings closely to Navigator.

If it comes down to nitpicking, **Outlook Express** starts quicker, is more stable, and handles multiple mail accounts superbly. Its most unique feature is support for **Hotmail** (see p.118) and other Webmail accounts. In fact, if you don't have an email address you can start a Hotmail account on the spot through the Tools menu. Not surprising if you consider that Microsoft owns Hotmail. If you intend to use more than one email account – and you probably will – Outlook Express is the superior option.

**Messenger** concentrates more on getting the basics perfect than trying to be clever. That means there's never a hitch carrying out simple everyday tasks such as replying to a message, or forwarding it to someone else. It also gives you greater hands-on control of your formatting. Outlook Express isn't quite as well polished in this regard as we'll explain later. It does have some annoying quirks of its own though, as you'll soon find out. Going online to pick up ads isn't its most endearing aspect.

It's not worth trying to mix and match the browser suites as neither Outlook Express nor Messenger can be installed without their respective browsers.

## Other mail programs

Microsoft has put out some real email stinkers over the years such as **Exchange** (built into Windows 95) and **Outlook 97** (part of Office 97). Exchange should be avoided at any cost, but Outlook 97 can be improved by installing the Office 97 upgrades at http://officeupdate.microsoft.com

**Outlook 98** was touted as the next step up from Outlook Express. Although it adds contact, calendar, and task-management tools along with some neat features such as mapping and return receipt, you can safely get by without them. And unless you're using it for internal office mail, ensure you choose the **Internet mail only** installation – it loads faster. Its successor **Outlook 2000** adds more bulk that you can safely do without.

**Internet Mail & News**, which accompanies IE3.0x, however, is simple, elegant, and ample for the task if you're strapped for disk space.

If you'd prefer a custom-built email program, Eudora (http://www.eudora.com) remains the choice option. You can have it free, but you'll have to view a few ads.

### Where to get email programs and tools

If these options can't satisfy your email appetite you'll find plenty of alternative mail programs and tools at:

http://www.download.com (Mac and PC)
http://www.winfiles.com
http://www.davecentral.com

This includes utilities for polling your accounts and downloading just the headers, selectively deleting mail from your server, and attaching all sorts of multimedia such as video and voice. You're unlikely to need them though.

## Setting up for email

Before you can start you need to fill in a few **configuration details** for whoever supplied your email account (usually your ISP). Even if this process is automated by a wizard or your ISP's software, take some time to understand your email profile so you can enter it on other machines. For more on email addresses (see p.16).

To **start a new account in Outlook Express**, open **Accounts** under the Tools menu, choose "Add Mail" and follow the prompts. To change the settings select the account and choose Properties.

In **Messenger**, close the browser, open **Profile Manager**, click on **New** and follow the prompts. To change your details later, open **Mail & Newsgroups** under Navigator's Preferences.

## The settings

Let's say you're Anton Lavin and your email address is anton@leisureprince.com

Open your settings in any mail program and here's what you'll strike:

**Name:** Anton Lavin
(Who or what will appear as the sender of your mail.)

**Email Address:**
anton@leisureprince.com
(Where mail you send will appear to come from.)

**Return Address:**
anton@leisureprince.com
(Where replies to your mail will go. Most users opt for their regular email address but you could divert it to a work account, for example.)

**Outgoing Mail (SMTP):**
mail.leisureprince.com
(The server to handle your outgoing mail – usually your own provider.

**Incoming Mail (POP3):**
mail.leisureprince.com
(Where your mail is stored. This should be the same as the last part of your email address, though often with pop. or mail. added at the start.)

**Account Name:** anton
(The first part of your email address.)

**Password:** ******
(Careful, don't let anyone see you enter this one.)

**Note** that the above applies only to **POP3-based mail systems**, which at present doesn't include AOL. For more on POP3, see p.263.

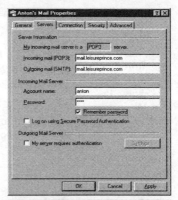

## Sending and receiving email

You needn't be connected to the Net to **compose an email message**. Simply open your mail program, start a new message, address it either by entering an address manually or by selecting a name from your **address book**, add a **subject**, write the note, and then click **Send**. But before you can actually deliver it you need to **go online**. Sending is usually tied in with receiving (read on for more detail on both operations). Normally you do both at the same time, although it's possible if necessary to separate the two. If you're offline, you'll want to **Send Later**. This is automatic in Outlook Express, but you'll have to choose it from the new message's File menu in Messenger. Then once you're online, you'd choose **Send Unsent Messages** from the File menu.

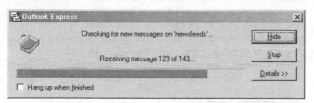

Outlook Express and Messenger store **unsent mail** in a folder either called the **Outbox** or **Unsent Messages**. Once it's dispatched, it moves into the **Sent** folder. Other programs may do it differently. For instance, Eudora marks unsent mail with a Q, which changes to an S after it's sent.

**Incoming mail** arrives in the **Inbox** or wherever your filters (message rules) dump it. When it arrives, you'll hear a sound, get a message and/or see a little envelope in your system tray. That depends on what you configure in your settings. You can change the new mail sound in Windows 95/98 under Sounds in the Control Panel.

Outlook Express and Messenger both let you **read mail as it arrives**, as well as preview messages in a separate window. You can tell which messages are new as they'll be bold and the little envelopes next to them will be closed. Outlook Express displays a number beside each folder to tell you how many unread messages it contains.

### Addressing email

Open up a new mail message window, and you'll see a line starting with **To:** which is where you type in your **recipient's address**. Internet email addresses should be along the lines of someone@somewhere where someone is the recipient's account name and somewhere identifies the server where they collect their mail.

If you submit a wrongly constructed or a non-existent address, your message should bounce back to you with an **error message** saying what went wrong. This tends to happen within a matter of minutes. Sometimes, however, mail bounces back after a few days. This usually indicates a physical problem in delivering the mail rather than an addressing error. When it occurs, just send it again. If it's your end that's caused the problem, you might have a whole batch of mail to resend.

### The address book

Despite first appearances, Internet email addresses aren't so hard to recall. Their name-based components are stacks easier to remember than telephone numbers and street addresses. However, there's no real need to memorize them, nor do you have to type in the whole address every time. Not when you have an **address book**.

Start your address book by putting yourself in. Open it in Outlook Express from under the Tools menu or by clicking on the book icon. In Messenger it's under the Communicator menu. Choose **New Card** or **New Contact** and fill in the

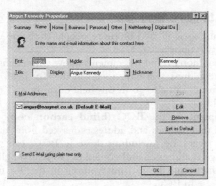

blanks. To **import addresses from messages** simply right-click (or click in Macs) on the sender's name and choose **Add to Address Book** from your mouse menu.

You can **send a message to someone in your address book** in several ways, from within the Address Book or the New Message window. Start off by adding every email address you know, and click on all the options until you know it inside out. With most email programs you can **click** or **double-click** on addresses in your address book to create new mail, or with Netscape **drag and drop addresses** into the **To**: or **CC** fields of a new message.

You can also **assign nicknames** to act as shortcuts – and even if you don't the programs are smart enough to help you out. For example, you might only have to enter a few letters of a name, an address or a nickname and it will search the address book for the closest matches. Just be careful it does enter the right address – otherwise it could prove embarrassing.

It's worthwhile experimenting to see which way you prefer. Understanding your address book's capabilities will save you time and tedium in the long run. But the simplest way to address a message is by replying to a previous one.

## Sending to more than one

If you want to send two or more people the same message, you have two options.

When you don't mind if recipients know who else is receiving it, one address will have to go in the **To**: field, and the other addresses can also go in this field or in the **CC** (**carbon copy**) field.

Put recipients in the **BCC** (**blind carbon copy**) field if you want their names and addresses masked from all others. However, everyone, including those in BCC, can see who the message is addressed and copied to. To send a bulk mailer without disclosing the list, put yourself in the To: field and everyone else in BCC.

If you don't see a BCC option in Outlook Express, open a new message and tick All Headers under the View menu.

## The subject

Let your email recipients know what your message is about. Put something meaningful in the **Subject:** heading. It's not so important when they first receive it – they'll probably open it even if it's blank. However, if you send someone your résumé and you title it "Hi dude", two months down the track when they're looking for talent, they'll have a hard time weeding you out of the pile.

Filling in the subject is optional when replying. If you don't enter anything, it will retain the original subject and insert **Re:** before the original subject title to indicate it's a reply.

## Replying

Yet another great thing about email is how you can quote received mail. To **reply to a message**, simply select it, and click on the **Reply** button or choose **Reply** from under the

Message or mouse button menu. This will automatically copy the original message and address it back to the sender.

Depending on your settings (check your Help file or experiment), this new message will contain the original, with **quote tags (>)** prior to each line, or underneath a dotted line perhaps with a bar down the side. It will also contain the **header** of the original message detailing the sender, subject, and delivery date.

To change the quote style in Outlook Express go to the Send tab in Options, and play with the Mail Sending Formats. Start with the **Send format set to Text** as not all mail programs understand HTML. Then you can select to send HTML on a per message basis under the Format menu in the New Message window. Messenger gives a far greater depth of control over reply formatting. Its settings are within Preferences under the **Messages** and **Formatting** tabs in Mail & Newsgroups.

You can **keep parts or the entire original message**, including the subject – or delete the lot. So when someone asks you a question or raises a point, you're able to include that section and answer it directly underneath or above. This saves them having to refer back and forth between their message and your answer. It also saves keying their address.

Don't fall into the habit of including the entire contents of the original letter in your reply. It wastes time for the receiver and its logical outcome (letters comprising the whole history of your correspondence) hardly bears thinking about.

Note also that the **Reply all** option addresses your message not only to the sender but also to all recipients of the original. That's not something you'll always want to do.

You can normally tell if a message is a reply because the **subject will start with Re:**

## Forward a message

If you'd like to share an email with someone, it's possible to **forward it on**. Forwarded messages are just like replies except they're not addressed to the original sender. You'll have to add the addresses manually. Unfortunately Outlook Express treats forwarded messages under the same rules as replies. That means if your replies come with quote tags, your forwarded messages will follow suit. It's better to forward them **inline**, that is, **beneath a dotted line**. The only way to switch over in Outlook Express is to re-enter Options. That's quite a pain. Alternatively, you could **forward the message as an attachment**. This isn't a bad option.

To forward in Outlook Express, select the message and either select **Forward** or **Forward as an attachment** from the mouse menu, toolbar, or under the Message menu. The same for Messenger, except it differentiates between Forward Quoted and Forward Inline (three cheers!)

You can tell if a message has been forwarded to you because the subject line will start with **Fwd:** or **Fw:**

## Resend a message

There isn't a menu option to resend a message in either Outlook Express or Messenger, so the easiest way is to right-click on the message, choose "select all", then copy and paste the text into a new message and reenter the subject and recipients.

## Signatures and vCards

All mailers let you add your personal touch at the end of your composition in the form of a **signature file**. This appears automatically on the bottom of your email, like headed notepaper. It's common practice to put your address, phone number, title, and perhaps round off with a witticism. There's nothing to stop you adding a monstrous picture, frame, or your initials in ASCII art. Except you have more taste than that.

```
/////\\        //|||\\        //\|\\        ///||\
/`0-0'`        ` @ @\       //o o//         a a
   ]              >          ) | (          _)
   -              -              -              ~
 John          Paul         George         Ringo
```

To create and manage your signature(s) click on the "**Signatures**" tab in Outlook Express's Options, or under Identity in Messenger's Mail & Newsgroups' Preferences. In Messenger, you have to create the signature in a separate text file, say in Windows Notepad, and then locate it with the Choose button. You can do the same in Outlook Express, or simply create one in the box provided.

A **vCard** is an address book entry with as much contact details as you care to disclose. You might like to attach a copy to your mail so your recipients can add it to their address books. To set it up in Outlook Express, edit the Business card section under the Compose tab in Options. In Messenger, choose Edit Card under Mail & Newsgroups' Preferences.

## Attaching non-text files to your email

Suppose you want to send something other than just a text message – such as a **word processor document, spreadsheet, or an image** – via email. It's a piece of cake. To send a file, look in your mail menu for something along the lines of **Send Attachments** or **Attach File**. Either that or try dragging and dropping the file into the New Message window. It will normally work without a second thought from you.

Well, it's almost that simple. A residual problem, while people are using a variety of mailers, is that both parties' mailers need to support a common encoding standard, otherwise it will appear in gibberish. The most used methods are **MIME** and **UUencode**. It doesn't really matter which you use as long as it works every time, so try a practice run first.

If you have problems getting a file to someone, refer to your Help file on how to specify an encoding method, as it varies between packages. MIME is gaining acceptance across all platforms (it's all that Netscape's older mailers recognize), so if you have the option, set it as the default. Eudora for Macs includes **Binhex**, Apple Single and Apple Double. Always choose Apple Double.

If your mail program doesn't automatically decode attachments, ditch it for one that does. It's not worth the bother. Old office systems like early Microsoft Mail are notoriously fussy. If you're not allowed to use an email program that handles attachments with grace, consider a new job.

**Note**: Don't ever send an attachment of more than a few hundred kilobytes without prior warning or agreement. Large attachments can take ages to download and even crash meager machines. It's no way to make friends.

## How to send a CD track

If you'd like to share a tune from your new CD try encoding it with **Real Jukebox** (http://www.real.com) and attaching it to a message. All your friend will need is the RealPlayer from the same address. Alternatively, if you don't mind a bigger file, you'll get better sound quality by encoding it in MP3. For instructions, see p.229.

## HTML mail and sending Web pages

Not long ago, email was a strictly plain text affair. The odd mailer such as Microsoft Exchange allowed formatting, but it didn't really make an impact until Netscape introduced **HTML mail** as a new standard. Today, if your mailer lacks HTML support you'll feel a bit backward.

HTML mail blurs the distinction between email and the World Wide Web, bringing Web pages right into your email. This means Web publishers, particularly magazines and news broadcasters, can send you regular bulletins formatted as Web pages complete with links to further information. It also means you can send Web pages by email. Either drag and drop them into a message or choose Send Page from under the File menu. Just make sure your recipient also has an HTML compliant email program, otherwise they'll get all the formatting as a useless and time-wasting attachment.

Although the concept of fancying up your email with stationery and a business logo might seem more professional, it's entirely unnecessary, and perhaps even inappropriate. It actually detracts from one of email's strongest features – simplicity. So don't spend too much time worrying about the appearance of your email. Just get the words right.

For a quick lesson in Outlook Express HTML mail see:
http://www.mindspring.com/~majik/docs.htm
and the newsgroup:
microsoft.public.windows.inetexplorer.ie5.outlookexpress
.stationery

## Managing email

If your provider or phone company charges you by the minute to stay connected, it's best to **compose and read your mail offline** (ie, when you are not connected by phone). That way, while connected you're actually busy transferring data, and getting your money's worth. All programs allow you to send your messages immediately or place them in a queue, as well as to collect mail at regular intervals or on request.

Unless you're always online, you should choose: **not to send mail immediately; to check manually (not every x minutes)**; and **to not check for messages at startup**. Otherwise your software will try to send and collect when you're offline. It's best to go online, collect your mail, upload your unsent mail, reply to anything urgent, log off, deal with the rest, and send your new bag of letters next time you go online.

If you have **unsent messages** it will ask you if you wish to send them whenever you open or close the program. Choose **No** if you're offline.

### Filing

Just as you keep your work desk tidy, and deal with paper as it arrives, try to keep your email neat. Most programs can organize your correspondence into **mailboxes** or **folders** of some sort and offer you the option of automatically filing sent mail into a **Sent Mail** folder.

It's good discipline to use several folders for filing and to transfer your sent mail into periodic archives. Otherwise you'll be creating unwieldy folders containing thousands of messages that are possibly hard to open. Similarly, when you have dealt with mail, either send it to trash (and empty this folder regularly) or put it into a topic folder.

### Sorting

To **sort your messages** by date, sender, size or subject, click on the bar at the top of each column. Click again to sort in a different way. Sorting by date makes the most sense so you can instantly see what's most recent.

### Filtering

Most programs can **filter** incoming mail into designated mailboxes, either as it arrives or afterwards. It looks for a common phrase in the incoming message, such as the address

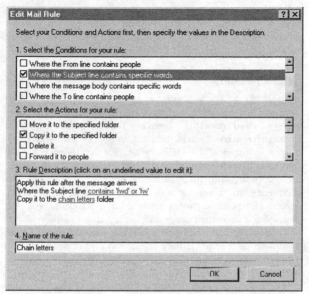

or subject, and transfers it to somewhere other than the default inbox. This is indispensable if you subscribe to a lot of mailing lists (see the following chapter, p.124) or get a ton of junk office email.

To set up your filters in Outlook Express, open **Message Rules** under the Tools menu. In Messenger, the **Message Filters** are located under the Edit menu.

### Tracking replies

Transfer email that needs attention into a special folder until it's dealt with so you can instantly see what's urgent. Do the same with your Sent box. Transfer the mail that's awaiting replies.

As email is quick, and people tend to deal with it immediately, if you don't get a reply within a few days you'll know what to follow up. Once you've received your reply, you can either archive or delete your original outgoing message.

## Return receipts

If you'd like to know if your mail has been delivered and/or opened, you could try requesting a "**delivery receipt**" and/or "**read receipt**". Delivery receipts verify that your message has arrived safely on your recipient's mail server, but only if it supports the Delivery Service Notification (DSN) standard. If it doesn't support it, you'll get no reply. Read receipts notify your message has been opened. But again, the recipient must be using a mail program that supports the Message Disposition Notification (MDN) standard. Not only that, even if their mail program supports it, when they receive your message, a box will pop up asking whether they'd like to acknowledge receipt. If they say no, you'll get no receipt. In other words, it's not a reliable system and really not worth the bother.

Still, if you feel like experimenting with it, you can easily enable either or both types in Messenger, on a per message, or per recipient, basis. Outlook Express only supports read receipts. For instructions, search on the keyword "receipt" in your help file.

## Sending your first email

The best way to start is to **send yourself some email**. That way you'll get to both send and receive something. If you're dialing in, start this exercise offline with your mail program in **offline mode**.

**1.** To set up **Messenger**, open Preferences, then Offline, and choose **Ask me**. Restart the program, and choose **Offline**. Open the Mail Servers tab in the Mail & Newsgroup Preferences, click on the Incoming Mail server and choose Edit. Uncheck the box to check the mail every 10 (or so) minutes.

In **Outlook Express**, open Options, then General and choose not to send and receive messages at Startup, not to check mail regularly, and not to **Send mail immediately** under the Send tab.

You can alter all these settings later when you know what you want.

**2.** Presuming you've completed your server details, the first step is to put yourself into the address book. Next, open up a new message, choose yourself from the address book, give the message a subject, enter something in the body and click **Send** in the **New Message** window. If you're **in offline mode**, that will place your message in a queue to be sent once you go online. Otherwise, it will call up your dialer and try to send it immediately.

**3.** Now attempt to retrieve/send your mail. If you're not connected, that should bring up your dialer. If not and you can't see how to make it happen automatically, call up your dialer manually, log in, and try again. Most mail programs pop up a progress window to tell you what's going on.

Once you've sent yourself the message keep checking every 30 seconds until you receive it. It shouldn't take more than a few minutes. Now repeat this exercise until you're confident to face the rest of the wired world.

# Get your free email address here

Need an email address that you can keep for as long as you like without paying a penny, or signing up for Internet access? Perhaps you already have one through work, but you'd like an alternative for personal mail – one that your boss can't read. Or you need a second one for junk mail. Or to take on vacation. No problem. You can score one (or more) online within minutes and it needn't cost you a thing, though you might have to suffer a little advertising.

There are three main options: **Webmail**, **POP3 mail**, and **mail forwarding**.

**W e b m a i l** accounts work through the Web. You have to log into a Web site to collect, write and send your mail.

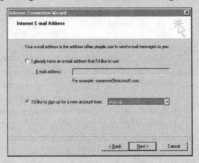

That means you don't need to set up a mail program. You can access your mail from any computer with a Web browser. Ideal, if you're at work, or at a cybercafé, but a bit inconvenient for everyday use. As you can give any details you like, it's perfect for anonymous mail – though abusers can still be traced by their IP address.

Webmail accounts are everywhere. Just about every major site will give you one in an attempt to get you to return. **Hotmail** (http://www.hotmail.com) is the most popular and heavily featured with junk mail detection and automatic virus scanning. Just log in, give a few details and you'll have a mail account in seconds. You can even do it through a menu entry in Outlook Express 5.x. **PlanetAccess** (http://www.planetaccess.com) is another with a good reputation for its speed. You might find it better for traveling. Or if you'd rather a more distinct address, try: http://www.another.com

At this stage, Outlook Express 5.x is the only mail program that can collect Webmail but others may follow suit. You'll find it much slower to send and receive than with the regular POP3

mail account you'd get from an ISP. You can also get free POP3 accounts but they're not as common. They usually require that you check your mail, before you can send, which can be annoying as Outlook Express likes to do it in the opposite order. The ideal solution is to specify your ISP's SMTP server as the outgoing mail server.

See **MailandNews** (http://www.mailandnews.com) and **Yahoo** (http://mail.yahoo.com).

If you already have an email address and simply want something funkier, you can get one ending in anything from @struth.com to @doglover.com through a **forwarding service**. What's sent to this address gets redirected to wherever you choose. You're then free to switch providers while retaining a fixed address. See: **Mail.com** (http://www.mail.com) and **V3** (http://www.v3.com)

For **thousands more free email providers**, see:
http://www.fepg.net
http://www.emailaddresses.com
http://www.internetemaillist.com

## Staying anonymous

Occasionally when sending mail or posting to a newsgroup, you might prefer to **conceal your identity** – for example, to avoid embarrassment in health discussions. There are three main ways to send mail anonymously. As mentioned in the box on p.118, **Webmail** is one.

The second is less ethical. You can **change your configuration** so that it looks like it's coming from somebody else, either real or fictitious. However, if anyone tries to reply, their mail will attempt to go to that alias, not you. But, be warned, it's possible to trace the header details back to your server, if someone's really eager – and your national law enforcement agency might be if you're up to no good.

The third way is to have your IP address masked by a third party, such as an anonymous remailer. This can be almost impossible to trace. See: http://www.anonymizer.com and http://www.andrebacard.com/remail.html

## Privacy

Although there's been a lot of fuss about hacking and Net security, in reality email is potentially more secure than your phone or post. In fact, most new-generation email programs (including Messenger and Outlook Express) have some kind of **encryption** built in. But it's not hackers who are most likely to read your mail – it's whoever has access to your incoming mail server and, of course, anyone with access to your computer. If it happens to be at work, then you can **assume your boss can read your mail**. In some companies it's standard practice, so don't use your work mail for correspondence that could land you in hot water. Instead, set up a private account and don't store your messages on your work machine. You can collect and send your POP3 mail from a Web interface such as Mail2Web (http://www.mail2web.com), or from within HotMail. Alternatively, set up a free Webmail account, the most private being HushMail (http://www.hushmail.com), which offers secure storage and encrypted messaging between users.

If you're really serious about privacy, you may want to investigate **PGP (Pretty Good Privacy)**, a powerful method of encryption, which generates a set of public and private "keys" from a passphrase. You distribute the public key and keep the private key secure. When someone wants to send you a private message, they scramble it using your public key. You then use the private key, or your secret passphrase, to decode it. For more, see: http://www.pgpi.org

## Digital signing and encryption

Internet Explorer, Netscape Communicator, and their associated mailers already support emerging encryption and digital signing standards but few use them.

**Digital signing** proves your identity via a third party certificate. Here's how to get yours. First up, fetch a personal certificate from Verisign (http://www.verisign.com) You can't go wrong if you follow the instructions. Once it's installed, open your mail security settings and see that the certificate is activated. You may choose to sign all your messages digitally by default, or individually. Then send a secure message to all your regular email partners, telling them to install your certificate. Those with secure mailers can add your certificate against your entry in their address books. From then on, they'll be able to verify that mail that says it's from you is indeed from you. Don't use it flippantly, though, because **it's a pain for your recipients**.

**Encryption** works similarly, though you'll also need your email partners' certificates to encrypt messages to them. Also, as each certificate only works on one installation, you'll need a different one for work and home. This makes it a bit cumbersome if you're collecting mail on the road. It also means anyone with access to your machine could pretend they're you.

Yes, it's all a bit flaky at this stage. So spend a few minutes in your Help file figuring out the finer details, try it with your friends, and decide amongst yourselves whether it's worth the bother.

## Finding an email address – and being found

If you'd like your long-lost childhood sweetheart to track you down by email, you'd better list yourself in a few online email directories. See "Email Search" (p.289) in our Web guide.

For advice on how to find someone else's email address, see our chapter on "Finding It" (p.178).

## Avoiding viruses

If you've updated Windows with the latest security patches, the only way you'll catch a virus from email is by clicking on an attachment. For a rundown on the precautions you should take see p.22.

## Coping with spam

If you start receiving piles of unsolicited mail (commonly known as **spam**), contrary to popular advice, **there's not a lot you can do about it**. You can employ various filters but there's really not much point. You might as well let them arrive and delete them on sight. If the option of unsubscribing from a mailing list is offered give it a go. That will stop the messages on any legitimate mailing list, but some unscrupulous marketeers regard any response, no matter how negative, as nothing more than a confirmation of receipt.

The best action is to **avoid exposing your main address** in the first place. Most importantly, always mask your email address, or **use an alternative account**, if posting to Usenet or an online forum of any type (see p.136). And whenever you hand over your email address to a Web site, use your secondary

account and ask not to be sent any occasional offers from their
"associates."

For instructions on how to complain to the spammer's ISP,
see: http://www.spamfree.org and http://www.whew.com

## Help

If you're frustrated by Microsoft's **Internet Mail & News**
or **Outlook Express** try
http://www.xs4all.nl/~koch01/index.htm
http://chattanooga.net/~scochran/oe5faq.htm
http://www.okinfoweb.com/moe/

Or the newsgroups:
microsoft.public.windows.inetexplorer.ie5.outlookexpress or
microsoft.public.internet.mail
For all versions of Outlook, try:
http://www.slipstick.com/outlook/faq.htm

For Eudora, try: http://www.eudora.com
and the newsgroups:
comp.mail.eudora.ms-windows or
comp.mail.eudora.mac

For Netscape, try:
http://help.netscape.com/nuggies/
and the newsgroups:
comp.infosystems.www.browsers.ms-windows or
comp.infosystems.www.browsers.mac

# 8

# Mailing Lists

## SUBSCRIBE YOURSELF

If you want email by the bucketload, join a mailing list. This will involve giving your email address to someone and receiving whatever they send until you beg them to stop. Mailing lists fall into two categories: closed (one way) or open. Closed lists are set up by some sort of authority or publisher to keep you informed of news or changes. That could be anything from hourly Antarctic weather updates to product release announcements. They're one way only: you don't contribute. What comes through an open list is sent by its members – and yes, that could be you.

The purpose of most lists is to broadcast news or encourage discussion about a specific topic – anything from alien abductions to Japanese jazz. In some cases, the list itself forms a group, like a social club, so don't be surprised if discussion drifts way off topic or into personal and indulgent rants. You'll see. But you'll also find lists are an easy way to keep up with news and to meet a few peers, maybe in person, too.

## How it works

Each mailing list has two addresses: the **mailing address** used to contact its members; and the **administrative address** used to send commands to the server or maintainer of the list. Don't get them mixed up or everyone else on the list will think you're a twit.

Most lists are **unmoderated**, meaning they relay messages immediately. Messages on **moderated** lists, however, get screened first. This can amount to downright censorship, but more often it's welcome, as it can improve the quality of discussion and keep it on topic by pruning irrelevant and repetitive messages. It all depends on the moderator, who is rarely paid for the service. Certain other lists are moderated because they carry messages from one source, such as the US Travel Warnings. Such lists often have a parallel open list for discussion.

If you'd rather receive your mail in large batches than have it trickle through, request a **digest** where available. These are normally sent daily or weekly, depending on the traffic.

As discussions are conducted entirely by email, **the only software needed is your standard mail program**.

## Climbing aboard a list

Joining should be simple. In most cases, you **subscribe** by sending a single email message or by filling out a form on a Web page. It depends who's running the list. Once you're on an open list, you'll receive all the messages sent to the list's address, and everyone else on the list will receive whatever you send. Your first message will either welcome you to the list, or ask you to confirm your email address (to stop prank subscriptions). Keep the welcome message, as it should also tell you how to **unsubscribe**, and in some cases set other parameters, such as ordering it in **digest format**.

### Subscribing and other list options

Mailing lists are typically run on **Listserv**, **Listproc** or **Majordomo** software. Generally, the list's administrator sets a few options and leaves it up to the program to handle subscription requests automatically, and bounce email out to the list members. So when you want to subscribe or unsubscribe, there's no point writing a courtesy letter as it will only confuse the program. You'll need to find the list's administrative address. Don't send requests to the list address, as it will simply be sent as a normal message to all the list members.

So, let's say you're called Caroline Appleton. Here's how you might subscribe to a list formally called gossip-list:

For **Majordomo:**
To: administrative address
Subject:
Message: subscribe gossip-list

For **Listproc** and **Listserv:**
To: administrative address
Subject:
Message: subscribe gossip-list Caroline Appleton

To unsubscribe, replace the word "subscribe"
with "unsubscribe".

And to find out about other list options in any program, send:

To: administrative address
Subject:
Message: help

# In-box Direct

You'll find the most organized collection of high-quality closed (or one-way) lists rounded up by Netscape and loosely known as **In-box Direct**. These range from fashion probes like Elle Direct to techie bulletins like PC Week. But they all have one thing in common: they're all sent as Web pages, less the images. This means you need a mail program – like those built into Netscape or Internet Explorer – that reads HTML mail.

The only hitch is you have to join Netscape's NetCenter, which involves filling out far too many details and choosing a password and log-in name. Don't tick any boxes that give Netscape the right to pass on your address, otherwise you'll be panhandled by email forever.

To sign up, go to: http://home.netscape.com/ibd/
and follow the instructions. It takes weeks to get on some lists, but persevere; it does eventually work. Or bypass this and go directly to each home site and sign up there. In the same way, keep an eye out for interesting lists as you browse the Web. Almost all the best sites have them. For more on **finding a list to join**, see our chapter on "Finding It" (p.163).

# Starting your own list

If you'd like to **create your own list** check out

| | |
|---|---|
| **Listbot**: | http://www.listbot.com |
| **Coollist**: | http://www.coollist.com |
| **Topica**: | http://www.topica.com |
| **eGroups**: | http://www.egroups.com |

They're free, and simple to manage from the Web. Or if you want to get serious, ask your provider or network manager to set you up a Listserv, Listproc or Majordomo account on their server.

## Privacy

You should consider anything sent to a mailing list to be **in the public domain**. That means discussions could end up archived on the World Wide Web (for instance, at: http://www.mail-archive.com). This isn't usually the case, and may not even be legal, but it's safer not to test it, so take care not to say anything you wouldn't like to see next to your name on the front page of your local paper.

## Coping with the volume

Before you set off subscribing to every list that takes your fancy **consider using separate email addresses** for mailing lists and personal mail. Apart from the obvious benefits in managing traffic and filtering, it protects your personal account from **evil spammers**. If nothing else, you should at least **filter your list messages** accordingly so your high-priority mail doesn't get buried amongst the junk. Remember, though, when posting to ensure you switch accounts first. It's easy with Outlook Express 5.x. You can select whichever identity you want to post from through the drop-down window in the From: field. Messenger (4.7x) is less flexible. You can set up a separate identity, but you'll have to close and re-open Netscape to switch.

## Vacation alert!

If you're trotting off from your mail for a while, consider unsubscribing from your high-volume lists. Otherwise you might face a serious mail jam when you return.

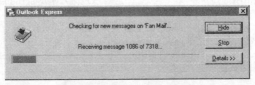

# 9

# Newsgroups

## THE MYSTERIES OF USENET

**W**ould you like: a deep and meaningful discussion on the matters closest to your heart; an answer to a question that's been bugging you forever; to share your expertise with others; or just hook up with people who think like you? If so, the place for you is Usenet news, the Net's prime discussion area. Don't be confused by its name, it's not about delivering the news as you know it. In this context, news relates to the messages stored in more than 85,000 discussion groups. These groups are called "newsgroups", and each one is dedicated to a specific topic.

With an Internet population of over 300 million, it's potentially possible to get access to the world experts (and loonies) in every field. Want to know the recipe for Lard Surprise, who sells Mach3 blades in Kabul, or where to sell that unexploded land mine in your garden? Easy, just find the right newsgroup, post your query, and wait for the results.

Whatever you do, **don't think the Net starts and ends with the World Wide Web**. If you miss Usenet, you miss the very best the Net has to offer.

This chapter covers the basics of how to jump on and join in.

## How it works

A **Usenet newsgroup** is a bit like a **public notice board** on the Internet. When you send (post) a message to a newsgroup, everyone who reads that group can see it. They can then **contribute to the discussion publicly** by posting a reply and/or **contact you privately** by email. You won't have a clue who's reading your messages unless they post. It's possible to read any message, in any group, as long as it remains on your news provider's system. That could be anywhere from a few days to a month depending on the policy it has set for each group.

## What you'll need

Apart from an Internet connection, the only two things you'll need to get Usenet happening on your machine is a **newsreader program** and **access to a news server**. You'll already have a newsreader if you've downloaded the latest versions of Netscape or Internet Explorer. And, as **most ISPs maintain a news server** as part of the access package, you should be ready to go. If you don't know your ISP's news server address, call its support line or check its home page.

## Choosing a newsreader

**Newsreaders** – the software you use for viewing and posting to newsgroups – are the most counterintuitive and inconsistent of all Internet programs. You can be proficient with one yet bewildered at first by another. So expect a tough time in your first session as you come to grips with its nuances. But after a couple of sessions, it'll all become second nature.

If you have **Netscape Communicator 4.x (Messenger)**, **Internet Explorer 4.x (Outlook Express) or later versions** you won't need to look for another newsreader unless you have high demands. (Earlier versions, Netscape Navigator 3.0x and Internet Mail & News, are satisfactory though not cutting edge).

However, if you want more power and value from your session, **or you're using any version of Outlook for your mail,** you should grab a dedicated client. For PCs, try **Agent** from Forté (http://www.forteinc.com). It has two versions: Free Agent, which is free; and Agent, the registered, full-featured, Swiss-army-knife edition.

On the **Mac**, go straight for **MT NewsWatcher** (http://www.best.com/~smfr/mtnw/)

You can also access Usenet through a Web interface such as:

| | |
|---|---|
| **Deja.com** | http://www.deja.com/usenet/ |
| **Remarq** | http://www.remarq.com |
| **Talkway** | http://www.talkway.com |

They're handy if you couldn't be bothered installing a program or don't have access to a news server, say at work or in a cybercafé, but you'll find them tediously slow by comparison.

## How to read newsgroup names

Newsgroups are divided into specific topics using a simple naming system. You can usually tell what a group's about by looking at its name. The first part is the **hierarchy** (broad category) it falls under. Here are just some of the top-level and most popular (asterisked) hierarchies:

| Hierarchy | Content |
|-----------|---------|
| alt. | Alternative, anarchic, and freewheeling discussion* |
| aus. | Of interest to Australians |
| ba. | San Francisco Bay Area topics |
| bionet. | Biological topics |
| bit. | Topics from Bitnet LISTSERV mailing lists* |
| biz. | Commercial bulletins |
| clari. | ClariNet subscription news service |
| comp. | Computing* |
| de. | German groups |
| k12. | Education through to grade 12 |
| microsoft. | Microsoft product support |
| misc. | Miscellaneous* |
| news. | About Usenet itself* |
| rec. | Hobbies and recreational activities* |
| sci. | All strands of science* |
| soc. | Social, cultural, and religious groups* |
| talk. | The most controversial issues* |
| uk. | British topics |

Note that **newsgroup names** contain dots, like domain names, but they're interpreted differently. Each part of the name distinguishes its focus, rather than its location. The top of the hierarchy is at the far left. As you move right, you go down the tree and it becomes more specific. For instance **rec.sport.cricket.info** is devoted to information about the compelling recreational sport that is cricket. Also, though several groups may discuss similar subjects, each will have its own angle. Thus while **alt.games.gravy** might have light and anarchic postings, **biz.gravy.train** would get right down to the business.

To find which newsgroups discuss your interests, think laterally and use your newsreader's filtering capabilities to **search its newsgroup list** for key words. Or easier still, search **Deja.com discussions** (http://www.deja.com/usenet/), the biggest newsgroup directory on the Web.

## Getting access to more groups

**No news server carries every group**. Some groups are restricted to a local geographical area or within one ISP's network. Other groups, which are deemed unpopular or irrelevant, might be cut to conserve disk space, or there might be a **policy to ban certain groups** and hierarchies. The decision on what you see and what you don't falls with whomever supplies your newsfeed.

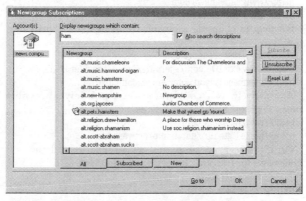

This is not entirely a bad thing as it takes less bandwidth to keep the Usenet file up to date and thus reduces the general level of Net traffic. And **most providers are flexible**. If, say, your provider has arbitrarily decided to exclude all foreign-language and minor regional groups, and you're interested in Icelandic botany and Indian plumbing, you might be able to get the **groups added to the feed** simply by asking. However, sometimes omissions are due to **censorship**. Many providers remove groups on moral grounds, or to avoid controversy. The usual ones to get the chop are the `alt.binaries.pictures.erotica` (pornography), `alt.sex` and `alt.warez` (software hacking and piracy) hierarchies. No great loss.

If you can't get the groups you want from your provider, your account doesn't come with a newsfeed (eg, at work), or you have privacy concerns, you needn't resort to another ISP. You could sign up to a **news-only account** with a Usenet specialist, such as:

http://www.newsguy.com

http://www.supernews.com

http://www.usenetserver.com

For help in choosing a **commercial newsfeed provider**, see:

http://www.newsreaders.com/

http://www.exit109.com/~jeremy/news/providers/

http://members.tripod.com/~newscompare/

Alternatively, you could jump on a **publicly accessible news server**. For the latest lists, see:

http://www.newzbot.com

http://home1.gte.net/docthomp/servers.htm

Or, if you're really desperate, it's possible to read and post your news for free **via the Web** at **Deja.com**.

## Getting started

Before you can get your news you'll need to tweak a few knobs on your **newsreader**. It's hard to give definitive instructions because the features differ so markedly between programs. However, here's what to look for.

## Configuring your newsreader

To start with, you'll need to specify your **news server**, **identity**, and **email address** (see overleaf). It should be part of your initial set-up routine. If not, to add a new Usenet service in **Outlook Express**, open Accounts from under the Tools menu, select "Add News" and follow the prompts. In **Netscape Messenger**, open "Preferences" from under the Edit menu, and add your Newsgroup server under Mail & Newsgroups.

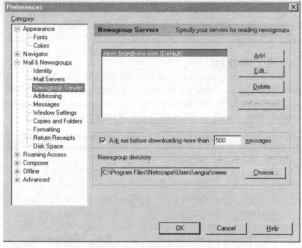

Most newsreaders offer a whole bunch of options for how long you want to keep messages after you've read them, how much to retrieve, how to arrange your windows and so forth. Leave those in the default settings and go back when you understand the questions and know your demands. Right now, it's not so important.

### Very important – mask your address!

Spammers regularly extract all the email addresses from Usenet to add to their bulk mail databases. Consequently all savvy users doctor their addresses in an obvious way to fool bulk mailers but not genuine respondents. For example, henry@plasticfashions.com might enter his address profile as henry@die-spammer-die.plasticfashions.com or henry@remove-this-bit.plasticfashions.com

**It's essential to do the same, before you post your first message,** otherwise you'll be bombarded with junk email for years to come. Alternatively, you could use a second address, perhaps under a pseudonym, for privacy's sake. It'll only take you a few minutes at Hotmail.

### Building a group list

Before you can jump in, you'll need to compile a list of the **newsgroups** available on your server. Your newsreader should do this automatically the very first time you connect to your news server. It's a big file, so expect to wait a few minutes.

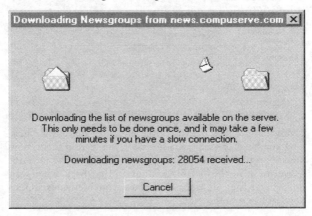

Downloading Newsgroups from news.compuserve.com ✕

Downloading the list of newsgroups available on the server. This only needs to be done once, and it may take a few minutes if you have a slow connection.

Downloading newsgroups: 28054 received...

Cancel

As the newsgroups arrive on your list, they'll either appear in a window titled **New Groups** or go straight into the main list (commonly called All Groups). **To compile your newsgroup list** in Outlook Express, go online and click on your news server entry at the bottom of your mail folder list. In Messenger, go online, select the news server entry in your folder list and click on **Subscribe** under the File menu.

### Browsing the groups

If your ISP has a decent newsfeed you should be faced with a list of at least 20,000 groups. Don't be put off by the volume; your newsreader can sift through them in a flash. But before you start filtering, scroll down and see what's on offer.

In **Outlook Express**, click on your news server's entry in the folder list. Wait a few seconds for the buttons to appear, and then click on Newsgroups to bring up the **Newsgroup Subscriptions** box. To browse the groups, click inside the Newsgroups window and scroll up and down using your arrow keys or mouse wheel. To filter on the fly, click in the box marked "Display newsgroups which contain" and enter your search term. There's also a further check box option to search the brief descriptions that accompany some groups. You might as well check that box, although it's rarely useful.

In **Netscape Messenger**, select your news server's entry in the folder list and choose Subscribe, either from your right mouse button menu, or under the File menu. Messenger will then take a minute or two to download a message count for all the displayed groups. To browse through the groups, click on the hierarchy folders to reveal the tree below. To search through the newsgroup names, click on the Search tab, enter your query, and click on the Search Now button.

### Finding groups to join

Unlike the Web, newsgroups aren't scattered across the Net in a chaotic mess. Your newsgroups list is effectively a complete directory of Usenet – or at least the part that your news provider carries. By browsing and filtering you should see a few groups that look interesting at first glance. However, you won't know whether they contain active discussions, or whether they're appropriate, until you subscribe and check them out. Although you can generally tell what groups are about just by looking at their names, sometimes it's not always so obvious. There might also be several groups that appear to discuss the same thing. You'll find, though, there will always be some distinction, or if not, a dominant group. While filtering and browsing is fine for locating groups by their name, it's not always the quickest route. To fast-track the process, run a keyword search at Deja.com (http://www.deja.com/usenet/), take note of the "discussion forums", and then locate them in your newsgroups list.

Don't overlook the local hierarchies (aus, uk, etc) for regional topics such as TV, politics, for sale, employment, and sport. For instance, if you want to find out what happened last week on Buffy in the UK, you might find uk.media.tv.buffy.v.slayer more in tune with your season than alt.tv.buffy.v.slayer

## Reading messages

The newsgroup list contains only the group names, not the actual messages. You have to **retrieve the messages** in a separate two-part process. But first you might need to **subscribe** to the group. This simply means putting a newsgroup into a special folder, or marking it in some way, so that it's away from the main list. You might be able to give it priorities, such as automatically updating headers or retrieving all message bodies upon connection, or it might just make it easier to locate. It differs between news readers.

To **subscribe to a group in Outlook Express**, click on the news server entry and choose "Newsgroups" from the Tools menu, toolbar or mouse menu. When the list appears,

select a group, click **Subscribe**, and then **Goto** to commence downloading the message **headers**. The **headers**
contain the message subject, posting date, and contributor's
name. They can be threaded (bundled together) by subject,
or sorted by date or contributor. Once all the headers have
arrived, clicking on a message will download its body. You
can then read it in the preview panel. If you wish to read
the group at a later date, just select it from under the news
server folder and wait for the new headers to arrive. To
**remove a newsgroup**, choose **Unsubscribe** from your
mouse menu.

The process is almost identical in **Messenger**. Choose
**Subscribe**, from the File menu, open the folders until you find
your group, click on **Subscribe**, then close the window. Click
on the group to start downloading headers. Selecting a message
will download its body and display it in the preview panel.

**Other newsreaders**, and probably later versions of these,
will use a different combination of menu choices to go
through the same motions. So to get this right, you'll either
have to read the **Help File** or randomly click everything the
first time. Yes, really: it's the only way. As long as you understand the process, it will all come together, whatever the
terms and instructions.

## Reading Offline

Reading articles one at a time online is convenient, but not if
it's costing you to stay connected or you're tying up your only
telephone line. Consider **downloading the article bodies
along with the headers** to read offline at your leisure.

This is simple in Outlook Express. Before you go online,
choose **Work Offline** from under the File menu, select the
group, open its **Properties** from under the File or mouse
menu, and make your selection under the **Synchronize** tab.
Click on the group when you're next online, and choose

**Synchronize** from under the Tools menu to retrieve whatever you've sent. Once you're offline, switch to **Work Offline** mode and browse through the articles as if you're online.

**Messenger** makes a bit of a meal of the same operation, but it's still possible. One way is to select the group while online, choose **Newsgroup Properties** from under the Edit or mouse menu, then mark your preferences under the **Download Settings** tab. If you choose **Download Now**, it will bring down all the headers. Just follow the prompts.

## Contributing to a discussion

When a newsgroup message raises a new topic, it's called **starting a thread**. Replies to that initial message add to this thread. You can configure your newsreader to **sort threads** together to follow the progress of a discussion. But if you follow a group regularly you might find it more convenient to sort by date, to see what's new. You can sort by date, sender, subject or size, by clicking the bar at the top of that column – except in Free Agent, which has it disabled to annoy you into shelling out for the full version.

### Posting

**Posting** is like sending email – and equally simple. You can start a new thread, follow up an existing one, and/or respond privately by email.

When you post, most programs automatically insert the newsgroup you're reading in the **Newsgroups**: line. When starting a thread, enter a **subject** that outlines the point of your message. That way it will catch the eye of anyone who's interested or can help. The subject line will then be used to identify the thread in future.

To post a new message in Outlook Express, enter a group and click on the **New Message** toolbar icon or select **New Message** from under the Message menu. The process is identical in Messenger.

To **crosspost** (post a message to more than one group), just add those groups after the first group, separated by a comma, and then a space. Replies to crosspostings are displayed in all the crosspostings groups. If you attempt to crosspost too many groups your message is likely to be identified as spam and cancelled by one of the roving cancelbots.

## Replying

**Replying** (or responding) is even easier than posting. You can send your contribution to the relevant newsgroup(s) and/or email the poster directly.

It's doesn't hurt **to reply by email as well as post**, so the original poster gets it instantly. It's also more personal and saves scanning the group for replies. Don't forget to edit the address if they've masked it. They'll normally provide some clue to their real address either in their signature, or within the address. And, of course, if they've used an obviously bogus address – which is very common – there's no point sending an email.

It's quite acceptable to continue communicating outside Usenet as long as it serves a purpose. A lot of new friendships start this way.

Like email, you also have the option of **including parts or all of the original message**. This can be quite a tricky choice. If you cut too much, the context could be lost when the original post is deleted. If everyone includes everything, it creates a lot of text to scan. Just try to leave the main points intact.

You'll find the various reply options beside or below your **New Message** menu entries in all newsreaders.

## Sending a test post

As soon as anyone gets Usenet access, they're always itching to see if it works. With that in mind, there are a few **newsgroups dedicated to experimenting**. You can post whatever you like to any group with test in the name, such as **alt.test**, or misc.test, but remember not to use your main email address as it might generate a pile of responses, some unwelcome.

## Canceling a message

If you've had second thoughts about something you've posted, select it in the newsgroup and choose **Cancel Message** from under the Message menu in Outlook Express or the mouse menu in Messenger. Unfortunately it won't be instantly removed from every server worldwide so someone still might see it.

## Kill files

If you don't like a certain person on Usenet, you can "kill" their mail. If your newsreader has a **kill file**, just add their email address to that, or use your **Filters**. Then you'll never have to download messages they've posted again. You can also trash uninteresting threads in the same way, by setting a delete filter on the subject. But don't make it too broad or you might filter out interesting stuff as well. See:
http://www.kibo.com/kibokill/

# Decoding binaries (pictures, programs, audio, etc)

As with email, Usenet can carry more than plain text. Consequently there are entire groups dedicated to the posting of **binary files** such as images, sounds, patches, and even full commercial programs. Such groups should have .binaries in their address.

Again like email, binary files must be processed, most commonly in UUencoding or MIME, before they can be posted or read. This is something you needn't think about, as your newsreader will do it automatically. Sometimes larger files, like movies, get chopped into several messages. Each part will have the same subject heading followed by its number. The problem is sometimes that parts go astray, which makes it impossible to reassemble the file.

Depending on your newsreader, to **retrieve a binary file** you might have to highlight all the parts and decode them in one go. Agent/Free Agent recognizes a set, just by clicking on one part. **Messenger** and **Outlook Express** both decode automatically within the window, but are very slow. You'd be better off with Agent or one of the many newsreaders dedicated to binary decoding.

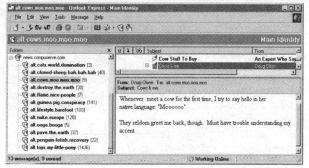

To decode a multi-part attachment in Outlook Express, select the components and choose **Combine and Decode** from the Tools menu. With some newsreaders, you might need to retrieve the message body and decode in two stages. In Messenger, for example, it's a pain. It might work if you select all parts in the right order using Ctrl or Shift, then click on Save As under the File menu, and wait for all the segments to download. Give the file a name ending with the extension .UUE, and then drop it on Winzip or Stuffit Expander. For other newsreaders, it's best to read your Help file to get it straight.

To **post a binary**, just attach it as in email and your newsreader will look after the rest.

**Warning:** Virus check any programs you download from Usenet. Or better still, don't go near them, or Word documents with macros. And just because you can find **full PlayStation CDs** posted to **alt.binaries.cd** doesn't make it legal for you to burn them to disk – even for your own use.

## Newsgroup netiquette

Apart from your provider's contract, the Net largely has no formal rules. Instead, there are certain established, or developing, codes of conduct known as **Netiquette** (Net-etiquette). These apply mainly to Usenet.

People who behave **really badly** on Usenet sometimes get reported to their ISP or news provider, which might result in them losing their account, or even being sued. The address for reporting someone is generally **abuse@serviceprovider** where **serviceprovider** is the name of their news server.

But mostly, they just get ignored, or **abused**. On the Net, personal abuse is called **flaming**. You don't have to breach netiquette to get flamed – just expressing a contrary or naive opinion should do the trick. When it degenerates into nothing but name calling, it's called a **flame war**. Just about every busy group will have a flame war in progress within one of the threads, and sometimes, for example in the alt.flame.* hierarchy, that's about all that's in there. You'll probably be swinging insults yourself before too long. It's all part of the fun.

But, before you charge in armed with barbs, read the ground rules, so at least you'll know where you stand.

### Read the Frequently Asked Questions (FAQs)

Most newsgroups have at least one FAQ (Frequently Asked Question) document. This will describe the newsgroup's charter, give guidelines for posting, and compile common answers to questions. They should always be your first source

of information. FAQs are periodically posted and usually updated every few weeks. You can usually find them by searching Deja.com, or the FAQ archive at:
http://www.faqs.org

## Post to the right group

It's wise to **get the feel of a newsgroup** before posting. If it's a big group you should get a fair idea within one session, but don't be in a hurry. Read all the **relevant FAQs** first, to ensure your message isn't old hat. Some newsgroupies are not too tolerant of repeats. But that's no rule.

Next, make an effort to **post in the most relevant group**. If you were to ask for advice on fertilizing roses in rec.gardening you might find yourself politely directed to rec.gardening.roses but if you want to tell everyone in talk.serious.socialism about your favorite Chow Yun Fat film, don't expect such a warm response.

## Keep your cool

**Never post in anger**. You'll regret it later, especially when everything you send is archived at Deja.com. And beware of **Trolls**. These are baits left to start arguments or make you look stupid. If someone asks something ludicrous or obvious, says something offensive or inappropriate, or attacks you personally, don't respond. Let it pass. Tread carefully with sarcasm, too, as not everyone will get it, especially those nationalities with no sense of irony. (This is meant to be a joke, but how can you be sure?)

Less obviously, **NEVER POST IN UPPERCASE** (ALL CAPS) unless you're **shouting** (emphasizing a point in a big way). It makes you look rude and ignorant. And keep your **signature file** short and subtle. Three to five lines, no ASCII art. Got it?

Express yourself in plain English (or the language of the group). Don't use **acronyms** or **abbreviations** unless they reduce jargon rather than create it. And avoid over-using **smileys and other emoticons** (see "Net Language" – p.469). They spell "newbie".

Finally, don't post **email you've received from someone else** without their consent.

### Get in there

These warnings aside – and they're pretty obvious – don't hold back. If you can forward a discussion in any way, contribute. That's what it's all about. **Post positively** and invite discussion rather than make abrasive remarks. For example, posting "Hackers are social retards" is sure to get you flamed. But: "Do hackers lead healthy social lives?" will get the same point across and invite debate, yet allow you to sidestep the line of fire.

Overall it's a matter of courtesy, common sense and knowing when to contribute. In Usenet, you're a complete stranger until you post. They'll get to know you through your words, and how well you construct your arguments. So if you want to make a good impression, think before you post, and don't be a loudmouth.

If you're a real stickler for rules you should read: http://www.albion.com/netiquette/ If all this seems a tad stiff, you might appreciate: **Usenet Tomfoolery at:** http://www.elsop.com/wrc/humor/usenet.htm or check out **Emily Postnews** http://www.psg.com/emily.html

## Posting ads

Having such a massive captive audience pre-qualified by interests is beyond the dreams of many marketeers. Consequently you will frequently come across **advertisements and product endorsements** crossposted to inappropriate newsgroups.

This **spamming** is the surest way to make yourself unpopular in Usenet. If you try, you'll be bombed with hate mail and more than likely reported to your provider. In other words, it's not good publicity. As a rule no-one who uses this technique to advertise is reputable, as with those who send mass emails.

If you'd like to make **commercial announcements**, you could try the groups in the .biz hierarchy; after all that's what they're for. The catch is no-one reads them because they're chock-full of the usual network marketing schemes. In other groups, tread more subtly with mentions of your new book, CD, or whatever; otherwise you might come in for a hard time. You can still do it, but only in the right groups and in the right context.

Ironically, nobody minds what you put in your **signature**, so if you put in your Web address it's sure to attract a few visitors.

## How it gets from A to B

Usenet articles are like email messages but are transmitted in a separate system called **NNTP** (Network News Transport Protocol). Your Usenet provider (eg, your ISP) maintains an independent database of Usenet messages, which it updates in periodic exchanges with neighboring news servers. It receives and dispatches messages anything from once a day to instantly. Due to this pass-the-ball procedure, messages might appear immediately on your screen as you post them, but propagate around the world at the mercy of whoever's in between. Exactly how much newsfeed you get, and what you see, depends on your provider's neighbors and how often they update their messages. Most of the time, these days, it's almost as fast as email.

No provider, however, can keep messages forever, as it needs the space for new ones, so it **expires postings** after a certain holding period. It's usual to delete messages after about four days and even sooner for large groups and **binaries**. Each provider has its own policy.

In addition, some newsgroups are **moderated** which means that postings are screened before they appear. Officially moderated groups are screened by whoever started the group or an appointee, but it's possible, though uncommon, that messages could be censored anywhere between you and the person who posted.

## Starting your own newsgroup

With Usenet already buckling under the weight of 85,000+ newsgroups, you'll need fairly specialized tastes to get the urge to start another – plus a fair bit of technical know-how and a monk's patience. It's one of the more convoluted and arcane procedures on the Net. For instructions, see:
http://www.geocities.com/nnqweb/ncreate.html
http://homepages.go.com/~eacalame/create.html

## Searching Usenet

See our chapter on "Finding It" (p.163).

## Further help

For beginners' guides, and more on Usenet in general, see:
http://www.geocities.com/nnqweb/nnqlinks.html
http://www.newsreaders.com
And for tips and hacks to **enhance Agent**:
http://www.skuz.net/madhat/agent/patch.html

# 10

# Downloading Software

## FREEWARE, SHAREWARE
## AND HOW TO USE FTP

**W**hether you're after a browser upgrade, the latest Quake
patch, or some obscure CD mastering software, the
Internet is the very first place you should look. Just about
every program that's released nowadays finds its way on to the
Net, and most of the time you can download a full working
copy. If not, at the very least, you should be able to order it
on disk by email direct from the publisher.

What you certainly will be able to find is all the **Internet
software** you'll ever need. And the good news is you can
download the pick of the crop, for free. So don't be afraid to

replace your starter kit. Once you're online, you can use whatever you like.

## What you'll need

Before you can download anything, you'll need a program that handles **FTP (File Transfer Protocol)**. You can use a stand-alone dedicated program such as **CuteFTP**, **WS_FTP, Anarchie**, or **Fetch**, but it's usually more convenient to use your **Web browser**. However, dedicated programs are still worth checking out for serious use. They have more features. And if you're uploading or accessing password-protected sites, you might find one necessary.

We've dedicated a chapter to **Net software** (see p.439), which includes the download addresses. You may want to refer to it in conjunction with this section.

## Free software from the Net

While the Internet might be a veritable clearinghouse of freely available software, it's not all genuinely free. There are four types of programs you're allowed to use, at least for a while, without paying. They are called **freeware**, **adware**, **shareware**, and **beta programs**.

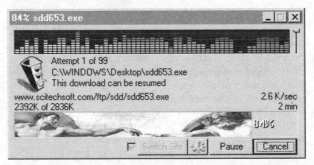

## Freeware

**Freeware** is provided by its author(s) with no expectation of payment. It could be a complete program, a demonstration sample with crippled features, a patch to enhance another program, or an interim upgrade. If you like the program, write and thank the developers.

## Adware

Adware is freeware that serves you advertising banners. The banners themselves aren't usually a hindrance, but sometimes the mechanism of getting them to you can cause nasty crashes. Then there's the question of whether they're spying on you. See: http://grc.com/optout.htm

## Shareware

**Shareware** comes with strings attached, which you accept when you install or run the program. Commonly, these may include the condition that you must pay to continue to use it after an initial free trial period, or that you pay if you intend to use it commercially. Sometimes a shareware program, while adequate, is a short form of a more solid or better-featured registered version. You might upgrade to this if you like the shareware, usually by paying a registration fee, in return for which the author or software distributor will mail you a code to unlock the program or its upgrade.

## Beta programs

**Betas (and Platform Previews)** are distributed as part of the testing process in commercial software development. You shouldn't pay for them as they're not finished products. But they're often good enough for the task, and usually right at the cutting edge of technology. Take Netscape and Internet Explorer betas, for example. They've been the most popular programs ever to hit the Net.

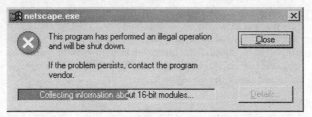

With all betas, expect to encounter **bugs and quirks** now and again and don't be too upset by having to restart the program (or your computer) occasionally – it's all part of the development process. Do report recurring faults to the developers; that's why they let you have it free. If you notice a pattern, email the distributors and ask for a fix. If it's just too buggy, get an alternative.

## Downloading from the Web

**Netscape Navigator** and **Microsoft Internet Explorer** are fine for both **FTP** and **HTTP** transfers. You can kick off multiple transfers and then surf the Web while you wait for downloads to finish.

That's pretty convenient because most of your file leads will come from Web pages. And not just from specialist software guides either (see our Web guide, p.291). For instance, if you were to read a review of a computer game you can bet your back door it will contain a link to download a demo.

To retrieve it, all you need do is **click on the link and follow the prompts**. You might have to supply a bit of information, but all should be self-explanatory. Once the transfer is initiated (you might have to wait a little longer than it takes to load a Web page), a window will pop up asking you whether you'd like to **open or save the file**. Choose **Save** and browse to where you'd like to put it on your computer. Once that's done a new window will appear with a running estimate of the transfer rate and time to completion. The **Mac version of Internet Explorer** will automatically place all downloads in a **Download folder** unless you specify elsewhere within the Receiving Files section of Preferences. It also combines all downloads into a single Download Manager window.

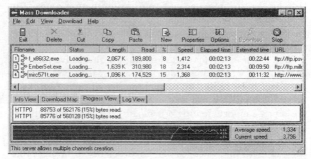

As with any FTP transfer, if the file has moved, you'll either be defaulted back to a higher directory or face an error message. If the file isn't where it should be, or you want to **enter an unlinked location**, just enter it as a Web address but instead of keying http: use ftp: as the first part of the address.

So, to look for a file at: ftp.chook.com in the path: /pub you enter: ftp://ftp.chook.com/pub Once connected, just click on what you want in the usual fashion.

## Resume downloads

As FTP downloads can take some time – hours, even, if it's a big program and your link is slow – it's helpful if your transfer program supports resume downloads. Then if you drop out, you can go back and pick up where you left off. That's a real lifesaver if you're 90 percent through downloading a 35 MB game demo. Netscape and Internet Explorer are supposed to support resume downloads, but it rarely works in practice. All the more reason to get a dedicated **download manager.**

### Download managers

If you're serious about your downloads, get yourself a download manager, such as **Download Accelerator** (http://www.downloadaccelerator.com) or **Mass Downloader** (http://www.metaproducts.com). Mass Downloader is particularly nice, as it integrates into your mouse button menu. But try them both and see which you prefer. You can assign them to take over whenever they detect a file download of a certain type such as .zip, .exe, or .mp3.

They can search FTP space looking for alternative locations and tell you which one is quickest, and speed up downloads considerably by setting up parallel transfer streams. And if you break the transfer it can take over where it left off (as long as the server supports resume downloads). Experiment with the option of letting them monitor your clipboard and browser clicks. But you might find they get in the way and prefer to just call them up as needed. There are plenty of similar products, but steer clear of Go!Zilla, which causes nasty crashes in Internet Explorer.

## Using an FTP program

Dedicated FTP clients are much alike – any of them will do to start. And if you don't like one, you can use it to download another.

Unless you've been granted special permission to log into an FTP server to transfer files, you'll have to use one that permits **anonymous FTP**. Such sites follow a standard log-in. Once you're in, you can look through the contents of a limited number of directories and transfer files to, and sometimes from, your computer.

Many **Net servers** have areas set aside for anonymous FTP. Some even carry massive specialist **file archives**. And most **software houses** provide updates, patches, and interim releases on their own anonymous FTP sites. No single server will have everything you need, but you'll soon find favorites for each type of file. Your ISP should have an FTP area, too, where you can transfer files for updating Web pages, download access software, and exchange files with colleagues.

### FTP domain addresses

**FTP domains** are often prefixed by ftp. but that's not a rule. When you're supplied a file location it could be in the form ftp.fish.com/pub/dir/jane.zip That tells you that the file jane.zip is located in the directory pub/dir on the ftp.fish.com server.

## Browsing an FTP site

FTP programs use different lingo, so it won't hurt to read its Help or Read Me file. It should tell you what to key in where. Basically, though, the procedure is fairly routine and goes like this:

To retrieve ftp.fish.com/pub/dir/jane.zip
enter the server's address ftp.fish.com as host name
enter anonymous as user name and your Internet
email address (in the form user@host) as a password.

Next, enter the **directory** in which you wish to start looking, in this case /pub/dir Make sure the path and file details are entered in the correct (upper/lower) case. If you enter Dir instead of dir on a UNIX host, it will return an error because UNIX is case sensitive. If you have the file's full location, try entering that as the initial directory. However, don't be surprised if a file isn't where it's supposed to be – system managers are forever shuffling directories. And it's not necessary to get the location exactly right: once you're in, you can always browse around until you find it.

Having entered the details above, you're ready to **log in**. If it's busy, you may not be admitted the first time. Don't let that discourage you. If you can't get in within ten attempts, try again later, perhaps outside the local peak hours. If you're accessing a foreign site, try when that continent is asleep. You're likely to get a better transfer rate.

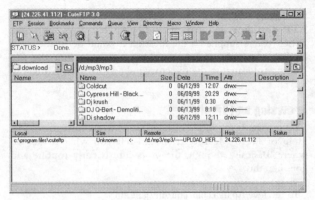

Once you're accepted, you'll see a listing of the initial **directory's contents**. Look for a contents file called **readme**, **index**, or the like. Read it if you're unsure of the contents, and read, too, any accompanying **text files** before downloading a program. You can usually do that by either clicking on them or selecting **view** or **read** from the menu.

Most FTP programs work in a similar way to Windows' file manager or the Macintosh folder system. That means when you click, something happens. Look at the top of the directory contents. **Clicking on ".."** will send you up a directory level. Directories should stand out from files by having a different color, typeface, folder icon, or at least not having extensions. **Clicking on a directory** will open it, clicking on a file or dragging and dropping it should start the download.

Always select **binary transfer** when downloading. It's usually set as the default. But if you're playing around you might accidentally change it and any graphic, sound, or program you download as **text** will be useless.

Your FTP client should give you a **transfer progress report** to tell you how long it's going to take. You can either sit back and watch the bits zip into your hard drive or relegate it to the background while you do something else, such as explore the Web. But, if the **transfer fails or is canceled**, or your line drops out, you won't be able to pick up where you left off unless your FTP program and the server both support **resume downloads**. Bear this in mind when choosing an FTP client.

## Uploading files

FTP isn't just for scoring files, you can **upload** as well. It might be more practical to submit stories, documents, graphics, and applications this way, rather than burden the email system with bulky attachments. For example, suppose you want to submit artwork to a magazine. You could FTP the scans to an area set aside for downloads (often a directory called **incoming**), and then notify your editor by email. The editor could then instruct staff to upload them for approval. If they're okay they could then be processed and moved to an outgoing directory for print house access.

In some cases an area is set aside where files can be uploaded and downloaded to the same directory. Useful maybe if you want to transfer files to a colleague who's having problems with handling mailed attachments (it happens!). It's frustrating waiting for several megabytes of mail attachments to download and decode before you can read your mail. Especially if it has to be resent.

You can upload through your Web browser but it's simpler with a dedicated program. You'll need to log into the site, probably with a legitimate user name and password, switch to the directory and start the transfer. With most programs it's as simple as dragging and dropping the file. Check your Help file if it's not obvious.

## FTP by email

Several services offer **FTP by email**. They can take up to a few days, but may save access charges over slow networks – it might be quicker to download your mail from a local server than to transfer files from a distant busy server. If you're in more of a hurry to get offline than get the file, give it a shot. See: http://www.emailfile.com

## File types and compression

There are two good reasons to compress files. One is to decrease their storage demands, the other to reduce transfer times. After you download a compressed file, you must decompress it to get it to work. Before you can decompress it you need the right program to do the job.

In general, it's easy to tell which technique has been used by looking at the file name or where it's located. Unless the site is specifically targeted at one platform, you're usually offered a **folder choice** between DOS, PC/Windows, Mac, and UNIX. Once you've taken that choice everything contained in that folder and its subfolders will be for that platform only. If not, you can usually tell by the file extensions.

### PC archives

PC archives mostly end in **.exe** or **.zip**. The **.exe** files are usually self-extracting archives, which means they can decompress themselves. To do this, transfer the file to a temporary directory and double-click on it. If you're on a PC, get the latest copy of **WinZip** (http://www.winzip.com), and the latest **Aladdin Expander** (aka **Stuffit Expander**) for Windows (http://www.aladdinsys.com) and place their shortcut icons on your desktop. The great thing about this combination is that it will handle just about everything, including files compressed on Macs. And it's easily configurable to extract archived files automatically just by double-clicking on them in Explorer, or by dropping them onto the Stuffit or WinZip icons.

### Mac files

Compressed **Macintosh files** usually end .bin, .cpt, .sit, .sea, or .hqx. The .sea files **self-extract** by clicking on them, the rest by dropping on, or opening with **Stuffit Expander**.

If you're **expanding a Mac file for PC use**, set the options under Cross Platform to "convert text files to Windows format when the file is known to contain text" and "never save files in MacBinary Format".

Internet Explorer will **automatically decode** MacBinary and Binhex files unless you specify otherwise within Download Options in Preferences.

### Useful helper programs

All recent Web browsers add support above your standard multimedia software to cope with the most common **audio and video** formats. Anything else is likely to need a browser plug-in or specialist program. If it's something odd, there'll probably be a link to download the player on the Web site where you found the file. Otherwise, browse through the file archives in our Web guide (p.291) for a solution.

### Watch out for viruses

See our Frequently Asked Questions section (p.22).

## How to set up your folder structure

Before you start installing every Internet program you can find, sort out your **directory structure**. Otherwise, you'll make a jungle of your hard drive.

Hard drives are organized into tree-like structures. In DOS, UNIX and Windows 3.x, each level is called a **Directory**. In Windows 95/98 and Macs it's called a **Folder** – they mean the same thing. For simplicity's sake we'll call them folders. The top level of a drive is called the **Root**. It's for system start-up files only, so don't lob anything in there. No matter what system you're running, you should create the following first-level folders:

## Programs

Install all **programs** into their own separate subfolders under a first-level folder called **Program Files**, **Apps**, or similar. Most Windows programs will install themselves by default in the Program Files folder. It's wisest to take that choice if possible, as it's less likely to cause problems later.

## Download

Configure your **browser, newsreader and any FTP programs or download managers** to download to a common **Download folder** and create a shortcut (alias) on your desktop to open it. Think of it as an in-tray and clear it accordingly. Alternatively, save files onto your **Desktop**, but deal with them straight away.

## Temporary

Once you've downloaded the installation program, extract it to an empty **Temporary folder** and then install it under the **Programs hierarchy**. Once done, delete the contents of the Temporary folder. If you have space, keep the original installation file in case you need to re-install it. Put it in your **Archive** folder.

## Archive

Rather than clog up your Download folder, create a dedicated **Archive folder** with enough **subfolders** to make it easy to find things again. As you download new versions of programs, delete the old one.

You could open your archive to your peers through an FTP server or a file-sharing program like Gnutella. It should be the first place to delete files to make space.

### Data

Put irreplaceable files, such as those you create, into a **Data directory** tree and regularly back it up onto another medium such as a floppy disk, Zip drive, CD, or even an FTP site. Use WinZip or Stuffit to compress it all into manageable chunks.

## Free storage online

Need somewhere to stash your most precious files for safe-keeping, to free up some room on your hard drive or backup your iMac? Then, see:

| | |
|---|---|
| **MySpace** | http://www.myspace.com |
| **FreeDrive** | http://www.freedrive.com |
| **i-drive** | http://www.idrive.com |
| **X:drive** | http://www.xdrive.com |

## Sending a file to a friend

If you use **ICQ** (chat – see p.188) to stay in touch online, rather than attach files by email, try sending them directly using its File option. It's more efficient. Alternatively, set up a file-sharing server on your system, or an online drive as mentioned above, and let them log in and grab it.

## Where to find an FTP client

See "Software Roundup" (p.439).

## Finding files

See the following chapter, "Finding It".

### File extensions and decompression programs

The following table shows some common **file extensions** and the **programs needed to decompress** or view them. For a list of every file format in the world, see: http://www.whatis.com/ff.htm

| Extension | Filetype | Program to decompress or view |
|---|---|---|
| .asf | Advanced streaming format | Windows Media Player |
| .bin | MacBinary | MacBinary, usually automatic in Macs |
| .bmp | Bitmap | Graphics viewer |
| .cpt | Mac Compact Pro archive | Compact Pro, Stuffit Expander |
| .doc | MS Word document | Word processor such as MS Word or Wordpad |
| .exe | PC executable | Self executing from DOS or Windows |
| .gif | Graphic Interchange Format | Graphics viewer |
| .hqx | Mac BinHex | BinHex, Stuffit Expander |
| .jpg | Compressed graphic | Graphics viewer |
| .mov | Quicktime movie | Quicktime Player |
| .mp3 | MP3 audio file | Media player |
| .mpg | Compressed video | Media player |
| .pls | MP3 playlist | Media player |
| .pit | Mac PackIt | PackIt |
| .ra, .ram | RealAudio | RealPlayer |
| .sea | Mac Self-extracting archive | Click on icon to extract |
| .sit | Mac Stuffit compressed archive | Stuffit Expander |
| .txt | Plain text | Notepad, text editor, word processor |
| .wav | WAV audio file | Media player |
| .wma | Windows media file | Windows Media Player |
| .uu, .uue | UNIX UU-encoded | UUDECODE, Stuffit Expander |
| .zip | PC PKZip compressed archive | PKZip, WinZip, Stuffit Expander |

# 11

# Finding It

## SEARCH TOOLS AND DIRECTORIES

O nce you're installed, setup, online, and the whole thing's purring along to perfection, you'll face yet another dilemma. How on earth do you find anything? Relax, it's not too hard once you've learned a few tricks. Before you set off on a search for something, you'll need to take into account what it is, how new it is, where it might be stored, and who's likely to know about it. In this chapter, we show you the first places to look, and as you gain experience the rest will fall into place. We also show you how to fix Web addresses that won't work. Assuming you have Web access, the only program you'll definitely need is a browser. You already have one? Fantastic. Well, here's how to wind it out to its full potential.

## Become an instant know-it-all

The art of **finding something** pinned up on the world's biggest scrapboard is, without doubt, **the most valuable skill** you can glean from your time online. If you know how to use the Net to find an answer to almost anything quickly and comprehensively, you'd have to consider yourself not only useful, but pretty saleable too. As it stands, **most people simply bumble their way around**, and that includes a fair share of Net veterans. Yet it's a remarkably basic skill to master once you've been pointed in the right direction. So read this chapter, then get online and start investigating. Within an hour or two you'll be milking the Net for what it's worth. It might turn out to be the best investment you'll ever make!

## How it works

The Net is massive. Just the Web alone houses well over a billion pages of text, and millions more are added daily. So if you need to find something – particularly if you want to research it in depth – you're going to need some serious help. Thankfully, there's a wide selection of search tools to make the task relatively painless. The job usually entails keying your **search terms** into a form on a Web page and waiting a few seconds for the results.

We'll introduce you to **search tools** that can locate almost anything: on the Web; linked to from the Web; or archived into an online Web database, such as email addresses, phone numbers, program locations, newsgroup articles, and news clippings. Of course, first it has to be put online, and granted public access. So just because you can access US government servers doesn't mean you'll find a file on DEA Operative Presley's whereabouts.

Let's start by examining the main search tools. You'll find even more listed in the "Search Tools and Directories" section of our Web guide (see p.281).

# The main search tools

There are three basic types of Web search tools: **search engines**, **hand-built subject directories** and **search agents**. Apart from the odd newspaper archive, they're almost always free. Because they're so useful and popular, there was a trend towards tacking other services onto the side and building themselves into so-called **portals**, **communities**, and **hubs**. More recently, that trend has begun to reverse with the launch of several skeletal search tools free of fancy overheads. Irrespective of which you use, ignore the quantity of froufrou and concentrate on the quality of the results. The next few pages discuss each category in detail, and show you how to torture them for answers.

## Read me!

As with just about everything on the Net, the easiest way to learn is to dive straight into the search engines and explore how they work. But before you do, it's worth pausing to **read the instructions first**. Every search engine and directory has a page of Read Me tips on how to use them to their full potential. A few minutes' study will make your searching more effective.

## Search engines

Use a search engine when you're looking for specific mention of something on a Web page. These are just a few of the best:

| | |
|---|---|
| **AltaVista** | http://www.av.com |
| **Excite** | http://www.excite.com |
| **Fast Search** | http://www.alltheweb.com |
| **Go** | http://www.go.com |

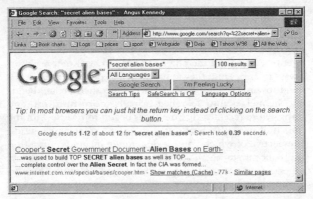

| Google | http://www.google.com |
| HotBot | http://www.hotbot.com |
| Lycos | http://www.lycos.com |
| Northern Light | http://www.nlsearch.com |
| Raging Search | http://www.raging.com |
| Snap | http://www.snap.com |

**Search engines** enable you to search the contents of **millions of Web pages simultaneously**. You simply go to the search engine's Web page and **submit keywords**, or **search terms**, into a simple form. It runs these terms past its database and, almost instantly, returns a list of results or "hits". For example, if you were to search on the expression "Rough Guide to the Internet", here's what might come up on top:

### 1. Welcome to the Rough Guide to the Internet
The Rough Guide to the Internet is the ultimate guide to the Web, complete with a 2500+ site directory.
www.roughguides.com/internet/index.html

In this case the top line tells us the name of the page or site. Followed by a description excerpted from the page, and then the page's address. If it suits, click on the link to visit the site.

> **Tip:** Don't just click on a result, and then hit the Back button if it's no good. Instead, run down the list and open the most promising candidates in new browser windows. It will save you tons of time. Do this by **holding down the Shift key** as you click.

It's important to know **you're not searching the Web live**. **You're merely searching a database** of Web pages located on the search engine's server. This database is compiled by a program that crawls around the Web looking for new sites, as well as changes to the ones it already knows. How much text is retrieved from each site varies between search engines. The better ones scavenge almost everything.

## Choosing a search engine

You rarely need to use more than one search engine, and you'll end up using it all the time, so **make sure the one you pick is up to speed**. Some are definitely better all round than others, but none can claim to catch everything. Even the worst engines are capable of finding unique hits. On top of this some give very similar results because they share technologies. **HotBot**, **Snap**, **Goto,** and **MSN**, for example, currently use the **Inktomi** system, which means their results won't differ greatly, but that may change over time. **Raging Search** and **AltaVista** presently share the same database, but they may display results differently. What will definitely differ are the forms in which you enter your search terms. And this can make all the difference.

Because these engines source, store, and retrieve data differently, shop around to see which you prefer. You'll want the **biggest**, **freshest**, **database**. You'll want to be able to **fine-tune your search** with extra commands. And you'll want the most hits you can get on one page with the most **relevant results on top**.

Our choice would be a toss-up between **Google**, **Fast Search**, and **Raging Search**. They're all big, fast, clutter free, and can deliver a long page of relevant hits. At the top, **Google** probably, because of its uncanny knack of getting it right in the first few hits, both from within its search engine database and its association with the **Open Directory** (see p.173). It also provides local cache access to pages that have disappeared since it's crawl or are otherwise unavailable.

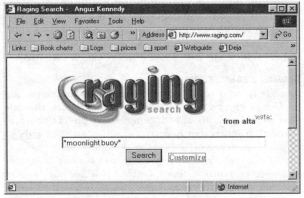

Next up, **Northern Light** is worth a shot. It's also big, but not so fast or user-friendly despite its curious system of organizing hits into folders. Check out its special collection. It comes at a cost – and much of it's free at the source – but it might save you time getting it in one spot.

**As for the rest?** They're certainly not without merits, but unless you're after extra hits, you're unlikely to need them. Of course, that changes if they suddenly improve.

But if you seriously need **more results**, rather than visit several engines in turn, query them simultaneously using an agent such as **Copernic** (see p.175). You can tell how each engine ranks from the results. For more detailed analysis see:

**Search Engine Watch**
http://www.searchenginewatch.com

**Search Engine Showdown**
http://www.searchengineshowdown.com

They keep tabs on all the finer details such as who owns what, how they tick and who's currently biggest.

## Limitations

Search engines aren't the be all and end all of what's on the Web. **They're only as good as their most recent findings**, which might be just a small proportion of what's actually there and, possibly, months old. So just because you can't find it through a Web search doesn't mean it's not there. If you're after something brand new, they may not be much use. You might be better off searching **Usenet** (see p.177) or a news service.

## How to word your search terms

Now here's the art. Get this right and you'll find anything. The trick is to think up a **search term** that's unique enough to get rid of junk results, but broad enough not to miss anything useful. It will depend entirely on the subject, so be prepared to think laterally!

Each search engine has its own quirks to learn – otherwise you'll waste a lot of time weeding through poor results. Try all the main search engines and study their instructions. The main things to glean are how to **create a phrase,** how to **search on multiple phrases**, and how to **exclude certain words.** Let's start with a complex example. Suppose we want to search for something on the esteemed author, Angus Kennedy. Let's see how you'd do it in **Raging Search**. If you were to enter:

```
angus kennedy
```

it would return all pages that contain "angus" **or** "kennedy" **or both**. That means there'd be lots of pages about Angus cattle and JFK. We don't want to sift through those so let's make sure the pages contain **both words**. In AltaVista, and most other search engines, you can use a **plus sign (+)** to state that the page **must contain a word**. So let's try:

```
+angus +kennedy
```

That's better. All the pages now contain both words. Unfortunately, though, there's no guarantee that they'll be next to each other. What we really want is to **treat them as a phrase**. A simple way to do this is to enclose the words within quotes, like this:

```
"angus kennedy"
```

Now we've captured all instances of Angus Kennedy as a phrase, but since it's **a person's name**, we should look for Kennedy, Angus as well. So let's try:

```
"angus kennedy" "kennedy, angus"
```

As with the first example we now catch pages with **either or both phrases**. Now suppose we want to narrow it down further and exclude some irrelevant results, for example, others with the same name. Our target writes books about French literature, so let's start by getting rid of that pesky Rough Guide author. To **exclude a term**, place a minus sign (-) in front. So let's ditch him:

```
"angus kennedy" "kennedy, angus" -"rough guide"
```

That's about all you need to know in most instances. These rules should work in most engines, as well as the search forms on individual sites. However, there are exceptions. **Google** and **Deja.com**, for example, don't support "or" searches. That means searching on:

```
angus kennedy
```

would search for pages containing "angus" AND "kennedy." If you want to search for pages containing either, you would have to do two separate searches. You'll find this isn't really a problem, and in most cases, is actually preferable.

Most engines also have a **drop down menu** with the options of "any of the words", "all the words", or "the exact phrase". If the meaning of that isn't instantly obvious, try it.

For more complex searches in other search engines, look for an **advanced search** link, or refer to the help or search tips page. Observe how they interpret **capitals**, dashes between words, brackets, wild cards, truncations, and the **Boolean** operators such as AND, OR, NEAR, and NOT.

In particular, watch out for "**stop words**". These are words that are normally ignored. In Google, for example, single letters are ignored unless you place a "+" sign in front of them. So to search for Angus J Kennedy, you'd enter:

```
"angus +j kennedy"
```

Just because search engines can't find something, doesn't mean it's not on the Web. It just means their trawlers haven't visited that site yet. Which means you'll have to turn to another, maybe fresher source. **Read on.**

**Tip:** You'll be using your favorite engines often, so drop their addresses onto your browser Links bar. But rather than save the front page, go for the one with advanced options. At **Fast Search**, for example, click on "Advanced search" to bring up an assortment of tuning boxes, including the friendlier 100 hits per page option. At **Google** and **Raging Search**, click on "Language, Display, & Filtering Options" and "Customize" respectively to increase the default number of hits per page. You can then save the front page, as your preferences will be stored in your cookies.

## Subject directories

If you'd like to browse the **range of sites under a topic**, or by other common criteria, it's usually more helpful to refer to a **subject directory**. These aren't compiled by trawling the Web, **they're put together by human beings**. That means everything is neatly filed under various categories, like a phone directory, making it easy for you to drill down to what you're after.

You usually have the choice of browsing directories by **subject group** and sometimes by other criteria such as **entry date or rating**. Or sometimes you search the directory itself through a form, rather like a search engine. Unlike search engines, directories don't keep the contents of Web pages but instead record titles, categories, and sometimes comments or reviews, so adjust your search strategy accordingly. Start with broad terms and work down until you hit the reviews.

The best **general directories** are:

| | |
|---|---|
| **Yahoo** | http://www.yahoo.com |
| **Open Directory** | http://dmoz.org |
| **About.com** | http://www.about.com |

**Yahoo** is the best place to start any search. If the Web has seven wonders, it would probably be the first. You should spend at least one session online exploring its reaches. Chances are, you'll be back there every day. If you're located outside the USA, or looking for country specific information, then switch to the relevant regional guide, if available.

**The Open Directory** is a relatively recent project, that's compiled by about 25,000 volunteers. As yet, it's not quite up to Yahoo's standard across the board, but in some areas it beats it hands down. But like everything online, it's a work in progress so is bound to get better.

**About.com** deserves a special mention, because unlike most broad directories, its topics are researched and introduced by expert guides. Which makes it an excellent jumping off point if you need a helping hand. If you like this approach, **Suite101** (http://www.suite101.com) is attempting the same tack.

There's no shortage of alternatives, which might prove useful if the above fail, such as:

| | |
|---|---|
| **AltaVista** | http://www.av.com |
| **Excite** | http://www.excite.com |
| **Go** | http://www.go.com |
| **LookSmart** | http://www.looksmart.com |
| **Lycos** | http://www.lycos.com |

But broad subject directories aren't always the best at digging up everything within a category, or giving you expert guidance. For that you need a specialist directory – or as the suits call them, vortals.

## Specialist sites and directories

Whatever your interest, you can bet your favorite finger it will have several dedicated Web pages and there's probably a page somewhere that keeps track of them all. Such **specialized directories** are a boon for finding new, esoteric or local interest pages – ones that the major directories overlook. How do you find a specialist directory? Well, you could start by searching a directory that specializes in listing specialist directories such as:

| | |
|---|---|
| **Directory Guide** | http://www.directoryguide.com |
| **GoGettem** | http://www.gogettem.com |
| **Search Bug** | http://www.searchbug.com |
| **Search Engine Guide** | http://www.searchengineguide.com |
| **Search IQ** | http://www.searchiq.com |
| **SuperSeek** | http://www.super-seek.com |
| **Webdata** | http://www.webdata.com |

Specialist sites often maintain a **mailing list** to keep you posted with news and, in some cases, they run **discussion lists** or **bulletin boards** so you can discuss issues with other visitors. If you feel you can contribute to the site in any way email the Webmaster and introduce yourself. That's how the Web community works. You'll find hundreds of specialist sites all through our Web guide.

## Search agents

**Search agents**, or **searchbots**, gather information live from a limited number of sites. For example, to find new information, to compare prices or stock, or combine the results from several search engines. Metasearch agents such as **Copernic** (http://www.copernic.com), **Search.com** (http://www.search.com), and **MetaCrawler** (http://www.metacrawler.com) can query multiple search engines and directories simultaneously; shopping agents, like **Shopper.com** (http://www.shopper.com), can look for the best deal across several online shops; and Web agents, like **NetAttaché** (http://www.tympani.com), can scan specific sites for pages which have changed or contain instances of an expression. Though many are accessible through a Web interface, the better ones are generally standalone clients.

If you're a serious researcher, once you've tried **Copernic** you'll never want to use an individual search engine again. It's a standalone program that can query hundreds of search engines, directories, Usenet archives, and email databases, at

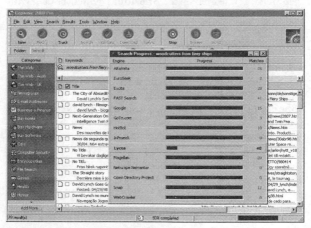

once. It filters out the duplicates, displays the results on a single page in your browser and even retrieves them automatically for offline browsing. It comes in versions for both PC and Mac, so don't pause for thought, **download it now!**

Unfortunately, the Web equivalents aren't as useful. Sure, they can query multiple search resources, but even the best, **MetaCrawler**, will return only up to 30 hits per site. The whole point of searching multiple engines is to get more hits, so you'd be better off starting with **Fast Search**.

You might find the same goes for the bewildering layers of **search aids built into IE5.x and Windows 98**. Click on IE5.x's Search button, or "Find on the Internet" from Windows 98's Start menu, and a search form will appear on the left-hand side of your browser. Click **Customize** to choose from an impressive array of search engines, directories, email databases, maps, and more. It looks promising but again you'll probably get better value at the source.

**Apple's** metasearch agent, **Sherlock**, which comes with MacOS 8.5 and later, also looks promising at first but suffers from the same problems as MetaCrawler. Before you condemn it as entirely worthless, download all the plug-ins from Apple (http://www.apple.com/sherlock/), choose Update Search Sites from under the Find menu and search for a common phrase. Compare the result with Google or Fast search and then decide. Perhaps the next version…

**Shopping agents** are about to take over the Net by storm. Some attempt to find you the best product by features and price within a category. Others can instantly compare the price and availability of various products across a number of online stores. See our shopping section for more details; (p.201).

For searchbot news, reviews and a listing of all known strains, see: BotSpot (http://bots.internet.com)

# Finding stuff

If you start your search with the search engines and directories they'll invariably lead you to other sites, which in turn point you closer toward what you're after. As you get more familiar with the run of the Net, you'll gravitate toward specialist sites and directories that index more than just Web pages, contain their own unique content, and shine in specific areas. What's best depends largely on what you're after. When you find a useful site, **store it in your Favorites or Bookmarks**, so you can return. Here are a few examples, using a mixture of techniques.

## Find answers to the most common questions

Where else would you look for answers to the most Frequently Asked Questions than the repository for Usenet FAQs? If the answer's not in http://www.faqs.org try Usenet itself.

## Find out what others think on Usenet

You want to, but you don't know how. You want one, but you don't know which one. You have one, but you can't get it to work. You want more than just a second opinion. You want a forum on the subject. That's Usenet (see p.129).

There's no better place to find opinions and personal experiences than Usenet, but it's a lot of text to scan. Although it's sorted into subject bundles, if you had to find every instance of discussion about something, it could take you days. And if it was tossed around more than a couple of weeks ago, the thread might have expired.

With **Deja.com Discussions** (http://www.deja.com/usenet/), however, not only can you scan close to all Usenet now, but a fair chunk of its history as well. That includes over 20,000 newsgroups going back, in many cases, to March 1995. You can pursue entire threads and profile each contributor, just by clicking on the results. Which means you can follow a whole discussion, as well as check out who's who and how well they're respected. And on top of that, you can identify which groups are most likely to discuss something and then join the group. You'll get to the bottom of even the most obscure subject.

Like all search engines, Deja.com is pretty self-explanatory, but do yourself a favor and start out by reading:
http://www.deja.com/help/help_ps.shtml

## Find someone's email address

When you're given an **email address** it's private unless you instruct someone to list it in a **directory** or make it public in some other way. So if you're looking for a long-lost friend's email address, there's no guarantee you'll find it. Nonetheless, it's worth trying the **email directories**, but don't give up if they're not there! The biggest directories are:

**Bigfoot**                                http://www.bigfoot.com
**WhoWhere**                          http://www.whowhere.com
**Yahoo PeopleSearch**        http://people.yahoo.com

These get most of their data from Usenet postings and visitors, so while they're not in any way comprehensive they're pretty vast databases – and growing by the day. You can also access them from the address books in Messenger and Outlook Express.

If these fail, try searching on your quarry's full name in a search engine or Deja.com. Alternatively, if you know where they work, search their company's Web pages – or (an old standby of detective agencies), **ring up and ask**.

For other tips, see:

**FAQ on finding email addresses**:
http://www.qucis.queensu.ca/FAQs/email/finding.html

**Yahoo's email search directory**:
http://dir.yahoo.com/Reference/Phone_Numbers_and_Address
es/Email_Addresses/

**ICQ Email directory**:
http://www.icq.com/search/email.html

## Find games, hints, and cheats

Try one of the big games sites such as the **Games Domain**, **Gamespot**, or **Happy Puppy**, or search through Usenet as explained above. Stuck on a level? Look for a walkthrough, or ask in Usenet.

## Find a product review

See our Shopping chapter (p.201).

## Find an online shop

Again, see our Shopping chapter (p.201).

## Find product support

Whenever you buy anything substantial, see if the company has a Web site offering **follow-up support** and **product news**. If it's not on the accompanying literature, try putting its name between www and .com and if that doesn't work, look it up in any of the search directories.

Most companies offer some kind of online product support and registration, but if you want advice from other users, go to Usenet.

## Find the latest news, weather, finance, sport, etc

Apart from hundreds of newspapers and magazines, the Net carries several large **news-clipping archives** assembled from all sorts of sources. Naturally, there's an overwhelming amount of technology news, but also an increasing amount of services dedicated to what you would normally find on the newsstands – and it's often fresher on the Net. Occasionally there's a charge for access, though that's more usual with the archives rather than what's current. For pointers, check our Web guide under News, Fashion, Finance, Weather, and so forth. The best place to start would be **Moreover** (http://www.moreover.com), where you can search or browse headlines from over 1500 newsfeeds and then link to the story. **Yahoo Daily News** (http://dailynews.yahoo.com) is another good starting point.

## Find out about a film or TV show

See the Film and TV section of our Web guide or try the entertainment section of any major directory for leads to specialist sites. The **Internet Movie Database**, for example, is exceptionally comprehensive and linked to Amazon in case you're tempted to order the video.

## Find the latest software

First off, try one of the specialist file directories such as **Stroud's**, **Tucows** or **Download.com** and look under an appropriate category. Failing that, try coining an appropriate search term and feeding it into the search engines, Usenet archives, and IT press archives such as **ZDNet** (http://www.zdnet.com). As a bonus you'll likely find a description or review to tell you whether it's worth getting.

Once you've found a file, if it proves slow to download, feed the file name into one of the **FTP engines** such as **Filez** (http://www.filez.com), **Shareware.com** (http://www .shareware.com), or **FTP Search** (http://www.ftpsearch.com), to find an alternative FTP site from which to download it.

## Find health support

Start by searching the Web. Try Yahoo listings of organizations and so forth, and then Google for mentions on Web pages. Chances are they'll in turn point you towards useful mailing lists and discussion groups. If not, try Deja.com to see if, and in which groups, it's being discussed on Usenet. Ultimately, though, you'd like to join a mailing list.

## Find a mailing list

The best place to find mailing lists is through a well-worded Web search, or through the small list directories at:

http://www.paml.net

http://www.meta-list.net

http://www.list-universe.com

http://www.liszt.com

If that's not satisfactory, try the same search in Deja.com and check the FAQs from groups with hits.

## Find something you've forgotten

Don't give up if you can't remember where you saw that hot tip last week. Just open IE5.x's History and search the cache. So long as it hasn't been deleted, you should even be able to recall it offline.

## Find advice

If all else fails – and that's pretty unlikely – you can always turn to someone else for help. Use Deja.com to find the most

appropriate newsgroup(s). Summarize your quest in the subject heading, keep it concise, post, and you should get an answer or three within a few days. Alternatively, try a mailing list or one of the "expert" advice services such as:

| | |
|---|---|
| **AskMe.com** (free) | http://www.askme.com |
| **ExpertCentral.com** (free) | http://www.expertcentral.com |
| **Exp.com** (pay) | http://www.exp.com |

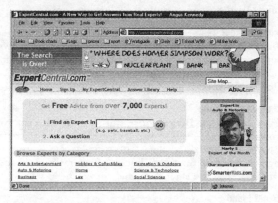

# Finding the right Web address

It won't be long before you encounter a **Web link or address that won't work**. Don't get too perturbed – it's common and usually not too hard to get around. We already know that many of the URLs in our Web guide will be wrong by the time you try them. Not because we're hopeless, they just change. For example, in the five months between the last edition of this book's first and fifth printings, almost 100 sites needed updating. That's the way of the Net. The most useful thing we can do is show you how to find their new homes.

# Error codes

When something goes wrong, your browser will pop up a box with a message and **error code, or display a page with an error message** – that or nothing will happen, no matter what you try. To identify the source of the problem, get familiar with the types of errors. Different browsers and servers will return different error messages, but they'll indicate the same things. As an exercise, identify the following errors:

## Incorrect host name

When the address points to a nonexistent host, your browser should return an error saying "Host not found" or "Cannot find server".

Test this by keying: http://www.rufgide.com

## Illegal domain name

If you specify an **illegal host name** or **protocol**, your browser should tell you. Try this out by keying http://wwwrufguide and then http:/www.ibm.com (noting the single slash before the www). Internet Explorer 5.x will automatically detect the latter error, and correct it.

## File not found

If the **file has moved**, **changed name**, or you've overlooked **capitalization**, you'll get a message within the page from the server telling you the file doesn't exist on the host. Test this by keying a familiar URL and slightly changing the path.

## Busy host or host refuses entry

Occasionally you won't gain access because the host is either **overloaded with traffic**, or it's temporarily or permanently **off-limits**. This sometimes happens with busy FTP servers, like Netscape's. It's a bit hard to test, but you'll come across it sooner or later. You might also make a habit of accessing foreign sites when locals are sleeping – it's usually quicker.

## When nothing works

Now that you're on speaking terms with your browser, you're set to troubleshoot that problem URL. When you get one, first check that you have a **working connection** to the Web. Try another site, like: http://www.yahoo.com

If it works, you know the problem's with that URL (more on which below). If you can't connect to any Web site, **close and then reopen your browser**. It might only be a software glitch. Otherwise, it's most likely a problem with your Net connection or proxy server (if you're using one).

**Check your mail**. If that looks dodgy, log off, then back on. Check it again. If your mailer connects and reports your mail status normally, you know that the connection between you and your provider is okay. But there still could be a problem between it and the Net or with your proxy server. Check you have the right proxy settings and if so, disable them. If it still doesn't work, **ring your provider** and see if there's a problem at their end or diagnose it yourself.

To do this, test a known host – say **www.yahoo.com** – with a **network tool** such as **Ping**, **TraceRoute** or **NetMedic** (see p.72) or try logging in to an FTP site. If this fails, either your provider's connection to the Net is down, or there's a problem with your **Domain Name Server**. Get on the phone and sort it out.

If you've verified that all connections are open but your browser still won't find any URLs, then the problem must lie with your **browser setup**. Check its settings and re-install it if necessary.

## When a page won't display

You'll sometimes find a page or frame inside a page instantly comes up blank. You can tell your browser hasn't tried to fetch the page because it happens too quickly. In this case hit the Refresh button. If that doesn't work, reboot your browser window, and re-enter the address. Failing that, open your set-tings and clear your Temporary Internet Files or browser cache. Finally, if you're still having problems and it appears to be related to Internet Explorer security, such as the acceptance of an ActiveX control at an online banking site, check your security settings within Internet Options, disable **Content Advisor**, and consider adding the site to your Trusted sites.

## When one address won't work

If only **one address fails**, you know its address is wrong or its host has problems. Now that you're familiar with error messages you can deduce the source and fix that address.

**Web addresses disappear and change** all the time, often because the address has been simplified, for example from: http://www.netflux.co.uk/~test/New_Book/htm to http://www.newbook.com

If you're lucky, someone will have had the sense to leave a **link to the new page** from the old address but sometimes even that pointer gets out of date. Since the Web is in a constant state of construction, just about everything is a test site in transit to something bigger and more glorious. Consequently, when a site gets serious, it might relocate to an entirely new host and forget the old address.

If you're convinced the address is fine, then try it later, per-haps even days later. It might be down for maintenance or experiencing local problems. If you can reach it on another machine, but not yours, the problem might lie with your Windows Hosts file – especially if you've ever installed any browser acceleration software. If so, first get rid of the offending program properly through the Add/Remove applet in Windows Control Panel. Then locate the file called Hosts in your Windows folder. It will have no file extension. Open it with Notepad and remove any lines not starting with # except for the localhost entry. Save the file, and exit.

## Finding that elusive URL

The error messages will provide the most helpful clues for **tracking elusive addresses**. If the problem comes from the host name, try **adding** or **removing the www part**. For example, instead of typing http://roughguides.com try http://www.roughguides.com Other than that you can only guess. It may only be that the host is busy, refusing entry, or not connecting, so **try again later.**

If you **can connect to the host but the file isn't there**, there are a few further tricks to try. Check capitalization, for instance: book.htm instead of Book.htm Or try **changing the file name extension** from .htm to .html or vice versa, if applicable. Then try **removing the file name** and then each subsequent directory up the path until finally you're left with just the host name. For example:

```
http://www.roughguides.com/old/Book.htm
http://www.roughguides.com/old/book.htm
http://www.roughguides.com/old/book.html
http://www.roughguides.com/old/
http://www.roughguides.com
```

In each case, if you succeed in connecting, try to locate your page from whatever links appear.

If you haven't succeeded, there's still hope. Try **submitting the main key words** from the URL's address or title to **Google** or **Fast Search**. Failing that, try searching on related subjects, or scanning through one of the subject guides like **Yahoo** or the **Open Directory**.

By now, even if you haven't found your original target URL, you've probably discovered half a dozen similar if not more interesting pages, and in the process figured out how to navigate the Net.

# 12

# Chat

## IRC, WEBCHAT AND USING
## THE NET AS A PHONE

**Y**ou won't really feel the full impact of having instant access
to a cast of millions until you jump into your first chat
session. You might even find it a touch spooky at first. The
way you can type something in, and within seconds, someone
replies. Even if chat doesn't quite sound like your sort of
thing, at least give it a go once or twice, just for fun.

You'll find Internet chat opportunities at almost every corner, particularly within the Online Services, and increasingly,
on the **Web**. AOL and CompuServe are known for their
**chat forums**, which often host interviews with notable
**celebrities**. You have to be a member, though, to join in.
But don't let that bother you because there are ample chat
forums on the Web, and way more again within an entirely
separate system called **Internet Relay Chat**, or **IRC.** We'll

cover IRC in step-by-step detail over the next few pages, and then investigate some other popular chat techniques such as **Instant Messaging** and **Internet Telephony**.

## How it works

Unlike Usenet and email, on Internet chat, **conversations are live**. Joining a **chat channel**, **chat room** or **chat forum** is like **arriving at a party**. It could be **full of people**, or you might be the first to arrive. Whatever you say in that channel is instantly broadcast to everybody else on the same channel, even if they're logged into a server on the other side of the world. And you can expect them to reply as instantly as if they were in the same room.

Some channels are obviously dedicated to **specific topics**, for example, #cricket, #dili, and #cosplay but most are merely **informal chat lines**. While chat might have business potential in areas such as customer support, it's overwhelmingly more orientated to **social banter.** Such idle natter between **consenting strangers** can lead to the online equivalent of **seriously heavy petting**, and inevitably makes it particularly attractive to teens. It can also make it unnervingly confrontational, so tread with caution.

## What you'll need

If you're only chatting in text, you won't need a particularly fast connection, nor a powerful computer. Voice and video are another matter: the more speed you throw at them, the better they work. Ideally, you don't want to be paying **timed online charges**, because once you're hooked, you'll end up squandering hours online.

Net software bundles don't always include a standard IRC program. But that's no problem, because there are plenty out on the Net to download. **mIRC** (http://www.mirc.co.uk) is by far the most popular under Windows, while **Ircle** (http://www.ircle.com) rules on the Mac. For more, check any of the major software archives in our Web guide (p.291).

## Getting started

There's not much to configure on most chat programs. First, you'll need to think up a **nickname** for yourself. That's what will identify you in the channel. So if you make it something rude you can expect to be ignored or treated accordingly. Next, you'll have to decide what to enter as your **real name** and **email address**. For privacy's sake and to avoid potential embarrassment, stick to an alias. Finally, enter **a chat server address**. You'll probably be offered a choice from a drop-down menu, either within your user options or upon connecting. Experiment with a few and settle on whichever takes your fancy.

If it's not obvious where to enter your details refer to the program's Help files. In fact, it wouldn't hurt to run through any tutorials either. It might sound a bit pedestrian but it will pay off. Chat programs have an array of cryptic buttons and windows that are less intuitive than most Internet programs. And before you start randomly clicking on things to see what they do, **remember people are watching**.

## The servers

There are hundreds of open IRC hosts worldwide; many of them linked together through networks such as **Undernet**, **DALnet,** and **EFnet**. To ease the strain on network traffic, start with a **nearby host**. The best place to get a fresh list of servers, or indeed any information about IRC, is from the alt.irc newsgroup. But the quickest would be from: http://www.irchelp.org/irchelp/networks/

For starters, choose a host from your chat program's Connect Setup menu or try: us.undernet.org on port 6667.

# A caution

Of all the Net's corners, IRC is the one most likely to trip up newbies – mainly because you can't hide your presence. For example, on Usenet, unless you jump in and post, no-one can tell you've been following the discussion. However, the second you arrive in an IRC channel **you'll be announced** to all and your nickname will remain in the names list for as long as you stay.

If you select someone's name in your channel, and click the right button, you'll be able to find out a little bit about them. Cross-reference that, and you might find out a little bit more. So bear in mind: others might be checking you out in the same way.

Whatever you do, **don't click on files sent to you** by a stranger. This is the most common way of spreading **Trojan horse** programs, which can do all sorts of damage such as hand over your PC to outsiders. While its file extension might say it's a harmless JPG image, it's possible that after the .JPG there's about one hundred spaces followed by an .EXE. In other words, it could be a program in disguise. And **don't rely on your virus checker** to pick them up. The kids on IRC are smarter than that. As an extra precaution against attacks, you should install a personal firewall, such as the excellent free program, **ZoneAlarm** (http://www.zonelabs.com). It will protect you from anyone trying to access your computer from outside, and alert you to any stealth programs trying to access the Internet from your machine.

For the same reasons, **don't enter any unfamiliar commands at the request of another person**. If someone is bothering you privately, protest publicly. If no-one defends you, change channels. If they persist, get them kicked out by an operator.

# IRC commands

IRC has **hundreds of commands**, but you can safely get by only knowing a few. However, the more you learn, the more you can strengthen your position. You can almost get away without learning any commands at all with modern programs, but it won't hurt to know the script behind the buttons, and you may even prefer it. Your client won't automate everything, so each time you're online test a few more. The Help file should contain a full list. If not, try: http://www.irchelp.org

There are far too many commands to list here, but those below will get you started. Note that **anything after a forward slash (/) is interpreted as a command**: if you leave off the slash, it will be transmitted to your active channel as a message and you'll look like a dork.

| Command | Description |
|---|---|
| /AWAY <message> | Leave message saying you're not available |
| /BYE | Exit IRC session |
| /CLEAR | Clear window contents |
| /HELP | List available commands |
| /HELP <command> | Return help on this command |
| /IGNORE <nickname><*><all> | Ignore this nickname |
| /IGNORE <*><email address><all> | Ignore this email address |
| /IGNORE <*><*><none> | Delete ignorance list |
| /JOIN <#channel> | Join this channel |
| /KICK <nickname> | Boot this nickname off channel |
| /LEAVE <#channel> | Exit this channel |
| /LIST <-MIN n> | List channels with minimum of n users |
| /MOP | Promote all to operator status |
| /MSG <nickname><message> | Send private message to this nickname |
| /NICK <nickname> | Change your nickname |
| /OP <nickname> | Promote this nickname to operator |
| /PING <#channel> | Check ping times to all users |
| /QUERY <nickname> | Start a private conversation with this nickname |
| /TOPIC <new topic> | Change channel topic |

/WHO* ................................................................ List users in current channel
/WHOIS <nickname> ....................................... Display nickname's identity
/WHOWAS <nickname> ................................. Display identity of exited nickname

## Step by step through your first session

By now, you've configured your client, chosen a **nickname
you'll never use again**, and are raring to go. The aim of
your first session is to connect to a server, have a look around,
get a list of channels, join one, see who's on, say something
public, then something private, leave the channel, start a new

channel, make yourself operator, change the topic, and then
exit IRC. The whole process should take no more than about
ten minutes. **Let's go**.

✦ Log on to a server and wait to be accepted. If you're not, keep trying others until you succeed. Once aboard, you'll be greeted with the MOTD (message of the day) in the server window. Read the message and see if it tells you anything interesting.

✦ You should have at least two windows available. One for input, the other to display server output. Generally, the two windows form part of a larger window, with the input box below the output box. Even though your client's point and click interface will replace most of the basic commands, since you probably haven't read its manual yet, you won't know how to use it. So instead just use the commands.

✦ To see what channels are available, type: **/LIST** You'll have to wait a minute and then a window will pop up, or fill up, with thousands of channels, their topics, and the number of users on them. To narrow down the list to those channels with six or more users, type: **/LIST -MIN 6** Now you'll see the busiest channels.

✦ Pick a channel at random and join it. Channel names are always preceded by #, so to join the lard channel, type: **/JOIN #lard** and then wait for the channel window to appear. (Clicking on its name should have the same effect in most programs.) Once the channel window opens, you should get a list of the channel's occupants, in yet another window. If not, type: **/WHO\*** for a full list including nicknames and email addresses.

✦ Now say something clever. Type: **Hi everyone, it's great to be back!** This should appear not only on the screen in your channel window, but on the screen in every other person's channel window. Wait for replies and answer any questions as you see fit.

✦ Now it's time to send something personal. Choose someone in the channel and find out what you can about them first, by typing: **/WHO** followed by their nickname. Your client might let you do this by just double-clicking on their nickname in the names window. Let's say their nickname is Tamster. To send a private message, just type: **/MSG Tamster Hey Tamster, I'm a clueless newbie, let me know if you get this so I won't feel so stupid.** If Tamster doesn't reply, keep trying until someone does. Once you're satisfied you know how that works, leave the channel by typing: **/LEAVE** Don't worry, next time you go into a channel, you'll feel more comfortable.

✚ Now to start your own channel. Pick any name that doesn't already exist. As soon as you leave, it will disappear. To start a channel called lancelink, just type: **/JOIN #lancelink** Once the window pops up, you'll find you're the only person on it. Now promote yourself to operator by typing: **/OP** followed by your nickname. Others can tell you have channel operator status because your nickname will appear with an @ in front of it. Now you're an operator – you have the power to kick people off the channel, change the topic, and all sorts of other things that you can find out by reading the manual as recommended. To change the topic, type: **/TOPIC** followed by whatever you want to change the topic to. Wait for it to change on the top of your window and then type: **/BYE** to exit IRC.

That's it really; a whirlwind tour but enough to learn most things you'll need. Now before you can chat with other chatsters, you'll need to speak their lingo.

## The language of IRC

Just like CB radio, IRC has its own **dialect**. Chat is a snappy medium, messages are short, and responses are fast. Unlike CB, people won't ask your "20" to see where you're from but they might ask your a/s/l – age/sex/location. **Acronyms and abbreviations** are mixed in with normal speech and range from the innocuous (BTW = by the way) to a whole panoply of blue phrases. But don't be ashamed to stick with plain English, Urdu or whatever. After all, you'll stand a better chance of being understood.

For just a taste of what you might strike, see "Net Language" on p.469.

## IRC netiquette

IRC is almost diversity defined. You're as likely to encounter a channel full of Indian expats following a ball-by-ball cricket commentary as a couple of college kids flirting. So long as no-one rocks the boat too much, coexistence can be harmonious. Of course, there's bound to be a little mayhem now and then, but that usually just adds to the fun of the whole event.

However, some actions are generally frowned upon and may get you kicked from channels, or even banned from a server. These include dumping large files or amounts of text, harassment, vulgarity, beeping constantly to get attention, and inviting people into inappropriate channels. Finally, if you make a real nuisance of yourself, someone might be vindictive enough to track you down and make you regret it.

## IRC games

Many IRC channels are dedicated to **games**. Sometimes you can play against other people, although more commonly you're up against programs called **bots**. Such programs are written to respond to requests in a particular way, and even learn from the experience. You'll also come across bots in standard chat channels. It might even take you some time to recognize you're not talking to a human.

For more about IRC games, see:

http://www.yahoo.com/Recreation/Games/Internet_Games

## Web chat

Like almost every other aspect of the Internet, chat too has moved onto the Web. About the best thing you can say about Web chat it is that it doesn't require a special IRC program. All you need is your Web browser.

Simple Web chat isn't as instant as IRC, as you have to wait a little while for the page to refresh to follow responses. However, most decent Web chat is done through Java, ActiveX

or a small program download, which makes it just like a crippled, but foolproof, version of the real thing. And in some
cases, you can circumvent the Web interface and log into the
server directly with your normal chat program. You only need
find out the server address, and then enter the channel name.

Just about all the top line portals, such as **Yahoo**
(http://chat.yahoo.com), **Excite** (http://chat.excite.com), and
**MSN** (http://chat.msn.com) have strong chat facilities, cou-
pled with planned events guides. You'll also find chat (or at
least a bulletin board) at any site that's attempting to create a
community around their content, such as most investment
sites and newspapers.

For a rundown of the **most popular Web chat channels**,
see: http://www.100hot.com/chat/

## What's on

Although most of what goes on in IRC is spontaneous, it also
plays host to loads of organized events, including **celebrity
interviews and topical debates**. The big ones tend to hide
behind the Online Service curtain but the Net still attracts its
share. For a calendar of what's planned across all forms of
Internet chat, including the structured Web-based alternatives, such as **Talk City** (http://www.talkcity.com), see **Yack**
(http://www.yack.com). Also check the **events guides** at the
various portals, such as http://guide.yahoo.com

For a directory of themed, regularly inhabited, and most
popular channels across almost 30 networks, see:
http://www.liszt.com/chat/

And to **keyword search** the text currently orbiting the
networks, see: http://www.enow.com

## Instant messaging – ICQ and AIM

IRC, Web chat, and Online Service forums are great for
meeting complete strangers, but they're not the best for talking

privately amongst friends. If you'd like to corner your pals as soon as they pop online get them to grab **ICQ** (http://www.icq.com) or **AOL Instant Messenger** (http://www.aol.com/aim/) which comes with Netscape Communicator. Oddly, both programs are owned by AOL. Other alternatives include **PowWow** (http://www.tribal.com), **MSN Messenger** (http://messenger.msn.com) and **Yahoo Messenger** (http://messenger.yahoo.com). All are fine, and free, but it's best to use whatever you're friends are on, because they're not compatible. ICQ is by far the most popular.

These "**buddy lists**" are even threatening email as the pre-ferred tool for quick messages – and often lead to impromptu chat sessions if you're both online. But they can be a **major source of distraction** when your online chums buzz you as you're trying to work. They're also a potential security risk. As with any other medium, never run any files sent to you by strangers, and preferably operate behind a firewall such as **ZoneAlarm.** If you install ICQ, at least read the following: http://www.icq.com/features/security/

## Internet telephony

The concept of using the **Internet as an alternative to the telephone network** is getting some quarters quite frisky – mainly because it can **cut the cost of calling long distance** to that of a local call plus Internet charges (at both ends). It works but don't expect the same fidelity, convenience, or reliability, as your local regular phone network. In other words, give it a go for curiosity's sake, but don't invest any money in it.

To place a Net call through your computer, you need a **soundcard**, **speakers**, and a **microphone** – standard multi-media fare. If your soundcard permits duplex transmission, you can hold a regular conversation, like an ordinary telephone; otherwise it's more like a walkie-talkie where you take turns to speak. As for your modem, 14.4 Kbps is generally ample for the task but the higher the bandwidths at each end the better your chance of decent sound quality.

## Phone programs

You have plenty of choice in **Net phone programs**. Some, like **Internet Phone**, are similar to IRC – you log into a server and join a channel. Others, such as **WebPhone**, are more like an ordinary phone and start a point-to-point connection when you choose a name from a directory. It's worth trying a few to see what works best for you.

**Microsoft NetMeeting** is as good as any. It has **real-time voice and video conferencing**, plus things like collaborative application sharing, document editing, background file transfer, and a whiteboard to draw and paste on. Plus it's free with Windows 98 and Internet Explorer. Grab the latest version through Windows Update or from:
http://www.microsoft.com/netmeeting/

## Internet to telephone

It's also possible to initiate a call from your PC to a normal telephone at the other end. Within DialPad (http://www .dialpad.com), you can talk as long as you like to any number in the US, from anywhere in the world, entirely free. With Net2Phone (http://www.net2phone.com), you can call phones worldwide, for a fraction of the usual cost.

Alternatively, there's **Aplio Phone** (http://www.aplio.com), which looks like an ordinary telephone and works similarly except it automatically initiates a call through each end's ISP. The sound is passable, albeit with slight delay, but you'll need to tally the combined cost of both party's Internet access and local call charges, and factor in the cost of the units at each end, to tell whether its cheaper than a discount calling card. It seems very unlikely.

## Video conferencing

You might like the idea of seeing who you're talking to, but you'll need serious bandwidth to make **Internet video conferencing** any more than a slide show. But if it means seeing live footage of a loved one across the world, perhaps it's worth it. All you need's a relatively cheap video cam, and **Netmeeting**.

## Chat worlds

There's no doubt virtual reality can look quite cute, but there's not much call for it. The best applications so far seem to be among the plethora of **chat worlds**, **virtual cities**, and **avatars**. These tend to work like IRC, but with an extra dimension or two. So rather than channels, you get rooms, playgrounds, swim-

ming pools, and so forth. To switch channels, you might walk into another building or fly up into the clouds. You might be represented by an animated character rather than a text nickname and be able to do all sorts of multimedia things such as build 3D objects and play music.

This all sounds pretty futuristic and it's certainly impressive at first, but whether you'll want to become a regular is another matter. The most popular are **World's Chat** (http://www.worlds.net) and **The Palace** (http://www.thepalace.com).

If it's action and hi-tech graphics you're after, however, ditch chat, and head straight to the world of **Online Gaming**. See p.232.

# 13

# Shopping

## STORES, SECURITY
## AND AUCTIONS

If you suspect your main mission on Earth is to shop, then destiny must be leading you online. Because in case you haven't heard, the Net and commerce have moved on from a mere flirtation to a serious item. In fact, the Net is starting to look like the greatest bazaar ever built, with new stalls popping up daily across the planet. Whether you're after a ticket to the **monster trucking safari** (http://www.ticketmaster.com) or a **midget tourist submarine** (http://www.ussubs.com), all you have to do is click, and of course, have your credit card handy.

So is it merely catalog mail order made complicated by computers? Sometimes, maybe, but that's only part of the story. The Net hasn't entirely killed off catalogs just yet, but it already blitzes them in many ways. To start with it's interactive not static. That means you can sift large inventories in seconds. And get the latest information, be it new releases, stock levels or recommendations based on your tastes. So, if you're shopping for music, for example, you could plough through a performer's entire back catalog, listening to samples as you read what other customers have to say about each album. Plus you can **visit several stores, in different parts of the world, all at once**, simply by opening multiple browser windows. Or send a search engine to forage for the best prices or availability across hundreds of shops simultaneously. Catalogs don't even come close.

But **you might be concerned that it's unsafe**. Fair enough, but you needn't worry too much. As long as you follow the advice here you'll find it's considerably less risky than the offline world.

## Pros and cons

The Net mightn't be as neatly arranged as your average shopping center, but it does offer some advantages – particularly when you can't find something as cheaply, if at all, locally. Nonetheless, while you can't rule anything out completely, some products are definitely more suited to selling online. **Books** and **CDs**, for example, fit perfectly because you can sample and read reviews before you buy. And if you don't like your purchase, you can return it for a refund. Or if you couldn't be bothered, you haven't blown your life savings. Clothes, on the other hand, are much trickier. You might squeeze by on generics like jeans and t-shirts, but anything that requires trying on will cause problems. While you can always return them if they don't fit, it's a hassle involving extra postage costs and monetary risk.

In essence, the Net isn't suitable if: you need to examine the goods; the weight or size makes shipping too costly; they can't deliver in time; or it costs more without being more convenient. **So just because you're on the Net doesn't mean you'll never have to leave the house again.**

# Shop safe

Without wishing to scare you unduly, you should be aware that sharks do lurk out there. Not that many, but enough to keep you on your toes. Contrary to the popular notion, the biggest threat isn't some boy hacker sneaking off with your card number. They mostly only break into sites to show off. In the unlikely chance one does get your number, they probably won't even use it. Besides, **there are easier ways to nab your credit details**. Like getting a part-time job in a shop, for instance. You should be more concerned with con artists running seemingly legitimate sites, or approaching you by unsolicited email. Ignore the following warnings at your own peril:

● If anything at all seems fishy, don't shop there.

● If a site hasn't gone to the effort of registering its own domain name, then don't expect it to be professional in any other way. **Merchants using free servers like Geocities should be regarded as classified ads** rather than shops. And regard any business operating out of a collective shopping mall as a **market stall**.

● **Never deal with a site that doesn't give a street address** and phone number. An email address isn't enough. And a free email address, like Hotmail, spells trouble. Mind you, failure to display a phone number doesn't make them instantly dodgy. It's an all too common omission on even the best-known sites. And some, for example Amazon, bury their contact details at the bottom of a help file. **Feel free to abuse them about it**. Tell them we sent you.

● Any site or email that uses **LOADS OF BOLD UPPER CASE TEXT** isn't to be trusted.

● Always **switch to a secure connection** when modifying your account details or checking out. When a connection becomes secure the beginning of the address will change from http:// to https:// and a closed lock will appear in the bottom bar of your browser. If a shop doesn't offer secure purchasing, it's not serious about its online presence. Shop elsewhere, or phone through your order. **Never send your credit card details by email**.

● To make an online purchase you should only need to provide your name, billing address, delivery address, credit card number, account name, expiry date and shipping preferences. **You should never need any other form of identification** such as your social security, health insurance, driver's license, savings account, or passport number.

● The **username/password combination** you choose for a site, applies to that site only. Never give it to another site, or to anyone by email or phone. Avoid using the same combination at every site, and especially don't use your mail or dial-up connection password.

● **Don't respond to spam** (unsolicited email). Those "get paid to surf", "work from home", "recruit new members", "clear your credit rating", and various network-marketing schemes **are** too good to be true.

● **Don't install free browser or mouse cursor enhancements**, including so-called Web accelerators. Or let any site make itself your "home page". They're only interested in collecting marketing data. Your browser is just fine the way it is.

● Avoid any site that pops up a new window when you try to leave, or spawns multiple windows. Don't deal with, or download software from, any site that seems to consist of top lists of other sites, which in turn point you to more lists. These are merely trying to milk click-through referrals. It mightn't cost you anything but it wastes your time.

● It has to be said: **almost all online scams revolve around porn** sites. More than is let on, because their victims are often too embarrassed to own up. **Don't pass over your credit details to adult sites unless you're prepared to be stung**. And whatever you do, don't download any connection software, picture viewers, or browser add-ons from adult sites. These have been known to drop your line and redial somewhere like Vanuatu, racking up a massive phone bill in the process. If you must delve in porn, go wallow in the binary newsgroups.

● Never accept **ActiveX controls** unless you're absolutely positive they're from a reputable firm.

● Beware free trials and **subscription services** that require your credit details. You might find it harder to cancel than you anticipated. Or they might bill you whether you use the service or not. Check your bill carefully each month for discrepancies, and make sure the subscription doesn't renew itself automatically.

● Don't believe everything you read. As much as the Net is the greatest source of consumer advice, it's also the great source of **misinformation**. Look for a second opinion before you fork out cash on the basis of a recommendation.

● And don't forget: **keep a record of your order**, so you can balance it against your bank statement.

Like to know more about Net scams? Subscribe to: http://www.scambusters.com

## Are you covered?

Credit and debit cards provide varying degrees of **protection against fraud**. You'll need to read the fine print on your agreement for specifics, but normally you're only liable for a set amount. You also might be able to pay a yearly surcharge to fully protect your card against fraud. Ask your bank, along with what to do if you suspect you've been wrongly charged.

Some sites also offer to pick up the balance if you can show they're at fault.

## Know your product

Whether you're buying online or off, the Net is an invaluable mine of consumer advice. However, consumer written reviews can often be more anecdotal than scientific, and somewhat prone to rigging. So while you can't take it all at face value, the more you know the better your chance of a happy purchase. Usenet (p.129) is the best place to ask advice, but search **Deja.com – discussions** (http://www.deja.com/usenet/) first to see if it's already been discussed. **Productopia** (http://www .productopia.com) is the most thorough collection of buying guides, customer opinions, ratings and links to external reviews. It should be your first port of call, followed by these:

| | |
|---|---|
| **Amazon** | http://www.amazon.com |
| **ConsumerReview** | http://www.consumerreview.com |
| **Deja.com** | http://www.deja.com |
| **Dooyoo (EUR)** | http://www.dooyoo.com |
| **Epinions** | http://www.epinions.com |
| **eSmarts** | http://www.esmarts.com |
| **ProductReviewNet** | http://www.productreviewnet.com |
| **Rateitall.com** | http://www.rateitall.com |

You could also query Yahoo or a search engine to locate trade magazines or sites that specialize in your desired product category. And perhaps one of the consumer organizations, like:

http://www.consumersdigest.com (US)
http://www.choice.com.au (AUS)
http://www.which.net (UK)

But if you need hands-on experience you should examine the goods in a shop first, and then check whether you can get a better deal online.

# Buying foreign

With the entire Net at your fingertips, you're empowered to shop the world. And placing an order with a foreign store should be no harder than doing it locally, especially if you're paying by credit card. But, it does require a little more effort on the vendor's part, and certain products aren't suitable for export, so some stores won't accept foreign orders. You can usually find this out fairly quickly by looking up the store's shipping and handling section.

Before you leap on a bargain, **ensure it will work at home**. Phone or power plugs can be adapted quickly, but if the conversion involves something complex like replacing a power transformer, question if it's worth the effort. Other things that may differ between countries include: DVD region codes; console games; TV and video devices (check whether they're PAL or NTSC); PC keyboard layouts; software editions; and of course, anything where measurements could cause confusion such as recipes, clothing and space exploration vehicles.

Finally, when applicable, ask if it's covered by an **international warranty**, whether spares are available locally, where you'd have to send it for repairs, and who's responsible for shipping.

# But is it really a steal?

Sure, you can save money by shopping abroad, but if saving cash is your primary motive, you'll need to do your figures carefully. To start with you'll need to work out what it costs in your own currency. Call your bank for the going forex rate less transaction charges, and compare it with the wholesale rate at http://quote.yahoo.com. Then you'll be able to work it out in future.

Next, balance the shipping costs against transit time. Heavy items will naturally cost more, and cheaper options will take longer. How long can you wait? If you need it pronto, you'd better check they have the stock at hand.

And not least, the **sticky issue of tax**. The ideal scenario is to
buy duty free, and have it arrive untaxed by local customs. That
can happen, but it will depend on the countries involved, the
nature of the product, what it's worth, and whether anyone
could be bothered to chase it up. The US is the most complex
due to its state taxes. Technically, you should be able to buy duty
free between states as long as the shop doesn't have an office in
your home state. If you need more info on your tax laws, call
your local post office or customs helpdesk. Or if you live in the
UK, US, or Australia, try unpicking some sense from this lot:

  http://www.customs.gov.au (AUS)
  http://www.hmce.gov.uk (UK)
  http://www.customs.ustreas.gov (US)

## Auctions

If you've seen a paper in the last year, you've surely heard of
**eBay**. It was the first auction house to take the Net by storm.
Since then hundreds more have appeared, but eBay remains the
biggest player. You know how auctions work: the sale goes to the
highest bidder, as long as it's above the preset reserve price.
Or in the case of a Dutch auction, the price keeps dropping
until a buyer accepts. Well, it's the same online, but with several
advantages. Most obviously, you don't have to drive across
town and waste a day. You simply set a starting bid and then
leave an instruction to raise the bid in preset increments up to a
ceiling. If no-one outbids you, the deal is struck at your highest
offer – which could be your starting bid if it's above the reserve
and there aren't any other bidders.

Once the deal's been settled it's up to the buyer and seller to
arrange delivery and payment, though both can be arranged
via trusted third parties. The auction house typically takes a
cut of the vendor's taking. There are millions of goods for sale
in thousands of categories across hundreds of online auctions.
This is merely a selection of the biggest:

| | |
|---|---|
| **Amazon** | http://www.amazon.com (all branches) |
| **Auctions.com** | http://www.auctions.com (US) |
| **eBay** | http://www.ebay.com (US, UK, AUS, CAN) |
| **Gofish** | http://www.gofish.com.au (AUS) |
| **QXL** | http://www.qxl.com (US, UK, Europe) |
| **Sold.com.au** | http://www.sold.com.au (AUS) |
| **Yahoo** | http://auctions.yahoo.com (all branches) |

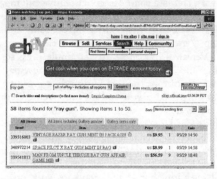

While these sites carry most items, sometimes you might prefer a specialist dealer. For a more comprehensive list, try Yahoo or a dedicated directory such as:

| | |
|---|---|
| **AuctionInsider.com** | http://www.auctioninsider.com |
| **Bidfind** | http://www.bidfind.com |
| **Internet Auction List** | http://www.internetauctionlist.com |

To search across hundreds of auctions simultaneously try **Auctionwatch.com** (http://www.auctionwatch.com), **Bidder's Edge** (http://www.biddersedge.com) or one of the many auction programs – search for "auction" at Download.com or Tucows (http://www.tucows.com). And check out **Esnipe** (http://www.esnipe.com), which can help you get a better price at eBay by waiting until the last minute to bid.

The Net has added a raft of new twists on the bidding game. At **Priceline** (http://www.priceline.com), **eWanted** (http://www.ewanted.com) and **Lastminute.com** (http://www.lastminute.com) for example, you state how much you'd like to pay and wait to see if anyone accepts. At **ReverseAuction.com** (http://www.reverseauction.com) the price keeps dropping until someone buys. **Ybag** (http://www.ybag.co.uk), **BuyersEdge** (http://www.buyeredge.com) and **myGeek** (http://www.mygeek.com) approach merchants on your behalf looking for the best deal. While **LetsBuyIt.com** (http://www.letsbuyit.com) and **Mercata** (http://www.mercata.com) use collaborative buying power to clinch lower prices across Europe and the US respectively. And at **NexTag** (http://www.nextag.com) and **Hagglezone** (http://www.hagglezone.com) you can barter for a better price. Ventures like these attract ample press so watch the shopping and Internet sections of your newspaper for further leads. But be warned, although they promise the world, don't be surprised if you end up inconvenienced or lumped with a so-so deal.

**Online classifieds** need no explanation. They're like the paper version, but easier to search and possibly more up to date. In fact most papers are moving their classifieds onto the Net, though you might have to pay to see the latest listings. Here's just a small selection, but as they tend to work on a local level check your hometown papers, or regional Yahoo for listings in your area:

| | |
|---|---|
| **Excite Classifieds** | http://www.classifieds2000.com |
| **Loot** | http://www.loot.com (UK, NY, IE) |
| **Newsclassifieds** | http://www.newsclassifieds.com.au (AUS) |
| **Trader.com** | http://www.trader.com |
| **Trading Post** | http://www.tradingpost.com.au (AUS) |
| **Zshops** | http://www.amazon.com |

Or if you'd rather swap than deal in cash, try:
**WebSwap** (http://www.webswap.com) and
**Webswappers** (http://www.webswappers.com).

## Let's shop!

Shopping's the same the world over: you collect your booty, head to the checkout, fix the bill and carry it home. As you'd expect, that's also how it works online. While the intricate details might differ between sites, once you've used one, the rest should fall into place. Let's use **Amazon** as an example:

### A journey through Amazon.com

Getting online and not visiting Amazon would be like going to Cairo and skipping the pyramids. Although it hasn't yet reported a profit, it's without argument the very model of online shopping excellence. Since launching in 1995 as a not so humble bookstore – allegedly the world's biggest – it's

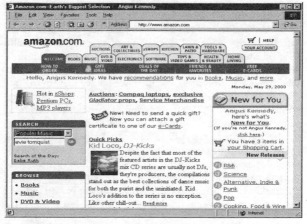

blossomed into a massive department store carrying music, DVD, electronics, furniture, cosmetics, tools, the next biggest auction house after eBay, classifieds, and loads more. But as you'll soon see, it's not the sheer bulk of stock alone that makes it so special. Amazon has branches in:

| **US** | http://www.amazon.com |
| **UK** | http://www.amazon.co.uk |
| **Germany** | http://www.amazon.de |

Although their inventories and editorials overlap, they're really three separate outlets, with local stock and distribution hubs. The US operation is ahead of the rest, stocking a wider range of products and features. But, it's worth checking both the UK and US operations, especially if you're after music.

### Sifting the inventory

Point your browser at: http://www.amazon.com. You'll find no time-wasting intro there. Everything's linked from the front page, so save it into your favorites. Explore the links around the page. You can either search the inventory using the form at the top left, or browse through the categories. Information about the vendor, including shipping and help is located at the bottom of the page. This is standard practice at all well-designed sites. After you've clicked a little, it will soon become clear how it works. But it might take you an hour or two to fully appreciate everything on offer. We'll leave that up to you.

But for now, try searching music for your favorite performer. Within seconds it will return a listing of entries from each section of its inventory. Click on any title to display the album details. Sometimes this will include a full track listing, along with editorial and customer reviews. Track entries that look like links are short RealAudio samples. Clicking on the performer's name will bring up a listing of their entire works, or at least those that Amazon carry. Now that you've worked that out, you should have no trouble navigating the rest of the site.

### The shopping basket

Although you can't actually purchase anything until you set up an account, you can add items to your "**shopping basket**". This is just like a shopping basket in the familiar sense. If you see something you like, drop it into your basket by clicking the "add to basket" button. All good sites use this system. Don't worry about how much you add to your basket. You're not committed to buy until you move the items through the checkout. You can always take items out later, or simply leave them there for another time. To return to shopping, hit your back button or start another search. You can return to your basket at any time by clicking on the basket icon at the top of the screen or on the link at the bottom of the page.

## Starting an account

When you're ready to buy, go to your basket and examine its contents. At this point, you can remove items, change the quantities or save them for later. But again, don't worry because you'll be given the chance again. Clicking "**proceed to checkout**" will bring up the "**signing in**" page. If it's your first visit you'll need to create a new account. Just choose "**I am a new customer**" and follow the prompts. You can change your account details later by clicking on "your account" at the top of the page, or when you're checking out. Once you move into the account phase, the server goes into secure mode – the address changes to **https://** and a closed lock appears on the bottom bar. If your browser doesn't support secure purchasing, then either download one that does, or don't shop online!

## Your privacy

Whenever you give your details to any site it will ask whether you'd like to receive mail from them, or associated parties. **Say no.** You don't need junk mail from them or anyone else.

## Checking out

Once you've logged in with your password, checking out is as straightforward as following the prompts. The most difficult part will be deciding between the various shipping options. If you've bought more than one item you'll have to decide whether to ship them all at once, or as they arrive at their warehouse. One item might take weeks to arrive, delaying the rest of the order. You'll see an indication of how long Amazon thinks each item will take to arrive underneath its entry in the basket. The rest should be all self-explanatory. Just read the help files if you're unclear.

### Confirmation

Almost all shops send you an instant email confirming your order. Some shops need a reply to confirm acceptance, though Amazon doesn't. Keep all your orders and shipping notices together in a separate folder so you can refer to them later if something goes amiss.

### Tracking

To check the status of each item in your order at Amazon, click on "your account", sign in, and look under Order History. Some sites can give you order tracking details right down to the shipping hubs.

### Your next visit

Next time you arrive at Amazon it will welcome you by your name. This will only work if you're using the same computer, though, as it stores your ID in a cookie file. This isn't a bad thing generally as it learns from your purchases and attempts to recommend stuff you might like. It's not a security con-cern, as you still have to sign in with your password to make a purchase or change your account details.

## Finding shops

We listed individual shops in our previous editions but there are so many now it's no longer practical. Even the guides solely dedicated to shopping are feeling the strain. Soon it will be like trying to replicate the Yellow Pages. Nonetheless, you might find such a guide useful if it's well researched.

Otherwise, it's tough to advise you where to start. It depends where you live, what you're after, and of course, what you like. The major search portals like Yahoo, Excite and AltaVista index shopping sites within their normal directories, but they don't make it obvious. Instead, when you click on "Shopping" you're shunted towards their own hybrid shopping malls that favor their partnered vendors. Still, if you're looking for a specific product rather than a type of shop, this can be a good way to go. **The Open Directory** (http://dmoz.org), on the other hand, treats shopping like any other category, making it much easier to browse.

There are also hundreds of specialist shopping directories. None, however, can claim to list every shop, and even with the few they do carry, they make fossicking hard work. Such as:

| | |
|---|---|
| **Buyersguide** | http://www.buyersguide.to |
| **eDirectory (UK)** | http://www.edirectory.com |
| **Internetshopper** | http://www.internetshopper.com |
| **MyTaxi (UK)** | http://www.mytaxi.co.uk |
| **Nobags (UK)** | http://www.nobags.com |
| **Ozshopping (AU)** | http://www.ozshopping.com.au |
| **Premierstores** | http://www.premierstores.com |
| **Shopfind** | http://www.shopfind.com |
| **Shopfinger** | http://www.shopfinger.com |
| **Shopnow** | http://www.shopnow.com |
| **ShopSmart (UK)** | http://www.shopsmart.com |
| **UKShopping (UK)** | http://www.ukshopping.com |

For more, see: http://dmoz.org/Shopping/Directories/

Directories usually provide a description, but if you'd rather a rating or review, see: http://www.bizrate.com and http://www.shopping-sites.com

If your needs are more specialized try a search engine, or scan **Deja.com** for an appropriate newsgroup. For example, if you ask about coffee grinders in **alt.coffee**, you'll get the rundown on various brands and vendors, and be pointed to several FAQs. A shopping directory is less likely to be so helpful.

Given the wealth of information online, this might sound like an odd suggestion, but the best way to keep up with what's hot in online shopping is to follow the regular media, especially the full-page ads in the glossy magazines.

Finally, if you can't find what you're after, try posting your request at **iWant.com** (http://www.iwant.com), and see if someone comes to your rescue.

## Compare prices

Comparing prices across shops has become the latest craze amongst shopping portals. Whether they're called comparison engines, **shopping bots**, or bargain finders, they more or less do the same thing. Which is, you enter a product or keyword and they return a listing of prices and availability across a range of retailers. Sounds great, but unfortunately few seem capable of consistently keeping their databases current. Which kind of defeats the point of the exercise.

Generally the bots that specialize in one product group do better than the Swiss army knife variety. Particularly if they scan a lot of shops, including all the big names. Take **Shopper.com** and **Pricewatch.com**, for example. If you're after anything computer related, they're definitely the best place to start.

But it also depends on the shops queried, and whether they're passing out correct information. You'll find some, for example Altavista's **Shopping.com**, query a lot of products but across a very limited and often obscure selection of shops. In the end you might get a better deal at Amazon.

So again, like the shopping directories, it's a hit and miss affair. Try a few and see what works for you:

  http://shopping.egg.com (UK)
  http://www.addall.com (books worldwide)

http://www.bestbookbuys.com (books)
http://www.bottomdollar.com (US, UK, CAN, FR, DE)
http://www.dealtime.com (US, UK, DE)
http://www.evenbetter.com
http://www.mysimon.com
http://www.shopgenie.com (UK)
http://www.shopmart.com (UK)
http://www.valuemad.com (UK)

## Try our Web guide

You'll find short guides to buying music, cars, books, travel, financial services, groceries, and more in our Web guide, which starts on p.277.

## Prefer it on paper?

Then drive your postie crazy by ordering every catalog in the world:

http://www.catalogworld.com
http://www.buyersindex.com
http://www.catalogs2go.com
http://www.catalogsite.com

# 14

# MP3 and Online Radio

## PLAYING AND DOWNLOADING
## MUSIC FILES FROM THE NET

**Y**ou can sometimes learn more about someone by rifling through their records than knowing how they paid for them. Which might explain why back in the early days of vanity home page publishing, when the Web was anarchistic and thoroughly geeky, listing your entire music collection was deemed cooler than posting your résumé.

Back then it wasn't practical to put audio samples online. Digitized music eats buckets of bytes, which makes it time consuming to download – especially with the old 14.4 Kbps modems. But since then technology has advanced. Both in the speed at which we connect, and in the way we store music. As a result, people can now place their actual collections online, much to the anguish of the music biz.

## How it works

Music as it's stored on a CD is too bulky to put online. A minute of sound needs roughly 10 megabytes of disk space. Which means a four-minute track could take more than three hours to download with a 56K modem. But thankfully, there are several techniques that can compress the music to eat less space, thus making it quicker to transfer. Which one you'd use would depend on whether you want to listen to the music live (**streaming**) or download it to your computer and play it later (**MP3**).

## Stream it live

Getting music to play in real time over a modem connection takes some pretty clever footwork in the **audio compression** department. Put very simply, this involves stripping out the bits that  matter least to your ears. The catch is the more you take out, the worse it sounds.

An online radio station can only work with as much data as it can transfer live across your connection. So **the slower the connection, the lower the fidelity**. But just because you have a nice clean fast connection doesn't mean you'll get better sound. The files are encoded at a fixed rate low enough to cater for the average connection speed.

Sometimes, though, there'll be separate choices for low and high bandwidth connections. If you choose high bandwidth over a modem you won't be able to download the data fast enough to play it live. It will take ages to load and then drop out constantly. The same will happen if you choose low bandwidth and there's too much traffic between you and the server. Because heavy traffic and packet loss is a way of life on the Net, most players "**buffer**" a small amount of data in advance to cover up intermittent hiccups. You can set the buffer in the player's options. But normally once you've entered your connection speed at setup, you shouldn't need to worry about it again.

As you can imagine, this amount of audio compression takes its toll on fidelity. So when you tune into Radio Nova (http://www.novaplanet.com) across the Net, it won't sound as good as straight off the radio in Paris. But you might be surprised that it doesn't sound too bad either. Somewhere **between AM and FM** is a fair comparison.

## Play it again with MP3

**Tinny sound** might be okay for taste-testing CDs at Amazon, or when it's your only chance of hearing a foreign station, but there are better options if you have time to download the tracks. The one that's all the rage right now is **MP3**. It sounds much better than streaming audio as it doesn't need to be compressed to the same extent. This compression level is called the **bitrate**. It tells you the average number of bits used to store one second of audio data. The more bits you use, the better it sounds, but the longer it takes to download.

Most MP3s on the Net are encoded at a bitrate of **128 Kbps**. This isn't far off **CD quality**. You won't be able to tell the difference over your PC speakers, but you might if you played it through your home stereo. A four-minute track recorded at 128 Kbps would need 3.8 megabytes. So with a 56K modem, this should take less than twenty minutes to download. MP3s can be encoded at a range of rates, depending on the quality required.

## Here's the catch

While it's fine to rip MP3s from your own CDs and listen to them on your PC or portable MP3 player, unless the artist or publisher has granted you express permission, **it's illegal to distribute these copies or post them to your Web site**. That means most of what you find through file-sharing agents like **Napster** is in flagrant breach of copyright. In practice, if you're caught lobbing a few MP3s onto your Web site you might simply be told to pull them down. But if you're caught attempting to profit from them, you'll almost certainly be prosecuted. So irrespective of whether you believe exposure through illegal copying might increase sales to the benefit of all, beware that it could land you in the stew. If you need the point belted into you, see: http://www.riaa.com and http://www.bpi.co.uk

## Get the software first

Before you can listen to anything, you'll need the right playing software. See what you already have and then build from there. Make sure your speakers work, and go online. The main formats in order of popularity are **RealMedia**, **MP3**, **Windows Media**, **QuickTime**, **SHOUTcast** and **Liquid Audio**. The annoying part is the main players will happily take over playing all these formats (and more), but they most likely won't do them all properly. You're better off installing a few players and assigning the formats to whichever player handles them best. You might already have enough to get started, as most are optional add-ons with browser installations. While some of the following have commercial versions, you should download the free options first.

Let's start with **RealMedia**. This incorporates both RealVideo and RealAudio, the formats most commonly used for live radio and television broadcasts, and music samples at online CD shops. Drop by the **Real.com Guide** (http://realguide.real.com) and click on one of the broadcasts. Does it call up the **RealPlayer**? If not, click on the link to download the player and install it. When it asks which formats it should play, let it take over everything for the time being. You can always change it back later. If you already have the player, click on the option under Help to update it to the latest version. While you're there you might also investigate **RealJukebox**, its MP3/CD player and playlist organizer.

If you're running Windows, update **Windows Media Player**. It's the native player for a variety of new streaming formats. They should be supported by other programs such as the RealPlayer and **WinAmp**, but Media Player should do them better. Again, it can handle all sorts of other formats, including WAV, AU, and MP3, as well as play your CDs. However, unless Microsoft has fixed things somewhat since this was written, **leave RealPlayer to handle Real Media**. You can get the latest version through **Windows Update**, by clicking the option under the Help menu in Windows Media Player, or by downloading it from the **Windows Media guide** (http://www.windowsmedia.com).

Next, stop by Apple's **QuickTime** Guide at: http://www.quicktime.com and see if you can play what's on offer. Don't be surprised if Windows Media Player or RealPlayer attempts to open the file, but gives you a useless error message. If so, download the QuickTime player and assign it to associate with only the native Macintosh file types – under Preferences/Registration. While the QuickTime player can also handle other types, it's pretty rustic compared to the competition, and persistently nags you to pay. Still, Apple's proprietary video technology is highly regarded within the industry, particularly amongst Mac users, so it's worth having support for it, especially if you have a **high bandwidth connection**.

**SHOUTcast** is another streaming audio format, which lets you turn your MP3 library into an online radio station within about half an hour of reading and tweaking. You can listen by logging into http://www.shoutcast.com and choosing a station. While you can get by with RealPlayer, you'll get better results with Nullsoft **WinAmp** (http://www.winamp.com), the player behind the technology. WinAmp is also by far the most popular MP3/CD player. If you like what you hear, grab **RadioSpy** (http://www.radiospy.com) to help find stations.

By now you should be able to play everything that's thrown your way. Apart from the main formats, there are a few less

popular alternatives such as **Liquid Audio** (http://www
.liquidaudio.com). Generally, all you'll need to play them is to
download a RealPlayer plug-in. You'll be offered a range of
these when you check for new updates with auto-update. But
generally, if you strike an unsupported format somewhere,
they'll usually provide a link to the player. Until then, most of
them you can safely do without so don't bother adding them
until required.

## Pick your players

If you've been paying attention you'll have at least one program that can play MP3s. But once you start to accumulate a
large collection of MP3 files, you'll want a MP3/CD jukebox such as WinAmp, RealJukebox, Sonique, MusicMatch
Jukebox or Windows Media Player 7 in that role. Try a few
to see which you prefer. When you've made a choice, completely uninstall the rejects so they don't interfere. Typically,
these all-in-one jukeboxes can play your music CDs, automatically look up the track listings at the **CDDB** online
database (http://www.cddb.com), rip tracks from a CD and
encode them into MP3s, search your hard drive for media
files, and organize your music library into **playlists**. Again,
you can get by without paying, but you mightn't get the full
product. Sometimes if you pay to upgrade to the full version
you'll get more features such as being able to encode your
own MP3s at a higher fidelity.

| | |
|---|---|
| **AudioSoftware.com** | http://www.audiosoftware.com |
| **MP3.com** | http://www.mp3.com |
| **MP3site** | http://www.mp3site.com |
| **Shareware Music Machine** | http://www.hitsquad.com/smm/ |
| **Stroud's** | http://cws.internet.com/mp3.htm |
| **ZDnet** | http://music.zdnet.com |

# What plays what

The worst part of installing another media player is that it will try to hijack all your media settings. Once you've established a preferred player for a format, go through its Options/Preferences/Settings and specify that you'd like it to be the default for that media type. It's something that's often well hidden. In RealPlayer, for example, it's under the Upgrade tab in Preferences. If you can't find the option, refer to the help file, try the publisher's support page, or ask in Usenet.

## Finding streaming music

Real-time audio comes in two forms: **live** broadcasts and **on-demand** pre-recordings. Tapping into a live broadcast is like switching on a radio. Except you have a lot more choice. For starters, you're not restricted to your local reception area. That means you can tune into real world stations from right around the globe. And as anyone can set up a broadcast without a special license, there are also thousands of "stations" you won't hear anywhere else. On top of that there are loads of special events and concerts being piped online. All you need to know is where to look. To help you on your way, see the Radio section of our Web guide: p.391.

The difference with on-demand audio is the material is pre-recorded. So no matter when you join, the clip will start at the beginning. You might come across the odd archived radio broadcast, but its biggest use is for **previewing CDs** at online music stores like Amazon. There's no better way to shop for music – as long as your credit card can handle the pressure. For a guide to CD shopping, see p.363.

## Finding MP3s

Go to any search engine, type in MP3 and you'll get the impression they're taking over the Net. To a certain extent they are. Music is the new pornography for consuming network bandwidth. Which means you won't have any trouble finding MP3s. Like any search, though, you might need to try a few places if you're after something very specific or obscure. And of course, it has to be put online in the first place.

The MP3s you'll strike will fall into three main categories: free previews authorized by the artist or publisher; tracks you can pay to download; and illegal bootlegs. Free previews tend to be from acts that can't get radio airplay and are eager for exposure, but that's no rule. You can usually preview pay tracks in a low-fi format, such as RealAudio or streaming MP3, before purchasing. Here are a few commercial sites that have both free and pay-to-download **legal MP3s**:

| | |
|---|---|
| **Dmusic** | http://www.dmusic.com |
| **Emusic** | http://www.emusic.com |
| **Epitonic** | http://www.epitomic.com |
| **iCrunch** | http://www.icrunch.com |
| **IUMA** | http://www.iuma.com |
| **Launch.com** | http://www.launch.com |
| **Liquid Audio** | http://www.liquidaudio.com |
| **Listen.com** | http://www.listen.com |
| **Mjuice** | http://www.mjuice.com |
| **MP3.com** | http://www.mp3.com |
| **MP3.com.au** | http://www.mp3.com.au |
| **Peoplesound** | http://www.peoplesound.com |
| **RioPort** | http://www.rioport.com |
| **UBL** | http://www.ubl.com |
| **Vitaminic** | http://www.vitaminic.co.uk |

Not until you start using search engines and file sharing agents will you start seeing the contraband. That's not to say they only index bootleggers. They don't, but once you come across lots of songs you recognize you'll know you're in dodgy waters. Don't be impressed by an engine just because it returns hundreds of hits. You might find they're mostly dead links. To search using a Web page front end, try:

**AudioFind**                    http://www.audiofind.com
**ChangeMusic**             http://www.changemusic.com
**Findsongs**                  http://www.findsongs.com
**Look4Mp3**                http://www.look4mp3.com
**Lycos**                         http://mp3.lycos.com
**Scour**                        http://www.scour.com
**Spinfrenzy**              http://www.spinfrenzy.com

There are several software agents that can poll various search sites at once. They're okay, but not outstanding. Such as:

**Copernic**                  http://www.copernic.com
**MP3Fiend**                http://www.mp3fiend.com

Much to the alarm of artists and labels most of the activity in MP3 isn't happening at the commercial and official sites, but within Usenet, IRC and the underground networks created by the file-sharing utilities, such as:

**CuteMX**                    http://www.cutemx.com
**Gnutella**                http://gnutella.nerdherd.com
**iMesh**                      http://www.imesh.com
**Macster (Mac)**    http://www.blackholemedia.com/macster/
**Napster**                   http://www.napster.com
**Scour Exchange**      http://www.scour.com

These programs enable you to share your own library online, and of course, pick through everyone else's. Despite protestations, they're rampant right now, especially across college networks.

Set your **newsreader to filter on MP3** and you'll uncover a bevy of groups dedicated to posting music binaries, though again predominately bootlegs. As always, **read the FAQ** first: http://www.mp3-faq.org

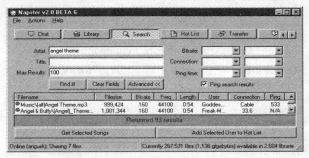

IRC isn't only used for idle chatter. It's also a hotbed of file trading, thanks to the **DCC** command and mIRC scripts like **Multimedia Jukebox** (http://spr.hurricaneweb.com). Log onto any server, and list the channels and topics that match MP3. But don't accept any programs – they'll be Trojans for sure.

Finally, try searching the Web using a normal search engine for fan pages, which might lead you to all sorts of gems like outtakes, rare singles and live bootlegs.

## Let's play the music

Clicking on a streaming audio (or lo-fi MP3) link should call up the appropriate player. After a few seconds of buffering, you should hear the clip or broadcast. If you can't hear any sound, but it appears to be playing, check the player's volume control. If that's up full, try your master volume settings. You can reach these in Windows by clicking on the speaker in your system tray. If nothing opens when you click on the link, or a player opens but fails to recognize the format, you'll either need to reset the file associations in the preferred player, or reinstall it.

Unless you have a very fast connection you'll need to download hi-fi MP3s to your machine in order to play them. If clicking on the link starts your player, rather than a download, right-click and choose "Save Target As" from the mouse menu.

Think about where you'd like your downloads to arrive. Straight onto the Desktop isn't a bad choice. Then once you've listened to them, transfer them into a music library with sensible subfolder names. And as MP3s are big files, it's wise to relegate the transfer to a **download manager** that supports resume downloads. See (Downloading software – download managers – p.154).

## Roll your own MP3s

If your CD drive supports DAE (digital audio extraction), and it should, you can extract MP3s from your own CDs. Technically this is a two-step process that involves "ripping" an audio track from the CD into a WAV file, and then encoding it into an MP3. But most ripper/encoder programs can copy straight from the CD into MP3. The program you choose could make a difference to the sound quality, so read some reviews and try a few before coding up your entire CD collection. This test, for example, http://arstechnica.com/wankerdesk/1q00/mp3/mp3-1.html favors encoders using the **Fraunhofer compression algorithm**. While this report: http://www.r3mix.net favors **LAME**: but bear in mind that the algorithms are a work in progress, so situations will change.

Still, the bitrate will always be the **biggest determinant of sound quality**. Although 128 Kbps has become the defacto standard online, if you intend to convert them back to WAV files to create a **compilation CD**, encode them at upwards of 192 Kbps. Under that, you will definitely hear the artifacts on a decent sound system.

For better sound, also consider ripping your CDs into WAVs, before encoding into MP3. The best ripper around is the free program **Exact Audio Copy** (http://www.exactaudiocopy.de). For more on encoding, see: http://www.r3mix.net and http://www.mp3-faq.org

## Keep your CDs online

If you'd like access to your CD collection from any computer online, beam your CDs to **My MP3** (http://www.mp3.com). You simply insert your CD and it will look it up in its database. If it has the album in its library, it adds the tracks to your personal collection. You can then access them at any time without ever having to upload any MP3s. And any CDs bought from their online music store partners can be beamed across instantly. Incredible, but true.

## MP3 hardware

Part of MP3's recent surge in popularity has been due to the proliferation of **portable players**. These are like a Walkman, but somewhat less convenient in that to "change a disk" you have to upload tracks from your computer. Being mainstream consumer items, you'll find them at any electrical outlet or airport duty free. Things to look out for when shopping:

**USB or Parallel Port uploads?** USB is faster, if your computer supports it.

**Supports your system?** Especially if you use a Mac or Windows 2000.

**Memory?** Figure on about one-megabyte per minute of music. Is it expandable and how much to add extra storage?

**Power?** What's the battery life and does it come with a charger?

**Upgradeable?** Not being able to upload software upgrades could render the unit obsolete before its time.

**Display?** Does it display track names?

**Size?** Smaller might mean a short battery life.

For opinions on the latest models, try the computer press and techno toy mags like Stuff and T3. Or on the Web: **MP3.com**, **Deja.com**, **Epinions**, **Productopia**, and **Amazon**.

If you want to **play them on a regular CD player** you'll need to convert them to the WAV format and burn them to CD. For instructions see:

| | |
|---|---|
| **CDR FAQ** | http://www.fadden.com/cdrfaq/ |
| **CDR Info** | http://www.cdrinfo.com |
| **DailyMP3** | http://www.dailymp3.com/how4.html |

## Rather buy the CD?

Then see our guide to buying music online (p.363).

## For more

If the following FAQs:
http://webhome.idirect.com/~nuzhathl/mp3-faq.html
http://www.mp3-faq.org
don't answer your questions, try the newsgroup:
alt.music.mp3

For the latest news and reviews on MP3 and streaming audio, drop by the MP3 supersites:

| | |
|---|---|
| **About.com** | http://about.mp3.com |
| **MP3.com** | http://www.mp3.com |
| **MP3Place** | http://www.mp3place.com |
| **MP3site** | http://www.mp3site.com |
| **ZDNet** | http://music.zdnet.com |

You'll find more at Yahoo by searching on the keywords: format MP3.

# 15

# Online Gaming

## PLAYING GAMES
## WITH STRANGERS

**C**omputers aren't very bright. It doesn't take much skill to get through games like Quake, Half-Life and War Craft in single player mode – just loads of practice. But over the Internet, playing against real people – even strangers – such games take on a whole new dimension. And things become way more serious. In fact, once you've played in multi-player mode, you'll never want to play alone again.

When home computers first appeared in the late 1970s, they weren't good for much else but games like Pong and Breakout. Back then, gaming consoles and PCs sometimes let two players compete though joysticks or at either end of the keyboard. As computers became more useful in the 1980s, gaming took a back seat to business software, and game designers focused on players taking turns rather than playing together. Today, multi-player racing and martial-arts games dominate the arcade, while at home, players compete on the same games by **connecting their personal computers** together. These machines needn't be in the same room. Or even in the same country. Serious gamers no longer loiter with intent in arcades – they can have more fun at home.

**Multi-player capability** is becoming standard in most new games, not just in the action genre. Almost any computer game that can be played by two or more people can be played online. Current hot numbers include: Age of Empires, Chess, Command & Conquer, Delta Force, Duke Nukem Forever, Half-life, Kingpin, Midtown Madness, Myth 2, Red Alert, Rogue Spear, Sega Rally, Soldier of Fortune, Starcraft, Thief 2, Total Annihilation and Warcraft 3. And some, such as EverQuest, Ultima Online, Starsiege Tribes, Quake III: Arena, Unreal Tournament and Team Fortress can only be played online.

## Finding opponents

To bring in another player to a computer game, you'll need to connect to their machine. The simplest way is via a **serial link**. Just run a null modem cable between your serial ports. It's a fast connection, and quick to set up, but restricts it to two players at cable's length apart. The same can be done over a **telephone line**, using modems. Again it links only two players and is limited by modem speed.

To conscript more victims, you need a proper network. A **local area network (LAN)** is best. That's where you connect all the machines via network cards and cables. It doesn't cost much to set up at home, though players will have to bring their machines round. Easier still is to use a LAN at work. Just be sure to invite your boss to play, to take the flak if you crash the network.

A far easier way to find new opponents, or someone to play you at 4am, is to chime into a public network – such as the **Internet**.

## The problem with Internet gaming

Although it's by far the easiest way to meet other players, the Net has its drawbacks for games that require split-second reactions. **Latency** is the biggest issue. That's the length of time it takes data to reach its destination. If it takes too long, it makes a fast game such as Quake unplayable. Then there's **packet loss** – that's where segments of data fail to reach the other end and must be retransmitted. This has the same slowing effect as high latency.

Online games use latency correction algorithms that attempt to predict likely moves. However, players with lower latency (ping) times, usually those close to the server, will always be at a distinct advantage, giving the game an inbuilt bias.

## What you'll need

And now for the really bad news: 3D games (and these are the most popular), appreciate every bit of speed you can throw at them. If you want to win, you'll need to be more than just a quick draw on the mouse. You'll need a fat connection, a fast processor, plenty of RAM, and most of all, **3D video acceleration**.

Until recently, serious gamers shunned Macs, due to their substandard 3D graphic support. Consequently, games developers have been concentrating on the greater PC market. Mac versions often appear months after the PC release, if at all. In gaming terms, that makes the platform about as fashionable as last year's top 40.

PCs, however, are being challenged by the new generation of console machines, which are not only cheaper but have superior graphics. **Sega Dreamcast** (http://www.dreamcast.com), **Sony PlayStation 2** (http://www.playstation2.com), and **Microsoft XBox** (http://www.xbox.com) are all Net enabled. Dreamcast comes with a modem, PlayStation 2 can connect via a USB modem or broadband card, while the Xbox has both USB and Ethernet ports.

## So let's play

Once you're armed, online and ready to duel, you'll need to track down some willing chumps. That's usually not too hard, but how you go about it depends on what game you're playing. If it won't let you start midway, you'll need to meet in some kind of lobby and wait for a new game to start. Otherwise, you only need find the nearest available game and jump aboard. A few of the newer games such as **Starseige Tribes** and **Unreal Tournament** include inbuilt support for finding, and chatting to, opponents, but most require a third-party program.

The best way to start is to download **GameSpy** (http://www.gamespy.com) and **Kali** (http://www.kali.net). They enable you to find the closest games, with the lowest lag times, and then automate the connections. **When you're shopping for an ISP ask if it runs gaming servers**. It would be quite a bonus if it does, as it will mean playing with little or no lag – a major advantage.

You might also like to see what the Internet gaming networks such as Mplayer (http://www.mplayer.com),

Heat (http://www.heat.net), MSN Gaming Zone (http://www.zone.com), World Opponent Network (http://www.won.net) and Pogo (http://www.pogo.com) have to offer. Then there are **dial-up networks** set aside solely for gaming, such as **Wireplay UK** (http://www.wireplay.co.uk).

Some game software houses also set up their own **game servers** as part of the product package, such as **Battle.net** (http://www.battle.net) for Starcraft and **Bungie.net** (http://www.bungie.net) for Myth II.

## Quake

id Software's **Quake** was the first major game designed primarily for online play. Over a network, it's usual to switch off the 'monsters' and fight with or against other players. Serious Quakers form clans, complete with their own custom-designed outfits, called skins. Clan members compete side by side against other clans or individuals.

**Quake III** comes with its own Netplay support. For more see http://www.bluesnews.com and http://www.quake3.com

## Team play

The most recent trend is not to pit you against the world, but to join a team. The first generation of team play arrived in Quake's Team Fortress add-on, where you had to choose a team, pick a character type, and battle against one or more opposing teams. But there are now many more mission types such as Capture The Flag, where the goal is to raid the other team's base and pinch their flag.

## Breaker, breaker!

Want to chat with your teammates or opponents as you play? Try **Roger Wilco** (http://www.resounding.com). It works like an Internet telephone, but uses so few resources it shouldn't interfere with your game.

## Where to find the real eggs

Remember those ancient **text-based games** where you'd stumble through imaginary kingdoms looking for hidden objects, uttering magic words, and slaying trolls? Believe it or not, they're still going strong, and are now multiplayer, with some 100,000 players entwined in more than 3000 gaming worlds, like **Wheel of Time** (http://wotmud.org), **Lord of the Rings** (http://mume.pvv.org) and **Discworld** (http://discworld.imaginary.com).

What sets these apart from conventional arcade games is their community spirit, and the level of character involvement as players become absorbed in their alter-egos. This can make them especially addictive, and possible dangerous psychologically, as obsessive types can be prone to retreat to their fantasy worlds for comfort. Nonetheless, if it sounds your bag, see http://www.mudconnector.com and the newsgroup hierarchy rec.games.mud.*

Somewhat up the evolutionary ladder graphically, but along similar lines, **Ultima Online** (http://www.owo.com), the latest in the Ultima fantasy series, throws you into a continually evolving virtual world, complete with day and night. The idea is to create not only a battleground, but a social community for thousands of players. As does **EverQuest** (http://www.everquest.com), creating a spectacular fantasy world in the process.

## For games – and more info

Although you'll come across simple games such as chess, cards or backgammon that you can play through a Web interface, the best games are way too big to download as a Java applet. They're so big you might even balk at downloading demo versions from the Web. Check out the gaming magazines, such as **PC Gamer** (http://www.pcgamer.com), **Computer Gaming World** (http://cgw.gamespot.com), and **PC Zone** (http://www.pczone.co.uk). They're often the best place to find out what's hot in online gaming. Not just because gaming companies send them software evaluations early, but because they invariably come with a **free CD-ROM full of games**. Although you can generally get demos off the Net sooner, with most decent games weighing in at over 20 MB, it's a worthy saving in download time. Especially when you'll flick most of them out after a few minutes.

On the Net, the best source of news and downloads are the main games Web sites. For a listing of the most popular, see: http://100hot.com/directory/gaming/games.html and the games section of our Web guide (p.336).

# 16

# Creating Your Own Web Page

## HTML AND EDITING TOOLS

It won't be long before you'll want a crack at your own Web page. You don't need to be anyone particularly important, or a company with something to sell. You just need something to say, some way to convert it into Web code (HTML), somewhere to put it, and some way of putting it there. Finding a location isn't hard or expensive. The logical place would be your ISP's server. Most providers toss in a few megabytes' storage as part of your account. If not, we'll show you where to get it free. Though, if you're serious, you should get your own domain name and shop around for the best deal on server space.

Once you've found some Web space, you can publish anything you like such as how to build a psychotronic mind-control deflector (http://zapatopi.net/afdb.html) to your navel fluff collection (http://www.feargod.net/fluff.html). Or you can use it to publicize yourself, push causes, provide information, sell your products or entertain. But before you leap out of the closet and air your obsessions or dotty schemes, do check you're not breaking any laws of decency or trade. Your Web space provider will know.

## How it works

Dozens of programs can convert text to HTML in some fashion. Most attempt it in a What-You-See-Is-What-You-Get (**WYSIWYG**) manner, meaning you don't have to look at any of the underlying code. However well they succeed it's worth-

while devoting an afternoon to learning the basics. While it's simpler than computer programming in general, it's even more repetitive and tedious. So once you understand how it works, even though you'll do most of your work in a Web site edi-

tor, you'll know enough to be able to go in and tweak the raw code. And, trust us, you will.

Doing it from scratch basically boils down to writing the page in plain text, adding "tags" that make it look presentable, and creating links to other pages. As you get into the more advanced levels you'll also have to consider whether the browsers that visit your page can interpret your code. Unfortunately, some code will work fine in one browser but not in another.

## Choosing a site editor

The quickest way to get familiar with how HTML operates is to **create a simple page from scratch**. You won't need any complex software – a simple text editor like **NotePad** or **SimpleText** will do. However, an **HTML editor** can help by automating much of the process so you don't have to type in all the code manually.

There are plenty of editors to choose from, but your choices narrow quickly if you know what kind of Web site you want to create. Small, simple sites can be knocked together with small, simple editors that come free with browsers.

Internet Explorer's **FrontPage Editor/Express** is the friendliest. But you'll also need an FTP program to post your pages on the Net. **Netscape's Composer** can do FTP at a pinch but if you're at all serious, its limitations will force you to look elsewhere.

Spending US $40-100 opens the door to more powerful editors with extensive tag options, site management tools, FTP software, and support files. At the most affordable end, the semi-WYSIWYG **SiteAid** (http://www.siteaid.com) clearly justifies its loyal band of users. Meanwhile at the upper limit, **Microsoft FrontPage 2000** (http://www.microsoft.com/frontpage/), which comes with Office 2000 Premium, or by itself, makes the transition from familiar Office products like Word and Excel relatively painless. It's capable of producing highly professional sites, but is often criticized for producing bulky code.

Serious projects however demand serious editors. These pack in full support for Cascading Style Sheets, DHTML, ASP and other curiosities you really don't need to know about unless you're intent on doing it for a living. If you do, you'll want nothing short of **Macromedia Dreamweaver** (http://www.macromedia.com).

Once you read around, you'll quickly discover that, whatever the price, not one WYSIWYG editor offers full control over HTML. So whether you like it or not, you'll eventually end up grappling with raw code. So resign yourself to learning HTML. The rest of this chapter will give you ample information to start experimenting.

## Meet the tag

Next time you're online, examine the HTML that makes up any Web page. Choose "**View Source**" from your browser menu to see the raw code. The first thing you'll notice is that the text is surrounded with comments enclosed between less-than and greater-than symbols, like this:

```
<BOLD> My head hurts </BOLD>
```

These comments are known as **tags**. This tag makes the text appear bold when displayed in a browser. Most tags come in pairs and apply to the text they enclose. A forward slash signals the end of their relevance, as in: </BOLD>.

## The code

Want to make a Web page? Easy. Create a new blank page in a text editor like Notepad or SimpleText, name it webpage.html, then type in the following:

```
<HTML>(identifies the document as an HTML file)
<HEAD><TITLE>My First Page</TITLE></HEAD>
<BODY> I am a genius</BODY>
</HTML>(defines the end of the document)
```

Bravo, you've finished! You'll see it has two parts: a **head** and a **body**. The head contains the title, which is displayed in the top bar of your browser. The body defines what appears within the browser window. Everything else is a refinement.

## Using your browser's HTML editor

**Internet Explorer FrontPage Express** isn't always easy to find. If you're online and a page is fully loaded in your browser, Edit with FrontPage Express will appear under the File menu. If you're offline, click Start, point to Programs, point to Internet Explorer, and then click FrontPage Express. If it's not there, hunt it down via your Win98/2000 Windows Update link or download the custom install from the Microsoft site, selecting FrontPage Express in the download options (while you're at it, grab the Web Publishing Wizard, which is the FTP component).

It's worth the effort. To start a new page, click on the blank page symbol at the top left, type some words in the WYSI-WYG blank page. Then under View, choose HTML. You can swap between the code and actual page without having to save each time.

## Netscape Navigator Composer

Composer comes with Navigator's **basic install.** Click on Composer, under the Communicator menu. Type some words in the WYSIWYG blank page, save the file, then under Edit, choose HTML Source. The HTML will appear in a text editor. You can swap between these two interfaces, saving whenever you swap, watching the Web page and HTML coding grow.

## Saving your pages

When you call up a Web page by entering the domain name (such as `http://www.roughguides.com`) into your browser, it actually retrieves a file called `index.html` or `index.htm` that's stored on that host. It's the same as entering `http://www.roughguides.com/index.html`

So when you save the front page to your site you should call it: `index.html` or `index.htm` – all in lowercase. That way you'll have a shorter Web address to hand out. Unless you have a very good reason, save all your filenames in lowercase, as it's less likely to cause confusion. The rest of your pages should also use the same extension (.htm or .html). Name your other pages in a way that relates to their contents. The file names shouldn't contain spaces (use dashes or under-scores) or non-English language characters.

## Backgrounds and colors

You can specify styles and formats for the entire page by defining them within the <BODY> tag. For example, <BODY BGCOLOR="#FFFFFF"> changes the page's background color to #FFFFFF, the RGB (Red, Green, Blue) code for white. HTML editors work out these numbers for you. Most browsers also recognize literal words such as "blue", "red", and "purple".

You can also define the color of four types of text within the body tag: the standard text (TEXT="RGB code"), the text that links to other documents (LINK="RGB code"), any linking text that the browser detects has been visited already (VLINK="RGB code"), and linking text that you have just clicked on (ALINK="RGB code").

You aggregate all these definitions within the tag. So, applying all the above might look something like this:

```
<BODY BGCOLOR="#FFFFFF"
TEXT="#000000"
LINK="#0000A0"
VLINK="#008000"
ALINK="#FF0000">
```

## Playing with text

To change text size, use:

```
<FONT SIZE="x">(text here)</FONT>
```

where x is an increment above or below a standard font size (between "-7" and "+7"). You can also change sizes with the heading tags, where <H1> is the largest heading size and <H6> is the smallest. Unfortunately, with basic HTML, your control here is limited: the actual size the text appears depends on the type and configuration of the viewer's browser.

HTML ignores multiple spaces, tabs, and carriage returns. To get around that you can enclose text within the <PRE></PRE> (preformatted text) tag pair. Otherwise, any consecutive spaces, tabs, carriage returns, or combinations produce a single space. However it's more conventional to enclose paragraphs with <P> and </P> creating two line breaks above and below. You can also create extra spaces with   to create single or multiple line breaks, use:<BR>

Browsers automatically wrap text so there's no need to worry about page widths. To center text use:

<CENTER>(text here)</CENTER>

and to indent from both margins use:

<BLOCKQUOTE>(text here)</BLOCKQUOTE>

Three simple but effective ways to emphasize text are to use bold, italic (though beware; italics can be hard to read online), or colored type. To make text bold, enclose it within

<B>(text here)</B>

To italicize, use: <I>(text here)</I>
To change color:

<FONT COLOR="RGB code">(text here)</FONT>

## Viewing your page

To see how your page would look on the Web, open it up as a local file in your browser. Look under the File menu for "Open" or "Open Page". Alternatively, drag and drop it into your browser window. And then to see changes while editing, hit "Refresh" or "Reload".

## Images

Placing **graphics** on a Web page is easy. Planning and creating them is an art form. The smaller they are in bytes and the fewer you use, the quicker your page will load. So it's wise to reduce their file size using either an online facility like **GifWizard** (http://www.gifwizard.com) or a file reduction program like **JPEG Optimizer** (http://www.xat.com). The versatile and affordable **PaintShopPro** (http://www.jasc.com) incorporates Web compression facilities, but if you want to splash out, **Adobe PhotoShop 5.5** (http://www.adobe.com) provides the finest Web image compression. With practice, you can reduce byte size considerably without sacrificing quality.

The simplest way to display an image is to place it within the <IMG> tag, like this: <IMG SRC="(image location here)"> This displays it full size and bottom-aligned with adjacent text. The picture will appear faster if you insert dimensions too. You also add page layout commands here. For example:

```
<IMG HEIGHT=300 WIDTH=400 ALIGN=TOP VSPACE=60
HSPACE=70 BORDER=100 SRC="sinkingkiribati.gif">
```

would define sinkingkiribati.gif as 300 pixels high by 400 wide, align the top with the tallest item in the line of adjacent text, give it a border 100 pixels wide and separate it from the text by 60 pixels vertically and 70 horizontally.

Now, before planning a full-screen online photo album, bear in mind that your visitors will have to wait, often ages, for each separate image to load. That means the smaller they are, and the fewer of them, the faster they'll get to your text. Try to keep the combined image size on each page under 30 KB.

You can place links to other pages, sites or images within any image. Or you can go one further and create an "imagemap", which contains several links mapped to various co-ordinates around the image. While this might sound clever it's a pain in the pants for visitors. And the worst thing you can do is use one as your table of contents – making your visitors wait for it to load before they can move onto your content.

It's illegal to pilfer graphics from other sites without the owners' permission, as numerous Web developers have discovered in court. For free images visit:

http://www.graphxkingdom.com
http://www.zeldman.com/steal.html

## Alignments

You can specify all manner of image alignments including:

ALIGN=right

Aligns image with left margin. Text wraps on right.

ALIGN=left

Aligns image with right margin. Text wraps on left.

ALIGN=texttop

Aligns top of image with tallest text in line.

ALIGN=middle

Aligns the baseline of text with middle of image.

ALIGN=absmiddle

Aligns the middle of text with middle of image.

ALIGN=baseline

Aligns the bottom of image with the baseline of the current line.

ALIGN=bottom

Aligns the bottom of image with the bottom of the current line.

## Place text behind images

Sometimes images don't load, or load slowly, so place some text behind them if they contain links to elsewhere, or to show what they are. To do this, insert ALT="description of image" anywhere between IMG and SRC.

## Lines

Create a **horizontal line** using <HR> or, more precisely,

  <HR WIDTH=X% ALIGN=Y SIZE=Z>, where

X is the percentage proportion of page width,
Y is its positioning (CENTER, LEFT, or RIGHT) and
Z is its thickness.
The default is 100 percent, CENTER and 1.
Or you could insert an image of a line or bar, or legless lizard for that matter.

## Lists

HTML offers three types of lists: **ordered**, **unnumbered**, and **definition**.

### Ordered lists

Ordered lists are enclosed with the <OL></OL> pair. Each item preceded by <LI> is assigned a sequential number. For example:

  <OL> On the command, "brace! brace!":
    <LI> Extinguish cigarette
    <LI> Assume crash position
    <LI> Remain calm
  </OL>

produces:

  On the command, "brace! brace!":

1. Extinguish cigarette
2. Assume crash position
3. Remain calm

## Unnumbered lists

Unnumbered lists work similarly within the <UL></UL> pair, except that <LI> **produces a bullet**:

```
<UL> On your mark
    <LI>Get ready
    <LI>Get set
    <LI>Go!
</UL>
```

produces:

- On your mark:
- Get ready
- Get set
- Go!

## Definition lists

Definition lists indent lines to make lists easier to read. The <DT><DD> pair **splits the list into levels**:

```
<DL>
    <DT> Cars collide, colors clash
        <DD> Disaster movie stuff
    <DT> For a man with the Fu Manchu moustache
        <DD> Revenge is not enough
</DL>
```

produces:

Cars collide, colors clash
Disaster movie stuff
For the man with a Fu Manchu moustache
Revenge is not enough

## Frames

Frames let you organize your page into compartments that are like Web pages in themselves. The most common application is to place a static site index in a left-hand frame and the contents of the site in a frame beside it. However, frames cause so many problems that most professional sites avoid them. You should too.

## Tables

Tables are the building blocks of page formatting. You can create any number to build rows and columns, precisely placing text and graphics. The <TABLE> and </TABLE> tags define them, while Table Rows <TR></TR> and Table Data <TD></TD> draw the grids. Other tags lend detail. The code below would space a, b and c equally in a row in three boxes 20 pixels wide.

```
<TABLE>
<TR>
<TD width="20" align=center>a</TD>
<TD width="20" align=center>b</TD>
<TD width="20" align=center>c</TD>
</TR>
</TABLE>
```

## Links

The whole idea of HTML is to add a third dimension to pages by **linking them to other pages**. This is achieved by embedding clickable hot-spots to redirect visitors to other addresses. A hot-spot can be attached to text, icons, buttons, lines, or images. Items containing links usually give an indication of where the link goes, but the address itself is normally concealed. Most browsers reveal this address when you pass your mouse over the link.

You can direct hot-spots to anywhere on the Net. Here's how to:

## Create a link to another Web site

```
<A HREF="http://www.roughguides.com">Rough Guides</A>
```

Clicking on "Rough Guides" would load the Web page at: http://www.roughguides.com

## Create a link to a local page

```
<A HREF="trap.html">Step this way</A>
```

If the file trap.html is in the same directory as the file which links to it, clicking on "Step this way" will launch it.

## Embed links in images

```
<A HREF="fish.html"><IMG SRC="fish.gif"></A>
<A HREF="bigfish.gif"><IMG SRC="fish.gif"></A>
```

In both cases, the locally stored image fish.gif contains the hot-spot. The first case launches the local Web page fish.html while the second would display bigfish.gif, which could be a different image – for example a more detailed version of fish.gif

## Invite mail

```
<A HREF="mailto:bigflint@texas.net">bigflint@texas.net</A>
```

Clicking on "bigflint@texas.net" brings up the viewer's email program, with the email address field automatically filled in. Although you don't have to, it's best to spell out the full email address in the visible text, since the link won't work with all browsers.

## Route to a newsgroup

```
<A HREF="news:alt.elvis.sighting">Find Elvis</A>
```

Clicking on "Find Elvis" would bring up articles in the alt.elvis.sighting newsgroup.

### Log in to an anonymous FTP server

`<A HREF="ftp://ftp.bucket.com/gert.exe">Gert</A>`
`<A HREF="ftp://ftp.microsoft.com/">Microsoft</A>`

Clicking on "Gert" would commence the download of bucket.exe while clicking on "Microsoft" would bring up a listing of the root directory of ftp.microsoft.com

## But wait, there's more

Once you're comfortable with the logic, you can glean advanced techniques by analyzing other Web pages or plundering their code. Just find a page you like and from your browser menu, call up **"View Source"**. You can cut and paste selections into your own pages, or save the file and tweak it with a text or HTML editor.

That's about all you'll need to know in about 90 percent of cases, but if you're adventurous there are no bounds to the things you can do with a Web page. As you move up the levels of sophistication, you'll start to move out of the basic HTML domain, into DHTML, XML and more complex scripting and programming languages such as JavaScript, ActiveX, Shockwave, Java, PERL, CGI, and Visual Basic. You may also need access to the special class of storage space reserved for Web programs, known as the **cgi-bin directory**.

If you see a feature you like, and you can't work out how it's done by looking at the source code, ask the site's Webmaster, or search the Web for a good DIY document. There are plenty of books on the subject, but beware, the technology's moving so fast that they date instantly.

## Flash

**Flash** lets you create colorful interactive animations in very small files. For example a 10 second clip might only take up 10KB. But beware; the greatest design crime online is the use of flatulent Flash animations to welcome visitors to a site. It's about as likely to impress your visitors as making them walk across broken glass to read your Mission Statement. Apart from the obvious blunder of putting an obstacle between your guest and where they want to go, it might even crash their browser and lock them out of your site altogether. For more appropriate applications, visit **Macromedia** (http://www.macromedia.com). Then check out http://www.skipintro.com if you still don't get why Flash welcome screens are the pits.

## Java

Java is not a mark-up code like HTML, but a serious programming language designed to be interpreted by any computer. That makes it perfect for the Web as you can place an applet (Java program) on your site and activate it from your Web page. Most browsers have in-built Java interpreters, so visitors don't need any extra software to view it. Some useful online calculators, translators and interactive quizzes are powered by Java, but then so are countless useless applications that slow your browsing for no good reason. As for writing applets yourself; if you think C++ is a chuckle, it's probably right up your alley. Good luck.

## JavaScript

**JavaScript**, a Netscape innovation, extends the Java concept to HTML. Because it sits entirely within the HTML of the Web page, you can pinch the code from other pages, just like regular HTML. It can add tricks, which, with the odd exception in form creation for example, are just that: tricks. But if you want to create personalized messages for each visitor to your site, display a clock, or spawn twenty pop-up windows, look at The **Javascript Source** (http://javascript.internet.com) and **WebCoder** (http://www.webcoder.com). Just keep in mind that most of your visitors would rather you didn't.

## Free Web space and other stuff

Need some free Web space for your handiwork? Then visit **Free Web space** (http://www.freewebspace.net) for overviews of free sites. You'll get ample space, plus free homebuilding tools to ease the process of editing and uploading pages. There are even a few without the usual hindrances associated with free space such as pop-up windows and ad banners.

Other handy freebies, include:

Detailed visitor statistics: http://www.extremetracking.com

A free quiz, search form, chat room, bulletin board, guest book, and more: http://www.beseen.com

Your own search engine: http://www.freefind.com

## Be king of your own domain

Say you run a shop called Top Clogs and you want to flog your clogs over the Web. Don't even consider an address like: http://members.tripod.com/~clogs/topclogs.htm To be taken seriously; only http://www.topclogs.com will do.

Before you make any plans for a **dotcom** address, put your chosen domain name (the bit between the www. and the .com) into the search box at **Register.com** (http://www.register.com) or **DomainMonger** (http://www.domainmonger.com) – to make sure it hasn't been taken. Once that's done, you'll need to do two things: find two domain name servers to direct traffic to the Web server where you will eventually put your pages; then register the domain name. If you do it through the above mentioned, they will park your site until you're ready to move it to a hosting service. Alternatively, search on "domain registration" at Yahoo! for increasingly cheap deals.

Once you've registered, you'll want to find space on a Web server. Compare prices and services listed at http://www.tophosts.com and http://www.findahost.com. Check out the bandwidth and phone support thoroughly. You don't want to be stuck on a slow server and you want to be able to talk to support staff at the busiest times of day. Generally the best deals are in the US. However, it helps to locate close to your target audience, as your pages will load quicker.

There are a few operations that will host your domain free, but don't expect the same level of service, speed, reliability, lifespan, support or credibility that you'd get from a good commercial service. Such as:

**Webprovider**            http://www.webprovider.com
**Virtual Avenue**         http://www.virtualave.net
**Freeservers**            http://www.freeservers.com

Read the reviews at http://www.freewebspace.net before you commit.

## Name Registration with country codes

If you're outside the USA and would prefer to be associated with your country of origin, instead of a .com address, register a regional one, ending in a country code. See the list of available codes and relevant contacts at:
http://www.uninett.no/navn/domreg.html

You can register a wide range of countries at Register.com (http://www.register.com). Alternatively, to register Australian and UK names, see http://www.netregistry.com.au and http://www.thename.co.uk respectively.

## Almost your own domain

**MailBank** (http://www.mailbank.com) will rent you a cheap personalized Web/email address combination from a range of more than 12,000 domains. Or, if you don't want to spend a penny but still want a short, memorable Web address, visit any of these:

    http://come.to
    http://beam.to
    http://i.am
    http://www.iscool.net

## Uploading your site

The usual way to deliver files to a Web server is by **FTP**. This process requires a User ID, password and FTP address for your pages, which your Web space provider will give you. Along with FTP software, probably.

Most HTML editing packages incorporate FTP software. They also usually synchronize the content to ensure you have the same files live and locally, as well as check for broken links and dead files.

But if you're building a serious site with a basic HTML editor and want a tool that caters to all servers and upload conditions, invest a little in a powerful and easy drag-and-drop FTP client like **FTP Voyager** (http://www.ftpvoyager.com). You may also benefit from a standalone link validator such as **SiteManager** (http://www.merc-int.com/products/astrasitemanager/) or **Alert Linkrunner** (http://www.alertbookmarks.com/lr/).

## A Web or FTP server at home

Most people store their Web pages on a dedicated Web hosting service. However, once your computer's connected to the Net, it can also act as a Web or FTP server, just by running the right software. You can even run your own server on a regular dial-up account, though of course your pages or files will only be accessible while you're online – and you'll have a different IP address each time you log in, so you won't be able to pass it on until you're online. This is functional enough if you just want to demo a couple of Web pages to a colleague or friend. However, if you want a serious Web presence, you'll need a permanent connection to run your own server.

Servers are remarkably simple to install – read the Help file and you'll be up within half an hour. But take the time to set up your **security options** to allow only appropriate access to appropriate directories. That means things like making your

Web pages read-only and your FTP incoming write-only. Otherwise you might get hacked.

## How to publicize your site

Once you've published your page and transferred it to your server, the real problems begin. How do you **get people to visit it?**

Before you crank up the publicity campaign, consider how you'd find such a site yourself and whether, if you stumbled across it, you'd bother stopping or returning. Most of all, decide whether publicity now would be good, or whether teething problems need to be solved before you take out **full-page adverts in the *Brisvegas Bugle*.**

On a basic level, most people will arrive at your site by taking a link from another site or by typing in the URL. That means if other pages link to yours, or people can find your address written somewhere, you'll stand a chance of getting traffic. Look around the Web for sites of parallel interest to your own and send them email suggesting reciprocal links. Most will oblige, especially if you offer them useful content to put on their site. This sometimes starts a wonderful relationship. If you want to move up a step to sell or buy commercial syndicated material, visit **iSyndicate** (http://www.isyndicate.com).

The best publicity machines of all are the search engines and directories. Before you submit your URL to them (and you should), find out how they work. Establish whether they accept brief reviews, if they scan your page for key words, or if they index your site in full. To study the black art of how they tick, visit **Search Engine Watch** at http://www.searchenginewatch.com

Whether you register or not, the biggest search engines should eventually find your site. You can skew their results in your favor by dotting appropriate words and phrases in key places in your HTML code. The <title> is most important, as search engines rely heavily on it as an indicator of the page's subject matter. Reproduce its contents as below and the page will rank higher in search results on that topic.

<TITLE>Heavy Breathing Hamsters do Honolulu</TITLE>
<META NAME="DESCRIPTION" CONTENT="Furry friends get fresh."> This will appear in search listing results.
<META NAME="KEYWORDS" CONTENT="ham, pineapple, mozzarella, david attenborough">

Also add key words to the <alt> tags behind graphics, and repeat them in the text itself.

To save time tracking down all the various engines, several services such as

| | |
|---|---|
| **Addme!** | http://www.addme.com |
| **Broadcaster** | http://www.broadcaster.co.uk |
| **Easy Submit** | http://www.easysubmit.com |

will **send your details to multiple engines and directories** at once. And if what you're doing is **new**, ask Yahoo to create you a new category. Once you've done all that, the online tool, **Did It Detective** (http://www.did-it.com), can email you how you're ranked, though for a fuller service you'll want to invest in **Web Position Agent** (http://www.webposition.com). You can also check how many sites link to yours at **LinkPopularity** (http://www.linkpopularity.com)

Next, generate some off-Web interest. Announce your site in relevant **newsgroups and mailing lists**. You can get away with posting the same message periodically in Usenet, and as many times as you like if it's part of a signature file, but don't post to a mailing list unless you have something new to say.

Don't forget about the old world, either. **Include the URL** on your stationery, business cards, and in all your regular advertising. And flash it in front of everyone you can.

Finally, if it's really newsworthy, send a press release to whatever media might be interested. And just quietly, it mightn't hurt to throw a party, invite some scribes, and wave some free merchandise and t-shirts about.

Since most people go to a site once only, seduce them back by asking them to **register their email address** (and nothing else) promising them you'll send them a short note when there's something genuinely new and interesting on your site.

## Where to next?

For beginners' guides, and more about HTML, Web programming, style, and publicity, try the following sites:

| | |
|---|---|
| **Developer.com** | http://www.developer.com |
| **HTML Goodies** | http://www.htmlgoodies.com |
| **Link Exchange** | http://www.linkexchange.com |
| **Useable Info Technology** | http://www.useit.com |
| **Web Developer's Virtual Library** | http://www.stars.com |
| **CNET's Builder.com** | http://www.builder.com |
| **Web Pages That Suck** | http://www.webpagesthatsuck.com |
| **WebMonkey** | http://www.webmonkey.com |
| **WebPromote** | http://www.webpromote.com |

And the newsgroup: alt.html

You should find everything you need either on or linked to these sites, while for HTML editors, try any of the software guides listed in our Web guide (p.291) or look for demo copies on PC magazine cover mount disks.

And to check your site's health, for example how it looks in different browsers and whether all the links work, drop in to the **Web Site Garage** (http://www.websitegarage.com).

# 17

# On the Road

**W**herever you travel, if you can get to a phone line, or a Net-connected terminal, you can get to your email. Unlike a phone number, fax number, or postal address, you can take your email address anywhere, picking up and sending your mail as if you were at home. Read on and we'll show how the Internet can liberate you from your desk.

## Going portable

Anyone who's serious about work mobility has a **laptop (notebook) computer**, often as a desktop replacement. After all, almost anything you can do on a desktop you can do on a portable. And although at present they're still more expensive than their bulkier equivalents – and lag slightly in chip, video, and sound technology – that margin is rapidly closing. When shopping around, here are a few things to look out for:

**Weight:** No matter how small a laptop might seem in the shop, it's a different experience carrying it over your shoulder for a few hours. Get one that's thin and light.

**Power:** If you plan to use it on a plane, in your car, or anywhere away from a power socket, go for long battery life (lithium ion is best) and consider a spare. Also ensure your power adapter supports dual voltage (100-240 V and 50/60 HZ). They usually do, but check anyway.

**Modem:** A built-in modem's an added bonus, but PCMCIA models sometimes have better specs, plus you can swap them between machines. Make sure it supports V.90 and that it'll work with a cellular phone. There are also several PC cards that combine a **cellular phone and modem**, if that sounds useful.
  Something most travelers don't consider is whether their modem is approved internationally. Technically, you could be breaking the law if you're caught using a non-approved modem. If you're trotting the globe, check out 3Com's Global Modem PC cards. They have built-in digital line guards, tax impulse filtering, widespread approval, and software to tweak your modem to the tastes of almost every country's telephone network. See: http://www.3com.com

**Network card or USB to Ethernet adapter:** Modems are convenient but nowhere near as fast or as cheap as hooking into a corporate network. If you're on business, visiting a branch office, ask the IT manager to fill in your network settings. Now, that's luxury but only practical if you plan to spend extended time there. Otherwise it's back to the phone jack.

**Warranty:** Having a notebook go down with all your mail and data onboard is one of life's least rewarding experiences. If you can have a replacement shipped to you anywhere in the world the minute you have problems you'll never regret having paid a bit extra.

## Scaling down

If the risk of having your technological triumph shorted by tropical rain, or filched from your daypack, makes your skin creep, look at taking something smaller and/or cheaper. Exactly what, depends on how small or cheap you want to go, and why you need it. There are plenty of options, but many are little more than expensive novelties.

You can reduce size and weight without losing features, by moving towards **sub-notebooks** and **palmtops** that can run Windows programs. Don't expect big savings though. If price is the key, or you just need a powerful organizer, try something like the **Psion Organiser**, **3Com Palm Pilot**, or one of the many other **PDAs**, which combine basic office programs with Net connectivity, and can upload later to your main machine.

Scaling down further, you can collect your email, and surf the Web (just), with various new mobile phones. Or, if you only need to receive mail, see what your local paging services have to offer. These, however, work only within one country.

## Wireless access

Going cordless seems the way of the future but right now the offerings are more suited to gadgeteers than everyday use. You can hook a GSM-ready PC card modem to a cellular phone and dial your ISP, but it's slow and usually prohibitively expensive. A better option is to connect your Palm Pilot, Notebook, or PDA to a dedicated wireless ISP such as **GoAmerica** (http://www.goamerica.net) using one of the new wireless PC card standards. Rates and services vary, but it's not hard to find unlimited access for a reasonable monthly charge. Well, in the US anyway. The rest of the world hasn't quite caught on yet.

**WAP**, on the other hand, appears to be everywhere, accompanied by hearty hype but as yet few applications. Drop into any phone sales shop to hear the spiel, then see: http://wireless.yahoo.com

For more on wireless access, see:

http://mobile.yahoo.com
http://www.everythingwireless.com
http://www.gsmworld.com
http://www.wireless.com
http://www.wirelessadvisor.com

## An address that moves with you

Once you have a **reliable fixed email address**, no matter where you roam, people can reach you. Put it on your business card and say, "If you want a swift reply, email me." You might shift house, business, city, or country, but your email address need never change. So, take care when choosing your address as it might become your virtual home for years to come. For more on email addresses, see p.98. Here's how to use the various types on the move:

### POP3 and IMAP

Almost all ISP mail accounts these days are **POP3** or **Webmail** (ask your provider if you're unsure), which means that if you can get onto the Internet, you should be able to collect your mail. **POP3 mail** is collected via an email program such as Outlook Express, whereas **Webmail** is collected through your Web browser by logging into a Web site and entering your account details.

If you're taking **your computer** with you, it's doubly easy to collect your POP3 mail. You mightn't even have to change your mail settings – only your dial-up configuration, and perhaps your outgoing mailserver.

To collect mail using an email program on **another computer**, you need to enter your **user name**, your **incoming mail server** address, and your **password**, when prompted. To send email you also need to enter your **identity** (who you want your mail to appear it's come from) and your **return**

**address** (your email address). Although you can sometimes use your regular **outgoing mailserver** address **if you collect your mail first**, you'll get a faster response if you use the one maintained by the ISP through whom you're dialing. So if the machine you're using has one set, leave it be.

If your connection's slow or difficult, you can **configure your mail program** to download the first 1 KB or so of each message and then select which you want to read. Alternatively, if your mailserver supports **IMAP** (a superior form of POP mail which allows you to manage mail on the server – again, ask your provider), you can download just the headers. So when you're up in a plane paying 14¢ per second to download at 2400 bps you can leave all those massive mail list digests for later.

One day, you'll also be thankful that you **maintain an alternative address for priority mail**.

## Webmail

With **Webmail accounts** such as **Hotmail, YahooMail**, and **Planet Access** you can send and collect email on any machine with access to the Web. If you don't already have an account, stop by their sites (see p.118 – "Get your free email address here") and you'll be granted one free, right away. **Planet Access** (http://www.planetaccess.com) is particularly suited to traveling as it's much faster than most.

What makes Webmail so different, is no matter what computer you're on, you won't need to change any settings; you just log into your account using a Web browser. Plus, you can scan through your headers first and retrieve only what interests you.

The problem with Webmail is that you need Web access, which can make things slow or impossible over low bandwidth connections. It also has zero prestige – if that's an issue – so try not to use a Webmail address as your permanent business address.

## The easiest way to collect your POP3 mail

If you're using a machine only briefly, you needn't tamper with the email program. You can do it all through the Web. You can configure Hotmail to collect your POP3 mail and retain the headers in your mailbox. It's worth setting up a dummy account just for this purpose, and forgetting about it until you need it. Alternatively, if you're in a real hurry, try **Mail2Web** (http://www.mail2web.com). Just enter your **long email address**\* and password to **collect** and **send** your mail on the fly. No need to set up an account. Messages aren't deleted from the server so they'll still be there next time you collect.

\* Your long email address is your mail account name @ your incoming mailserver name. For example, the long email email address of angus@easynet.co.uk is angus@mail.easynet.co.uk (mail.easynet.co.uk is the incoming mailserver address)

## Telnet

Some universities and workplaces don't maintain POP3 mail accounts. If that applies to you, you might have to use **Telnet** to log in. Once you get over the indignity of not being able to point and click, it's not so bad. You can access Telnet in Windows 95/98 by opening **Run** on the **Start** menu and typing telnet. Collecting this way will involve logging into your mail server over the Net, supplying identification, then typing commands into a UNIX mail program. **You can also read your POP3 email by Telnetting to your mailserver** on port 110 (you'll have to add this in manually in Windows), entering user then your user name, pass then your password, and list to list your messages. To read messages selectively, type retr followed by the message's number. This is the best way to collect mail when you're operating over a very low bandwidth, under poor conditions, or limited by software, for example with a palmtop. Ask your ISP or systems manager for further instructions.

### AOL Netmail

You can collect your AOL mail from any computer by firing up your Web browser and pointing it at:
http://www.aol.com/netmail/

## How to stay connected

Keeping in touch needn't mean expensive long-distance calls home to your provider. It's possible to travel the world on a single **ISP account**, dialing locally wherever you are. Depending on your deal and where you travel between, that should work out considerably cheaper – though if you need to dial in only every few days, then calling long distance with a discount calling card may be both practical and economical. Only you can tell what suits you best, but these are your most likely options:

### Cybercafés and Net terminals

When you're traveling without hardware you have to use someone else's machine. If you can't get to one through a friend or work, look for somewhere to rent Internet time. That's most commonly available through so-called **cyber-cafés**. These are basically coffee shops or bars, with a few Net-connected terminals up for public use. Lately, though, the concept of mixing cakes, coffee, and computers is giving way to **communication centers** complete with fax, discount phones, and printing. Whatever the case, you can generally buy half-hour blocks of Net time.

If you're new to the Net, these also make the ideal places to test-drive it under supervision. Or if you're after a temporary account on your travels they can point you to a provider. Most of all, though, they're an easy access point to do your email, and coincidentally meet other wired travelers.

Whether you're using a cybercafé or someone else's computer, the procedure is the same. Either open the browser and do your stuff through Mail2Web or Hotmail or look for a **mail program**. In the latter case, open the settings, and fill out your details as described earlier (under "POP3" – see p.263). Then set it to "leave mail on server", and "CC" yourself everything you send. That way when you get back to your main machine, and download for the first time, you'll have a record of all your correspondence. Once you've finished, delete all your mail (don't forget the "sent" box), and change the settings back.

To **find a cybercafé** before you leave, try Yahoo or the following directories:

| | |
|---|---|
| **Cybercafe Guide** | http://www.netcafes.com |
| **Cybercafe Search Engine** | http://www.cybercaptive.com |
| **Cybercafés of Europe** | http://www.kiosek.com/eurocybercafes/ |
| **Easyeverything** | http://www.easyeverything.com |
| **Internet Café Guide** | http://www.netcafeguide.com |

Or, just ask at any backpacker's guesthouse once you arrive. Even if there's only one cybercafé in town, you can bet it will be close to the main tourist district. And keep your eye out for **Netbooths** in places like airports, major hotels, or shopping malls. They're like public phones, except with a computer screen instead of escort ads. The biggest drawback of all these options is that **they're generally very slow**, especially if they're busy. It's not unknown to be unable to log into Hotmail, without timing out, for example.

## National ISPs

Most of the **ISPs in our directory** (see p.485) have national coverage or at least multiple dial-up points across a country. But this doesn't mean they'll have local call access everywhere – it may be restricted to major urban areas. Before you sign with a provider, ensure it covers your territory at local call rates. Many ISPs, particularly in the US and Australia, have a national number charged at a higher rate. Check that first and do your sums. All our listed UK providers have local call access throughout Britain.

## International ISPs

Several **Online Services** and **ISPs** have **international points of presence** (POPs). These include:

**AOL:** Although AOL has POPs in more than 100 countries, many are serviced by third-party networks. Outside the UK, North America, Australia, and select European cities, you'll be hit with a surcharge. For full details, log onto AOL and type the keyword Access

**APC:** Set up mainly to link non-governmental organizations and social activists worldwide. Has member POPs in a few offbeat locales, but don't expect blistering speed: http://www.apc.org

**AT&T:** Full reciprocal Internet access in over 50 countries – though steep premiums apply away from home. See http://www.attbusiness.net

**CompuServe:** Nothing gets off the plane and online faster than a CompuServe account. But as ever, premium charges make it an expensive option. Ditch its kludgy software, and treat it like a normal ISP dialing through Windows Dial-up Networking or its Mac equivalent. Like AOL, though, it relies on a variety of networks once you stray a little, so you might need a different script from usual. You can get the right script on CompuServe at: GO SOFTSUP, Files, PC Modems/Scripts. **Better still; call support to make doubly sure you're prepared.** You'll find access numbers at: GO Phones or on the Web, at: http://www.csi.com

**EUNet:** Some 3000 POPs worldwide through its own connections and iPass. Can work out expensive. See: http://traveller.eu.net

**Microsoft Network:** MSN has scaled back its operation worldwide and now offers reciprocal access only in the US, UK, and Japan. For access numbers and rates, see http://free.msn.com

## Global roamers

The surest way to gain international access is to join an ISP that belongs to a global roaming group. This means you can dial into any ISP in the group. You'll be handsomely charged by the minute for the convenience, which is fine for urgent email but if you plan to surf the Web abroad, you'd do better signing up with a local.

Quickly test the foreign numbers before you leave – better to risk the expense of an international call than wait until you have to wrestle the hotel's system and a directory enquiries that can't understand your accent. See GRIC (http://www.gric.com) and the i-Pass Alliance (http://www.ipass.com) for their lists of participating ISPs.

# Jacking in

No matter what your account, you'll get nowhere fast if you can't **get your modem talking** to the phone system. This is where it can get a bit technical, especially when you're abroad, so be prepared to roll up your sleeves. Here's what you should know:

## Foreign plugs

If you think the variety of power plugs is crazy, wait until you travel Europe with a laptop and modem. There are six different varieties of phone jacks in Germany alone. Nevertheless, thanks to wired travelers, the US **RJ11 plug** is becoming
somewhat of a world standard. Trouble is, some countries use this plug but connect the two wires to different pins. So, before you set out, get a **lead/adapter** that plugs into your modem at one end with a US-wired RJ11 plug/socket at the other. As long as you travel with this setup, you'll have no trouble finding an adapter at a local airport, electrical store, or

market. To prepare in advance, grab a plug bundle such as TeleAdapt's Laptop Lifeline (http://www.teleadapt.com).

### Dial tone detect

It's a rare modem that's smart enough to recognize every foreign dial tone, and if it's been instructed to **wait for a tone before dialing**, you mightn't get anywhere. If dial tone errors persist, or your modem refuses to dial, switch this setting off. It's usually as simple as checking a box in your dialer. If not, you'll need to insert the **Hayes command X1** into the modem's initialization string. Refer to your modem manual for more on initialization strings.

Then there is the question of **pulse or tone**? Pick up a phone and dial. If it sends beeps, set it to tone dialing. If it makes clicking sounds, set it to pulse.

### Manual dialing

Sometimes you need to dial with a **phone in parallel**. For example, if you have to go through an operator or calling card company, or if the phone system won't recognize your modem's tones. If that's the case, **turn the dial detect off** and set it to dial a short number, say 123. Have it ready to dial with one key press or mouse click. Now, dial your provider with the phone. When the other modem answers, press or click to fire off your dialer. As soon as you hear the two modems handshaking, hang up the phone and you'll be away.

### Public phones

In the US, Australia, and Asia (though rarely at present in Europe), an increasing number of phones at airports, convention centers, and hotel lobbies have **modem ports** – generally RJ11 sockets. If not you can use an **acoustic coupler**, which you just strap over the handset. **Roadwarrior** (http://www.warrior.com) and **TeleAdapt** have units that will transfer at up to 28.8 Kbps.

If the handset has a carbon microphone, give it a tap first to loosen the grains, but don't expect better than 2400 bps. However you connect, you'll need to dial manually (see above).

## Planes

Don't set your hopes too high on surfing the Net at 35,000 feet. Yes, with the wide-scale introduction of satellite telephony in planes, it's possible. But, at present it's limited to a speed of 2400 bps, with 9600 bps some way on the horizon. At up to US$10.00 per minute, it'd need to be important.

## Digital PBX

Most offices and hotels run their own **internal PBX phone systems**. What matters to you is whether the extensions are hooked to the exchange using **digital** or **analogue** techniques. If it's digital, your modem won't like it. At worst, it could turn to toast. You can't always tell at first, so when you're shopping for a PCMCIA modem, look for one with a **digital line guard**. If you strike a digital system, look around for an alternative line. Try the fax line, for starters. Otherwise, you might need an acoustic coupler or a device like TeleAdapt's **TeleSwitch** or Road Warrior's **Modem Doubler** to tap you in between the handpiece and the phoneset.

## Hard wiring

More often than not, hotel phones are wired directly into wall sockets. If you don't have an acoustic coupler, you'll have to tap in. In that case, before you set out, pick up a **telephone line tester** and a **short patch cord** with an RJ11 female socket at one end and a pair of alligator clips on the other. You can get both from TeleAdapt, Road Warrior, or any good computer store. If you can't get a patch cord it's easy enough to make – just find an extension lead, cut off the male end, and crimp clips to the right two wires (usually the red and green, but use your line tester for confirmation). You'll find clips at any electronic store.

When you're ready to operate, fish around for something to unscrew that will expose wires. Inside the mouthpiece is sometimes a good bet. Once you've tapped in, check the polarity with the line tester. Keep trying wires until you get the green light. That's all there is to it. Just plug in to your new extension and dial.

## Dropouts

If you keep losing your connection, it could be something simple. First, check that **call waiting** is switched off. Those beeps that tell you someone's waiting will knock out your modem every time. Next, **unplug any phones that share the same line**. Some phones draw current from the line every few minutes to keep all those numbers stored in memory.

Maybe the **secret police** is bugging your line. Don't laugh, it happens in certain countries. After all, if your hotel cleaner spots you hunched on the floor tapping in messages, jacked in through a nest of clips and wires, don't say you won't look a bit suspicious. Mostly, however, it's just a noisy line and there's nothing you can do.

## Tax impulsing

A few countries – Austria, Belgium, Czech Republic, Germany, India, Spain, and Switzerland, among them – send metering pulses down the line to measure call times. Unless your modem is approved in these countries, the pulses will slow down or knock out your connection. Better PC card modems, and certainly all those approved in the above countries, have filtering built in. If not, you can fit a filter, such as TeleAdapt's **TeleFilter**, between your modem and the line.

# Faxes and voicemail

Although thanks to email, the fax's days are clearly numbered, not everyone is quite up to speed. So what do you do if your fax is in Houston, and you're in Hochow? **Jfax** (http://www.jfax.com)

and **Efax** (http://www.efax.com) have the answer. They can allocate you a free phone number in the US or UK, or an inexpensive number in about a hundred cities worldwide. Faxes sent to these numbers are converted to email attachments, redirected to your email address or online mailbox, and can be converted to text by OCR. Callers can also leave voice messages, which are forwarded as compressed audio files. Sending faxes from your desktop is also a breeze, and the whole thing can even integrate with your mobile Internet toyphone. **So forget fooling around with faxmodem software, this is the way to go.**

## Further info

As the world wakes up to the era of computer mobility, you'll see loads of new products and new opportunities.

For **general news** read:
**On the Road**                              http://www.roadnews.com

For tips on how to **connect worldwide**, see:
**Help for World Travelers**        http://www.kropla.com
**Laptop Travel**                  http://www.laptoptravel.com

For a guide to **wired hotels**:
**Rooms with a Clue**   http://www.forbes.com/tool/toolbox/clue/

For the latest in **ultra-slim notebooks**:
**Japan Palmtop Direct**                     http://www.jpd.com

For **adapters, insurance, advice, and support** see:
**TeleAdapt**                      http://www.teleadapt.com
**Road Warrior**                    http://www.warrior.com
**Port**                            http://www.port.com

For reviews on the full range of **Net devices**, see:
**AllNetDevices**                  http://www.allnetdevices.com

For the latest in **wireless connectivity**, see:
**Yahoo Mobile**                   http://mobile.yahoo.com

# 18

# World Wide Web Sites

## INTRODUCTION

**N**o-one can tell exactly how many addresses are accessible from the Web. If you were to try to work it out you'd have to factor in not only every Web page, but all the off-Web links as well. That means every newsgroup on every news server, every chat room, every music sample, and potentially every computer hooked to the Internet in any way. The Web proper, though, is the most popular part, and it's what we'll deal with in this guide. As you'll see from the following listings, it's more than just the world's biggest library; it's something you'll have to experience for yourself to understand.

Technically, Web site addresses start with the prefix **http://** – anything else, although accessible from the Web, really belongs to another system. What sets the Web apart is the way you can move around by clicking links. Most Web sites have links to other sites strewn throughout their pages. Plus, as a bonus, they might devote a section to listing similar sites (or simply ones they think might interest you). Just look for a section called "Links". Of course if you take such a link, you'll arrive at another site that could link to even more related sites. So although we only list a couple of thousand sites in the following pages, they'll lead you to millions more.

## Finding what you want

The keys to finding your way around the Web are the **Internet search tools and directories**. They're listed first. See "Finding It" (p.163), for how to use them.

## How to get there

To reach a site, carefully enter its **address** (taking note of any capital letters) into your browser's **URL, Location, or Address** bar. This is normally located directly underneath the menu. Although formal Web addresses start with http:// you don't need to enter this bit unless you have a very old browser. **So if the address is listed as** http://www.abc.com **simply type** www.abc.com

## An easier way to get there

**You'll also find this entire listing on the Rough Guides' Web site**. So rather than type these addresses individually, simply browse this chapter, get an idea of what you'd like to see, go online, type: www.roughguides.com/internet/ and follow the links from there.

## How to find a site again

When you see something you like, save its address to your **Favorites, Bookmarks,** or **Links bar**. To find it later, simply click on its name in the list. You could also read it offline by saving the page to disk or switching to Offline mode. For instructions, see p.88.

## When it's not there

Some of the following sites will have moved or vanished altogether but don't let that deter you. For advice on how to track them down, see p.183. The easiest way is to enter the title, and/or related subjects, as keywords into one of the search engines such as Google, Fast Search, or Raging Search. Once you've mastered the Internet Search Tools and Directories, you'll be able to find anything. So, wax down your browser and get out there!

## Web sites directory

So far no-one has succeeded in creating a Dewey Decimal System for Web sites, and chances are they never will. Some Web sites sit across several categories, while others almost defy categorization. We've had a crack at shuffling them under sensible headings, but you still might need to use your lateral thinking a little. So check under a few categories, especially "Reference" before giving up hope. To search the Net by **subject or keyword**, try out some of the entries in our "Search Tools and Directories" section (see overleaf).

---

### The Rough Guide to the Internet – On the Net

We've posted the whole of this Web guide section on the Net itself at the Rough Guides' home site. So rather than type each of these addresses individually, simply browse this chapter, get an idea of what you'd like to see, go online, then type: **http://www.roughguides.com/internet/** and follow the links from there.

---

## SEARCH TOOLS AND DIRECTORIES

## SUBJECTS

# PART ONE

# Search Tools
# and
# Directories

**L**et's start with the **most useful addresses** on the Net: the main **search engines** and **directories**. Armed with these, you should be able to find just about anything you might want. Get to know them all in depth, compare their services, and come to your own conclusions about which is best for what. Save these addresses in your **Bookmarks**, **Favorites,** or **Links** bar, as you're sure to return often.

Start with **Yahoo, Open Directory** and **About.com**. These are the most useful directories: Yahoo, because it's the biggest; Open Directory, because it's the next big thing; and About.com because it offers a little more guidance. Next, move on to the search engines.

Try **Google** first. Don't ask us how, but it seems to be the best at getting it right in the first few hits, and you don't have to wait for graphics. Next try **Fast Search** and **Raging Search,** which are bigger, equally quick and also clutter free. And bookmark the advanced settings so you get more hits per page! (See p.172)

Finally try **Deja.com**. If you haven't already fired up your newsreader, you'll soon find out what Usenet is all about. Browse the ratings, and then search for answers to whatever's puzzling you.

Most of these sites have international versions, personal editions, free Webmail, picture and audio searches, chat communities, and a host of other services tacked on – usually fed from other sites. So much, that it's quite possible to spend your entire session within their bounds.

## The Search Powerhouses

### About.com

http://www.about.com

Cozy directory built by a team of "expert guides". Often the best place to find the picks of a genre. Along similar lines, try:
http://www.suite101.com

### AltaVista/Raging Search

http://www.av.com
http://www.raging.com

One and the same, but the latter strips away all the directory fluff and gives you what you want: lightning fast responses, fifty at a time (if you customize), from one of the biggest Web page databases online. The AltaVista front end is still worth investigating for its peripheral services such as language translation, multilingual searches and an okay directory.

## Deja.com (Discussions)

http://www.deja.com/usenet/

Here's where to come when you're looking for opinions, advice, first-hand experiences, or the right newsgroup to join. Search Usenet archives going back several years or browse the user surveys. Arguably the Net's greatest treasure.

## Excite

http://www.excite.com

Poor search engine, but a reasonable site directory. Comes in several international editions all padded out with a plethora of services such as TV listings, news, weather, stock quotes, people-finding, email lookup, flight booking, maps, and yellow pages. Its strength is in its community.

## Go

http://www.go.com

Similar to Excite and AltaVista, but blessed with the Walt Disney stamp. The Web search is fast and gives accurate results, but not enough of them.

## Google

http://www.google.com

Not the biggest database, but its results are fast, impressively relevant, and able to be fed back 100 per shot. Check out the "Show matches" link to see the page as stored in its cache. Useful if the original has since vanished.

## HotBot

http://www.hotbot.com

Once the pick of the crop but sadly neglected by new owner Lycos. Will a new surge of data from Inktomi bring it back to life? We've yet to see.

## LookSmart

http://www.looksmart.com

Another big directory that's strong on individual country guides. Every link includes a tightly edited comment. Snap (http://www.snap.com) is similar.

## Lycos

http://www.lycos.com

Has poached some of the best sites online, but none seem to look better for it. You'll need to dig through the directories to find anything worthwhile. Like Excite, give the search engine a miss. Whoever's driving this buggy's fast asleep at the wheel.

## Northern Light

http://www.nlsearch.com

Massive Web database, possibly the biggest online, but nobbled by serving only 10 hits per page. Yet it's the pay per view "special collection" of press clippings that you'll come here to free-trial, and possibly revisit.

## Open Directory Project

http://dmoz.org

Netscape's Yahoo killer aims to be the world's largest hand-built directory. It's not quite that yet, but its bare-bones approach is a pleasure to navigate.

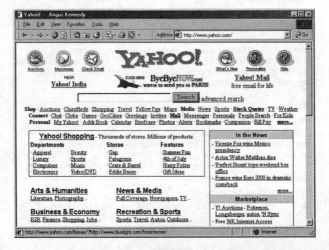

## Yahoo

http://www.yahoo.com

The closest the Net has to a central directory. Big and easy to navigate by subject, but light on reviews. Loads of specialist stuff such as national and metropolitan directories, weather reports, kids' guides, seniors' guides, yellow pages, sport scores, plus outstanding news and financial services. And don't overlook the local area Yahoos, which often include a few sites not in the main directory. There's also regional content such as TV listings. If you don't know this site back to front, you don't know the Net!

# Other Directories and Search Aids

For specialist searches, such as News (p.373) try the relevant sections in Part Two of the Web guide. Product searches, price comparisons and shopping directories are covered in Shopping (p.201), and music searches in MP3 and Online Radio (p.218). And of course don't overlook Finding It (p.163).

Yahoo and the Open Directory might have the most exhaustive lists of **specialist search engines** and directories, but a chaff-free specialist directory of **specialist directories** could still get you there faster. Try:

http://www.beaucoup.com
http://www.clearinghouse.net
http://www.directoryguide.com
http://www.internets.com
http://www.searchengineguide.com
http://www.searchpower.com
http://www.webdata.com

To find **regional directories** that specialize in sites about or within a specific area, try searching Yahoo and the Open Directory by the country or region name, and click through from there. Don't forget, most of the **leading portals** have international branches, so check for links at the main (.com) site. Alternatively, there's a reasonable list at: http://www.beaucoup.com. For a helping hand, a bit of news, and pointers to what works in search tools, try: http://www.traffick.com

### Ask Jeeves

http://www.ask.com

Works on the premise that you're such a moron you can't work a search engine. You're not; so don't let us catch you wasting your time here.

### Big Hub

http://www.thebighub.com

Metasearch over 2000 Web and specialist databases. While it's usually more efficient to search the sites directly, this is a neat way to find them.

### Britannica Internet Guide

http://www.britannica.com

Reviews and rates sites by category. Not that big, but it's top quality and cleverly integrated with a certain encyclopedia.

### EuroSeek

http://www.euroseek.net

Multilingual European Web search and directory.

### MetaCrawler

http://www.metacrawler.com

Bug several Web search engines at once. Limited to thirty results per engine, which in many circumstances renders it useless. See also: http://www.mamma.com

### Mirago (UK)

http://www.mirago.co.uk

Search the British Web and medical sites.

### Quickbrowse

http://www.quickbrowse.com

Doesn't query as many engines as MetaCrawler, but merges up to 200 results from each all on one page. Can also combine multiple sites into one page. Which makes it interesting, and in contrast, possibly useful.

### Search Engine Watch

http://www.searchenginewatch.com
http://www.searchengineshowdown.com
http://www.searchlores.org

Know your search engines and you'll know the Net.

### SearchIQ

http://www.searchiq.com

Lists, reviews and ranks broad, specialty and meta search engines and directories. A useful directory, but don't take its rankings as the final word.

### Spyonit

http://www.spyonit.com

Spy on sites, such as auctions, TV listings, directories and search engines. It will notify you by email, pager, SMS or ICQ, whenever your search term scores a hit.

### Tracerlock

http://www.peacefire.org/tracerlock/

Emails you whenever AltaVista finds a new hit on your terms.

### Webgator

http://www.inil.com/users/dguss/wgator.htm

Become an online private dick.

### Women's Portals

http://www.women.com • http://www.wwwomen.com
http://www. iVillage.com • http://www.icircle.com (UK)

Guides to the Web's man-free zones.

# Business and Phone Directories

### 192.com (UK)

http://www.192.com

Search the UK phone directories and electoral roll.

### Big Yellow

http://www.bigyellow.com

Millions of North American business listings, plus links to international
business directories and people finders. See also:
http://www.bigbook.com

### BT PhoneNet

http://www.bt.com/phonenetuk/

UK business and home phone directory.

### dot com directory

http://www.dotcomdirectory.com

Business directory that's linked in with Network Solutions' dot com
registry. Might be useful for finding a company's Web site.

### Scoot

http://www.scoot.co.uk

Business, people, and product finder for Britain, Holland and
Belgium. Business searches return all the contact and payment
details, plus Web pages if available. See also:
http://www.192enquiries.com

### Switchboard

http://www.switchboard.com

Trace people and businesses in the US. Also try:
http://www.anywho.com and http://www.infospace.com

## Telstra White and Yellow Pages

http://www.whitepages.com.au • http://www.yellowpages.com.au

Australian phone directories complete with street maps.

## World Pages International Directories

http://www.worldpages.com/global/

Find a phone number in almost any country.

# Email Search

To make your email address public you'll need to submit it to these directories individually. Likewise don't expect to find someone who hasn't done the same. The downside is it can lead to spam.

| | |
|---|---|
| **Bigfoot** | http://www.bigfoot.com |
| **Internet Address Finder** | http://www.iaf.net |
| **WhoWhere?** | http://www.whowhere.com |
| **Yahoo People Search** | http://people.yahoo.com |

# Lists, Picks and Weblogs

## 100 Hot Websites

http://www.hot100.com • http://www.top100.com.au (AUS)

The hundred most visited Web sites each week, overall or by category. Not necessarily accurate, but close enough. Bear in mind that browser startup pages skew results. Compare with Alexa: http://www.alexa.com

## Cruel Site of the Day

http://www.cruel.com

Something horrid daily.

## Losers.org

http://www.losers.org

Here's a list you don't want to make.

## MemePool

http://www.memepool.com

Daily Weblog from multiple authors, archived by subject. Always a good source of interesting links.

## Netsurfer Digest

http://www.netsurf.com/nsd/

Subscribe to receive weekly site updates and reviews.

## Portal of Evil

http://www.portalofevil.com

At least three guaranteed jaw-droppers from the Web's outer limits daily. Not for the squeamish.

## Top Ten Links

http://www.toptenlinks.com

Large directory of links sorted by votes.

## Useless Pages

http://www.go2net.com/useless/ • http://www.worstoftheweb.com

The sludge festering at the bottom of the Net.

## Web100

http://www.web100.com

Reviews and ranks the Web's one hundred "top" sites in many categories.

## Weblogs

http://beebo.org/metalog/ratings/
http://www.jjg.net/portal/tpoowl.html

Lists and ranks a few hundred Web wandering journals.

## WebSoup

http://www.ursus.net/WebSoup/

Collates what's being singled out as coolest, newest, or must-see, across about 50 Web review sites.

# Discussion Directories

### Enow

http://www.enow.com

Keyword search the text currently orbiting the chat networks.

### Forum One

http://www.forumone.com

Search or browse over 310,000 Web-based discussion groups.

### Liszt

http://www.liszt.com

Find a mailing list, chat channel, or newsgroup on your favorite topic.

### Publicly Accessible Mailing Lists

http://paml.net

Thousands of specialist email discussion groups organized by name or subject, with details on traffic, content, and how to join. See also: http://www.meta-list.net and http://www.list-universe.com

### Yahoo Clubs

http://clubs.yahoo.com

Too lazy to start a newsgroup? Then start a club. No holds barrod.

# Software Guides

### Browser News

http://www.upsdell.com/BrowserNews/ • http://www.browsers.com

All the latest on Web browsers.

### Cool Tool of the Day

http://www.cooltool.com

New Windows or Mac program of merit each day.

### Download.com

http://www.download.com

Latest notable downloads in all categories, for PC and Mac, from CNET.

### Em@ilfile

http://www.emailfile.com

Rather than wait for a file to download, have it sent to you via email.

### Freesite

http://www.freesite.co.uk

Small, but high quality, collection of assorted freebies from email autoresponders to Web site extras. Worth a look to see what's out there.

### Hotfiles

http://www.hotfiles.com

Mac and PC shareware reviewed by ZDNet.

### Jumbo Shareware

http://www.jumbo.com

Mammoth shareware archive for all platforms.

### Mac Software

http://www.macorchard.com • http://www.pure-mac.com
http://www.chezmark.com • http://hyperarchive.lcs.mit.edu

Apple software releases updated daily.

### Shareware.com

http://www.shareware.com

Search several major file archives for all platforms.

### SoftSeek

http://www.softseek.com

PC downloads reviewed.

Also, see: http://www.slaughterhouse.com

### Stroud's Consummate Winsock Applications

http://www.stroud.com

Top spot for Windows Internet software reviews. Misses a few but keeps you up to date with daily releases.

### Tucows

http://www.tucows.com

Another esteemed Internet applications archive with mirrors all over the world. Covers all platforms, even PDAs. For similar, see: http://www.filedudes.com and http://www.davecentral.com

### Version Tracker

http://www.versiontracker.com

Keep your Mac up to date.

### Walnut Creek CD-ROM

http://www.cdrom.com

Download direct from this massive shareware archive or get it all at once on CD-ROM.

### Winfiles

http://www.winfiles.com

Find obscure Windows programs, for just about every task, as they're released.

# Other Internet Stuff

### Coalition against Unsolicited Commercial Email

http://www.cauce.org

Enlist in the war against junk email.

### Cyber-Geography Research

http://www.cybergeography.org

Maps the nest of wires girdling the globe.

### FAQ Consortium

http://www.faqs.org

The place to find all the Frequently Asked Questions from Usenet newsgroups. Look here before you post.

### Hackers.com

http://www.hackers.com • http://www.cyberarmy.com

Stop and stare at the Net's raw underbelly.

### Internet Traffic Report

http://www.internettrafficreport.com

Monitor the state of the world's main Internet arterials.

### NetMind

http://www.netmind.com

Know when a Web page changes.

### NUA Internet Surveys

http://www.nua.org/surveys/

Leading Internet survey results straight off the press. More stats and Web marketing news at: http://cyberatlas.internet.com and http://www.internetstats.com

### Proxys 4 All

http://proxys4all.cgi.net

Hide your tracks online.

### Scambusters

http://www.scambusters.org • http://www.worldwidescam.com

Exposes the sharks that prey on gullible newbies. To complain go to https://www.ifccfbi.gov

### Zaplet

http://www.zaplet.com

Create invitations, schedules, polls, lunch orders, and all sorts of interactive things you never knew you could do with email. Try it yourself to see how it works. Just follow the prompts.

# PART TWO

# Web Sites

## SUBJECT GUIDE

First off, a disclaimer. This isn't meant to be a definitive guide to the best Web sites. That just isn't possible any more. There are too many sites, and besides, it's a matter of personal taste or interests. That said, we think you'll find this selection broad enough to get you well and truly on your way. So, get clicking!

## Amusements

### Assassin

http://www.newgrounds.com/assassin/

Toast a few excess celebrities.

### Brain Candy

http://www.corsinet.com/braincandy/

Riddles, jokes, insults and general word play.

### Cartoon Bank

http://www.cartoonbank.com

Every cartoon ever published in The New Yorker.

## Comic Book Resources

http://www.comicbookresources.com • http://www.bigpanda.net
http://www.zapcartoons.com • http://www.cartoon-links.com
http://www.geocities.com/Area51/Aurora/2510/greatest_comics/
Comic and cartoon sites, shops, and fanfare.

## Complaint Letter Generator

http://www-csag.cs.uiuc.edu/individual/pakin/complaint/
Punch in a name for an instant dressing down.

## Dobe's Punny Name Archive

http://www.eskimo.com/~dobe/
Thousands of unwise baby names.

## Hidden Mickeys

http://www.hiddenmickeys.org
Subliminal Mickeys hidden around Disneyland?
Must be something in the drinks. Confirm those rumors:
http://www.snopes.com/disney/

## Humor Database

http://www.humordatabase.com • http://www.humournet.com
http://www.humor.com • http://www.goofball.com
http://www.looniebin.mb.ca
So many jokes it's not funny.

## Japanese Engrish

http://www.lumine.net/engrish/
Copywriters wanted, English not a priority.

## Jester: the Online Joke Recommender

http://shadow.ieor.berkeley.edu/humor/

It knows what makes you laugh.

## Mr T'inator

http://firefly.sparse.org/~mrt/

Pity that page, sucka!

## National Lampoon

http://www.nationallampoon.com

Daily humor from the satire house that PJ built. Not what it was in the 70s as you'll see from the vault.

## Newspaper Comic Strips

http://www.kingfeatures.com • http://www.comics.com

The entire works of the Phantom and friends.

## The Onion

http://www.theonion.com

News satire to die for. Don't miss.

## Pocket Internet

http://www.thepocket.com

Gadgets, games, greeting cards, cartoons and more, updated daily.

## Pranksta's Paradise

http://www.ccil.org/~mika/

All the practical jokes from alt.shenanigans

## Pythonline

http://www.pythonline.com

Take a Gilliam-drawn carriage down Monty Python memory lane.

## Rec.humor.funny

http://www.netfunny.com/rhf/

Archives of the rec.humor.funny newsgroup, updated daily.

## Sissyfight

http://www.sissyfight.com

Scratch, tease and tattle your way to playground supremacy.

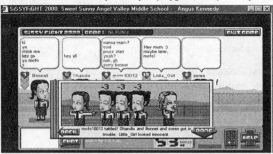

## Spumco's Wonderful World

http://www.spumco.com

Shockwave cartoons from the creators of Ren & Stimpy.

## Stick Figure Death Theater

http://www.sfdt.com

Stickcity citizens meet their sticky ends.

## Surrealist Compliment Generator

http://www.geek-boy.com/scg/

Makes not a shred of sense, but at least it's positive.

## Tony's Illustrated Guide to Unpleasantness

http://www.geocities.com/SouthBeach/Marina/1743/

Refresher course in insults.

## UnderGround Online

http://www.ugo.com

Vigilante gang of counterculture sites that's close to the antithesis of AOL.

# Art, Museums, and Photography

If you're an artist, photograph your work (preferably with a digital camera) and post it online. It's cheap gallery space that your disciples can visit at any time without leaving home. But don't expect them to stumble across it randomly. You'll need to hand out its address at every opportunity. And, don't forget to include news of your exhibitions and contact details.

Like the real world, **finding art online** is very much a **click and miss** (http://www.badart.com) **affair**, and of course entirely a matter of taste. Most major galleries are finding their feet online with limited exhibitions, and any artist who's at all switched on will have their work on the Web. If you're up for clicking, these link banks will locate just about everything that could be considered a bit arty:

| | |
|---|---|
| **ADAM** | http://adam.ac.uk |
| **Art Planet** | http://www.artplanet.com |
| **Artcyclopedia** | http://www.artcyclopedia.com |
| **World Wide Arts Resources** | http://www.wwar.com |

Or if the prospect of an art portal sounds more like your scene:

| | |
|---|---|
| **Artnet.com** | http://www.artnet.com |
| **Artstar** | http://www.artstar.com |
| **Art Advocate** | http://www.artadvocate.com |

To find museums:

| | |
|---|---|
| **MuseumNetwork.com** | http://www.museumnetwork.com |
| **Museums around the World** | http://www.icom.org/vlmp/world.html |
| **24 Hour Museum (UK)** | http://www.24hourmuseum.org.uk |

## 24 hours in Cyberspace

http://www.cyber24.com

One thousand photographers save the day.

## 3D Artists

http://www.raph.com/3dartists/

Art that looks too real to be real.

### A Life Garden

http://alifegarden.com • http://www.technosphere.org.uk
Watch your virtual organism fight for its life.

### Aliens and UFO Art

http://www.wiolawa.com
Defy the Government by becoming as one with alien sculptures.

### AllPosters.com

http://www.allposters.com • http://www.allaboutart.com
Plaster over the cracks in your bedroom walls.

### American Museum of Photography

http://www.photographymuseum.com
Exhibitions from back when cameras were a novelty.

### Amico.org

http://www.amico.org
Art thumbnails from the top North American galleries.

### Anime Pitstop

http://www.animepitstop.com • http://anime.about.com
Today Japan; tomorrow a schoolyard near you.

## The Art Connection

http://www.art-connection.com
Buy British art.

## Art Crimes: Writing on the Wall

http://www.graffiti.org • http://www.grafcafe.com
Spray for recognition, but don't call it art:
http://www.ci.eugene.or.us/nograffiti/

## ArtMuseum

http://www.artmuseum.net
Infrequent exhibitions of modern US classics.

## Artist's Exchange

http://artistexchange.about.com
Artists for artist's sake.

## Cereal Box Archive

http://www.ticktock.simplenet.com/cbarch.html
Identify your breakfast from a line-up of known suspects.

## Core-Industrial Design Resources

http://www.core77.com
Get a hand with industrial design.

## Dia Center for the Arts

http://www.diacenter.org
Web exclusives from "extraordinary" artists, plus the low-down on the
NY Dia Center's upcoming escapades.

## Elfwood

http://www.elfwood.com
Sketches and tales
from a gaggle of
junior fantasy and
sci-fi buffs.

## The Exploratorium

http://www.exploratorium.edu

Kid-friendly online exhibitions from San Francisco's Exploratorium.

## Fine Art Lease

http://www.fineartlease.com

Borrow posh pictures to hang in your snooker room.

## Gallery of Psychiatric Art

http://www.tiac.net/users/smisch/home/mupsyeum.shtml

Three decades of pushing psychoactives.

## Great Buildings Collections

http://www.greatbuildings.com

Shuffle knowingly through 3D models of some 750 of the world's most notable structures.

## Grove Dictionary of Art Online

http://www.groveart.com

Freeload on the definitive art reference for a day.

## Interactive Collector

http://www.icollector.com

Bid on art and collectibles like celebrity cast-offs.

## Labelcollector.com

http://www.labelcollector.com

Salute to the golden era of fruit crates and jars.

## Library of Congress

http://www.loc.gov

Research tools, exhibitions, library services, current hot bills, and an unparalleled multimedia showcase of American history.

## Life

http://www.pathfinder.com/Life/

View Life magazine's picture of the day, then link through to some of the world's most arresting photographs. There's even more over at **Time's Picture Collection** (http://www.thepicturecollection.com) and Australia's **Newsphotos** (http://www.newsphotos.com.au).

THE FLAG IN GAZA CITY Islamic Jihad supporter in Gaza City waves burning American and Israeli flags during a rally to mark the assassination of Mahmoud Khawaja. Photo by ADEL HANA/AP

## Museum of Modern Art NY

http://www.moma.org

About to expand this small online exhibit, or so we're told.

## Online Photo Albums

Got some snaps you'd like to show to the world, or just your friends through selective password access? Upload them here:

| | |
|---|---|
| **Club Photo** | http://www.clubphoto.com |
| **PhotoLoft** | http://www.photoloft.com |
| **Photopoint** | http://www.photopoint.com |
| **Yahoo! Photos** | http://photos.yahoo.com |

### Photodisc

http://www.photodisc.com

Plunder these photos free, or pay for the hi-res versions.

### Soda Connector

http://sodaplay.com/constructor/

Train ingenious spring models that obey the laws of physics and the whims of your idle mind.

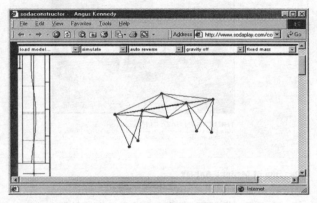

### Stelarc

http://www.stelarc.va.com.au

No artist has given his body to the Net like Prof Stelarc.

### Vincent Van Gogh Gallery

http://www.vangoghgallery.com

So, where else could you see his entire works in one place?

### Year in the Life of Photojournalism

http://www.digitalstoryteller.com/YITL/

Tag along with voyeuristic pros and see what they do in their day to day.

# Books and Literature

If a squillion Web pages aren't enough to satisfy your lust for the written word, then maybe you should use one to order a book. You'll be spoiled for choice with hundreds of shops offering millions of titles for delivery anywhere worldwide. That includes bumper showings from most of the major chains alongside exclusively online book havens such as Amazon and BOL. The superstores typically lay on all the trimmings, such as user ratings, reviews, recommendations, sample chapters, author interviews, bestseller lists, press clippings, publishing news, secure ordering, and sometimes even gift wrapping.

## Major Chains

| | |
|---|---|
| Barnes & Noble (US) | http://www.bn.com |
| Blackwells (UK) | http://bookshop.blackwell.co.uk |
| Book Passage (US) | http://www.bookpassage.com |
| Borders (US) | http://www.borders.com |
| Collins (AUS) | http://www.collinsbooks.com.au |
| Dymocks (AUS) | http://www.dymocks.com.au |
| Hammicks (UK) | http://www.thebookplace.com |
| McGills (AUS) | http://www.mcgills.com.au |
| Waterstone's (UK) | http://www.waterstones.co.uk |
| WHSmith (UK) | http://books.whsmithonline.co.uk |

## Only on the Web

| | |
|---|---|
| Alphabet Street (UK) | http://www.alphabetstreet.com |
| Amazon (UK) | http://www.amazon.co.uk |
| Amazon (US) | http://www.amazon.com |
| BOL (UK, Europe, Asia) | http://www.bol.com |
| Buy.com (US) | http://www.buy.com |
| Fatbrain (US, Technical) | http://www.fatbrain.com |
| Internet Bookshop (UK) | http://www.bookshop.co.uk |

Not listed here? Try browsing or subject-searching this directory of booksellers worldwide: http://www.bookweb.org/bookstores/
For a rundown on British merchants see: http://www.books.co.uk

While Barnes & Noble and Amazon may rightly jostle over the title of "world's most ginormous bookstore", you'll find they all offer a staggering range, usually at substantial discounts. But because books are heavy, savings may be offset by freight. And naturally, the further away you are, and the sooner you want it, the more it adds up. So, before you check out in a frenzy, see that you have the best deal:

| | |
|---|---|
| **AddAll (Worldwide)** | http://www.addall.com |
| **Best Book Buys (US)** | http://www.bestbookbuys.com |
| **BookBrain (UK)** | http://www.bookbrain.co.uk |
| **BookFinder (US)** | http://www.bookfinder.com |
| **ShopGenie (UK)** | http://www.shopgenie.com |

## Atomic Books

http://www.atomicbooks.com

"Insane books about every kind of extreme". For more trashy treasures: http://www.fringeware.com/shop/
http://www.loompanics.com

## Banned Books Online

http://digital.library.upenn.edu/books/banned-books.html

Extracts from books that riled the righteous.

## Bibliofind

http://www.bibliofind.com • http://www.usedbooks.com

Old, used, and rare books from sellers worldwide.

## Book-A-Minute

http://www.rinkworks.com/bookaminute/

Knock over the classics in a lunch hour.

## BookCloseouts

http://www.bookcloseouts.com

Millions of books slightly past their shelf life – including this one's first edition!

## Bookwire

http://www.bookwire.com

US book trade news, bestseller lists, and author road schedules with content from the Publisher's Weekly and Library Journal. For UK publishing news, see: http://www.thebookseller.com

## CrimeBoss

http://www.crimeboss.com

Shock comic covers from the mid-20th century.

## The Damnedest Thing I Ever Saw

http://www.thedamnedestthing.com

Push your credibility to the edge.

## Dave's List of Words that are Fun to Say

http://members.tripod.com/~DeathInPlaid/list.html

Read them aloud for the time of your life.

## Femaledetective

http://www.femaledetective.com

She always gets her man.

## The Internet Public Library

http://www.ipl.org

Browse online books, magazines, journals, and newspapers.

## January Magazine

http://www.januarymagazine.com

Dissecting books and authors.

## JournalismNet

http://www.journalismnet.com

Tips and tools for tapping into the big cheat sheet. More facts for hacks at: http://www.facsnet.org • http://www.usus.org

## MysteryNet

http://www.mysterynet.com

Hmm, now what could this be?

## Poetry Society

http://www.poetrysoc.com • http://www.poets.org

Halfway-house for budding poets and their victims. You have to start somewhere: http://crappypoetry.com

## Project Gutenburg

http://www.gutenberg.net

Fifty years or so after authors croak, their copyrights expire. With this in mind, Project Gutenburg is gradually bringing thousands of old texts online, along with some more recent donations. Sounds great but you might prefer the convenience of hard copy. See also: http://digital.library.upenn.edu/books/

## Pure Fiction

http://www.purefiction.com

For pulp worms and writers alike. Not a word of it is true.

## Shakespeare

http://the-tech.mit.edu/Shakespeare/

The Bard unbarred online.

## The Slot: a Spot for Copy Editors

http://www.theslot.com

Soothing words of outrage for grammatical pedants.

### Tech Classics Archive

http://classics.mit.edu

Hundreds of translated Greek and Roman classics. For more ancient and mediaeval literature, see: http://argos.evansville.edu

### Text files

http://www.textfiles.com

Chunks of the junk that orbited the pre-Web Internet. For a slightly more modern slant, see: http://www.etext.org

### Urban Legends

http://www.urbanlegends.com

Separate the amazing but true, from the popular myths.

### The Word Detective

http://www.word-detective.com • http://www.quinion.com/words/

Words never escape him.

### The Yarn

http://www.theyarn.com

A story that offers you the choice of two paths at the end of each chapter. If one leads you to a dead end, you're asked to contribute.

# Business

### AccountingWeb

http://www.accountingweb.co.uk

Safe playpen for British beancounters.

### Ad Critic

http://www.adcritic.com • http://www.superbowl-ads.com

Make a cuppa while you wait for this year's best US TV ads. For the best of the last twenty, see: http://www.commercial-archive.com And for UK and Australian ads going back to the fifties: http://www.televisioncommercials.com

### Advertising Age

http://www.adage.com

Newsbreaks from the ad trade.

### Bizymoms

http://www.bizymoms.com

Crafty ways to cash up without missing the afternoon soaps.

### Business.com

http://www.business.com

Portal of business sites.
For more European sites and data, see:
http://www.dis.strath.ac.uk/business/

### Clickz

http://www.clickz.com

The Web as seen by the marketing biz.

### Companies Online

http://www.companiesonline.com

Get the score on almost a million
US companies.

### Customers Suck!

http://www.customerssuck.com

Grumbly dispatches from the retail
front.

### Dot Com Failures

http://www.dotcomfailures.com
http://fuckedcompany.com

Gloat over startup shutdowns.

### Entrepreneur.com

http://www.entrepreneur.com

Get rich now, ask us how.

### The Foundation Center

http://fdncenter.org

Companies who might happily spare you a fiver.

### Freemerchant.com

http://www.freemerchant.com • http://www.bigstep.com

Set up an online shop for next to nothing.

### Garage.com

http://www.garage.com

Matchmaking agency for entrepreneurs and investors founded by Apple's Guy Kawasaki. For more help milking funds for your online white elephant, see: http://www.moneyhunter.com

### Guerilla Marketing

http://www.gmarketing.com

Get ahead by metaphorically butchering your competitor's families and poisoning your customer's water supply.

### IBM Patent Server

http://www.patents.ibm.com

Sift through US patents back to 1971, plus a gallery of obscurities. Ask the right questions and you might stumble across tomorrow's technology long before the media. For UK patents see: http://www.patent.gov.uk

### InfoUSA

http://www.infousa.com

Find likely Americans to bug with your presentation.

### Killer Internet tactics

http://www.killertactics.com

How to murder brain-dead Web surfers with HTML.

### Patent Café

http://www.patentcafe.com

Protect your crackpot schemes and see them through to fruition.

### Super Marketing: Ads from the Comic Books

http://www.steveconley.com/supermarketing.htm

The ads that kept you lying awake at night
wishing you had more money.

### UBrandit

http://www.ubrandit.com

Refab a kit commerce site in your own name.

### The Wonderful Wankometer

http://www.cynicalbastards.com/wankometer/

Measure corporate hyperbole. Couple with:
http://www.dack.com/web/bullshit.html

# Computing and Tech News

Every decent PC brand has a site where you can download the
latest drivers, get support, and find out what's new. It won't be
hard to find. Usually it's the company name or initials between a
www and a com.

So you'll find **Dell** at: http://www.dell.com, **Compaq** at:
http://www.compaq.com, **Gateway** at: http://www.gateway.com, and
so forth. Most of the big names also have international branches,
which will be linked from the main site. Consult Yahoo if that
fails. If you're in the market for new computer bits, check out
the best price across US online vendors:

**Shopper.com**          http://www.shopper.com
**Price Watch**          http://www.pricewatch.com
**Lowerbound**           http://www.lowerbound.org

Popular package software vendors include:

**Jungle.com (UK)**      http://www.jungle.com
**Beyond.com**           http://www.beyond.com
**Chumbo.com**           http://www.chumbo.com

Bear in mind, if you live outside the US, it might be taxed upon
arrival.

## Apple

http://www.apple.com

Essential drop-in to update your Mac, pick up QuickTime, and be hard sold the latest hardware. To top up with news, software, and brand affirmations, see: http://www.macaddict.com http://www.tidbits.com • http://www.macintouch.com http://www.macnn.com • http://www.macslash.com

Don't even think of looking at http://www.ihateapple.com It will only upset you.

## Bastard Operator from Hell

http://members.iinet.net.au/~bofh/

If you work in a big office, you know this man.

## Chankstore FreeFont Archive

http://www.chank.com/freefonts.htm

Download a wacky Chank Diesel display font free each week. If there's still space in your font sack, arrive hat in hand at: http://www.printerideas.com/fontfairy/ • http://zapo.virtualave.net http://www.fontface.com • http://www.fontaday.com/

## Clip Art

http://webclipart.about.com

Bottomless cesspit of the soulless dross used to inject life into documents.

## CNET

http://www.cnet.com

Daily technology news and features, plus reviews, shopping, games, and downloads, along with schedules, transcripts, and related stories from CNET's broadcasting network.

## Desktop Publishing

http://desktoppub.about.com • http://desktoppublishing.com
Get off the ground in print.

## Dingbats

http://dingbats.i-us.com
For when you just can't get enough symbol fonts.

## Easter egg archive

http://www.eeggs.com
A racing game in Excel 2000, a basketball game in Windows 95, and a raygun-wielding alien in Quark Xpress? They're in there all right, but you'll never find them on your own. Here's how to unlock secrets in scores of programs.

## FreeDrive

http://www.freedrive.com • http://www.myspace.com
http://www.xdrive.com • http://www.idrive.com
Free storage space on the Net that's perfect for backups.

## Free-Help

http://www.free-help.com • http://virtualdr.com
http://www.tek-tips.com • http://www.help.com
Post your computer problems, though Usenet might be quicker.

## HotWired

http://www.hotwired.com
The Net's best source of breaking technology news plus archives of Wired magazine.

## Internet Type Foundry Index

http://www.typeindex.com
Typeface news plus a directory of font and design resources.

## MacFix-it

http://www.macfixit.com • http://www.mac-conflicts.com
Diagnose what's ailing your Mac. Some things are known to conflict.

## Microsoft

http://www.microsoft.com

If you're running any Microsoft product, and the chance of that seems to be approaching 100 percent, drop by this disorganized scrapheap regularly for upgrades, news, support, and patches. That includes the latest free tweaks to Windows, Office, and all that falls under the Internet Explorer regime.

## Modem Help

http://www.modemhelp.com • http://www.56k.com

Solve your dial-up dramas for modems of all persuasions including cable, ISDN, and DSL. And be sure to check your modem maker's page for driver and firmware upgrades, especially if it's X2 or K56flex.

## Need to Know

http://www.ntk.net

Weekly high-tech wrap-up with a sarcastic bite.

## Newslinx

http://www.newslinx.com

Have the top Net technology stories, aggregated from around 50 sources, delivered to your mailbox daily. Or for the highlights in a digest: http://classifieds.news.com.au/ni/netnews/

## Palmgear

http://www.palmgear.com

Know your Palm like the back of your hand.

## PC Mechanic

http://www.pcmech.com/byopc/

How to build, or upgrade, your own computer.

## PC Tweaking

http://www.anandtech.com

http://www.arstechnica.com

http://www.pcextremist.com • http://www.pureperformance.com

http://www.sharkyextreme.com • http://www.shugashack.com

http://www.tomshardware.com • http://www.tweaktown.com
http://www.ugeek.com • http://www.angelfire.com/biz/serenitymacros/

How to overclock your processor into the next millennium, tweak your bios, and upgrade your storage capacity to attract members of the opposite sex.

## PCWebopaedia

http://www.pcwebopedia.com

Superb illustrated encyclopedia of computer technology.

## The Register

http://www.theregister.co.uk

Punchy tech news that spins to its own tune.

## Scantips

http://www.scantips.com

Become a scan-do type of dude.

## Slashdot.org

http://slashdot.org

News for those who've entirely given up on the human race.

## Techtales

http://www.techtales.com • http://www.helpdesktech.com

Customers – they might always be right but they sure do ask the darndest things.

## Virus Myths

http://www.vmyths.com

If someone sends you an email insisting you forward it on to everyone you know, send them here instead. And tell them, if they don't want to catch a virus DON'T OPEN ATTACHMENTS. For more on real viruses, see: http://www.getvirushelp.com and p.23

## Windrivers

http://www.windrivers.com

Driver file updates and hardware reviews compiled by a Windows fanatic of such maniacal proportions he even named his son "Gates". More Windows news and assistance at: http://www.annoyances.org http://www.windows98.org • http://www.wugnet.com/wininfo/ http://www.activewin.com • http://www.win98central.com http://members.aol.com/Knows98/

## Woody's Office Portal

http://www.wopr.com

Beat some sense out of Microsoft Office. For Outlook, see: http://www.slipstick.com/outlook/faq.htm

## Yahoo Computing

http://www.yahoo.com/Computers/

The grandpappy of all computing directories.

## ZDNet

http://www.zdnet.com

Computing info powerhouse from Ziff Davis, publisher of PC Magazine, MacUser, Computer Gaming World and scores of other IT titles. Each magazine donates content such as news, product reviews, and lab test results; plus, there's a ton of prime Net-exclusive technochow. The best place to start researching anything even vaguely computer-related.

# Employment

If you're looking to move on up, beware that if you post your résumé online your boss could find it – embarrassing at the very least. The same situation could also arise if you leave it online once you're hired. Most job agencies have sites these days, and the better ones update at least daily. Consequently there are far too many to attempt to list here. What's best for you will depend on what field you're in and where you want to work. Bigger isn't always better, as you'll find yourself competing with more applicants.

So maybe you'd be better off searching the newspaper classifieds, or checking out the agencies that advertise in your vocation's trade mags. Better still, if you have a company in your sights check its Web site for vacancies, or write to its "Human Resources Officer". It should go without saying that you should never interview with any company without fully surveying its Web site along with its main competitors, and other voices within the industry. Whether you're looking for a job, or to fill a vacancy, try:

http://www.adecco.com (INT) • http://www.monster.com (INT)
http://www.topjobs.com (INT) • http://www.drakeintl.com (INT)
http://www.careermosaic.com/cm/gateway/ (INT)
http://www.hotjobs.com.au (AUS) • http://www.seek.com.au (AUS)
http://www.ajb.dni.us (US) • http://www.flipdog.com (US)
http://www.careerbuilder.com (US) • http://www.joboptions.com (US)
http://www.futurestep.com (US) • http://www.headhunter.net (US)
http://www.hotjobs.com (US) • http://www.jobsite.co.uk (UK)
http://www.fish4jobs.co.uk (UK) • http://www.jobsearch.co.uk (UK)
http://www.reed.co.uk (UK) • http://www.jobsunlimited.co.uk (UK)
http://www.peoplebank.com (UK)

### Cool Works

http://www.coolworks.com

Seasonal jobs in US resorts, national parks, camps, ranches, and cruise lines.

### Integrity Based Interviewing

http://www.interviewing.net

Ex-federal agents show you how to get to the truth without drawing any blood.

### The Riley Guide

http://www.rileyguide.com

Messy, but massive, directory of job-hunting resources.

### Salary Info

http://www.salary.com • http://jobsmart.org/tools/salary/

See what you're worth, and then how much you'd need in another town: http://www2.homefair.com/calc/salcalc.html

### WorkExchange

http://www.workexchange.com

Find a freelancer for your project, or vise versa.

### Yahoo Careers

http://careers.yahoo.com

As ever, Yahoo is in on the act, and as ever, does it superbly. This arm, however, handles only US placements. But key "employment" as a search term, or click on "international", and you'll be awash with options spanning the globe.

# Entertainment and Events

Finding out what's on in town, and booking your perch, has never been easier – once you settle on a trusty online source. Your local newspaper's site would be the first logical port of call. Then see how these multicity guides cater to your locale and interests:

| | |
|---|---|
| CitySearch | http://www.citysearch.com |
| Sidewalk (AU) | http://www.sidewalk.com.au |
| Time Out | http://www.timeout.com |
| Tribes | http://www.tribe.com.au |

## Aloud (UK)

http://www.aloud.com

Book UK music, festival, and event tickets online. For theatre tickets, see: http://www.whatsonstage.com and for what's on listings see: http://www.eventselector.co.uk

## CultureFinder (UK)

http://www.culturefinder.com

What's on guide to classical music, theatre, opera, dance, and visual arts in around a thousand US cities.

## London Techno Events

http://www.sorted.org/london/

What's spinning around London's techno circuit.

## Music Festival Finder

http://www.festivalfinder.com

Daily-updated listings of more than 1500 forthcoming Portaloo playtime across North America. Covers all genres. For the UK, see: http://www.timeout.com/festivals/

## NME Ticketshop (UK)

http://www.nmetickets.com

http://www.tickets-online.co.uk

Reserve music tickets across the UK.

## Ticketmaster/Ticketek

http://www.ticketmaster.com • http://www.ticketmaster.co.uk

http://www.ticketmaster.com.au • http://www.ticketek.com.au

Book event tickets online in the US, UK, and Australia.

## Fashion

Unless it entirely erodes your reading time the Net isn't likely to cut your guilty expenditure on glossy mags. While there's a spree of fledgling style zines and something of sorts from nearly all the big rack names, none of it compares to getting it in print. Nonetheless, it will certainly supplement your vice. What you will find the Net better for is researching products, checking out brands and saving money on consumables like cosmetics at stores such as:

http://www.beautyjungle.com • http://www.beautyspot.com.au

http://www.drugstore.com • http://www.gloss.com

http://www.ibeauty.com • http://www.perfumania.com

http://www.reflect.com • http://www.sephora.com

http://www.theperfumeshop.com • http://www.hqhair.com

http://www.beu.co.uk • http://www.vitago.co.uk

http://www.thinknatural.com • http://www.classcosmetics.co.uk

Buying **clothes**, however, is tougher. They're out there, if you know what you're doing, but you'll soon see why **Boo.com** failed. The best place to find fashion sites is in your regular glossies and newspaper's style section – both in editorial and ads. Label sites are sometimes interesting for new season looks, stockists and sometimes, direct ordering. For more on shopping, see p.201.

### 1-800-SURGEON

http://www.surgeon.org

Adjust your imperfection without pills or creams.

### Elle International

http://www.elle.com

Morsels plucked from Elle's global lunchbox plus a shop on the side.

### FashionBot

http://www.fashionbot.com

Search several UK high-street retailers' catalogs.

### Fashion Information

http://www.fashioninformation.com

Pay for trend forecasting reports.

### Fashion Net

http://www.fashion.net

Handy shortcut to the highest profile shopping, designer, magazine, modeling and fashion industry sites, with enough editorial to warrant an extended stopover.

### Fashionmall.com

http://www.fashionmall.com • http://www.brandsforless.com
http://www.bluefly.com • http://www.designersdirect.com

Mail order familiar, and mostly American, labels.

### Fashion UK

http://www.fuk.co.uk

Minimal, but fresh, vanity monthly out of London.

### Firstview

http://www.firstview.com

See what's trotting the catwalks – sometimes at a price.

### InShop (US)

http://www.inshop.com

Track shop sales and promotions in your area.

## The Lipstick Page

http://www.thelipstickpage.com

Cosmetic appliances for fun and profit.

## Moda Italia

http://www.modaitalia.net

Patch through to the Italian rag traders.

## Mullets of the Gods

http://www.mulletgods.com • http://www.mulletjunky.com

Don't touch the back.

## Solemates: The Century in Shoes

http://www.centuryinshoes.com

Stepping out in the 20th century.

## Victoria's Secret

http://www.victoriassecret.com

Order online or request the catalog preferred by nine out of ten teenage boys.

## Vogue (UK)

http://www.vogue.co.uk

Celebrity sightings, threadwear news, jobs, catwalk reports, assorted features, and of course incessant coverage of the you-know-who's. Still not had enough of them? Then try this for an overdose: http://www.supermodel.com

# Film, TV, and Stars

Most TV stations maintain excellent sites with all kinds of extras such as live sports coverage and documentary follow-ups. We won't need to give you their addresses because they'll be flashing them at you at every opportunity. In any case, you'll find them all at: http://www.tvshow.com

For personalized listings, perhaps delivered by email, try your local Yahoo, or:

http://www.sofcom.com.au/TV/ (AUS) • http://www.clicktv.com (CAN)

http://www.unmissabletv.com (UK) • http://www.radiotimes.beeb.com (UK)

http://www.digiguide.co.uk (UK) • http://www.ananova.com/tv/ (UK)

http://www.gist.com (US) • http://www.tvguide.com (US)

http://www.tvgrid.com (US) • http://tv.zap2it.com (US)

For other countries:

http://www.tvshow.com/tv/scheds/

To be notified when something's on:

**Spyonit**                                            http://www.spyonit.com

Several sites specialize in TV episode guides:

**Epguides.com**                                       http://epguides.com
**Hu's Episode Guides**                   http://www.episodeguides.com
**Mighty Big TV**                              http://www.mightybigtv.com

But if you want obsessive detail along with picture galleries and rumors, search Yahoo for a site dedicated to that show. For nostalgia:

**TV Cream (UK)**                                       http://tv.cream.org
**Yesterdayland**                           http://www.yesterdayland.com

Or if you'd prefer a video or DVD, you won't find a bigger range than:

**Reel.com**                                            http://www.reel.com
**Amazon**                                http://www.amazon.com (.co.uk)
**Black Star (UK)**                           http://www.blackstar.co.uk

To compare prices:

http://www.dvdpricesearch.com • http://www.formovies.com

For more on **DVD hardware and software**:
http://www.7thzone.com • http://www.dvdfile.com

When it comes to **movies**, one site clearly rules:
**The Internet Movie Database**    http://www.imdb.com

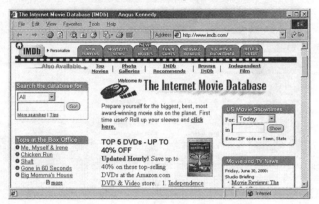

To say it's impressive is an understatement. You'll be hard pressed to find any work on or off the Net as comprehensive as this exceptional relational database of screen trivia from over 100,000 movies and a million actors. It's all tied together remarkably well – for example, within two clicks of finding your favorite movie, you can get full filmographies of anyone from the cast or crew, and then see what's in the cooker. Still, it's not perfect, or without competition. For example, you'll find a similar service with superior biographies and synopses at the colossal:

**All Movie Guide**                              http://www.allmovie.com

Or for more Chan, Li and Fat:

**Hong Kong Movie Database**                     http://www.hkmdb.com

They'll also direct you to external reviews, as will these search engines:

**Movie Review Query Engine**                    http://www.mrqe.com
**Cinemachine**                                  http://www.cinemachine.com

But perhaps you'd prefer a summary:

**Rotten Tomatoes**                http://www.rottentomatoes.com

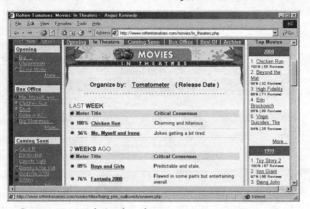

Or a recommendation based on your tastes:

**MovieLens**                http://movielens.umn.edu

While at least one site picks the all-time greats:

**Greatest Films**                http://www.filmsite.org

Far more are content to trash:

**Bad Movie Night**                http://www.hit-n-run.com

**Mr Cranky**                http://www.mrcranky.com

**The Stinkers**                http://www.thestinkers.com

Or roll in it:

**Astounding B Monster**             http://www.bmonster.com

**Bad Movie Report**        http://www.stomptokyo.com/badmoviereport/

**Badmovies.org**                http://www.badmovies.org

**Losman's Lair of Horror**          http://www.losman.com

**Oh the Humanity**              http://www.ohthehumanity.com

**Shock Cinema**           http://members.aol.com/shockcin/

**Trash City**                http://www.trshcity.demon.co.uk

But none unveil **box office evil** like:

**Childcare Action Project**   http://www.capalert.com

For whispers on **what's in production**:

| | |
|---|---|
| **Ain't It Cool News** | http://www.aint-it-cool-news.com |
| **CHUD** | http://www.chud.com |
| **Coming Attractions** | http://www.corona.bc.ca/films/ |
| **Dark Horizons** | http://www.darkhorizons.com |
| **IMDB** | http://www.imdb.com/Sections/Inproduction/ |

To reach out to a star:

**CelebrityEmail.com**   http://www.celebrityemail.com

Every celebrity has at least one **obsessive fan site** (http://www.ggower.com/fans/) in their honor. Finding them can sometimes be tricky. If they're not listed in Yahoo, try:

http://www.celebhoo.com • http://www.celebrityweb.com
http://www.celebsites.com • http://www.fansites.com
http://www.webring.org

Search engines tend to find porn scuttlers who've loaded their HTML metatags with celebrity names. Easy bait, when you consider that most fans could go a glimpse of their idol in **various states of undress** (http://www.cndb.com). If they succeed in catching your attention, at least have the sense not to pull out your credit card. Adding -naked -nude to your search term might help weed them out.

## asSeenonScreen

http://www.asseenonscreen.com
Buy stuff you've seen on TV or in movies.

## Atom Films

http://www.atomfilms.com
Watch entertaining short films.
For sixteen-color silliness see:
http://www.pixelfest.com

## Drew's Script-O-Rama

http://www.script-o-rama.com

Hundreds of entire film and TV scripts. Need help writing or selling your own? Try here: http://www.celluloidmonkeys.com

### E! Online

http://www.eonline.com

Daily film and TV gossip, news, and reviews.

### Empire Magazine

http://www.empireonline.co.uk

Reviews of every film showing in the UK.

### Friends Place

http://www.friendsplace.com

Every script of every episode ever. But, if you have that much spare time it might make you wish you had some of your own.

### Gil*galad's Martian Theaethyr

http://www.televar.com/~gnostran/

Applying AstroTarotry to old movies makes them so much clearer.

### Hollywood Reporter

http://www.hollywoodreporter.com

Tinseltown tattle, previews and reviews daily, plus a flick biz directory.

### India Talkies

http://www.indiatalkies.com

Take a stroll down Bollywood boulevard.

### Live TV

http://www.comfm.fr/live/tv/

Tune into live video feeds from hundreds of real world television stations. To record US cable shows and play them back in Real Video (court case pending) see: http://www.recordtv.com

### Melon Farmer's Video Hits

http://www.dtaylor.demon.co.uk

Question British screen censorship.

## Movie Cliches

http://www.moviecliches.com
Nothing unfamiliar.

## Moviemags.com

http://www.moviemags.com
Directory of film print and ezines.

## Movies.com

http://www.movies.com • http://www.mca.com • http://www.film.com
Preview box office features and trailers.

## SciFi.com

http://www.scifi.com • http://scifi.ign.com • http://www.fandom.com
Science fiction news, reviews and short films.

## Screen Network Australia

http://www.sna.net.au
Gateway to Australian film and TV sites. For news, reviews, and
interviews, see: http://www.urbancinefile.com.au

## Showbizwire

http://www.showbizwire.com
Entertainment newsbreaks from about 50 major sources.

## The Smoking Gun

http://www.thesmokinggun.com
http://www.apbnews.com/media/gfiles/
Celebrity shame dug up from police records complete with the
photocopied sources.

## Soap City

http://www.soapcity.com/ • http://www.soapdigest.com
http://members.tripod.com/~TheSoapBox/
Keep up with who's doing what to whom, whom they told, and who
shouldn't find out, in the surreal world of soap fiction.

### TV Eyes

http://www.tveyes.com

Informs you when your search term is mentioned on TV.

### TV Show

http://www.tvshow.com

Everything TV, from schedules of every station worldwide and links to just about every show ever made, to the technical aspects of production and broadcasting. Start all your TV-related searches here.

### TV Tickets

http://www.tvtickets.com

Secure your chance to clap on cue.

### Variety

http://www.variety.com

Screen news fresh off the PR gattling gun.

### VCR Repair Instructions

http://www.fixer.com

How to take a VCR apart and then get all the little bits back in so it fits easier into the bin.

### Who would you kill?

http://www.whowouldyoukill.com

So who would you toss into Dawson's Creek?

# Food and Drink

When following recipes, note where they're from so you don't mix up the measures. For example, an Australian tablespoon is four, not three, teaspoons.

## BarMeister.com

http://www.barmeister.com

Experimental cocktails with companion games to ensure the misfires aren't wasted.
Tons more at: http://www.idrink.com

## Beershots

http://micro.magnet.fsu.edu/beershots/

Beers of the world put under a microscope. Literally!

## Bevnet

http://www.bevnet.com

Know your new age beverages. Here's how to brew the "real thing": http://www.sodafountain.com

## Birdseye Recipe Search

http://www.birdseye.com/search.html

Cast your line into the Fish Finger king's own recipe database or trawl through hundreds of other Net collections. See also: http://www.lycos.com/search/recipedia.html

http://recipes.alastra.com • http://www.mymenus.com

## Breworld.com

http://www.breworld.com

None of the usual beer yarns like waking up in a strange room stark naked with a throbbing head and a hazy recollection of pranging your car. Here, beer is treated with the same dewy-eyed respect usually reserved for wine and trains. Like to send your chum a virtual beer? Stumble over to: http://www.pubworld.co.uk

## Chile-Heads

http://chileheads.netimages.com

http://easyweb.easynet.co.uk/~gcaselton/chile/chile.html

Get 'em while they're hot.

## Chocolate Lover's Page

http://chocolate.scream.org

The good gear: where to find recipes and dealers.

## Cigar Aficionado

http://www.cigaraficionado.com

Archives, shopping guides, and tasting forums from the US glossy that sets the benchmark in cigar ratings. Modeled on: http://www.thethirdrail.com/crack/

## Cocktail

http://www.cocktailtime.com • http://cocktails.about.com

http://www.webtender.com

Guzzle your way to a happier home. Yes, do buy the book.

## Cook's Thesaurus

http://www.foodsubs.com

Find substitutes for fatty, expensive, or hard-to-find ethnic ingredients.

## Buying Groceries Online

Your chances of being able to order home-delivered groceries online will be much higher if you live in a big city. Expect to pay a premium for the convenience. Although most of the following have physical stores, they mightn't offer their full range online:

http://www.colesonline.com.au (AU)
http://www.greengrocer.com.au (AU)
http://www.shopfast.com.au (AU) • http://www.woolworths.com.au (AU)
http://www.telegrocer.com (CAN) • http://www.sainsbury.co.uk (UK)
http://www.somerfield.co.uk (UK) • http://www.tesco.co.uk (UK)
http://www.waitrose.com (UK) • http://www.iceland.co.uk (UK
http://www.egrocer.com (US) • http://www.ethnicgrocer.com (US)
http://www.homegrocer.com (US) • http://www.homeruns.com (US)
http://www.netgrocer.com (US) • http://www.peapod.com (US)
http://www.kozmo.com (US)
Or name your price at: http://webhouse.priceline.com (US)

### DineNet

http://menusonline.com

Thousands of US restaurant menus, plus maps to aid fulfillment.

### Epicurious

http://www.epicurious.com

Online marriage of Condé Nast's **Gourmet**, **Bon Appetit**, and **Traveler** magazines, crammed with recipes, culinary forums, and advice on dining out worldwide.

### The Espresso Index

http://www.espresso.com • http://www.espressotop50.com

Kickstart your morning with the FAQs on coffee.

### Final Meal Requests

http://www.tdcj.state.tx.us/stat/finalmeals.htm

The prospect's enough to spoil your appetite.

## Internet Chef

http://www.ichef.com

Over 30,000 recipes, cooking hints, kitchen talk, and more links than you could jab a fork in.

## Kim Chee

http://www.kim-chee.com • http://www.kimchi.or.kr

Learn to love Korean spicy cabbage even if it makes you smell like a rendering plant.

## The Kitchen Garden Online

http://www.taunton.com/kg/

For cooks who love to garden, or perhaps vice versa.

## Kitchen Link

http://www.kitchenlink.com

Points to more than 10,000 galleries of gluttony.

## Moonshine

http://moonshine.co.nz

Get blind (possibly literally) on homemade spirits.

## An Ode to Olives

http://www.bayarea.net/~emerald/olive.html

You'll never look at an olive ambivalently again.

## Restaurant Row

http://www.restaurantrow.com

Key in your dining preferences and find the perfect match from hundreds of thousands of food barns worldwide.

## Spice Guide

http://www.spiceguide.com

Encyclopedia of spices covering their origins, purposes, recipes, and tips on what goes best with what.

## Tasty Insect Recipes

http://www.ent.iastate.edu/Misc/InsectsAsFood.html

http://www.eatbug.com

Dig in to such delights as Bug Blox, Banana Worm Bread, Rootworm Beetle Dip, and Chocolate Chirpie Chip Cookies (with crickets).

## Tea & Sympathy

http://www.enteract.com/~robchr/tea/

Home of the Rec.Food.Tea FAQ.

## Thai Recipes

http://www.importfood.com/recipes.html

Just click if you don't have an ingredient.

## Tokyo Food Page

http://www.bento.com

Where and what to eat in Tokyo, plus recipes. More help packing sushi at: http://www.learn-sushi.com and http://www.sushi101.com Now read your fortune: http://www.astprince.com/english/sushi/

## Top Secret Recipes

http://www.topsecretrecipes.com • http://www.copykat.com

At least one commercial recipe, such as KFC coleslaw, revealed each week. Many are surprisingly basic.

## The Ultimate Cookbook

http://www.ucook.com

Pinch recipes from hundreds of popular cookbooks. More food porn unplugged at: http://www.cook-books.com

## Vegetarian Society of the UK

http://www.vegsoc.org

Support for fussy eaters.

## Wine Spectator

http://www.winespectator.com

Research your hangover.

# Games

As outlined in **Online Gaming** (p.232) most multiplayer games can be played across the Net. There are also thousands of simple table, word, arcade, and music games as diverse as Chess, Blackjack, Connect 4, and Frogger that can be played on the Web courtesy of Java and Shockwave. In some cases you can contest online opponents for prizes. Peruse the selection on offer at:

| | |
|---|---|
| **Flash Kit** | http://www.flashkit.com |
| **Flazoom** | http://www.flazoom.com |
| **FreeArcade.com** | http://www.freearcade.com |
| **Gamesville** | http://www.gamesville.com |
| **Playsite** | http://www.playsite.com |
| **Pogo.com** | http://www.pogo.com |
| **Shockwave.com** | http://www.shockwave.com |
| **The Riddler** | http://www.riddler.com |
| **The Station** | http://www.station.sony.com |
| **Won.net** | http://www.won.net |
| **Yahoo Games** | http://games.yahoo.com |
| **Web Games** | http://www.happypuppy.com/web/ |

## The Best Games Music in the World Ever

http://gamemusic.siliconcircus.co.uk
Put someone special in the mood.

## Blues News

http://www.bluesnews.com
Keep up with what's Quakin'.

## ContestGuide

http://www.contestguide.com • http://www.contestworld.com
http://www.iwon.com
http://www.uggs-n-rugs.com.au/contests/ (AUS)
http://www.loquax.co.uk (UK)
Get junk mailed for life by entering loads of competitions.

### Game Downloads

http://www.fileplanet.com • http://www.freeloader.com

Stock up on gaming software.

### GameFAQs

http://www.gamefaqs.com

Stuck on a level or just want to know more?

### Grrl Gamer

http://www.grrlgamer.com

Team up with other game grrls and prepare to kick dweeb boy butt right across their own turf. More reinforcement at: http://www.gamegirlz.com and http://www.womengamers.com

### Kasporov Chess

http://www.kasparovchess.com

http://chess.about.com

Take tips from the Russian master and then find an opponent.

### PC Game Finder

http://www.pcgame.com

Search the leading game lairs.

### Vintage Gaming

http://www.vintagegaming.com

http://www.emux.com

http://www.download.net

Revive old school arcade games like Xevious on your home PC.

## PC Games

For reviews, news, demos, hints, patches, cheats, downloads, and other PC game necessities try:

| | |
|---|---|
| **Adrenaline Vault** | http://www.avault.com |
| **Daily Radar** | http://www.dailyradar.com |
| **Gamecenter** | http://www.gamecenter.com |
| **Gamers.com** | http://www.gamers.com |
| **Games Domain** | http://www.gamesdomain.com |
| **Gamespot** | http://www.gamespot.com |
| **Happy Puppy** | http://www.happypuppy.com |
| **Macintosh Gamer's Ledge** | http://www.macledge.com |
| **Old Man Murray** | http://www.oldmanmurray.com |

## Console Games

| | |
|---|---|
| **Console Domain** | http://www.consoledomain.com |
| **Daily Radar** | http://www.dailyradar.com |
| **Hotgames.com** | http://www.hotgames.com |
| **Psx Extreme** | http://www.psxextreme.com |
| **Video Game Strategies** | http://vgstrategies.about.com |

# Health

While the Net's certainly an unrivaled medical library, it's also an unrivaled promulgator of the 21st-century equivalent of "old wives' tales". So by all means research your ailment and pick up fitness tips online, but like the pill bottles say, check with your doctor before putting it to work. While you're with your GP, ask if they use the Net for research and if so, which sites they recommend. While not being online by now doesn't necessarily make them a bad doctor, it does suggest they're a little complacent.

Don't expect to go online for first aid advice. If it's an emergency, you won't have time. The Net is better for in depth research and anecdotal advice. None of which comes quickly. But once you've spent a few sessions online studying your complaint, you'll be fully prepared to state your case. You'll know straight away whether your GP knows their stuff. To find a **doctor**, **dentist** or **specialist**, try: http://www.medavenue.com (US) or http://www.netdoctor.co.uk (UK).

**WorldClinic** (http://www.worldclinic.com) provides phone fax or email response that could save your life on the road.

It's hard to say where to start your research. Perhaps a directory: Yahoo et al have seriously stacked medical arms, or you could try one of the specialist health portals:

| | |
|---|---|
| **Achoo** | http://www.achoo.com |
| **Hospitalweb UK** | http://www.hospitalweb.co.uk |
| **Patient UK** | http://www.patient.co.uk |
| **SearchBug** | http://www.searchbug.com/health/ |

Or a government gateway:

| | |
|---|---|
| **Healthfinder** | http://www.healthfinder.gov |
| **HealthinSite (AUS)** | http://www.healthinsite.gov.au |
| **Health on the Net** | http://www.hon.ch |
| **NHS Direct (UK)** | http://www.nhsdirect.nhs.uk |
| **US National Library of Medicine** | http://www.nlm.nih.gov |
| **World Health Organization** | http://www.who.int |

You'll find tons of excellent self-help megasites, though the presence of sponsors may raise ethical questions. Their features vary, but medical encyclopedias, personal health tests and Q&A services are fairly standard fare. Starting with the **former US Surgeon General**'s site, try:

| | |
|---|---|
| **Dr Koop** | http://www.drkoop.com |
| **HealthCentral** | http://www.healthcentral.com |
| **HealthWorld** | http://www.healthy.net |
| **Intellihealth** | http://www.intelihealth.com |
| **Mayo Clinic** | http://www.mayoclinic.com |
| **Netdoctor.co.uk** | http://www.netdoctor.co.uk |
| **ThriveOnline** | http://www.thriveonline.com |
| **UKHealthNet** | http://www.ukhealthnet.co.uk |
| **WebMD** | http://webmd.lycos.com |
| **Yahoo Health** | http://health.yahoo.com |

But for serious research go straight to **Medline**, the US National Library of Medicine's database. It archives, references, and abstracts thousands of medical journals and periodicals going back to 1966. You can get it free at **PubMed**, but the subscription services may have access to more material. These are aimed more at health pros and students:

| | |
|---|---|
| **BioMedNet** | http://www.bmn.com |
| **Medscape** | http://www.medscape.com |
| **Ovid** | http://www.ovid.com |
| **PubMed** | http://www.ncbi.nlm.nih.gov/PubMed/ |

Despite appearances, **Martindale's** has the best set of medical science links:

**Martindale's Health Science guide**
http://www-sci.lib.uci.edu/HSG/HSGuide.html

If you know what you have and you want to contact other sufferers, use a search engine such as Google to find organizations and personal home pages. They should direct you to useful mailing lists and discussion groups. If not, try Deja.com to find the right newsgroups, and PAML (p.291) for mailing lists.

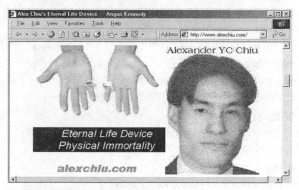

## Alex Chiu's Eternal Life Device

http://www.alexchiu.com

Live forever or come back for your money.

## All Nurses

http://www.allnurses.com

Springboard to chat groups, research data, professional bodies, jobs, and other nursing resources.

## Alternative Medicine

http://altmedicine.about.com • http://www.alternativemedicine.com

Part of the Net's ongoing research function is the ability to contact people who've road-tested alternative remedies and can report on their efficacy. Start here and work your way to an answer.

## Ask Dr Weil

http://www.drweil.com

Popdoctor Andrew Weil's eagerness to prescribe from a range of bewildering, and often conflicting, alternative therapies has seen him called a quack in some quarters, but not by Warner. TIME put him on the front cover and gave him a job peddling advice beside vitamin ads. Whether or not you believe in food cures, his daily Q&As are always a good read.

### Biorhythm Generator

http://www.facade.com/attraction/biorhythm/

Generate a cyclical report that can double as a sick note.

### Color Vision Test

http://www.umist.ac.uk/UMIST_OVS/UES/COLOUR0.HTM

Do you dress in the dark or are you merely colorblind?

### Dr Squat

http://www.drsquat.com • http://www.weightsnet.com/Links/docs/

Avoid getting sand kicked in your face through deep full squats.

### Drugs

http://www.erowid.org • http://www.lycaeum.org

http://www.trashed.co.uk

http://www.perkel.com/politics/issues/pot.htm

http://www.neuropharmacology.com

http://www.druglibrary.org

Everything you ever wanted to know about the pleasure, pain and politics of psychoactive drugs and the cultures built around them.

### GYN101

http://www.gyn101.com

Swot up for your next gynecological exam. But if you're after honors go straight to: http://www.obgyn.net

### Gyro's Excellent Hernia Adventure

http://www.cryogenius.com/mesh/

Holiday snaps from under the knife.

### Medicinal Herb Faq

http://metalab.unc.edu/herbmed/mediherb.html

If it's in your garden and it doesn't kill you, it can only make you stronger. More leafy cures and love drugs at:
http://www.algy.com/herb/

## Mental Health

http://www.mentalhealth.com

Guaranteed you'll come out of this site convinced there's something wrong with you. Worry your way along to:
http://www.anxietynetwork.com or http://www.onlinepsych.com

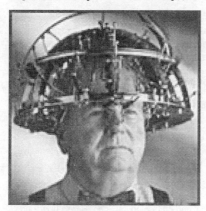

## Museum of Questionable Medical Devices

http://www.mtn.org/quack/

Gallery of health-enhancing products where even breaks weren't bundled free.

## Nutritional Supplements

http://www.nutritionalsupplements.com

First-hand experiences with vitamins, bodybuilding supplements, and other dubious health-shop fodder.

## Online Surgery

http://www.onlinesurgery.com

Human panel beating performed live for the camera by Dr Jake Riviera and associates.

## Phys: In Fitness and in Health

http://www.phys.com

Assess and improve your fitness and diet. Net exclusives plus select features from Condé Nast's **Sports for Women**, **Mademoiselle**, **Glamour**, **Vogue**, **Allure**, and **Self**.

## Pregnancy Calendar

http://www.pregnancycalendar.com • http://www.parentsoup.com
http://www.parenthoodweb.com • http://www.motherchild.com.au
http://www.babycenter.com • http://www.virtualbirth.com

Count down the nine months from conception to pregnancy and get prepared to juggle your life around your new family member. If bub gets sick and you can't get to a doctor try pediatrician Dr Greene for advice: http://www.drgreene.com

## Quackwatch

http://www.quackwatch.com

Separating the docs from the ducks. Don't buy into any alternative remedies until you've read these pages.

## RealAge

http://www.realage.com

Compare your biological and chronological ages. Here's how long you can expect to live:
http://www.msnbc.com/modules/quizzes/lifex.asp

## Reuters Health

http://www.reutershealth.com

Medical newswires, reviews, opinion, and reference.

## RxList

http://www.rxlist.com • http://www.virtualdrugstore.com
http://www.pharminfo.com

Look up your medication to ensure you're not being poisoned.

## The Virtual Hospital

http://www.vh.org

Patient care and distance learning via online multimedia tools such as illustrated surgical walkthroughs.

## The Visible Human Project

http://www.nlm.nih.gov/research/visible/

Whet your appetite by skimming through scans of a thinly filleted serial killer, and then top it off with a fly-through virtual colonoscopy. For higher production values, see the **Virtual Body**: http://www.medtropolis.com/vbody/

## World Sexual Records

http://www.sexualrecords.com

Go for gold in slap and tickle.

## Yoga

http://www.timages.com/yoga.htm

Stretch yourself back into shape with a personalized routine. More at: http://www.yogasite.com

# Home and Garden

## Ask the Master Plumber

http://www.clickit.com/bizwiz/homepage/plumber.htm

Save a small fortune by unblocking your own toilet.

## Australian Real Estate

http://www.propertiesaustralia.com.au • http://propertyweb.com.au

Combines listings from hundreds of Australian brokers.

## Buy.co.uk

http://www.buy.co.uk/Personal/

Clinch the best deal on British utilities.

## Feng Shui

http://www.qi-whiz.com • http://www.fengshui-fanzine.co.uk

Recreate the ambience of a Chinese restaurant.

## FinanCenter

http://www.financenter.com

Figure out your monthly payments or what you can't afford.

## GardenInfo

http://www.gardeninfo.com

Home of Australia's Encyclopedia Botanica and portal to gardening sites worldwide.

## GardenWeb

http://www.gardenweb.com

Hosts a multitude of gardening forums both here and on its European and Australian sister sites, plus a gardening glossary, plant database, calendar of garden events, plant exchange and plenty of meaty articles. Here's more:

http://www.gardensonline.com.au (AU)

http://www.gardenbed.com.au (AU)

http://www.talkingplants.com • http://www.gardenguides.com

http://gardening.about.com • http://www.gardening.com

http://www.vg.com • http://www.gardening365.co.uk (UK)

http://www.e-garden.co.uk (UK) • http://www.expertgardener.com (UK)

## Gothic Gardening

http://www.gothic.net/~malice/

Grow a little greenhouse of horrors.

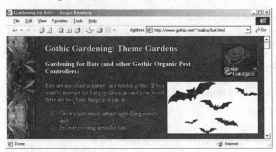

## HomeAdvisor (US)

http://homeadvisor.msn.com

Slick one-stop shop for finding homes and loans.

## Home Improvement Network

http://www.improvenet.com (US) • http://www.improveline.com (UK)
http://www.homepro.com (UK)

Peruse the latest design ideas and find someone to do the job. You can even screen your local builders against public records and find the one least likely to quaff all your home brew and sell your nude holiday snaps to the National Enquirer:
http://www.nationalenquirer.com

## Home Scout (US)

http://www.homescout.com

Scan hundreds of US and Canadian real estate listings.

## Home Tips

http://www.hometips.com • http://www.housenet.com
http://www.doityourself.com • http://www.naturalhandyman.com

Load your toolbox, roll up your sleeves, and prepare to go in.

## HouseWeb (UK)

http://www.houseweb.co.uk • http://www.findaproperty.com
http://www.propertylive.co.uk • http://www.propertyfinder.co.uk
http://www.propertyfile.co.uk • http://www.property-sight.co.uk

Rent, buy, or sell property within the UK.

## ihavemoved.com (UK)

http://www.ihavemoved.com

Bulk notify UK companies of your new address.

## International Real Estate Digest

http://www.ired.com

Locate real estate listings, guides, and property-related services worldwide.

## Postcode Plants Database (UK)

http://fff.nhm.ac.uk/fff/

Find the right native trees, shrubs, and flowers for your area.

### Realtor.com (US)

http://www.realtor.com

Lists over a million US properties.

### Spring Street

http://www.springstreet.com • http://www.apartments.com

Rent or buy a US apartment.

### This to That

http://www.thistothat.com

So what would you like to glue today?

### UpMyStreet

http://www.upmystreet.com

Astounding wealth of house price, health, crime, schools, tax, and other statistics on UK neighborhoods. Mighty useful if you're shifting base.

## Kids (mostly)

It's your choice whether you want to let them at it headlong or bridle their experience through rose-colored filters. But if you need guidance, or pointers towards the most kidtastic chowder, set sail into these realms:

| | |
|---|---|
| **About.com (Kids)** | http://www.about.com/kids/ |
| **American Libraries Assoc** | |
| http://www.ala.org/parentspage/greatsites/ | |
| **Australian Families Guide** | http://www.aba.gov.au/family/ |
| **Kids Click** | http://www.worldsofsearching.org |
| **Kids Domain** | http://www.kidsdomain.com |
| **Kids Identifying and Discovering Sites** | http://kids.library.wisc.edu |
| **Lightspan** | http://www.lightspan.com |
| **Open Directory: Kids** | http://dmoz.org/Home/Kids/ |
| **Scholastic International** | http://www.scholastic.com |
| **Surfing the Net with Kids** | http://www.surfnetkids.com |
| **Yahooligans (Yahoo for kids)** | http://www.yahooligans.com |

The search engines Google and AltaVista can also be set to filter out adult content. For encyclopedias and dictionaries see p.394.

### Adolescent Adulthood

http://www.adolescentadulthood.com

How to flirt, date, kiss, and ultimately dump, so you won't spend the rest of the year being teased at the bus stop.

### Beakman & Jax

http://www.beakman.com

Answers to typical kid questions from the likes of "why poop is brown" and "why farts smell" to "why your voice sounds different on a tape recorder" and "why the TV goes crazy while the mixer is on".

### Bizarre Things You Can Make In Your Kitchen

http://freeweb.pdq.net/headstrong/

Rainy-day science projects and general mischief such as volcanoes, stink bombs, cosmic ray detectors, fake blood, and hurricane machines.

### The Bug Club

http://www.ex.ac.uk/bugclub/

Creepy-crawly fan club with e-pal page, newsletters, and pet care sheets on how to keep your newly bottled tarantulas, cockroaches, and stick insects alive.

### Children's Literature Web Guide

http://www.ucalgary.ca/~dkbrown/

Critical roundup of recent kids' books, and links to texts.

### Club Girl Tech

http://www.girltech.com

Encourages smart girls to get interested in technology without coming across all geeky.

## Cyberteens

http://www.cyberteens.com

Submit your music, art, or writing to a public gallery. You might even win a prize.

## Decoding Nazi Secrets

http://www.pbs.org/wgbh/nova/decoding/ • http://www.thunk.com

Use World War II weaponry to exchange secret messages with your clued-in pals.

## Disney.com

http://www.disney.com

Guided catalog of Disney's real world movies, books, theme parks, records, interactive CD-ROMs and such, plus a squeaky-clean guide to the Net. For an unofficial Disney guide, see:
http://laughingplace.com

## eHobbies

http://www.ehobbies.com

Separating junior hobbyists from their pocket money.

## Funbrain

http://www.funbrain.com

Tons of mind-building quizzes, games, and puzzles for all ages.

## Funschool

http://www.funschool.com

Educational games for preschoolers.

## The History Net

http://www.thehistorynet.com • http://www.historybuff.com

Bites of world history, with an emphasis on the tough guys going in with guns.

## Homework Central

http://www.homeworkcentral.com

Study collections for all grades through to college.

## Kids' Games

http://kidsnetgames.about.com • http://dmoz.org/Home/Kids/Games/
http://www.wicked4kids.com • http://www.kidsdomain.com/games/
http://www.randomhouse.com/seussville/games/
http://games.yahoo.com/games/yahooligans.html

Give the babysitter a break.

## Kids' Jokes

http://www.kidsjokes.com
http://www.users.bigpond.com/lander/default.htm

Reams of clean jokes, riddles and knock-knocks.

## Kids' Space

http://www.kids-space.org

Hideout for kids to swap art, music, and stories with new friends
across the world.

## Learn2

http://learn2.com

Figure out how to do all sorts of things from fixing a zipper to
spinning a basketball. While the interests aren't strictly for kids,
there's nothing here that's too hard for a whippersnapper.

## The Little Animals Activity Centre

http://www.bbc.co.uk/education/laac/

The second the music starts and the critters start jiggling you'll know you're in for a treat. Let your youngest heir loose here after breakfast and expect no mercy until morning tea. You won't find cuter.

## Magic Tricks

http://www.magictricks.com • http://www.trickshop.com

Never believe it's not so.

## Poketech

http://www.poketech.com

Study at the academy of Pokemon trainers.

## Roper's Knots

http://www.realknots.com

It's not what you know; it's what knots you know.

## Sing Along Midis and Lyrics

http://www.niehs.nih.gov/kids/musicchild.htm

Gather round for a spot of keyboard karaoke.

## StarChild

http://starchild.gsfc.nasa.gov

Nasa's educational funhouse for junior astronomers. See also:
http://www.earthsky.com

## Starwars Origami

http://fyl.xymox.net/sworigmi.htm

Graduate from flapping birds onto Destroyer Droids and Tie Fighters.
Prefer something that will actually fly? See: http://www.artcraft.com

## Toy Stores

http://www.etoys.com (.co.uk) • http://www.toysrus.com (.co.uk)
http://www.faoschwartz.com • http://www.imaginarium.com

It's just like Xmas all year round.

## Web66: International School Web Site Directory

http://web66.coled.umn.edu/schools.html

Add your school's Web page if it's not already listed.

## White House for Kids

http://www.whitehouse.gov/WH/kids/html/kidshome.html

Follow Socks through the White House to uncover its previous
inhabitants, including the kids and pets. Then, write to the resident
moggy and get the goss on what goes down in DC after dark.

## The Yuckiest Site on the Internet

http://www.yucky.com

Fun science with a leaning towards the icky-sticky and the creepy-
crawly. But if you want to get thoroughly engrossed in the gross,
slither right along to: http://www.grossology.org

# Law and Crime

For legal primers, lawyer directories, legislation and self-help:

| | |
|---|---|
| **Australian Legal Info Inst** | http://www.austlii.edu.au |
| **Dan's Index (AU)** | http://www.spirit.net.au/~dan/law/ |
| **Delia Venables (UK)** | http://www.venables.co.uk |
| **FindLaw (INT)** | http://www.findlaw.com |
| **Free Advice (US)** | http://www.freeadvice.com |
| **InfoLaw (UK)** | http://www.infolaw.co.uk |
| **Law.com (US)** | http://www.law.com |
| **Lawoffice.com (US)** | http://www.lawoffice.com |
| **Lawrights (UK)** | http://www.lawrights.co.uk |
| **'Lectric Law (US)** | http://www.lectlaw.com |
| **Nolo.com (US)** | http://www.nolo.com |
| **UKLegal (UK)** | http://www.uklegal.com |

## Copyright Myths

http://whatiscopyright.org

http://www.templetons.com/brad/copyright.html

Just because it's online, doesn't make it yours.

## Crime Magazine

http://www.crimemagazine.com

Encyclopedic collection of outlaw tales.

## CrimeNet (AU)

http://www.crimenet.com.au

Pay to search a database of Aussie crims.

## Cybercrime

http://www.cybercrime.gov

How to report online crooks.

## Desktop Lawyer (UK)

http://www.desktoplawyer.net

Cut legal costs by doing it online.

### Dumb Laws

http://www.dumblaws.com

Foreign legislation with limited appeal.

### ECLS

http://www.e-commercelawsource.com

Global monitor and directory of online business law.

### Police Officer's Directory

http://www.officer.com • http://www.cops.aust.com (AUS)
http://www.crimespider.com

Top of the pops cop directory with more than 1500 baddy-nabbing
bureaus snuggled in with law libraries, wanted listings, investigative
tools, hate groups, special ops branches, and off-duty home pages.
To see who's in Scotland Yard's bad books:
http://www.met.police.uk

### PursuitWatch

http://www.pursuitwatch.com

Get paged when there's a live police chase on TV.

### Rate your risk

http://www.nashville.net/~police/risk/

See if you're likely to be raped, robbed, stabbed, shot, or beaten to
death in the near future.

# Money

If your bank's on the ball it will offer an online facility to check your balances, pay your bills, transfer funds, and export your transaction records into a bean counting program such as Quicken or Money. If that sounds appealing, and your bank isn't already on the case, start looking for a replacement. Favor one you can access via the Internet rather than by dialing direct. That way you can manage your cash through a Web browser whether you're at home, work, or in the cybercafé on top of Pik Kommunisma. For help finding a true online bank:

| | |
|---|---|
| **MyBank** | http://www.mybank.com |
| **Online Banking Report** | http://www.netbanker.com |
| **Qualisteam** | http://www.qualisteam.com |

As long as you can resist the urge to daytrade away your inheritance, the Net should give you greater control over your financial future. You can research firms, plot trends, check live quotes, join tip lists and stock forums, track your portfolio live, trade shares, and access more news than is fit to read in a life-time. By all means investigate a subscription service or two – at least for the free trial period – but unless you need split second data feeds or "expert" timing advice you should be able to get by without paying. Start here:

| | |
|---|---|
| **Yahoo Finance** | http://quote.yahoo.com |

or local counterpart such as

| | |
|---|---|
| **Yahoo Australia** | http://quote.yahoo.com.au |
| **Yahoo UK** | http://quote.yahoo.co.uk |

Apart from housing the Net's most exhaustive finance directory, Yahoo pillages data from a bunch of the top finance sources and presents it all in a seamless, friendly format. Enter a stock code, for example, and you'll get all the beef from the latest ticker price to a summary of insider trades. In some markets stocks have their own forums, which, let's face it, are only there to spread rumors. In other words, be very skeptical of anything you read or that's sent to you in unsolicited email.

Yahoo is by no means complete nor necessarily the best in every area, so try a few of these as well:

| | |
|---|---|
| **ABC (AU)** | http://www.abc.net.au/news/business/ |
| **Bloomberg (INT)** | http://www.bloomberg.com |
| **CBS MarketWatch** | http://cbs.marketwatch.com |
| **Egoli (AU)** | http://www.egoli.com.au |
| **FinancialWeb** | http://www.financialweb.com |
| **Free Real Time Quotes** | http://www.freerealtime.com |
| **Gay Financial Network** | http://www.gfn.com |
| **Interactive Investor (UK, SA, Asia)** | http://www.iii.co.uk |
| **Investorama** | http://www.investorama.com |
| **Market Eye (UK)** | http://www.market-eye.co.uk |
| **MetaMarkets** | http://www.metamarkets.com |
| **Microsoft MoneyCentral** | http://moneycentral.msn.com |
| **Money Extra (UK)** | http://www.moneyextra.com |
| **Quicken (US, AU)** | http://www.quicken.com (.au) |
| **Raging Bull** | http://www.ragingbull.com |
| **The Street (US, UK)** | http://www.thestreet.com (.co.uk) |
| **Wall Street City** | http://www.wallstreetcity.com |
| **Wall Street Research Net** | http://www.wsrn.com |

You'll no doubt be after a broker next. As with banking, any broker or fund manager who's not setting up online probably doesn't deserve your business. In fact, many traders are dumping traditional brokers in favor of the exclusively online houses. E★Trade (http://www.etrade.com), for example, offers discount brokerage in at least nine countries (click on "International" to find your local branch). But traditional brokers are catching on. Many have cut their commissions, and offer online services in line with the Internet competition. So it pays to shop around. You might find you prefer to research online and trade by phone. To compare US brokers:

| | |
|---|---|
| **Gomez.com** | http://www.gomez.com |
| **Ms Money** | http://www.msmoney.com |
| **Smart Money** | http://www.smartmoney.com |

If you're outside the US, try your local Yahoo for leads. A word of warning, though: some online brokers have experienced outages where they were unable to trade. So if the market crashes in a big way, it mightn't hurt to play safe and use the phone instead.

## BigCharts

http://www.bigcharts.com

Whip up family-sized graphs of US stocks, mutual funds, and market indices. Or if you'd prefer them streaming at you live, proceed to: http://www.livecharts.com

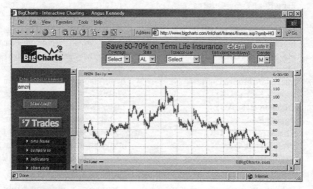

## Clearstation

http://www.clearstation.com

Run your stock picks through a succession of grueling obstacle courses to weed out the weaklings or simply copy someone else's portfolio.

## DataChimp

http://www.datachimp.com

Plain English primer in the mechanics of financial maths.

## Earnings Whispers

http://www.earningswhispers.com

When a stock price falls upon the release of higher than expected earnings, chances are the expectations being "whispered" amongst traders prior to open were higher than those circulated publicly. Here's where to find out what's being said behind your back. For the biggest surprises, see: http://biz.yahoo.com/z/extreme.html

## Financial Times

http://www.ft.com

Business news, commentary, delayed quotes, and closing prices from London. It's free until you hit the archives.

## Foreign Exchange Rates

http://quote.yahoo.com • http://www.xe.net/ucc/full.shtml

Round-the-clock rates, conversion calculators, and intraday charts on pretty close to the full set of currencies.

To chart further back, see:
http://pacific.commerce.ubc.ca/xr/plot.html

## iCreditReport

http://www.icreditreport.com

Dig up any US citizen's credit ratings.

## iExchange.com

http://www.iexchange.com

Tracks and ranks market prophets.

## Insider Scores

http://www.insiderscores.com

Get the inside on US and Asian directors' trades.

## Intermoney

http://www.intermoney.com

Daily technicals on the international money markets.

## Investment FAQ

http://www.invest-faq.com

Learn the ropes from old hands.

## InvestorWords

http://www.investorwords.com

Can't tell your hedge rate from your asking price? Brush up on your finance-speak here.

### Island

http://www.island.com

See US equity orders queued up on dealers' screens.

### Missing Money

http://www.missingmoney.com • http://www.findcash.com

Reclaim those US dollars you're owed.

### Money Origami

http://www.umva.com/~clay/money/

It's much more fun when you can make something out of it.

### Motley Fool

http://www.fool.com • http://www.fool.co.uk

Forums, tips, quotes, and sound advice.

### Paypal

http://www.paypal.com

Arrange online payments through a third party.

### RateNet

http://www.rate.net • http://www.bankrate.com

Tracks and ranks finance rates across over 11,000 US institutions in 175 markets. Also links to thousands of banking sites and investment products. For UK rates see: http://www.blays.co.uk

### Tax & Accounting Sites Directory

http://www.taxsites.com

Links to everything you need to know about doling out your annual pound of flesh.

### Wall Street Journal Interactive

http://www.wsj.com

Not only is this online edition equal to the print, its charts and data archives give it an edge. That's why you shouldn't complain that it's not free. After all, if it's your type of paper, you should be able to afford it, bigshot. You'll also find Forbes, Barrons, and Fortune at exactly the addresses you'd expect.

# Music

If you're at all into music you've certainly come to the right place. Whether you want to hear it, read about it, or watch it being performed, you'll be swamped with options. If you're after a specific band, label, or music genre, the Ultimate Band List should be your first port of call:

**Ultimate Band List**                           http://www.ubl.com

Followed by these directories:

**About.com**                    http://home.about.com/musicperform/
**Open Directory**                      http://dmoz.org/Arts/Music/
**SonicNet**                    http://www.sonicnet.com/allmusic/
**Yahoo**                              http://music.yahoo.com

For an astoundingly complete music database spanning most popular genres, with bios, reviews, ratings, and keyword crosslinks to related sounds, sites, and online ordering, see:

**All Music Guide**                           http://www.allmusic.com
**iMusic**                                    http://www.imusic.com

And don't overlook our own printed guides to Rock, Reggae, Drum & Bass, Jazz, Classical, House, Techno, Soul, World, and Opera:

**Rough Guides to Music**            http://www.roughguides.com

Feel like singing along but don't know the words? Try tapping the song, performer, or author into SongFile for a hyperconnected rundown on everyone concerned with the tune, and often the lyrics, sheet music and a link to buy it on CD. If it doesn't stock the sheet music, try Yahoo for another dealer.

**Songfile**                                  http://www.songfile.com


Or for rapping rhymes:

**Original Hip Hop Lyrics Archive**           http://www.ohhla.com


Much of the mainstream music press is already well established online. For the latest music news:

**iMusic Newsagent**          http://imusic.interserv.com/newsagent/


You'll find thousands of archived reviews, charts, gig guides, band bios, selected features, shopping links, news, and various sound artifacts courtesy of these familiar beacons:

**Billboard**                       http://www.billboard-online.com
**Blues and Soul**                  http://www.bluesandsoul.co.uk
**Dirty Linen**                     http://kiwi.futuris.net/linen/
**Folk Roots**                      http://www.froots.demon.co.uk
**NME**                                        http://nme.com
**Q**                               http://www.qonline.co.uk
**Rolling Stone**                   http://www.rollingstone.com
**Spin**                            http://www.spin.com
**Vibe**                            http://www.vibe.com


And if your concentration is up to it, MTV:

**Americas**          http://www.mtv.com • http://www.mtvla.com
**Asia Pacific**   http://www.mtvasia.com • http://www.mtv.com.au
**Europe**                          http://www.mtveurope.com
**UK**             http://www.mtv.co.uk • http://www.mtv2.co.uk


Don't buy a stereo component until you've consulted the world's biggest audio opinionbases:

**AudioReview.com**                 http://www.audioreview.com
**AudioWeb**                        http://www.audioweb.com
**What Hi-Fi**                      http://www.whathifi.com

Or if you wouldn't settle for less than a single-ended triode amp:

| | |
|---|---|
| **Audiophilia** | http://www.audiophilia.com |
| **GlassWare** | http://www.glass-ware.com |
| **Stereophile** | http://www.stereophile.com |
| **Triode Guild** | http://www.meta-gizmo.com |

Consult these directories for manufacturers, shops, and other audio sites:

| | |
|---|---|
| **AudioWorld** | http://www.audioworld.com |
| **Hifiheaven.com** | http://www.hifiheaven.com |
| **UK Hi-Fi Dealers** | http://hifi.dealers.co.uk |

## BUYING RECORDS ONLINE

Shopping for music is another area where the Net not only equals, but outshines, its terrestrial counterparts. Apart from the convenience of not having to tramp across town, you can find almost anything on current issue, whether or not it's released locally, and in many cases preview album tracks in RealAudio. You might save money, too, depending on where you buy, whether you're hit with tax, and how the freight stacks up. Consider splitting your order if duty becomes an issue.

The biggest hitch you'll strike is when stock is put on back-order. Web operators can boast a huge catalog simply because they order everything on the fly. This puts you at the mercy of their distributors. The trouble is your entire order might be held up by one item. The better shops check their stock levels before confirming your order, and follow its progress until delivery.

As far as where to shop goes, that depends on your taste. In terms of sheer innovation, Tunes.com stands out by profiling your preferences, recommending selections, linking to reviews, and serving up ample samples. You can't go too far wrong with most of the blockbusters:

| | |
|---|---|
| **Amazon (US, UK)** | http://www.amazon.com (.co.uk) |
| **AudioStreet (UK)** | http://www.audiostreet.co.uk |
| **BOL (INT)** | http://www.bol.com |
| **Book, Music, Video Store** | http://www.bmvs.com |
| **Borders** | http://www.borders.com |
| **Boxman (EUR, UK)** | http://www.boxman.com |
| **CDNow** | http://www.cdnow.com |
| **CD Universe** | http://www.cduniverse.com |
| **Chaos (AUS)** | http://www.cmm.com.au |
| **HMV (AUS, JP, UK, US)** | http://www.hmv.com |
| **Sam Goody** | http://www.samgoody.com |
| **Tower Records** | http://www.towerrecords.com |
| **Tunes.com** | http://www.tunes.com |
| **Virgin Megastore** | http://www.virginmega.com |

Or, if you're after something more obscure, you'll find no shortage of options under the appropriate Yahoo categories or at: http://www.offitsface.com/links.html

Like these, for example:

## CyberCD

http://www.cybercd.de • http://www.musicexpress.com
German outfits with enormous catalogs, though not so cheap.

## Dusty Grooves

http://www.dustygroove.com
Soul, jazz, Latin, Brazil, and funk on vinyl and CD.

## Funk45

http://www.funk45.com
Rare 70s funk and soul.

## Global Electronic Music Market

http://gemm.com

One-point access to over two million new and used records from almost two thousand sources. See also: http://www.musicfile.com and http://www.secondspin.com

## Hard to find records

http://www.hard-to-find.co.uk

Record-finding agency that specializes in house, hip-hop, soul, and disco vinyl.

## Penny Black

http://www.pennyblackmusic.com

Indie pop, punk and electronica.

## Record Finder

http://www.recordfinders.com

Deleted vinyl, including over 200,000 45s.

## Rockinghorse Records (AU)

http://www.rockinghorse.net

Indie, dance and Australian obscurities.

## X-Radio

http://www.x-radio.com

Dub, chill, leftfield, techno, and urban beats.

For a listing of price comparison agents see Shopping (p.216).

# COOKING YOUR OWN CD

Fancy whipping up your own custom CD? Then try out a DIY compilation shop. Simply run through their catalog, preview what looks good, submit your track listing, and they'll burn it to disk:

| | |
|---|---|
| **CD Now** | http://www.cdnow.com |
| **Emusic** | http://www.emusic.com |
| **imix.com** | http://www.imix.com |
| **MusicMaker** | http://www.musicmaker.com |
| **Razorcuts** | http://www.razorcuts.co.uk |

### Addicted to Noise

http://www.addict.com

Monthly news and reviews with a heavy bias towards the rowdy end of the pop rock spectrum.

### Art of the Mixed Tape

http://www.artofthemix.org

"If you have ever killed an afternoon making a mix, spent the evening making a cover, and then mailed a copy off to a friend after having made a copy for yourself, well, this is the site for you". Kind of says it all.

### Canonical List of Weird Band Names

http://www.geminiweb.net/bandnames/

Just be thankful your parents weren't so creative. Here's the story behind a few: http://www.heathenworld.com/bandname/

### CDDB

http://www.cddb.com

Automatically supplies track listings for the CDs playing in your PC drive.

### Classical Music on the Net

http://www.musdoc.com/classical/ • http://www.gmn.com/classical/

Gateway to the timeless.

### The Dance Music Resource

http://www.juno.co.uk

New and forthcoming dance releases for mail order, UK radio slots, and a stacked link directory. See also: http://www.fly.co.uk

### Dancetech

http://www.dancetech.com

One-stop shop for techno toys and recording tips. For more on synths: http://www.synthzone.com and http://www.sonicstate.com

### Dial-the-Truth Ministries

http://www.av1611.org

So why does Satan get all the good music?

### DJ University

http://dju.prodj.com

Become a wedding spinner.

### dotmusic

http://www.dotmusic.com

Top source of UK and global music news, weekly charts, and new releases in RealAudio. See also: http://www.music3w.com

### Getoutthere.bt.com

http://www.getoutthere.bt.com

Expose your unsung talents or listen to other unsigned acts.

### Harmony Central

http://www.harmonycentral.com

Directory and headspace for musicians of all persuasions.

### Independent Underground Music Archive

http://www.iuma.com

Full-length tracks and bios from thousands of unsigned and indie-label underground musicians.

### Jazz

http://www.jazzreview.com • http://www.allaboutjazz.com
http://www.downbeatjazz.com

Bottomless drawer of beard-stroking delights.

### Kareoke.com

http://www.kareoke.com

Sing along in the privacy of your own home.

### Live Concerts

http://www.liveconcerts.com

Major gigs live in RealAudio.

### MIDI Farm

http://www.midifarm.com

Synthesized debasements of pop tunes, TV themes, and film scores. Cheesy listening at its finest.

## Mr Lucky

http://www.mrlucky.com

Get smooth with rhythm 'n' booze.

## Launch.com

http://www.launch.com

Thousands of music videos, audio channels, record reviews and chat forums.

## Scorchin' Soul

http://www.scorchinsoul.co.uk • http://www.soulcity.ndo.co.uk

Listen to hundreds of 60s and Northern Soul clips.

## Scratch.dk

http://www.scratch.dk

Rated as the number-one hip-hop site by no less an authority than this site itself. More tough talk at http://www.thesource.com and http://www.hiphopsite.com and http://www.rebirthmag.com Gesticulating hands on decks at: http://www.wicked-styles.com and http://www.turntablism.com

### Shareware Music Machine

http://www.hitsquad.com/smm/

Tons of shareware music players, editors, and composition tools, for every platform.

### Sonic Net

http://www.sonicnet.com

Big-name live cybercasts, streaming audio and video channels, chats, news, and reviews.

### Sony

http://www.sony.com

Think about everything that Sony flogs. Now imagine it all squeezed under one roof.

### Sounds Online

http://www.soundsonline.com

Preview loops and samples, free in RealAudio. Pay to download studio quality. If it's effects you're after: http://www.sounddogs.com

### SS7x7 Sound System

http://www.ss7x7.com

Mix your own tracks in Shockwave. Or have a bit of a scratch: http://www.turntables.de

### Taxi

http://www.taxi.com

Online music A&R service. And guess what? You and your plastic kazoo are just what they're looking for.

### WholeNote

http://www.wholenote.com

Guitar resources and chat boards. For live lessons, see:
http://www.riffinteractive.com

For more music of the live streaming variety, fast forward to the Radio section (p.391) and for MP3s see: (p.218).

# Nature

### 3D Insects

http://www.ento.vt.edu/~sharov/3d/3dinsect.html

Whiz around a selection of 3D bugs. They're not real insects but at least they don't have pins through their backs. For a bigger range of bug bios see: http://insects.org

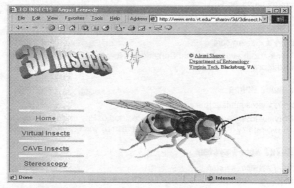

### Australian Botanical Gardens

http://www.anbg.gov.au

Guide to Canberra's Botanical Garden and flora down under.

### Bad Pets

http://www.geocities.com/bad_pets/

Animal owners speak out.

### Birding

http://birding.about.com • http://www.camacdonald.com/birding/
http://dmoz.org/Recreation/Birdwatching/

Birds are such regional critters no one site could hope to cover them all. Use these to find the chirpiest one on your block.

## Carniverous Plants FAQ

http://www.sarracenia.com/cp.html

Erect your first line of defense.

## The Complete Hamster site

http://www.hamsters.co.uk • http://www.direct.ca./hamster/

Definitive guides to online hamsters and their inevitable obituaries.

## Dog of the Day

http://www.dogoftheday.com

Submit a shot of that drooling retard that adores you unconditionally. Or if it has its own Web page enter it in Dog Site of the Day: http://www.st.rim.or.jp/~ito/d/dogmark.html

No prize for guessing what's at http://www.catoftheday.com and http://www.petoftheday.com

## eNature.com

http://www.enature.com

Vibrant field guides to North American flora and fauna.

## Environmental Organization Directory

http://www.webdirectory.com • http://www.eco-portal.com

Find primary production and green-minded sites.

## F@rming Online

http://www.rpl.com.au/farming/ • http://www.farmwide.com.au

Gateways to predominantly Australian agricultural resources.

## ForestWorld

http://www.forestworld.com • http://forests.org

Timber tales from both sides of the dozer.

## Internet Directory for Botany

http://www.botany.net/IDB/ • http://botany.about.com

Starting points for serious plantlife research.

### Interspecies Telepathic Communication

http://www.cyberark.com/animal/telepath.htm

Relax, you're not hearing voices. It's merely your pets playing mind games.

### Pet Shops

http://www.pets.com • http://www.dogtoys.com

http://www.petsonthebrain.com (UK) • http://www.pets-pyjamas.co.uk (UK)

Seduce your mate with a rubber love-toy.

### Planet Ark

http://www.planetark.org

Daily environmental news from Reuters.

### Predator Urines

http://www.predatorpee.com

Bewitch neighboring Jack Russells with a dab of bobcat balm.

### Sea turtle migration-tracking

http://www.cccturtle.org/satwelc.htm

Adopt a bugged sea reptile and follow its trail.

### Veterinary Medicine

http://vetmedicine.about.com • http://netvet.wustl.edu

Take good care of your little buddy.

the Hamster page

# News, Newspapers, and Magazines

Now that almost every magazine and newspaper in the world from Ringing World (http://www.luna.co.uk/~ringingw/) to the Falkland Island News (http://www.sartma.com) is discharging daily content onto the Net, it's beyond this guide to do much more than list a few of the notables and then point you in the right direction for more. The simplest way to find your favorite read would be to look for its address in a recent issue. Failing that try entering its name into a subject guide or search engine. If you don't have a title name and would prefer to browse by subject or region, try:

| | |
|---|---|
| **Open Directory** | http://dmoz.org/News/ |
| **Yahoo** | http://dir.yahoo.com/News_and_Media/ |

Or a specialist directory:

| | |
|---|---|
| **AJR NewsLink** | http://ajr.newslink.org/news.html |
| **Editor & Publisher** | http://www.mediainfo.com |
| **Metagrid** | http://www.metagrid.com |
| **NewsDirectory** | http://www.newsdirectory.com |
| **Publist** | http://www.publist.com |
| **Ultimate Collection** | http://pppp.net/links/news/ |
| **UK Media Directory** | http://www.mediauk.com/directory/ |
| **WebWombat** | http://www.webwombat.com.au |

Newspapers rarely replicate themselves word for word online, but they often provide enough for you to live without the paper edition. Not bad considering they're generally free online before the paper hits the stands. Apart from whatever proportion of their print they choose to put online, they also tend to delve deeper into their less newsy areas, such as travel, IT, entertainment, and culture. Plus they often bolster this with exclusive content such as breaking news, live sports coverage, online shopping, opinion polls, and discussion groups. In most cases they'll also provide a way to search and retrieve archives, though it might incur a charge. There are also a few sites that index multiple news archives, again, usually at a price. Such as:

| | |
|---|---|
| **Electric Library** | http://www.elibrary.com |
| **NewsLibrary (US)** | http://www.newslibrary.com |
| **Northern Light** | http://www.nlsearch.com |

The best free services for searching current or recent stories across hundreds of international news sources are:

| | |
|---|---|
| **Moreover** | http://www.moreover.com |
| **News Index** | http://www.newsindex.com |

A few of the more popular news bugles, to get you started:

# Australia

| | |
|---|---|
| **The Age** | http://www.theage.com.au |
| **The Australian** | http://www.news.com.au |
| **Sydney Morning Herald** | http://www.smh.com.au |

# UK

| | |
|---|---|
| **Economist** | http://www.economist.com |
| **Evening Standard** | http://www.thisislondon.co.uk |
| **Express** | http://www.express.co.uk |
| **Guardian** | http://www.guardian.co.uk |
| **Independent** | http://www.independent.co.uk |
| **Mirror** | http://www.mirror.co.uk |
| **The Sun** | http://www.the-sun.co.uk |
| **Telegraph** | http://www.telegraph.co.uk |
| **Times** | http://www.the-times.co.uk |

# USA

| | |
|---|---|
| **Boston Globe** | http://www.globe.com |
| **Chicago News Network** | http://www.chicago-news.com |
| **Christian Science Monitor** | http://www.csmonitor.com |
| **Detroit News** | http://www.detroitnews.com |
| **Houston Chronicle** | http://www.chron.com |
| **LA Times** | http://www.latimes.com |

| | |
|---|---|
| National Enquirer | http://www.nationalenquirer.com |
| National Geographic News | http://www.ngnews.com |
| Newsweek | http://www.newsweek.com |
| NY Post | http://www.nypost.com |
| NY Times | http://www.nytimes.com |
| The Onion | http://www.theonion.com |
| Philadelphia Newspapers | http://www.philly.com |
| San Francisco Gate | http://www.sfgate.com |
| San Jose Mercury | http://www.sjmercury.com |
| Seattle Times | http://www.seattletimes.com |
| Time Daily | http://www.time.com |
| USA Today | http://www.usatoday.com |
| Village Voice | http://www.villagevoice.com |
| Washington Post | http://www.washingtonpost.com |
| Weekly World News | http://www.wooklyworldnews.com |

## World

| | |
|---|---|
| Bangkok Post | http://www.bangkokpost.net |
| Daily Mail & Guardian | http://www.mg.co.za |
| El País | http://www.elpais.es |
| Frankfurter Allgemeine | http://www.faz.de |
| The Hindu | http://www.hinduonline.com |
| Irish Times | http://www.ireland.com |
| Jerusalem Post | http://www.jpost.com |
| La Stampa | http://www.lastampa.it |
| Le Monde | http://www.lemonde.fr |
| South China Morning Post | http://www.scmp.com |
| St Petersburg Times | http://www.sptimes.ru |
| Times of India | http://www.timesofindia.com |
| Toronto Star | http://www.thestar.com |

Like much you do online, reading news is addictive. You'll know you're hooked when you find yourself checking into newswires throughout the day to monitor moving stories. Try these for a fix:

## Breaking News

| | |
|---|---|
| ABC (Aus) | http://www.abc.net.au/news/ |
| ABC | http://www.abcnews.com |
| Ananova (UK) | http://www.ananova.com |
| Associated Press | http://wire.ap.org |
| BBC (UK) | http://news.bbc.co.uk |
| CBS | http://www.cbsnews.com |
| CNN | http://www.cnn.com |
| Fox | http://www.foxnews.com |
| ITN (UK) | http://www.itn.co.uk |
| NBC | http://www.msnbc.com |
| News24 (SA) | http://www.news24.co.za |
| Paknews (Pak) | http://www.paknews.org |
| Reuters | http://www.reuters.com |
| Satayam (Ind) | http://www.news.satyamonline.com |
| Sky (UK) | http://www.sky.com |
| Sydney Morning Herald (Aus) | http://www.smh.com.au/breaking/ |
| Wired News | http://www.wired.com |

To tap into several sources simultaneously:

## News Aggregators

| | |
|---|---|
| Arts & Letters Daily | http://www.cybereditions.com/aldaily/ |
| Excite Newstracker | http://nt.excite.com |
| FastAsia (Asia) | http://www.fastasia.com |
| Moreover (World) | http://www.moreover.com |
| NewsHub | http://www.newshub.com |
| NewsNow (UK) | http://www.newsnow.co.uk |
| Russian Story | http://www.russianstory.com |
| TotalNews | http://www.totalnews.com |
| Yahoo News | http://dailynews.yahoo.com |

Most of the major portals such as Excite, Yahoo and MSN, also allow you to create a custom news page that draws from several sources, though none do it quite so thoroughly as Crayon. Infobeat does similar but delivers by email.

**Crayon** http://www.crayon.net
**Infobeat** http://www.infobeat.com

While most magazines maintain a site, they're typically more of an adjunct to the print than a substitute. Still, they're worth checking out, especially if they archive features and reviews, or break news between issues. Again, check a recent issue or one of the directories for an address. If you'd rather subscribe to the paper edition try:

http://enews.com • http://www.mmnews.com
http://www.britishmagazines.com (UK) • http://www.acp.com.au (AUS)

Then there are the "ezines" – magazines that exist only online, or are delivered by email. However as almost any regularly updated Web page fits this description, the term has lost much of its currency. Although most ezines burn out as quickly as they appear, a few of the pioneers are still kicking on. The best known, or at least the most controversial, would be the Drudge Report, the shock bulletin that set off the Lewinsky avalanche. A one-hit wonder perhaps, but still a bona-fide tourist attraction on the info goat track. Salon, however, is the real success story. It spans the arts, business, politics, lifestyle, and technology in a style that's both smart and breezy. Microsoft's long-suffering Slate marks similar territory, but succeeds more in being terribly dull. While Suck, arguably the only ezine that ever mattered, sits in a smug class all by itself. Worth reading daily, if not for its cocked eye on all that's wired and painfully modern, then at least for Terry Colon's cartoons.

| | |
|---|---|
| **Drudge Report** | http://www.drudgereport.com |
| **Salon** | http://www.salon.com |
| **Slate** | http://slate.msn.com |
| **Suck** | http://www.suck.com |

While most ezines operate independently, there are two networks that will connect you to a slew of quality underground productions of almost opposite persuasions. You'll know instantly whether they're your scene:

| | |
|---|---|
| **Chick Click** | http://www.chickclick |
| **UGO** | http://www.ugo.com |

For more, try browsing one of the directories listed at: http://dmoz.org/News/Ezines/Directories/

# Personal, Friendship, and Advice

## Adoption.com

http://www.adoption.com • http://www.adopting.org
http://www.bastards.org

Find a child or your original parents. Or if you suspect Screaming Jay put a spell on your Momma: http://www.jayskids.com

## Alien Implant Removal and Deactivation

http://www.abduct.com/irm.htm

Discover, within a free three-minute phone call, how many times you've been abducted and which implants you're carrying. Then it's just a matter of surgically removing them: http://www.alienscalpel.com and sorting out your mental health. Perhaps the latter is all that's needed.

## Ask-a-Chick

http://www.ask-a-chick.com

Boys ask girls to set them straight.

## Astrology – Atlas and Time Zone Database

http://www.astro.com/atlas/

Know exactly what was happening upstairs the second of your birth.
Or if you prefer your zodiac readings with a touch less
pseudoscientific mumbo jumbo, try:
http://www.bubble.com/webstars/ or http://astrology.net
Now see what old sensible shoes has to say:
http://www.skepdic.com/astrolgy.html

## Breakup Girl

http://www.breakupgirl.com

How to mend a broken heart and get on with your life. Here's how not
to do it:

http://www.crazy-bitch.com

## ClassMates.com

http://www.classmates.com

You haven't forgotten. Now track them down one by one.

## Cyberspace Inmates

http://www.cyberspace-inmates.com

Strike up an email romance with a prison inmate; maybe even one on death row.

## Dating Directories

http://www.cupidnet.com • http://www.singlesites.com

http://www.100hot.com/directory/lifestyles/dating.html

Come aboard, they're expecting you.

## Digital Voodoo

http://www.pinstruck.com

Curse thy neighbor.

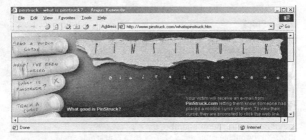

## DirectWish

http://www.directwish.com

Yearn into space.

## Famous Birthdays

http://www.famousbirthdays.com • http://us.imdb.com/OnThisDay

See who shares your birthday.

## Final Thoughts

http://www.finalthoughts.com • http://www.mydeath.net

Plot your legacy.

## Greeting Cards

http://www.postcardsindex.com • http://www.postcard-heaven.com
http://www.postcards.com • http://www.cardcentral.net

If stretching the bounds of good taste doesn't bother you, you'll find thousands of sites that will gladly speckle your message with multimedia tutti-frutti. Rather than forward your "card" directly, your victim will generally receive an invitation to drop by and collect it from the site. And of course being masked by a third party makes it perfect for harassing valentines and sending ransom notes. The above directories list hundreds of virtual card dispensers but check out the most popular ones first:

| | |
|---|---|
| **Blue Mountain** | http://www.bluemountain.com |
| **eGreetings** | http://www.egreetings.com |
| **Hallmark** | http://www.hallmark.com |
| **Pulp Cards** | http://www.pulpcards.com |
| **Tackymail** | http://www.tackymail.com |
| **Virtual Insults** | http://www.virtualinsults.com |
| **Yahoo Greetings** | http://greetings.yahoo.com |

### Guy's Rules

http://www.guyrules.com

Learn to conceal your latent femininity.

### Hotpaper.com

http://www.hotpaper.com

Fill in the blanks to create handy everyday documents like references, eviction notices, and credit card disputes.

## I Ching

http://www.facade.com/Occult/iching/

If the superior person is not happy with their fortune as told by this ancient Chinese oracle, one can always reload and get another one.

## Interflora

http://www.interflora.com

Punch in your credit card number, apology, and delivery details, and land back in the good books before you get home. Or for the opposite effect: http://www.dropdeadflorist.com

## Invites

http://invites.yahoo.com • http://www.mambo.com

http://www.egreetings.com • http://www.timedance.com

Throwing a slide night? Here's an easy way to create an instant email invitation and manage the thousands of RSVPs. For help planning: http://www.theplunge.com

## IPrint

http://www.iprint.com • http://www.cardcorp.co.uk (UK)

Need some business cards or invitations fast? Design them online for snappy delivery either via email or on the paper of your choice. Naturally, the latter option costs.

## Love Calculator

http://www.lovecalculator.com

Enter your respective names to see if you're compatible.

## Miss Abigail's Time Warp Advice

http://www.missabigail.com

Solve modern dilemmas with old school logic.

## National Center for Missing and Exploited Children

http://www.missingkids.org • http://www.missingkids.co.uk

Help locate missing children and nail abductors.

## Pen Pal Directory

http://www.yahoo.com/Society_and_Culture/Relationships/Pen_Pals/

Exchange email with strangers.

## PlanetOut

http://www.planetout.com • http://www.rainbownetwork.com (UK)
http://www.qrd.org • http://www.datalounge.com

Directories to all that's that way inclined.

## Random Access Memory

http://www.randomaccessmemory.org

Store your treasured memories in a safe place.

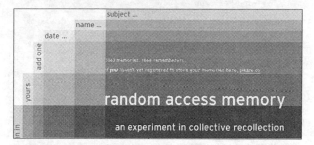

## Secret Admirer

http://www.secretadmirer.com • http://www.ecrush.com

Find out whether your most secret crushed one digs you back.

## So There

http://www.sothere.com

A place to post your parting shots.

## Swoon

http://www.swoon.com

Dating, mating, and relating. Courtesy of Condé Nast's Details, GQ, Glamour, and Mademoiselle. For desert, try: http://www.xseeksy.com and http://dating.about.com

## Toilet Tea Leaves

http://home.golden.net/~treleavn/toilet2.html

Predict your future using the most reliable technique.

## Trace your Ancestry

Don't expect to enter your name and produce an instant family tree, but you should be able to fill in a few gaps:

http://www.genhomepage.com • http://www.genealogytoday.com
http://www.familytreemaker.com • http://www.cyndislist.com
http://www.ancestry.com • http://www.familysearch.org
http://www.rootsweb.com

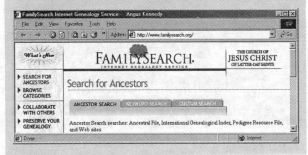

## Vampire Exchange

http://www.vein-europe.demon.co.uk
http://members.tripod.com/~Sanguinarius/
Give blood as an act of love.

## Virtual Presents

http://www.virtualpresents.com • http://www.it3c.co.uk
Why waste money on real gifts when, after all, isn't it the thought that counts?

## Weddings in the Real World

http://www.theknot.com • http://www.nearlywed.com
Prepare to jump the broom, or untie the knot:
http://www.divorcesource.com

# Politics and Government

Most government departments, politicians, political aspirants and causes maintain Web sites to spread the word and further their various interests. To find your local rep or candidate, start at their party's home page. These typically lay dormant unless there's a campaign in progress but can still be a good source of contacts to badger. Government departments, on the other hand, tirelessly belch out all sorts of trivia right down to the transcripts of ministerial radio interviews. So if you'd like to know about impending legislation, tax rulings, budget details and so forth, skip the party pages and go straight to the department. If you can't find its address through what we list below, try **Yahoo** (http://dir.yahoo.com/Government/), **GovSpot** (http://www.govspot.com), or better still, jump on the phone.

For the **latest counts from the tally room** check the breaking news sites (p.376) on **election night**. Below is a selection of the most useful starting points in Australia, Britain, and the US:

## Australia

| | |
|---|---|
| **Democrats** | http://www.democrats.org.au |
| **Federal Government** | http://www.fed.gov.au |
| **John Howard** | http://www.pm.gov.au |
| **Labour** | http://www.alp.org.au |
| **Liberals** | http://www.liberal.org.au |
| **Nationals** | http://www.npa.org.au |
| **State & Local entry point** | http://www.nla.gov.au/oz/gov/ |

## UK

| | |
|---|---|
| **Tony Blair** | http://www.pm.gov.uk |
| **British Politics Links** | http://www.ukpol.co.uk |
| **Government Portal** | http://www.open.gov.uk |
| **Labour** | http://www.labour.org.uk |
| **Liberal Democrats** | http://www.libdems.org.uk |
| **Natural Law** | http://www.natural-law-party.org.uk |
| **Scottish Parliament** | http://www.scottish-parliament.com |
| **Sinn Féin** | http://www.sinnfein.ie |
| **Tories** | http://www.conservative-party.org.uk |

# USA

| | |
|---|---|
| **Democratic National Committee** | http://www.democratics.org |
| **FedWorld** | http://www.fedworld.gov |
| **Friends of Jesse Ventura** | http://www.jesseventura.org |
| **Gov. Information Exchange** | http://www.info.gov |
| **Greens** | http://www.greenparty.org |
| **House of Reps** | http://www.house.gov |
| **Political Index** | http://www.politicalindex.com |
| **Political Resources** | http://www.politicalresources.com |
| **Republican National Committee** | http://www.rnc.org |
| **Senate** | http://www.senate.gov |
| **Thomas (search Congress)** | http://thomas.loc.gov |
| **WebActive Directory** | http://www.webactive.com/directory/ |
| **The Whitehouse** | http://www.whitehouse.gov |

### Adopt an MP (UK)

http://www.stand.org.uk

Pester your local member to protect privacy online.

### Amnesty International

http://www.amnesty.org

Join the battle against brutal regimes and injustice.

### Antiwar

http://www.antiwar.com • http://www.iacenter.org

Challenges US intervention in foreign affairs, especially the Balkans.

### The British Monarchy

http://www.royal.gov.uk • http://www.royalnetwork.com

Tune into the world's best-loved soap opera.

### Center for the Moral Defence of Capitalism

http://www.moraldefense.com • http://www.aynrand.org

Questions the DOJ's right to split Microsoft.

### Central Intelligence Agency

http://www.cia.gov

You're well informed. You watch TV and read the Weekly World News. So naturally you want the inside on political assassinations, arms deals, Colombian drug trades, spy satellites, phone tapping, covert operations, government-sponsored alien sex cults, and the X-files. Well, guess what? Never mind, you won't go home without a prize:

http://www.copvcia.com • http://www.magnet.ch/serendipity/cia.html

### Communist Internet List

http://www.cominternet.org

Angry intellectuals and workers unite.

### Conspiracies

http://www.mt.net/~watcher/ • http://www.conspire.com

There's no doubt about it. Certain people are up to something and what's worse they're probably all in it together. If these exposés of the sixty biggest cover-ups of all time aren't proof enough, then do your bit and create one that's more convincing:
http://www.turnleft.com/conspiracy.html

### Council for Aboriginal Reconciliation

http://www.reconciliation.org.au

Unfinished business in the Lucky (for some) Country.

### Disinformation

http://www.disinfo.com

The dark side of politics, religious fervor, new science, and current affairs you won't find in the papers.

### DOE Openness: Human Radiation Experiments

http://tis-nt.eh.doe.gov/ohre/

The improbable annals of Cold War research into nuking human flesh to see what happens.

### FBI FOIA Reading Room

http://foia.fbi.gov

FBI documents released as part of the Freedom of Information Act. Includes a few files on such celebrities as John Wayne, Elvis, Marilyn, and the British Royals. Check out who's most wanted now at: http://www.fbi.gov

### Foreign Report

http://www.foreignreport.com

Compact subscription newsletter with a track record of predicting international flashpoints well before the dailies.

### The Gallup Organization

http://www.gallup.com

Keep up to date with opinion trends and ratings such as the fickle swings of Free World Willy's popularity.

### German Propaganda Archives

http://www.calvin.edu/cas/gpa/

Who did you think you were kidding, Mr Hitler?

### Grassroots.com (US)

http://www.grassroots.com

Tracks political action and election policies across the board, aided by TV Nation champ Michael Moore: (http://www.michaelmoore.com).

### Greenpeace International

http://www.greenpeace.org

Rebels with many a good cause.

### Hatewatch

http://www.hatewatch.org • http://www.splcenter.org

Shining the public flashlight on hate groups.

### InfoWar

http://www.infowar.com

Warfare issues from prank hacking to industrial espionage and military propaganda.

## Jane's IntelWeb

http://intelweb.janes.com

Brief updates on political disturbances, terrorism, intelligence agencies, and subterfuge worldwide. For a full directory of covert operations, see:

http://www.virtualfreesites.com/covert.html

## National Charities Information Bureau

http://www.ncib.org

Investigate before you donate.

## National Forum on People's Differences

http://www.yforum.com

Toss around touchy topics such as race, religion, and sexuality, with a sincerity that is normally tabooed by political politeness.

## One World

http://www.oneworld.org

Collates news from over 350 global justice organizations.

## Open Secrets

http://www.opensecrets.org

Track whose money is oiling the wheels of US politics.

More keeping 'em honest at: http://www.commoncause.org

## Oxfam

http://www.oxfam.org

Pitch in to fight poverty and inequality.

## The Progressive Review

http://emporium.turnpike.net/P/ProRev/

Washington dirt dug up from all sides of the fence. For darker soil, try: http://www.realchange.org

## Protest.net – A Calendar of Protest Worldwide

http://protest.net

Riot down your alley.

## Revolutionary Association of the Women of Afghanistan

http://www.rawa.org

And you think you have problems with men: http://www.taleban.com.

## Spunk Press

http://www.spunk.org

All the anarchy you'll ever need organized neatly and with reassuring authority.

## Trinity Atomic Web Site

http://www.fas.org/nuke/trinity/

See what went on, and what went off, fifty-odd years ago, then file into the archives of high-energy weapon testing, and see who else has been sharpening the tools of world peace.

## US Census Bureau

http://www.census.gov

More statistics on the US and its citizens than you'd care to know. For UK stats, see: //www.statisitcs.gov.uk

## US Presidential Candidates and their Evil Genes

http://www.nenavadno.com/usaelections2000.html

Biocybernetic criminals from the 33rd dimension take America.

# Radio and Webcasts

While almost all radio stations have a Web site, only a fraction pipe their transmissions online. The ever-increasing percentage that do, usually broadcast (Webcast) in RealAudio and/or Windows Media Format (see p.221), so grab the latest copies of both before setting out. Both players come with inbuilt station directories along with Web-based event guides which are fine for starting out but nowhere near complete. Yahoo and Voquette also run services that keep tabs on notable audiovisual happenings:

| | |
|---|---|
| **RealGuide** | http://realguide.real.com |
| **Voquette** | http://www.voquette.com |
| **Windows Media Guide** | http://windowsmedia.com |
| **Yahoo Broadcast** | http://www.broadcast.com |

Not enough? Then try one of the specialist radio directories. These list physical radio stations with Web sites along with full-time stations that only exist online, normally lumped together by country or genre. If they don't provide a direct link to the live feed, visit the station's site and look for a button or link that says "live" or "listen". For a more complete listing of directories, see: http://radiodirectory.com/Stations/Web_Directories/

## Internet Radio Directories

| | |
|---|---|
| **ComFM** | http://www.comfm.fr/live/radio/ |
| **Internet Radio List** | http://www.internetradiolist.com |
| **Live Radio** | http://www.live-radio.net |
| **MIT List** | http://wmbr.mit.edu/stations/ |
| **RadioNow (UK)** | http://www.radionow.co.uk |
| **Sunset radio** | http://sunsetradio.com |
| **Virtual Tuner** | http://www.virtualtuner.com |

Apart from the traditional single stream broadcasters, dozens of sites host multiple feeds. These might be live, on demand, on rotation, archived, or once-off events. They tend to work more like inflight entertainment than radio.

## Multistream Webcasters

| | |
|---|---|
| 113 Audio | http://www.113audio.com |
| Anime Hardcore | http://www.animehardcoreradio.net |
| Betalounge | http://www.betalounge.com |
| GoGaGa | http://www.gogaga.com |
| House of Blues | http://www.hob.com |
| iCast | http://www.icast.com |
| Interface | http://interface.pirate-radio.co.uk |
| LiveConcerts | http://www.liveconcerts.com |
| NetRadio | http://www.netradio.net |
| Online Classics | http://www.onlineclassics.net |
| Radio SonicNet | http://radio.sonicnet.com |
| RadioSpy | http://www.radiospy.com/spycasts.shtml |
| Spinner | http://www.spinner.com |
| StreetSound | http://streetsound.pseudo.com |
| Wired Planet | http://www.wiredplanet.com |
| The Womb | http://www.thewomb.com |
| WWW.com | http://www.com |
| Yahoo! Radio | http://radio.yahoo.com |

If you fancy setting up your own station or listening to the online equivalent of pirate radio, try:

## DIY Stations

| | |
|---|---|
| GiveMeTalk (Talk only) | http://www.givemetalk.com |
| Icecast.org | http://www.icecast.org |

| | |
|---|---|
| **Live365** | http://www.live365.com |
| **MyPlay** | http://www.myplay.com |
| **Shoutcast** | http://www.shoutcast.com |
| **Spotlife** | http://www.spotlife.com |

To promote your own station or search for a song or artist currently playing across thousands of others:

| | |
|---|---|
| **RadioSpy** | http://www.radiospy.com |

For everything else related to professional or amateur radio broadcasting:

| | |
|---|---|
| **Radio Directory** | http://www.radiodirectory.com |

## Crystal Radio

http://www.midnightscience.com

Build a simple wireless that needs no battery.

## Phil's Old Radios

http://www.antiqueradio.org

If you ever drifted to sleep bathed in the soft glow of a crackling Bakelite wireless, Phil's collection of vacuum-era portables may instantly flood you with childhood memories.

## Pirate Radio

http://pirateradio.about.com

Stake your claim on the airwaves.

## Police Scanner

http://www.policescanner.com • http://www.apbnews.com/scanner/
http://www.javaradio.com

Live emergency scanner feeds piped into RealAudio. Eavesdrop on busts in progress. More on scanners at: http://www.strongsignals.net

## Satco DX Satellite Chart

http://www.satcodx.com

Where to point your dish and what you can expect to receive.

# Reference

With the Net threatening the very foundations of the encyclopedia industry, it should come as no surprise to find most of the household names well entrenched online. While they're not all entirely free, they're certainly cheaper and more up to date than their bulky paper equivalents.

| | |
|---|---|
| **Britannica** | http://www.eb.com |
| **Columbia** | http://www.bartleby.com/65/ |
| **Encarta** | http://www.encarta.com |
| **Funk & Wagnalls** | http://www.funkandwagnalls.com |
| **Macquarie** | http://www.macnet.mq.edu.au |

For one-point access to almost a thousand dictionaries and in every language:

| | |
|---|---|
| **Dictionary.com** | http://www.dictionary.com |
| **One Look** | http://www.onelook.com |
| **YourDictionary.com** | http://www.yourdictionary.com |

## Academic Info

http://www.academicinfo.net

Research directory for students and teachers.

## Acronym Finder

http://www.acronymfinder.com

http://www.ucc.ie/info/net/acronyms/acro.html

Before you follow IBM, TNT, and HMV in initializing your company's name, make sure it doesn't mean something blue.

## Altavista Translations

http://world.altavista.com

Translate text, including Web pages, in seconds. Run it back and forth a few times and you'll end up with something that wouldn't look out of place on a Japanese T-shirt. If you can't pick the language, try: http://www.dougb.com/ident.html

## alt.culture

http://www.altculture.com

Witty, digital A-Z of 90s pop culture. Fun to browse, maybe even enlightening, but don't blow your cool by admitting it.

## Alternative Dictionary

http://www.notam.uio.no/~hcholm/altlang/

Bucket your foreign chums in their mother tongue.

## American ASL Dictionary

http://www.handspeak.com

http://www.bconnex.net/~randys/

Learn sign language through simple animations.

## Anagram Genius

http://www.anagramgenius.com

Recycle used letters.

## Aphorisms Galore

http://www.aphorismsgalore.com

Sound clever by repeating someone else's lines.

## BabyNamer

http://www.babynamer.com

Why not give your bub a cutesy name like Adolph? It apparently means "noble hero". Sounds nice. More suggestions to scar babe for life at: http://bnf.parentsoup.com/babyname/

## Bartleby Reference

http://www.bartleby.com/reference/

Free access to several contemporary and classic reference works such as the American Heritage dictionaries, Columbia Encyclopedia, King's English, Emily Post's Etiquette, Cambridge History of English & American Literature, and the Anatomy of the Human Body.

## Biography

http://www.biography.com

Recounting more than 25,000 lives.

## Calculators Online

http://www-sci.lib.uci.edu/~martindale/RefCalculators.html

Awesome directory of some 10,000 online tools to calculate everything from how much sump oil to put in soap, to the burden of bringing up brats.

## Cliché Finder

http://www.westegg.com/cliche/

Submit a word or phrase to find out how not to use it.

## Didja Know

http://www.didjaknow.com

One fact, four fallacies daily – but which is which?

## Earthstation1

http://www.earthstation1.com

The 20th century captured in sound and vision.

## eHow

http://www.ehow.com

Make yourself useful through step-by-step tutorials.

## Encyclopedia Mythica

http://pantheon.org/mythica/

Hefty album of mythology, folklore, and legend.

## Evil House of Cheat

http://www.cheathouse.com

Thousands of college essays, termpapers, and reports.

## Expert Central

http://www.expertcentral.com • http://www.allexperts.com
http://www.abuzz.com • http://www.askme.com

Ask any question and let unpaid experts do the thinking.

## How to Speak to an Extraterrestrial

http://adrr.com/lingua/alien.htm

Crash course in ET101.

## InfoPlease

http://www.infoplease.com

Handy, all-purpose almanac for stats and trivia.

## LibrarySpot

http://www.libraryspot.com

Neat selection of the Net's best reference sources.

## Megaconverter

http://www.megaconverter.com

Calculate everything from your height in angstroms, to the pellets of lead per ounce of buckshot needed to bring down an overcharging consultant.

## Non-escalating Verbal Self Defence

http://www.taxi1010.com

Fight insults by acting insane.

## Princeton Review

http://www.review.com • http://www.collegeboard.org

Crack the SATs.

## Rap Dictionary

http://www.rapdict.org

Hip-hop to English. Parental guidance recommended.

### RhymeZone

http://www.rhymezone.com

Get a hoof up in putting together a classy love poem.

### Roget's Thesaurus

http://www.thesaurus.com

New format: useless as ever.

### Skeptic's Dictionary

http://www.skepdic.com

Punch holes in mass media funk and pseudo-sciences such as homeopathy, astrology, and iridology.

### Spellweb

http://www.spellweb.com • http://bodin.org/altameter/

Compare two words or phrases and see which gets more hits in a search engine. If it demonstrates anything, it's that the Web is strung together with a lot of bad spelling.

### The Straight Dope

http://www.straightdope.com

Cecil Adams's answers to hard questions. Find out how to renounce your US citizenship, what Kemosabe means, and the difference between a warm smell of colitas and colitis.

### Strunk's Elements of Style

http://www.bartleby.com/141/

English usage in a nutshell. For more on grammar, see: http://www.edunet.com/english/grammar/

## Study Abroad

http://www.studyabroad.com

Hop grass that's greener

## Study Web

http://www.studyweb.com

Ideal school research aid with thousands of leads split by topic.

## Symbols

http://www.symbols.com

Ever woken up with a strange sign tattooed on your buttocks? Here's where to find what it means without calling Agent Mulder.

4:32 · The Pythagoreans are said to have made use of the sign Υ, whose vertical line represented *life's path*. The point where the vertical line converges with the two diagonal lines represented the *choice between the good* (the right stem) *and the evil* (the left stem).

## US Postal Services

http://new.usps.com

Look up a Zip code, track express mail, sort out your vehicle registration or just get down and philatelic.

## What's in your name?

http://www.kabalarians.com/gkh/your.htm

The Kabalarians claim names can be cooked up to a numerical stew and served back up as a character analysis. Look yourself up in here and see what a duff choice your folks made. Then blame them for everything that's gone wrong since.

## What is?

http://www.whatis.com • http://www.webopedia.com

Unravel cumbersome computer and Internet jargon without having even more thrown at you.

# Religion

### Anglicans Online

http://anglicansonline.org

Gentle catapult into the Church of England worldwide.

### Avatar Search

http://www.AvatarSearch.com

Search the occult Net for spiritual guidance and lottery tips.

### The Bible Gateway

http://bible.gospelcom.net

Set your table with the Good Book.

### Catholic Church – God's One and Only Church

http://www.truecatholic.org

Yet more troops armed with the truth.

### Catholic Online

http://www.catholic.org

Saints, Angels, shopping, discussion and a portal to the online territory occupied by Catholics.

## Celebrity Atheist List

http://www.primenet.com/~lippard/atheistcelebs/

Big names you won't spot in Heaven.

## Chick

http://chick.com

Hard-core Christian pornography.

## Christians v Muslims

http://debate.org.uk • http://www.rim.org/muslim/islam.htm

http://members.aol.com/AllahIslam/

http://www.answering-islam.org

http://www.muslim-answers.org

http://www.biblicalchristianity.freeserve.co.uk

Put your faith on the line.

## Christian Naturists

http://home.vistapnt.com/markm/

Frolic with other Christian fun-seekers, the way God intended.

## Comparative Religion

http://www.academicinfo.net/religindex.html

Multifaith directory for religious academics.

## Crosswalk

http://www.crosswalk.com

Catch up with the latest on Jesus.

## Demon Possession Handbook

http://diskbooks.org/hs.html

Train for a job with the Watcher's Council.

## The Greatest Truth Ever Revealed

http://www.sevenseals.com

Revelations from survivors of the Waco siege.

## The Hindu Universe

http://www.hindunet.org

Hindu dharma – the philosophy, culture, and customs.

## The Holy See

http://www.vatican.va

Official hideout of the Pope and his posse.

## Islamic Gateway

http://www.ummah.net • http://www.musalman.com

Get down with Muhammed (sallallahu `alaihi wa sallam).

## Jesus of the Week

http://www.phoenixnewtimes.com/extra/gilstrap/jesus.html

The original Mr Nice Guy in 52 coy poses per year. Catch him wink at:
http://www.winkingjesus.com

## Jesus Puzzle – Was there no Historical Jesus?

http://human.st/jesuspuzzle/ • http://jesuspuzzlerings.com
http://www.jesusdance.com

Ask the question; buy the ring; do the dance.

## Maven

http://www.maven.co.il

The Yahoo of Jewish/Israeli links.

## Miracles Page

http://www.mcn.org/l/miracles/

Spooky signs that point towards a cosmic conspiracy.

## Peyote Way Church of God

http://www.primenet.com/~idic/peyote.html

Unless you're Native American, or live in select southern US states, you stand to be locked up for finding God through the psychedelic cactus. Otherwise, feel free to fry your brain; just don't drive home from church.

## Prophecy and Current Events

http://www.aplus-software.com/thglory/

You'll never guess who's coming to dinner. Don't bother cooking, though; he's supposed to be a real whiz with food.

## Religious Frauds

http://religiousfrauds.50megs.com

Esteemed reptile slayer David Icke sniffs out Christian cons.

## Religious Tolerance.org

http://www.religioustolerance.org

Sign up for a new faith. Certain rules and conditions may apply.

## Satinism 101

http://www.satanism101.com

Enter this address and go straight to Hell: http://www.what-the-hell-is-hell.com

## Ship of Fools: the Magazine of Christian Unrest

http://ship-of-fools.com

The lighter side of Christianity.

## Skeptics Annotated Bible

http://www.skepticsannotatedbible.com

Contends that the Good Book is a misnomer.

## Stories of the Dreaming

http://www.dreamtime.net.au

Selection of enchanting bedtime stories in text, video, and audio that explain creation from an Aboriginal perspective. Don't believe in creation? Go tell it to the jury: http://www.talkorigins.org

## Universal Life Church

http://ulc.org

Become a self-ordained minister.

## The Witches' Voice

http://www.witchvox.com • http://www.witchesweb.com

Expresses a burning desire to correct misinformation about witchcraft, a legally recognized religion in the US since 1985.

## Zen

http://www.do-not-zzz.com

Take a five-minute course in meditation.

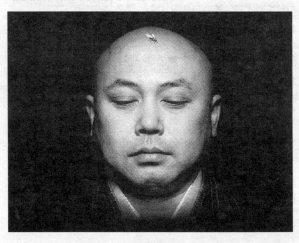

# Science

To keep abreast of science news and developments stop by Scitech, which aggregates stories from the leading scientific media:

**Scitech Daily Review**                         http://www.scitechdaily.com

Or go straight to one of the many science journals:

| | |
|---|---|
| **Archeology** | http://www.archaeology.org |
| **BBC** | http://news.bbc.co.uk |
| **Beyond 2000** | http://www.beyond2000.com |
| **British Medical Journal** | http://www.bmj.com |
| **Bulletin of Atomic Scientists** | http://www.bullatomsci.org |
| **Discover** | http://www.discover.com |
| **Discovery Channel** | http://www.discovery.com |
| **Earth Times** | http://www.earthtimes.org |
| **Edge** | http://www.edge.org |
| **Highwire Press** | http://highwire.stanford.edu |
| **The Lancet** | http://www.thelancet.com |
| **National Geographic** | http://www.nationalgeographic.com |
| **New Scientist** | http://www.newscientist.com |
| **Popular Mechanics** | http://www.popularmechanics.com |
| **Popular Science** | http://www.popsci.com |
| **Science à GoGo** | http://www.scienceagogo.com |
| **Science Magazine** | http://www.sciencemag.org |
| **Science News** | http://www.sciencenews.com |
| **Scientific American** | http://www.scientificamerican.com |
| **The Scientist** | http://www.the-scientist.com |
| **Skeptical Inquirer** | http://www.csicop.org/si/ |
| **Technology Review** | http://www.techreview.com |

## The Braintainment Center

http://www.brain.com • http://www.mensa.org
http://www.iqtest.com • http://www.mind-gear.com

Start with a test that says you're not so bright, then prove it by buying loads of self-improvement gear. Short on brains? Try:
http://www.brains4zombies.com

## Cool Robot of the Week

http://ranier.hq.nasa.gov/telerobotics_page/coolrobots.html

Clever ways to get machines to do our dirty work. More at:
http://www.robohoo.com

## Documentation and Diagrams of the Atomic Bomb

http://www.magnet.ch/serendipity/more/atomic.html

Let's hope this doesn't fall into the wrong hands. Imagine the effect
on your neighborhood:
http://www.pbs.org/wgbh/pages/amex/bomb/sfeature/mapablast.html

## History of Mathematics

http://www-groups.dcs.st-andrews.ac.uk/~history/

The life and times of various bright sparks with numbers.

## How Stuff Works

http://www.howstuffworks.com

Unravel the mysterious machinations behind all sorts of stuff from
Xmas to cruise missiles.

## Interactive Frog Dissection

http://teach.virginia.edu/go/frog/

Pin down a frog, grab your scalpel, and follow the pictures.

## The Lab (AU)

http://www.abc.net.au/science/

ABC science news and program info with Q&As from Aussie pop-
science superstar, Dr Karl Kruszelnicki.

## MadSciNet: 24-hour Exploding Laboratory

http://www.madsci.org

Collective of more than a hundred scientific smarty-pantses set up
specifically to answer your dumb questions. More geniuses for hire
at:
http://www.ducksbreath.com • http://www.wsu.edu/DrUniverse/
http://www.sciam.com/askexpert/ • http://www.sciencenet.org.uk

## MIT Media Labs

http://www.media.mit.edu

If you've read Being Digital or any of Nicholas Negroponte's Wired columns, you'll know he has some pretty tall ideas about our electronic future. Here's where he gets them.

## Museum of Dirt

http://www.planet.com/dirtweb/dirt.html

Celebrity dirt of an entirely different nature.

## Netsurfer Science

http://www.netsurf.com/nss/

Subscribe to receive weekly bulletins on science and technology sites.

## Personality Tests

http://www.keirsey.com • http://www.queendom.com/tests.html

http://www.emode.com • http://depts.washington.edu/iat/

So what breed of dog are you? Smug skeptics (http://www.skepdic.com/myersb.html) say you'll get closer to the truth here: http://www.learner.org/exhibits/personality/

## Rocketry Online

http://www.rocketryonline.com

Take on NASA at its own game.

## Skeptics Society

http://www.skeptic.com

http://www.csicop.org

Don't try to pull a swifty on this crowd.

## USGS National Earthquake Info Center

http://gldss7.cr.usgs.gov

http://www.gps.caltech.edu/~polet/recofd.html

Stats and maps of most recent quakes worldwide.

## Volcano World

http://volcano.und.nodak.edu

Monitor the latest eruptions, see photos of every major volcano in the world, and virtually tour a Hawaiian smoky without choking on sulfur fumes.

## Web-Elements

http://www.webelements.com · http://www.chemsoc.org/viselements/

Click on an element in the periodic table and suss it out in depth.

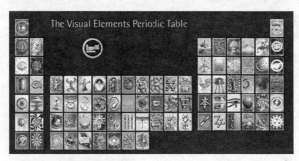

## Weird Science and Mad Scientists

http://www.eskimo.com/~billb/weird.html

http://www.student.nada.kth.se/~nv91-asa/mad.html

Free energy, Tesla, anti-gravity, aura, cold fusion, parapsychology, and other strange scientific projects and theories.

## Why Files

http://whyfiles.news.wisc.edu

Entertaining reports on the science behind current news.

## Yahoo Science

http://www.yahoo.com/science/

All the links you've come to expect plus news of the latest scientific breakthroughs.

# Space

If you have more than a passing interest in space, skip the popular science mags (p.405) and newswires (p.373), and go straight to the source:

**NASA**                                                    http://www.nasa.gov

Or any of these specialist space news portals:

| | |
|---|---|
| **Explorezone** | http://explorezone.com |
| **Human Spaceflight** | http://spaceflight.nasa.gov |
| **Jet Propulsion Lab** | http://www.jpl.nasa.gov |
| **Planetary Society** | http://planetary.org |
| **Space.com** | http://www.space.com |
| **SpaceRef** | http://www.spaceref.com |
| **SpaceScience** | http://www.spacescience.com |

## Alien Bases on Earth

http://www.earth-today.com

See, in great detail, where the Gods have parked their chariots.

## Area 51

http://www.terraserver.com/Area51.asp

See the first public satellite photos of the infamous no-fly zone.

## Astronomy Picture of the Day

http://antwrp.gsfc.nasa.gov/apod/astropix.html

Enjoy a daily helping of outer space served up by a gourmet astrochef.

## Auroras: Paintings in the Sky

http://www.exploratorium.edu/learning_studio/auroras/

If you're ever lucky enough to see the Aurora Borealis during a solar storm, you'll never take the night sky for granted again. The Exploratorium does a commendable job in explaining a polar phenomenon that very few people understand. Except maybe these champs: http://www.haarp.alaska.edu

### Deep Cold

http://www.deepcold.com

Artistic mockups of chic space racers that never left the hangar.

### Earth Viewer

http://www.fourmilab.ch/earthview/

View the Earth in space and time.

### Hubblesite

http://hubble.stsci.edu

Intergalactic snapshots fresh off the Hubble telescope.

### Inconstant Moon

http://www.inconstantmoon.com • http://www.starcity.freewire.co.uk

Click on a date and see what's showing on the Moon.

### International Star Registry

http://www.starregistry.co.uk

Raise your flag in outer space.

### Mars Home Page

http://mpfwww.jpl.nasa.gov

Get a bit more red dirt live from NASA's space safari before you stake out your first plot at: http://www.marsshop.com For the latest news, see: http://www.marsnews.com

### MrEclipse

http://www.mreclipse.com

Dabble in the occultations.

### Net Telescopes

http://www.telescope.org/rti/ • http://denali.physics.uiowa.edu/

Probe deep space by sending requests to remote telescopes.

### Seti@home

http://setiathome.ssl.berkeley.edu

Donate your processing resources to the non-lunatic end of the search for extraterrestrial intelligence by downloading a screensaver that analyzes data from the Arecibo Radio Telescope. Progress reports at:

http://www.seti.org • http://planetary.org • http://seti.uws.edu.au

### Solar System Simulator

http://space.jpl.nasa.gov

Shift camp around the solar system until you find the best view.

### Space Calendar

http://www.jpl.nasa.gov/calendar/

Guide to upcoming anniversaries, rocket launches, meteor showers, eclipses, asteroid and planet viewings, and happenings in the intergalactic calendar.

### Space Weather

http://www.spaceweather.com

http://windows.engin.umich.edu/spaceweather/

Monitor the influence of solar activity on the Earth's magnetic field.

### UFO Mania

http://www.ncircus.com/ufo/

Scrutize alien autopsy movies and saucer pics.

# Sport

For live calls, scores, tables, draws, teams, injuries and corruption inquiries across major sports, try the newspaper sites (p.374), breaking news services (p.376) or sporting specialists like:

| | |
|---|---|
| **CBS Sportsline** | http://www.sportsline.com |
| **ESPN Sportzone** | http://espnet.go.com |
| **LiveSport365** | http://www.livesport365.com |
| **SkySports (UK)** | http://www.skysports.co.uk |
| **Slam Sports (Can)** | http://www.canoe.ca/slam/ |
| **Sportal (INT)** | http://www.sportal.com |
| **Sport Live (UK)** | http://www.sportlive.net |
| **Sporting Life (UK)** | http://www.sporting-life.com |
| **SportList (Sport on UK TV)** | http://www.sportlist.com |
| **Sports.com (Euro)** | http://sports.com |
| **Sports Illustrated** | http://sportsillustrated.cnn.com |
| **SportsToday (Aus)** | http://www.sportstoday.com.au |
| **Total Sports** | http://www.totalsports.com |
| **Wide World of Sports (Aus)** | http://sports.ninemsn.com.au |

But if your interest even slightly borders on an obsession, you'll find far more satisfaction on the pages of something more one-eyed. For clubs and fan sites, drill down through Yahoo and the Open Directory. They won't carry everything, but what you'll find will lead you to the sites that understand you better than your partner:

| | |
|---|---|
| **Open Directory** | http://dmoz.org/Sports/ |
| **Yahoo Sports** | http://dir.yahoo.com/recreation/sports/ |

### Abdominal Training

http://www.timbomb.net/ab/
Build "abs ripped liked ravioli".

### Asimba

http://www.asimba.com
Log your training and nutrition regime online.

### Australian Football League

http://www.afl.com.au

Men in tight shorts play aerial ping-pong.

### Charged

http://www.charged.com

http://dmoz.org/Sports/Extreme_Sports/

For all that falls under the banner of "extreme sports", from taking your pushbike offroad to the sort of sheer recklessness that would get you cut from a will.

### Cric Info – the Home of Cricket on the Internet

http://www.cricket.org

Because every ball matters.

### Fishing Directories

http://www.thefishfinder.com • http://fishsearch.com

Trade tips and generally exaggerate about aquatic bloodsports.

### Goals – Global Online Adventure Learning Site

http://www.goals.com

Chase adventurous lunatics like Mick Bird, who's circling the globe in a canoe.

### NBA.com

http://www.nba.com

Pro basketball news, picks, player profiles, analyses, results, schedules, and highlight videos. See also Major League Baseball: http://www.majorleaguebaseball.com

and http://www.fastball.com

### NFL

http://www.nfl.com

Media schedules, chats, news, player profiles, stats, and streaming highlight videos from the National Football League's past and current seasons.

## Rugby League/Union

http://www.rleague.com • http://www.ozleague.com
http://www.scrum.com • http://www.rugbyheaven.com

Up to the minute coverage of hard men trotting in and out of the blood bin.

## Sailing Index

http://www.smartguide.com

Everything seaworthy: from swapping yachts to choosing a GPS.

## SkiCentral

http://www.skicentral.com

Indexes thousands of ski-related sites, such as snow reports, resort cams, snowboard gear, accommodation, and coming events in resorts across the world. For snowboarding, see:

http://www.soltv.com • http://www.boardtheworld.com.au
http://www.twsnow.com • http://www.board-it.com

## SoccerNet

http://www.soccernet.com

ESPN's shrine to football in England and beyond. Not enough news? Try:

| | |
|---|---|
| **Carling** | http://www.fa-carling.com |
| **Football365** | http://www.football365.co.uk |
| **Nationwide** | http://www.football.nationwide.co.uk |
| **When Saturday Comes** | http://www.wsc.co.uk |

For game, club, and player stats, see:

| | |
|---|---|
| **Matchfacts** | http://www.matchfacts.co.uk |
| **Soccerbase** | http://www.soccerbase.com |
| **Teamtalk** | http://www.teamtalk.com |

## Stats

http://www.stats.com

Pig in to an overflowing trough of US sport statistics.

## World Motorsport Index

http://www.worldmotorsport.com

Start here for your gasoline-induced pleasure.

## World Surfing

http://www.goan.com/surflink.html

Every day's like big Wednesday. For daily breaks and Aussie seaboard cams, see: http://www.coastalwatch.com

## Wrestling

http://www.wrestlezone.com • http://www.wrestlingdotcom.com

Vent the frustration of helplessly watching your boofhead heroes being piledriven, suplexed, and moonsplashed, by spilling some hardway juice virtually. If you'd prefer seeing them smack each other in the scone, see: http://www.boxingpress.com

# Telecommunications

## Campaign for Unmetered Telecommunications

http://www.unmetered.org.uk • http://www.telecom.eu.org

Rail against the call-charging system that's making Europe an Internet backwater. For a comparison of UK tariffs, see:
http://www.magsys.co.uk/telecom/

## Free Fax Services

http://www.tpc.int • http://easyfax.net

Transmit faxes via the Internet free.

## HomeIndia

http://www.homeindia.com

Type in a message. Have it faxed or delivered by post free anywhere within India.

Pay to send it worldwide at: http://www.letterpost.com

## J-Fax

http://www.jfax.com • http://www.efax.com

Free up a phone line by receiving your faxes by email.

## Mail2Wap

http://www.mail2wap.com

Collect your POP3 mail on a WAP phone.

## MobileWorld

http://www.mobileworld.org
http://www.unwin.co.uk/phonez.html

Assorted info on mobile phones and cellular networks.

## RelayOne (UK)

http://relayone.co.uk

Email your message or document for Royal Mail delivery.

### Reverse Phone Directory

http://www.reversephonedirectory.com

Key in a US phone number to find its owner. To find a UK location
see: http://www.warwick.ac.uk/cgi-bin-Phones/nng/

### SMS Text Messages

http://www.quios.com • http://www.mtnsms.com

Send free text messages to mobile phones worldwide.

### Stamps.com (US)

http://www.stamps.com • http://www.estamp.com

Buy your US stamps online.

### The Telegraph Office

http://fohnix.metronet.com/~nmcewen/tel_off.html

Salute to the bygone age of Morse telegraphy.

### UK.Telecom FAQ

http://www.gbnet.net/net/uk-telecom/

Satisfy your curiosity about the British phone network.

### What does your phone number spell?

http://www.phonespell.org

Enter your phone number to see what it spells. The reverse lookup
might help you choose a number.

### World Time & Dialing Codes

http://www.whitepages.com.au/time.shtml

International dialing info from anywhere to anywhere, including
current times and area codes.

# Time

### Calendarzone

http://www.calendarzone.com

Calendar links and, believe it or not, calzone recipes.

### DateReminder

http://www.datereminder.co.uk • http://www.cvp.com/freemind/

Remind yourself by email.

### The Death Clock

http://www.deathclock.com

Get ready to book your final taxi.

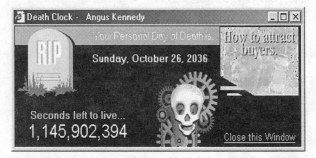

### International Earth Rotation Service

http://hpiers.obspm.fr

Ever felt like your bed's spinning? The truth is even scarier.

### iPing (US)

http://www.iping.com

Arrange free telephone reminders for one or many.

### Online Planners

http://www.dailydrill.com • http://www.appoint.net

http://www.when.com • http://www.visto.com

Maintain your planner online. Excite, Yahoo, MSN, and Netscape offer similar.

### Time and Date

http://www.timeanddate.com

http://www.smh.com.au/media/wtc/smhwtc.html

Instantly tell the time in your choice of cities.

Keep your PC clock aligned with a time synchronizer:
http://www.eecis.udel.edu/~ntp/software.html

### Time Cube

http://www.timecube.com

Disprove God through the simultaneous 4-day Time Cube.

## Transport

### Buying a Car

Before you're sharked into signing on a new or used vehicle, go online and check out a few road tests and price guides. You can complete the entire exercise while you're there, but it mightn't hurt to drive one first. Start here:

| | |
|---|---|
| Autobytel (INT) | http://www.autobytel.com |
| Auto Channel | http://www.theautochannel.com |
| Autohit (UK) | http://www.autohit.co.uk |
| Autolocate (UK) | http://www.autolocate.co.uk |
| Autotrader (UK, EUR, SA) | http://www.autotrader.co.uk |
| AutoWeb | http://www.autoweb.com |
| BBC Top Gear (UK) | http://www.topgear.beeb.com |
| CarClub | http://www.carclub.com |
| Car Importing (UK) | http://www.carimporting.co.uk |

| | |
|---|---|
| **Carnet (Aus)** | http://www.car.net.au |
| **CarPrice** | http://www.carprice.com |
| **CarsDirect** | http://www.carsdirect.com |
| **Carseekers (UK)** | http://www.carseekers.co.uk |
| **Carstreet (IND)** | http://www.carstreet.com |
| **DealerNet** | http://www.dealernet.com |
| **Drivers Seat** | http://www.driversseat.com |
| **Edmunds** | http://www.edmunds.com |
| **Exchange & Mart (UK)** | http://www.exchangeandmart.co.uk |
| **Kelly Blue Book** | http://www.kbb.com |
| **Microsoft CarPoint (Aus)** | http://carpoint.ninemsn.com |
| **Microsoft CarPoint** | http://carpoint.msn.com |
| **Oneswoop (UK)** | http://www.oneswoop.com |
| **What Car? (UK)** | http://www.whatcar.co.uk |

## Airdisaster.com

http://www.airdisaster.com • http://come.to/crashes/

http://www.aviationnewsweb.com • http://planecrashinfo.com

Way more goes wrong up in the air than you realize. Here's why you should be terrified to fly. For first-hand tales of terror, see:
http://www.pprune.com

## Airsafe

http://www.airsafe.com

Overcome your fear of plummeting.

## Air Sickness Bag Virtual Museum

http://www.airsicknessbags.com

Bring up some treasured memories.

## Aviation

http://aviation.about.com

http://www.airliners.net

If it takes off and lands, you'll find it here.

## BAC Testing

http://www.copsonline.com/bac2.htm

Slurring your swearwords, wobbling all over the road, mounting gutters and knocking kids off bikes? Pull over and blow into this site.

## FedEx

http://www.fedex.com

Book shipping, track parcels, or compare rates with UPS: http://www.ups.com and TNT: http://www.tnt.com

## Layover

http://www.layover.com

Long, wide loads of truckin' stuff for prime movers and shakers.

## License Plates of the World

http://danshiki.oit.gatech.edu/~iadt3mk/

Ring in sick, cancel your date, unplug the phone and don't even think about sleep until you've seen EVERY LICENSE PLATE IN THE WORLD.

## NMRA Directory of Worldwide Rail Sites

http://www.ribbonrail.com/nmra/ • http://www.trainorders.com

Locophilial banquet of online railway shunts.

## US Submarines

http:/www.ussubs.com

Scare the fish in your own custom-built U-boat.

## Woman Motorist

http://www.womanmotorist.com

The demographic group motor vehicle insurers prefer.

# Travel

Whether you're seeking inspiration, planning an itinerary, shopping for a ticket, or already mobile, there'll be a tool online worth throwing in your box. You can book flights, reserve hotels, research your destination, monitor the weather, convert currencies, learn the lingo, locate an ATM, scan local newspapers, collect your mail from abroad, find a restaurant that suits your fussy tastes, and plenty more. If you'd like to find first-hand experiences or traveling companions, hit the Usenet discussion archives at **Deja.com** (http://www.deja.com/usenet/), and join the appropriate newsgroup under the rec.travel hierarchy. Then see what the major guidebook publishers have to offer:

| | |
|---|---|
| **Fielding** | http://www.fieldingtravel.com |
| **Fodors** | http://www.fodors.com |
| **Frommers** | http://www.frommers.com |
| **Intrepid** | http://www.aurore2.demon.co.uk |
| **Let's Go** | http://www.letsgo.com |
| **Lonely Planet** | http://www.lonelyplanet.com |
| **Moon Travel** | http://www.moon.com |
| **Rough Guides** | http://www.roughguides.com |

While it might seem like commercial suicide for the **Rough Guides** to **give away the full text of its guides** to more than 10,000 destinations, the reality is books are still more convenient, especially on the road when you need them most. If you'd like to order a guide or map online you'll also find plenty of opportunities either from the above publishers, the online bookshops (p.305), or from **travel bookshops** such as:

| | |
|---|---|
| **Adventurous Traveler** | http://www.atbook.com |
| **Literate Traveler** | http://www.literatetraveller.com |
| **Stanfords (UK)** | http://www.stanfords.co.uk |
| **Travel Books & Maps** | http://www.travelbookshop.com |

Many online travel agents also provide destination guides, which might include exclusive editorial peppered with chunks licensed from guidebooks linked out to further material on the Web. For example:

| | |
|---|---|
| **Away.com** | http://away.com |
| **Escaperoutes (UK)** | http://www.escaperoutes.net |
| **Travel Vision (UK)** | http://www.travelvision.com |

Still, it won't hurt to hit the Web for more. Once you've exhausted the following directories, try a search engine:

| | |
|---|---|
| **Excite Travel** | http://travel.excite.com |
| **Open Directory** | http://dmoz.org/Recreation/Travel/ |
| **Virtual Tourist** | http://www.vtourist.com |
| **Yahoo Directory** | http://www.yahoo.com/Recreation/Travel/ |
| **Yahoo Travel** | http://travel.yahoo.com |

Or for entertainment, eating, and events, a city guide:

| | |
|---|---|
| **Citysearch** | http://www.citysearch.com |
| **Sidewalk (Aus)** | http://www.sidewalk.com.au |
| **Time Out** | http://www.timeout.co.uk |
| **Wcities.com** | http://www.wcities.com |
| **Yahoo Local (US)** | http://local.yahoo.com |
| **Zagat (Dining)** | http://www.zagat.com |

Is **Vindigo** the future of travel guides? Download its **Palm Pilot** city guides and decide for yourself:

| | |
|---|---|
| **Vindigo** | http://www.vindigo |

If you're flexible and/or willing to leave soon, you might find a **last-minute special**. These Net exclusives are normally offered directly from the airline, hotel, and travel operator sites, which you'll find through **Airlines.com** (http://www.airlines.com) or **Yahoo**. There are also a few Web operators that specialize in late-notice and **special Internet deals** on flights, hotels, events, and so forth, such as:

| | |
|---|---|
| **Bargain Holidays (UK)** | http://www.bargainholidays.com |
| **Best Fares** | http://www.bestfares.com |
| **Lastminute.com (UK)** | http://www.lastminute.com |
| **Lastminutetravel.com** | http://www.lastminutetravel.com |
| **Smarter Living** | http://www.smarterliving.com |
| **Travel Zoo** | http://www.travelzoo.com |

Then there are the reverse-auction sites such as **Priceline.com** where you bid on a destination and wait for a bite. You might strike up a good deal if you bid shrewdly and don't mind the somewhat draconian restrictions (see: http://www.angelfire.com/nt/priceline/). **Hotwire** offers similar discounts on undisclosed airlines but names the price up front. If you're super flexible, you could try **Airhitch** or a courier:

| | |
|---|---|
| **Air Courier Assoc.** | http://www.aircourier.org |
| **Airhitch** | http://www.airhitch.org |
| **Hotwire** | http://www.hotwire.com |
| **IAATC Air Courier** | http://www.courier.org |
| **Priceline.com** | http://www.priceline.com |

Booking a flight through one of the broad online ticketing systems isn't too hard either, but bargains are scarce. For example, unless you're spending someone else's money you'll want to sidestep the full fares offered on these major services:

| | |
|---|---|
| **Biztravel (US)** | http://www.biztravel.com |
| **Expedia (UK)** | http://www.expedia.co.uk |
| **Expedia (US)** | http://www.expedia.com |
| **Travel.com.au (AUS)** | http://www.travel.com.au |
| **Travelocity (Worldwide)** | http://www.travelocity.com |
| **Travel Select (Worldwide)** | http://www.travelselect.co.uk |
| **Travelshop (AUS)** | http://www.travelshop.com.au |

Although they list hundreds of airlines and millions of fares, the general consensus is that they're usually better for research, accommodation, and travel tips than cheap fares and customer service. So if you think it's worth the effort, drop in and check which carriers haul your route, offer the best deals, and still have seats available. You can then use their rates as a benchmark. Compare them with the fares on the airline sites and discount specialists such as:

| | |
|---|---|
| **Bargain Holidays (UK)** | http://www.bargainholidays.com |
| **Cheap Flights (UK)** | http://www.cheapflights.com |
| **Deckchair (UK)** | http://www.deckchair.com |
| **Ebookers.com (UK, EUR)** | http://www.ebookers.com |
| **Flight Centre (Aus, UK)** | http://www.flightcentre.com (.co.uk) |

| **Internet Air Fares (US)** | http://www.air-fare.com |
| **1 Travel.com (Worldwide)** | http://www.1travel.com |
| **Lowestfare.com (US)** | http://www.lowestfare.com |
| **TravelHub (US)** | http://www.travelhub.com |

Finally, see if your travel agent can better the price. If the difference is only marginal, favor your agent. Then at least you'll have a human contact if something goes wrong. See how the online bookers rate at:

**Gomez.com**        http://www.gomez.com

## A2Btravel.com (UK)

http://www.a2btravel.com • http://www.a2beurope.com
http://www.ukonline.co.uk/content/travel.html

Resources for getting into, around, and out of the UK, such as car-hire comparison, airport guides, train timetables and ferry booking.

## Africam

http://www.africam.com

Sneak a peek at wild beasts going about their business.

## Airtoons

http://www.airtoons.com

You'll never look at another flight card without smirking.

## Air Traveler's Handbook

http://www.cs.cmu.edu/afs/cs/user/mkant/Public/Travel/airfare.html

FAQ compiled from the **Rec.Travel.Air newsgroup** that's sure to leave you feeling worldlier. More useful Rec.Travel FAQs at: http://www.travel-library.com

## Art of Travel

http://www.artoftravel.com

How to see the world on $25 a day.

## ATM Locators

http://www.visa.com/pd/atm/ • http://www.mastercard.com/atm/

Locate a bowser willing to replenish your wallet.

### Bed & Breakfast Channel

http://www.bbchannel.com • http://www.babs.com.au (Aus)
http://www.innsite.com

Secure your night's sleep worldwide.

### CIA World Factbook

http://www.odci.gov/cia/publications/pubs.html

Vital stats on every country. For the score on living standards:
http://www.undp.org

### Concierge.com

http://www.concierge.com

Get packing with advice from **Traveler** magazine.

### Electronic Embassy

http://www.embassy.org

Directory of foreign embassies in DC plus Web links where available.
Search Yahoo for representation in other cities.

### Eurotrip

http://www.eurotrip.com • http://www.ricksteves.com

Look out Europe, here you come.

### Fielding's Danger Finder

http://www.fieldingtravel.com/df/

Adventure holidays that could last a lifetime.

### Find a Grave

http://www.findagrave.com

See where celebrities are buried, and maybe their graves.

### Hotel Discount

http://www.hoteldiscount.com • http://www.hotelnet.co.uk

Book hotels around the world. For backpacker rates, try:
http://www.hostels.com

### How far is it?

http://www.indo.com/distance/

Calculate the distance between any two cities.

### Incredible Adventures

http://www.incredible-adventures.com

Convert your cash into adrenaline.

### Infiltration

http://www.infiltration.org

Confessions of a serial trespasser.

### International Home Exchange

http://www.homexchange.com • http://www.sunswap.com

Swap hideouts with a foreigner until the heat dies down.

### International Student Travel Confederation

http://www.istc.org

Save money with an authentic international student card.

### Journeywoman

http://www.journeywoman.com

Reporting in from the sister beaten track.

### Mapquest

http://www.mapquest.com • http://maps.expedia.com

http://www.streetmap.co.uk (UK) • http://www.multimap.com (UK)

http://www.whereis.com.au (Aus)

Generate road maps for most cities worldwide and driving directions for North America and Europe. Check them all out as the features differ. To reconcile UK postcodes with addresses:
http://www.qas.com/html/body_demos.shtml

## Mungo Park

http://www.mungopark.com

If you'd rather New Year in Timbuktu than Times Square.

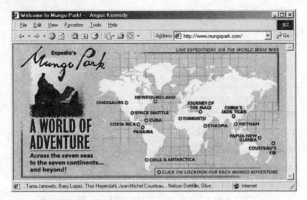

## No Shitting in the Toilet

http://www.noshit.com.au

Delighting in the oddities of low-budget travel.

## Roadside America

http://www.roadsideamerica.com

Strange attractions that loom between squished animals on US highways.

## Rooms with a Clue

http://www.forbes.com/tool/toolbox/clue/
http://www.geektools.com/hotels.html

Hotels that live up to your wired expectations.

## Sahara Overland

http://www.sahara-overland.com

Leave the city in a cloud of dust.

## Satellite and Aerial Imaging

http://www.terraserver.com • http://terra.nasa.gov
http://www.spaceimage.com • http://www.crworld.co.uk

See why nine out of ten Martian honeymooners prefer your planet.

## Subway Navigator

http://www.subwaynavigator.com • http://www.manhattanaddress.com

Estimate the traveling times between city stations worldwide, or find the right stop in NY.

## Topographic Maps & Atlases

http://www.nationalgeographic.com/mapmachine/
http://www.multimap.com/world/places.cgi
http://www.topozone.com (US)

Check them out, but you'll prefer it on paper. For more maps, geographical and GPS resources see:

http://geography.about.com • http://dmoz.org/Reference/Maps/

## Tourism Offices Worldwide

http://www.towd.com

Write to the local tourist office. They might send you a brochure.

## Traffic and Road Conditions

http://www.accutraffic.com • http://traffic.yahoo.com

Live traffic and weather updates across the US.

## Travel and Health Warnings

http://www.dfat.gov.au (Aus) • http://www.fco.gov.uk (UK)
http://travel.state.gov (US) • http://www.cdc.gov/travel/ (Health)

Don't ignore these bulletins if you're planning to visit a potential hot-spot or health risk, but seek a second opinion before postponing your adventure. If you're off on business, try a professional advisory such as **Kroll**: http://www.krollworldwide.com

## Travelmag

http://www.travelmag.co.uk

Several intimate travel reflections monthly.

### Travlang

http://www.travlang.com

Add another language to your repertoire.

### Unclaimed Baggage

http://www.unclaimedbaggage.com

You lose it; they sell it.

### Visit Britain

http://www.visitbritain.com • http://www.uktravel.com

Understand the British way of doing things.

### Walkabout

http://www.walkabout.com.au

Get the lowdown on the land down under.

### WebFlyer

http://www.webflyer.com

Keep tabs on frequent flyer schemes.

### Whatsonwhen

http://www.whatsonwhen.com

Annoyed you've missed Thaipusam or the Turning of the Bones yet again? Get your dates right here.

# Weather

### Climate Ark

http://www.climateark.org

Fret about coming changes in the weather.

### Ocean Weather

http://www.oceanweather.com • http://www.ssec.wisc.edu/data/sst.html

Mapping the swells and temperatures across the seven seas.

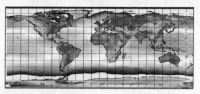

## WeatherPlanner

http://www.weatherplanner.com

Plan your washing around a long-term forecast.

## Weather Software

http://weather.hypermart.net/software.html

Stick out a wet thumb from the safety of your swivel chair.

## Wild Weather

http://www.wildweather.com

http://australiansevereweather.simplenet.com

http://www.storm-track.com • http://www.nssl.noaa.gov

Set your course into the eye of the storm.

## World Climate

http://www.worldclimate.com • http://www.weatherbase.com/

Off to Irkutzk next August? Here's what weather to expect.

## World Meteorological Organization

http://www.wmo.ch

UN division that monitors global climate.

## World Weather

http://weather.yahoo.com • http://cnn.com/WEATHER/

http://www.meto.govt.uk (UK) • http://www.bom.gov.au (AUS)

http://www.intellicast.com (US) • http://www.accuweather.com (US)

Forecasts, charts, storm warnings, allergy reports, and satellite photos for thousands of cities worldwide. For more national bureaus, see:
http://www.wmo.ch/web-en/member.html

# Weird

### Absurd.org

http://www.absurd.org

Please do not adjust your set.

### Aetherius Society

http://www.aetherius.org

Continue the legacy of the late Sir Dr George King, Primary Terrestrial Mental Channel of the Interplanetary Council.

### Bert is Evil

http://www.fractalcow.com/bert/

Sesame Street star exposed in photo shocker.

### Brother Ellis Society

http://www.freespeech.org/besna/besna.html

Appease God by eating unwanted pets. No details spared.

### Christian Guide to Small Arms

http://www.frii.com/~gosplow/cgsa.html

"He that hath no sword, let him sell his garment, and buy one"– Luke 22:36. It's not just your right; it's your duty!

### Circlemakers

http://www.circlemakers.org

Create crop circles to amuse New Agers and the press.

### Clonaid

http://www.clonaid.com

Thanks to the Raelians, we now know all life on earth was created in extraterrestrial laboratories. Here's where you can buy genuine cloned human livestock for the kitchen table. Ready as soon as the lab's finished.

## CNI Angel Gallery

http://www.cninews.com/CNI_Angels.html

Leading authorities point to evidence that angels may be alien frauds.
Backed up at: http://www.mt.net/~watcher/

## The Darwin Awards

http://www.officialdarwinawards.com • http://www.darwinawards.com

Each year the Darwin Award goes to the person who drops off the
census register in the most spectacular fashion. Here's where to read
about the runners-up and er ... winners.

## Derm Cinema

http://www.skinema.com

Know your celebrity skin conditions. But would you recognize them
under a gas mask?
http://www.geocities.com/TimesSquare/Alley/8207/

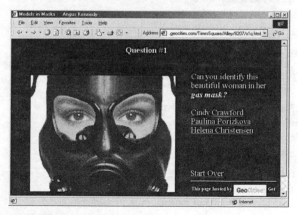

## Dolphin Society

http://www.dolphinsociety.org

Driftnet-eating submarines rescue humans who've shape-shifted into
dolphins.

### English Rose Press

http://www.englishrosepress.com
Diana sends her love from Heaven.

### Fortean Times

http://www.forteantimes.com
Updates from the print monthly that takes the investigation of strange phenomena more seriously than itself. See also:
http://www.parascope.com and http://www.bizarremag.com

### Freaks, Geeks, & Weirdness on the Web

http://www.rosemarywest.com/guide/
http://www.student.nada.kth.se/~nv91-asa/
Make that two big sacks of assorted nuts please.

### Future Horizons

http://www.futurehorizons.net
Snap off more than your fair share through solid-state circuitry.

### Gallery of the Absurd

http://www.absurdgallery.com
Strange ways to sell strange stuff.

## Great Joy In Great Tribulation

http://www.dccsa.com/greatjoy/

Biblical proof that Prince Chuck is the Antichrist and key dates leading to the end of the world. For more enlightenment, including how to debug the pyramids, see:
http://members.aol.com/larrypahl/lpahl.htm

## I Can Eat Glass Project

http://hcs.harvard.edu/~igp/glass.html

Deter excess foreign suitors and carpet dealers with the only words you know in their language.

## Illuminati News

http://mercury.spaceports.com/~persewen/illum_index.htm

Storm into secret societies and thump your fist on the table.

## Infamous Exploding Whale

http://www.perp.com/whale/

Take one beached whale carcass, add half a ton of dynamite, turn on the video, and run.

## International Ghost Hunters Society

http://www.ghostweb.com

They never give up the ghost.

## Itz Fun Tew Be Dat Kandie Kid

http://www.angelfire.com/ma/talulaQ/kandie.html

Mamas don't let your babies grow up to be ravers.

## Kaol's Ol' Sinkin' Hole

http://www.geocities.com/SoHo/8090/

What's sexier than sinking in quicksand? Nothing says Kaol, except perhaps being gassed, drowned, strangled or blown out into space:

http://www.fortunecity.com/lavendar/mockingbird/472/

### Mind Control Forum

http://morethanconquerors.simplenet.com/MCF/

http://www.mindcontrolmanual.com

Unpick Big Brother's evil scheme and then put it to work on the dancefloor.

### Mozart's Musikalisches Würfelspeil

http://sunsite.univie.ac.at/Mozart/dice/

Compose a minuet as you play Monopoly.

### Museum of Non-Primate Art

http://www.monpa.com

Become an aficionado of moggy masterpieces.

### Myrla's Korner

http://myrla.tripod.com

Thank goodness the ancient felinoid Ka'ats from planet Zimmorrah have Myrna. Otherwise no-one would take them seriously.

### Neuticles

http://www.neuticles.com

Pick your pet's pocket but leave his dignity intact.

### News of the Weird

http://www.nine.org/notw/ • http://www.thisistrue.com

Dotty clippings from the world press.

### Planetary Activation Organization

http://www.paoweb.com

Prevent inter-dimensional dark forces from dominating our galaxy by ganging up with the Galactic Federation of Light.

### Reptoids

http://www.reptoids.com

Was that an alien or merely the subterranean descendant of a dinosaur?

## Reverse Speech

http://www.reversespeech.com

They say we speak the overt forward and the covert backward. You're not going to believe what Bill Clinton, Tony Blair, and others are hiding. Or maybe you will. You have to watch what you write too: http://www.wildcowpublishing.com/paranormal/reverse.html

## Rocket Guy

http://www.rocketguy.com

Brian's about to launch himself into space. Bye-bye, Brian.

## Sensoterapia

http://www.sensoterapia.com.co

Master the sex secret you'll never see revealed in this month's Cleo.

## Sightings

http://www.sightings.com

Fishy newsbreaks from talk radio truthferret, Jeff Rense. For more real life X-file blather tune into: http://www.artbell.com

## Sulabh International Museum of Toilets

http://www.sulabhtoiletmuseum.org

Follow the evolution of the ablution at the world's leading exhibition of porcelain businessware. No need to take it sitting down: http://www.restrooms.org

## Things My Girlfriend and I Have Argued About

http://homepage.ntlworld.com/mil.millington/things.html

Add this page to that list.

## Time Travel Devices

http://home.inreach.com/dov/tt.htm

Step back to a time that common sense forgot.

## Toilet-train Your Cat

http://www.karawynn.net/mishacat/

How to point pusskins at the porcelain. Literally.

## WearCam

http://www.wearcam.org

Steve has a Netcam fixed to his head. You see what he sees. But that won't stop him having fun.

## World Database of Happiness

http://www.eur.nl/fsw/research/happiness/

Discover where people are happiest and statistically what they mean by that.

## Xenophobic Persecution in the UK

http://www.five.org.uk

If you're below British standards the MI5 will punish you by TV.

## ZetaTalk

http://www.zetatalk.com

Nancy's guests today are those elusive aliens that frolic in the autumn mist at the bottom of her garden.

# 19

# Software Roundup

## INTRODUCTION

**N**ow that Web browsers have become such Internet software lucky dips, it's no longer so important to scout around for accessories, and you certainly needn't pay for some "Internet made easy" kit. All the same, even though you can get by with the bare bones, there's no reason to rough it. One way to stack up with Net software is to install it from the free CDs given away with PC rags. A better way is to get the latest versions fresh from the Net. You could start by poking your snout into the software troughs listed in our Web guide (p.291). But before you trot off there, read this chapter, and get set with the crucial downloads first. They're all free – at least for a limited time – though some have superior commercial versions.

# Upgrade your browser

Your first concern will be to make sure your system has what it takes to dial up, connect to your ISP and then jettison you onto the Web. Your next operation should be to update your browser to its latest version and, if you like, gradually try some added extras. When you update Internet Explorer, for example, it will interrogate your system to see what you already have and offer you a list of upgrades and accessories. You simply tick the choices, select "Download", and your system will look after the rest. If you accidentally go offline during the process, it's smart enough to recover on your next attempt. The procedure with Netscape works similarly. We've covered this territory amply in earlier chapters (see p.55 and p.149), so let's assume you're online and snuggled up to the Web browser of your dreams. Just remember to **check in for updates regularly** (say, fortnightly) and always take any security patches. The rest is less important.

# Downloading, installing, and uninstalling

Downloading a program from the Net should be relatively painless. Just go to its developer's **Web page**, read about it first, decide whether it sounds useful, and if so, fill in any required details, and pick the appropriate version for your system.

It's good laboratory technique to download everything onto your **Desktop** or into a central folder called, say, "download". Once the program's downloaded, copy it to a temporary folder for installation. After it's installed, delete the contents of the temporary folder and either shift the original file into an archive or delete it. (See p.159 for "How to set up your folder structure").

Most files will **self-extract**, so installation should be as simple as following the prompts. If not, you'll need an archiving program such as **WinZip** or **Aladdin (Stuffit) Expander** (see p.158) to extract the installation files. Once extracted, read the accompanying text files for installation instructions. It's usually a matter of clicking on a file called "install.exe" or "setup.exe" in Windows, or on an install icon on the Mac. Try it for a few days. If it doesn't serve a purpose, remove it from your hard drive so you don't clog up your system with rubbish. In Windows, that means deleting it from within **Add/Remove Programs** in the Control Panel. If there's no entry in there, look for an uninstall icon in its Start menu folder. If neither exists, it will be safe to delete the file directly from its folder. Note that some programs will hijack your file associations, so to get file types to open automatically with a previous program you might have to go into that program's settings or simply reinstall it.

Most programs now offer the option to automatically check for updates. However, it's a common source of mystery crashes so switch it off and check manually.

## What to avoid – protect your privacy

It seems few people will pay for software if they can avoid it. Run a search on "crack" or "serial no" in any search engine, or check into **AstaLaVista** (http://www.astalavista.com) and you'll soon see how rife pirating has become. As a result, Internet software developers have been forced to prostitute their programs to ad serving networks and marketing sharks. At first glance this free **"adware"** alternative to full-featured registered software might seem a happy marriage – the advertisers get exposure, the marketers get their stats, the programmers get paid and you get the product for nix. Unfortunately, it's rarely that clean cut, and those **pesky ad banners** are the least of your worries. Gibson Research (http://grc.com /optout.htm), for example, has gone as far as labeling it **"spyware"** accusing the ad hustlers of all sorts of privacy infringements including tracking your online activities and calling home with the results. At the time of writing these allegations are a little on the wild side, with little concrete supporting evidence, but they're still plausible. And like all the best conspiracy theories, it's easier to prove guilt than innocence.

Invasion of privacy, however, is only half the story. Adware is also notorious for **crashing your system**. And some leave behind active remains after they're uninstalled, further adding to your woes.

On an even more cynical note, the adware concept has also sparked off a rash of **useless programs** that are little more than purpose-built ad servers or data collectors. You can usually spot them because they sound like "as seen on TV products" – that is, they're designed to sell, not to use. Don't even consider installing anything that claims to **accelerate your browser**, **optimize your modem**, enhance your **mouse cursor**, or **serve extra information on the sites you visit**. Your browser is touchy enough as it is, without adding more junk to it. You especially do not need **search aids that integrate into the browser**.

You'll find **RealNetworks** and **AOL/Netscape** will aggressively thrust third-party software your way during updates. Say no to it all. Read independent reviews before you download anything, and get it straight from the source.

If the prospect of browsing the Web entirely ad-free sounds appealing, try **Adfilter** (http://www.adfilter.com) or **WebWasher** (http://www.webwasher.com). They can automatically cull ad banners and pop-ups, which might even speed up your session. The downside is they could also cut useful information, or disable critical tasks like Windows Update. Take care.

## Manage your downloads

Although Internet Explorer will resume failed transfers (sometimes) it's not a feature that's either reliable or well implemented. If you find yourself downloading frequently, you'll soon appreciate the benefits of a trusty Download Manager that can queue up and schedule, set up multiple streams, and of course, recover dropped transfers. Oddly, there's one built into the Mac version of Internet Explorer, but not the PC version. There are plenty of PC options but none can be recommended without reservation, particularly those that fall into the adware category. Try **Mass Downloader** (http://www.metaproducts.com) first.

## Viruses and security

Contrary to popular opinion virus scanners aren't so important. What is important is that you understand how viruses, worms and Trojans spread. They can only get onto your PC if you run an infected program. If you keep your browser up to date, disable all Office document macros, and only run programs that come directly from a trustworthy publisher (either from the original install disk or its official Web site) you will NEVER get a virus. That means **never opening any attachment** sent to you through email, ICQ, Usenet, or chat, other than what is obviously a recognized document or media file format. Especially if it has the following extensions: .REG, .INF, .EXE, .COM, .VBS, .BAT, or .SHS. Even if it appears to be coming from your best friend! And tread cautiously with any program or registry file (.INF or .REG) offered on free Webspace (eg Geocities) or a site with a tilde (~) in the address. It doesn't say the author is dodgy but it does say they're unprofessional.

Still, it won't hurt to run all downloads and attachments through a virus scanner. But don't put too much faith in the results. Most scanners will pick up viruses but their record with Trojan horses isn't so hot. Try **Inoculate IT** (http://antivirus.cai.com). It's as good as any, and free. New PCs typically come with **McAfee's VirusScan** or **Norton AntiVirus**. They're supposedly the best in the field, but seem to cause more problems than they solve, especially if you let them run in the background (real-time protection). Instead switch them off and simply scan all new arrivals. Don't forget to keep the signature file up to date. Check in every couple of weeks or so. Refer to the help file for instructions. For more on viruses, see p.22.

As a line of defense against hackers, install a security **fire-wall**. For PCs you need look no further than the excellent, and free, **ZoneAlarm** (http://www.zonelabs.com). It will let you choose which programs can access the Net, and effectively make your PC invisible to outsiders, thus protecting you against inquisitive hackers, and Trojans that open remote control backdoors into your computer. A must!

## Update your drivers

To get the best from your hardware, grab all the latest device drivers – especially for your video card and modem. You'll find the newest drivers at the component manufacturer's Web site, or sometimes at your PC maker's site. They're normally located in the support section. Look for "files", "downloads" or "drivers", and follow the prompts. Alternatively, try **Windrivers** (http://www.windrivers.com).

## Sort out your media players

Next sort out your media players, image viewers and plug-ins. For both PC and Macs, grab the latest versions of:

| | |
|---|---|
| **Shockwave** | http://www.macromedia.com/shockwave/ |
| **RealPlayer** | http://www.real.com |
| **Windows Media Player** | http://www.windowsmedia.com |
| **QuickTime** | http://www.quicktime.com |

This will cover all the popular music and video formats, at least twice over, but you might still prefer to switch programs. You'll be able to assign what plays what within each program's settings. Alternatively, if you'd like a program to take over, just reinstall it. For a rundown on the various music players, see p.218.

It's also handy to have some **image viewing software** so you can flick through saved pictures and fool around with them. Try **ACDSee** (http://www.acdsee.com) as a viewer and set it to associate with all image formats. The full release becomes inoperative after 30 days, whereas the Classic version merely nags you to register. **Irfanview** (http://www.irfanview.com) is a free alternative, but it's not quite as polished. If you'd like to edit the images, try **Paint Shop Pro** (http://www.jasc.com), the next best thing to Adobe's professional, though somewhat overpriced, PhotoShop.

Finally, you're sure to encounter the odd **portable document file** (PDF), particularly at government sites. These are like laid-out brochures, and can be viewed within your Web browser using **Adobe's Acrobat Reader** (http://www.adobe.com/prodindex/acrobat/) plug-in. However, because they can contain fonts and images they're often quite bloated compared to their Word or Word Perfect equivalents. It's better to click on the link, choose "save target as" from your mouse menu, save them to your Desktop and then click on the file to view.

## Other Internet software

Despite Microsoft, AOL, Netscape and Real Networks, there's still competition left in the boutique end of the Internet software trade. You'll find numerous standout programs mentioned within the relevant sections throughout this book, but of course, there are many more, and new strains appear daily. So don't take our word for it. If you become embroiled in Usenet, for instance, investigate several newsreaders and ruthlessly toss them out if they fail to meet your expectations. Check into any of the software guides listed in our Web directory (p.291) and you'll be sure to leave with a few downloads in progress!

# 20

# A Brief History of the Internet

The Internet may be a recent media phenomenon but as a concept it's actually older than most of its users; it was born in the 1960s – a long time before anyone coined the buzz-words "Information SuperHighway". Of course, there's no question that the Net deserves its current level of attention. It really is a quantum leap in global communications, though – right now – it's still more of a prototype than a finished prod-uct. While Bill Gates and Al Gore rhapsodize about such household services as video-on-demand, most Netizens would be happy with a system fast enough to view stills-on-demand. Nonetheless, it's getting there.

## The online bomb shelter

The concept of the Net might not have been hatched in Microsoft's cabinet war rooms, but it did play a role in a previous contest for world domination. It was 1957, at the height of the Cold War. The Soviets had just launched the first Sputnik, thus beating the USA into space. The race was on. In response, the US Department of Defense formed the **Advanced Research Projects Agency (ARPA)** to bump up its technological prowess. Twelve years later, this spawned **ARPAnet** – a project to develop a military research network, or specifically, the world's first decentralized computer network.

In those days, no-one had PCs. The computer world was based on mainframe computers and dumb terminals. These usually involved a gigantic, fragile box in a climate-controlled room, which acted as a hub, with a mass of cables spoking out to keyboard/monitor ensembles. The concept of independent intelligent processors pooling resources through a network was brave new territory that would require the development of new hardware, software, and connectivity methods.

The driving force behind decentralization, ironically, was the bomb-proofing factor. Nuke a mainframe and the system goes down. But bombing a network would, at worst, remove only a few nodes. The remainder could route around it unharmed. Or so the theory went.

## Wiring the world

Over the next decade, **research agencies** and **universities** flocked to join the network. US institutions such as UCLA, MIT, Stanford, and Harvard led the way, and in 1973, the network crossed the Atlantic to include University College London and Norway's Royal Radar Establishment.

The 1970s also saw the introduction of **electronic mail**, **FTP**, **Telnet**, and what would become the **Usenet newsgroups**. The early 1980s brought **TCP/IP**, the **Domain Name System**, **Network News Transfer Protocol**, and the European networks **EUnet** (European UNIX Network), **MiniTel** (the widely adopted French consumer network), and **JANET** (Joint Academic Network), as well as the Japanese **UNIX** Network. **ARPA** evolved to handle the research traffic, while a second network, MILnet, took over the US military intelligence.

An important development took place in 1986, when the US National Science Foundation established **NSFnet** by linking five university super-computers at a backbone speed of 56 Kbps. This opened the gateway for external universities to tap in to superior processing power and share resources. In the three years between 1984 and 1988, the number of host computers on the **Internet** (as it was now being called) grew from about 1000 to over 60,000. NSFnet, meanwhile, increased its capacity to T1 (1544 Kbps). Over the next few years, more and more countries joined the network, spanning the globe from Australia and New Zealand, to Iceland, Israel, Brazil, India, and Argentina.

It was at this time too, that **Internet Relay Chat** (IRC) burst onto the scene providing an alternative to CNN's incessant, but censored, Gulf War coverage. By this stage, the Net had grown far beyond its original charter. Although ARPA had succeeded in creating the basis for decentralized computing, whether it was actually a military success was debatable. It might have been bombproof, but it also opened new doors to espionage. It was never particularly secure, and it is suspected that Soviet agents routinely hacked in to forage for research data. In 1990, ARPAnet folded, and NSFnet took over administering the Net.

## Coming in from the cold

Global electronic communication was far too useful and versatile to stay confined to academics. Big business was starting to notice. The Cold War looked over and world economies were regaining confidence after the 1987 stock market savaging. In most places, market trading moved from the pits and blackboards onto computer screens. The financial sector expected fingertip real-time data and that feeling was spreading. The world was ready for a people's network. And since the Net was already in place, funded by taxpayers, there was really no excuse not to open it to the public.

In 1991, the NSF lifted its restrictions on enterprise. During the Net's early years, its "**Acceptable Use Policy**" specifically prohibited using the network for profit. Changing that policy opened the floodgates to commerce with the greater public close behind.

However, before anyone could connect to the Net, someone had to sell them a connection. The **Commercial Internet eXchange (CIX)**, a network of major commercial access providers, formed to create a commercial backbone and divert traffic from the NSFnet. Before long, dozens of budding ISPs began rigging up points of presence in their bedrooms. Meanwhile, NSFnet upgraded its backbone to T3 (44,736 Kbps).

By this time, the Net had established itself as a viable medium for transferring data, but with one major problem. You had to know where to look. That process involved knowing a lot more about computers, and the UNIX computing language, than most punters would relish. The next few years saw an explosion in navigation protocols, such as WAIS, Gopher, Veronica, and, most importantly, the now-dominant World Wide Web.

## The gold rush begins

In 1989, Tim Berners-Lee of **CERN**, the Swiss particle physics institute, proposed the basis of the World Wide Web, initially as a means of sharing physics research. His goal was a seamless network in which data from any source could be accessed in a simple, consistent way with one program, on any type of computer. The Web did this, encompassing all existing infosystems such as FTP, Gopher, and Usenet, without alteration. It remains an unqualified success.

As the number of Internet hosts exceeded one million, the **Internet Society** was formed to brainstorm protocols and attempt to co-ordinate and direct the Net's escalating expansion. **Mosaic** – the first graphical **Web browser** – was released, and declared to be the "killer application of the 1990s". It made navigating the Internet as simple as pointing and clicking, and took away the need to know UNIX. The Web's traffic increased by 25-fold in the year up to June 1994, and domain names for **commercial organizations** (.com) began to outnumber those of educational institutions (.edu).

As the Web grew, so too did the global village. The media began to notice, slowly realizing that the Internet was something that went way beyond propeller heads and students. Almost every country in the world had joined the Net. Even the White House was online.

Of course, as word of a captive market got around, entrepreneurial brains went into overdrive. Canter & Seigel, an Arizona law firm, notoriously **"spammed"** Usenet with **advertisements** for the US green card lottery. Although the Net was tentatively open for business, crossposting advertisements to every newsgroup was decidedly bad form. Such was the ensuing wrath that C&S had no chance of filtering out genuine responses from the server-breaking level of hate mail they received. A precedent was thus established for **how not to do business on the Net**. Pizza Hut, by contrast, showed how to do it subtly by setting up a trial service on the Web. Although it generated wads of positive publicity, it too was doomed by impracticalities. Nevertheless, the ball had begun to roll.

## The homesteaders

As individuals arrived to stake out Web territory, businesses followed. Most had no idea what to do once they got their brand online. Too many arrived with a bang, only to peter out in a perpetuity of "under construction signs". Soon business cards not only sported email addresses, but Web addresses as well. And rather than send a CV and stiff letter, job aspirants could now send a brief email accompanied with a "see my Web page" for further details.

The Internet moved out of the realm of luxury into an elite necessity, verging toward a commodity. Some early business sites gathered such a following that by 1995 they were able to charge high rates for advertising banners. A few, including Web **portals** such as **InfoSeek** and **Yahoo**, made it to the Stock Exchange boards, while others, like **GNN**, attracted buyers.

But it wasn't all success stories. Copyright lawyers arrived in droves. Well-meaning devotees, cheeky opportunists, and info-terrorists alike felt the iron fists of Lego, McDonald's, MTV, the Louvre, Fox, Sony, the Church of Scientology and others clamp down on their "unofficial Web sites" or newsgroups. It wasn't always a case of corporate right but of might, as small players couldn't foot the expenses to test **new legal boundaries**. The honeymoon was officially over.

## Point of no return

By the beginning of 1995, the Net was well and truly within the public realm. It was impossible to escape. The media became bored with extolling its virtues, so it turned to **sensationalism**. The Net reached the status of an Oprah Winfrey issue. New tales of hacking, porn, bombmaking, terrorist handbooks, homebreaking, and sexual harassment began to tarnish the Internet's iconic position as the great international equalizer. But that didn't stop businesses, schools, banks, government bodies, politicians, and consumers from swarming online, nor the major **Online Services** – such as CompuServe, America Online, and Prodigy, which had been developing in parallel since the late 1980s – from adding Internet access as a sideline to their existing private networks.

As 1995 progressed, Mosaic, the previous year's killer application, lost its footing to a superior browser, **Netscape**. Not such big news, you might imagine, but after a half-year of rigorous beta-testing, Netscape went public with the third largest ever NASDAQ IPO share value – around $2.4bn.

Meantime, Microsoft, which had formerly disregarded the Internet, released **Windows 95**, a PC operating platform incorporating access to the controversial **Microsoft Network**. Although **IBM** had done a similar thing six months earlier with **OS/2 Warp** and its **IBM Global Network**, Microsoft's was an altogether different scheme. It offered full Net access but its real product was its own separate network, which many people feared might supersede the Net, giving Microsoft an unholy reign over information distribution. But that never happened. Within months, Microsoft, smarting from bad press, and finding the Net a larger animal even than itself, about-turned and declared a full commitment to furthering the Internet.

# Browser wars

As Microsoft advanced on the horizon, Netscape continued pushing the envelope, driving the Web into new territory with each beta release. New enhancements arrived at such a rate that competitors began to drop out as quickly as they appeared. This was the era of "This page looks best if viewed with Netscape". Of course, it wasn't just Netscape since much of the new activity stemmed from the innovative products of third-party developers such as **MacroMedia (Shockwave)**, **Progressive Networks (RealAudio)**, **Apple (QuickTime)**, and **Sun (Java)**. The Web began to spring to life with animations, music, 3D worlds, and all sorts of new tricks.

While Netscape's market dominance gave developers the confidence to accept it as the de facto standard, treating it as a kind of Internet operating system into which to "plug" their products, Microsoft, an old hand at taking possession of cleared territory, began to launch a whole series of free Net tools. These included **Internet Explorer**, a browser with enhancements of its own, including **ActiveX**, a Web-centric programming environment more powerful than the much-lauded **Java**, but without the same platform independence, and clearly geared toward advancing Microsoft's software dominance. Not only was Internet Explorer suddenly the only other browser in the race, unlike Netscape, it was genuinely free. And many were not only rating it as the better product, but also crediting Microsoft with a broader vision of the Net's direction.

By mid-1997, every Online Service and almost every major ISP had signed deals with Microsoft to distribute its browser. Even intervention by the US Department of Justice over Microsoft's (logical but monopolistic) bundling of Internet Explorer as an integral part of Windows 98 couldn't impede its progress. Netscape looked bruised. While it continued shipping minor upgrades it no longer led either in market share or innovation. In desperation, it handed over the project of completely reworking the code to the general programming public at Mozilla.org. When AOL bought Netscape in early 1999, little doubt remained. Netscape had given up the fight.

# Found on the internet

Skipping back to late 1995, the backlash against Internet freedom had moved into full flight. The expression "**found on the Internet**", became the news tag of the minute, depicting the Net as the source of everything evil from bomb recipes to child pornography. While editors and commentators, often with little direct experience of the Net, urged that "children" be protected, the Net's own media and opinion shakers pushed the **freedom of speech** barrow. It became apparent that this uncensored, uncontrollable new media could shake the very foundations of democracy.

At first politicians didn't take much notice. Few could even grasp the concept of what the Net was about, let alone figure out a way to regulate its activities. The first, and easiest, target was **porn**, resulting in raids on hundreds of **private bulletin boards** worldwide and a few much-publicized convictions for the possession of child porn. BBSs were sitting ducks, being mostly self-contained and run by someone who could take the rap. Net activists, however, feared that the primary objective was to send a ripple of fear through a Net community that believed it was bigger than the law, and to soften the public to the notion that the Internet, as it stood, posed a threat to national wellbeing.

In December 1995, at the request of German authorities, **CompuServe** cut its newsfeed to exclude the bulk of newsgroups carrying sexual material. But the groups cut weren't just pornographers, some were dedicated to gay and abortion issues. This brought to light the difficulty in drawing the lines of obscenity, and the problems with publishing across foreign boundaries. Next came the **US Communications Decency Act**, a proposed legislation to forbid the online publication of "obscene" material. It was poorly conceived, however, and, following opposition from a very broad range of groups (including such mainstream bodies as the American Libraries Association), was overturned, and the decision later upheld in the Supreme Court.

Outside the US, meanwhile, more authorities reacted. In **France**, three ISP chiefs were temporarily jailed for supplying obscene newsgroups, while in **Australia** police prosecuted several users for downloading child porn. NSW courts introduced legislation banning obscene material with such loose wording that the Internet itself could be deemed illegal – if the law is ever tested. In **Britain**, in mid-1996, the police tried a "voluntary" approach, identifying newsgroups that carried pornography as beyond the pale, and requesting that providers remove them from their feed. Most complied, but there was unease within the Internet industry that this was the wrong approach – the same groups would migrate elsewhere and the root of the problem would remain.

But the debate was, or is, about far more than porn, despite the huffing and puffing. For **Net fundamentalists**, the issue is about holding ground against any compromises in liberty, and retaining the global village as a political force – potentially capable of bringing down governments and large corporations. Indeed, they argue that these battles over publishing freedom have shown governments to be out of touch with both technology and the social undercurrent, and that in the long run the balance of power will shift toward the people, toward a new democracy.

## Wiretapping

Another slow-news-day story of the mid-1990s depicted **hackers** ruling networks, stealing money, and creating havoc. Great reading, but the reality was less alarming. Although the US Department of Defense reported hundreds of thousands of network break-ins, they claimed it was more annoying than damaging. While in the commercial world, little went astray except the odd credit card file. (Bear in mind that every time you hand your credit card to a shop assistant they get the same information.) In fact, by and large, for an online population greater than the combined size of New York, Moscow, London, Calcutta, and Tokyo, there were surprisingly few noteworthy crimes. Yet the perception remained that the Net was too unsafe for the exchange of sensitive information such as payment details.

**Libertarians** raged at the US Government's refusal to lift export bans on crack-proof **encryption algorithms**. But cryptography, the science of message coding, has traditionally been classified as a weapon and thus export of encryption falls under the Arms Control acts.

Encryption requires a secret key to open the contents of a message and often another public key to code the message. These keys can be generated for regular use by individuals or, in the case of Web transactions, simply for one session upon agreement between the server and client. Several governments proposed to employ official escrow authorities to keep a register of all secret keys and surrender them upon warrant – an unpopular proposal, to put it mildly, among a Net community who regard invasion of privacy as an issue equal in importance to censorship, and government monitors as instruments of repression.

However, authorities were so used to being able to tap phones, intercept mail, and install listening devices to aid investigations, that they didn't relish giving up their freedom either. Government officials made a lot of noise about needing to monitor data to protect national security, though their true motives probably involve monitoring internal insurgence and catching tax cheats – stuff they're not really supposed to do but we put up with anyway because if we're law-abiding it's mostly in our best interests.

The implications of such obstinacy went far beyond personal privacy. Business awaited browsers that could talk to commerce servers using totally snooper-proof encryption. Strong encryption technology had already been built into browsers, but it was illegal to export them from the US. The law was finally relaxed in mid-2000.

## The entertainment arrives

While politicians, big business, bankers, telcos, and online action groups such as **CommerceNet** and the **Electronic Frontier Foundation** fretted the future of privacy and its impact on digital commerce, the online world partied on regardless. If 1996 was the year of the Web, then 1997 was the year the **games** began. Netizens had been swapping chess moves, playing dress-up, and struggling with the odd network game over the Net for years, but it took id Software's **Quake** to lure the gaming masses online. Not to miss out, Online Services and ISPs took steps to prioritize game traffic, while hard-core corporate data moved further back on the shelves.

Music took off, too. **Bands** and **DJs** routinely simulcast, or exclusively played, concerts over the Net while celebrities such as Michael Jackson, Joe Dolce, and Paul McCartney bared their souls in public chat rooms. Web pages came alive with the sound of music, from cheesy synthesized backgrounds to live radio feeds. Many online music stores like **CDNow** reported profits, while **Amazon** became a major force in bookselling.

And then there was the Net as a prime news medium. As **Pathfinder** touched down on Mars, back on Earth millions logged into NASA sites to scour the Martian landscape for traces of life. China marched into Hong Kong, Tiger Woods rewrote golfing history, Australia regained the Ashes, and Mike Tyson fell from grace, all live on the Net. In response to this breaking of news on Web sites and newsgroups, an increasing number of **print newspapers** began delivering online versions before their hard copies hit the stands. In 1997, if you weren't on the Net, you weren't in the media.

## The casualties

Not everyone had reason to party in 1997. **Cybercafés** – the height of touted cool in 1995 – tended to flop as quickly as they appeared, as did many small **Internet Service Providers**, if they weren't swallowed by larger fish. From over thirty **browsers** in early 1996, less than a year later, only two real players – Netscape and Microsoft – remained in the game. The also-ran software houses that initially thrived on the Net's avenue for distribution and promotion faded from view as the two browser giants ruthlessly crammed more features into their plug-and-play Web desktops. Microsoft, and scores of other software developers, declared that their future products would be able to update themselves online, either automatically or by clicking in the right place. So much for the software dealer.

Meanwhile, **Web TV** arrived delivering Web pages and email onto home TV screens. It offered a cheap, simple alternative to PCs, but found its way to a smaller niche market than its fanfare predicted.

The whole **Web design industry** was due for a shakeout. Overnight Web cowboys – lacking the programming skills to code, the artistic merit to design, or the spelling standards to edit, yet who'd charged through the teeth for cornering the home-page design scam – were left exposed by the emerging professionalism. New media had come of age. The top Web chimps reworked their résumés and pitched in with online design houses. Major ad agencies formed new media departments, and splashed Web addresses over everything from milk cartons to toothpaste tubes.

Bizarrely though, 1997's best-known Web design team, **Higher Source**, will be remembered not for HTML handiwork, but for publishing their cult's agenda to top themselves in conjunction with the passing of the Hale Bopp comet. This was the Internet as major news story. Within hours of the mass suicide, several sites appeared spoofing both its corporate pages as well as its cult, **Heaven's Gate**. Days later, there were enough to spawn four new Yahoo subdirectories.

Back in the real world of **business and money**, major companies have played surprisingly by the book, observing netiquette – the Net's informal code of conduct. The marriage has been awkward but generally happy. Even the absurd court cases between blockbuster sites such as **Microsoft Sidewalk v. TicketMaster** and **Amazon v. Barnes & Noble** (over the "biggest bookstore in the world" claim) did little to convince Netizens that they were witnessing anything more than carefully orchestrated publicity stunts. Indeed, many felt launching a Web site without some kind of legal suit was a waste of free publicity. It seemed like just a bit of fun. And as big money flowed in, **bandwidths** increased, content improved, ma and pa scuttled aboard, and the online experience richened.

Alas, the same couldn't be said for the new school entrepreneurs. Low advertising costs saw **Usenet newsgroups and email in-trays** choked with crossposted get-rich schemes, network marketing plans, and porno adverts.

Further, unprecedented **banks of email** broke servers at AOL, MSN, and scores of smaller providers. Temporarily, Netcom was forced to bar all mail originating from Hotmail, the most popular free Web email service, and consequent safe haven for fly-by-night operators due to the level of spam originating from its domain. At the same time, in July 1997, a mislaid backhoe ripped up a vital US backbone artery darkening large parts of the Net – something many had presumed impossible – and reducing the worldwide network to a crawl. The Net was nuclear-proof maybe, but certainly not invulnerable.

## The world's biggest playground

By the end of 1997, the Net's population had skyrocketed to well over a hundred million. The media increasingly relied on it for research and, in the process, began to understand it. It could no longer be written off as geek-land when it was thrust this far into mainstream consciousness. Notable among the most recent arrivals were the so-called "grey surfers", predominantly retirees, who in some cases found it the difference between having few interests and few friends, and suddenly finding a reason to live. Indeed, the Net was looking not only useful, but essential, and those without it had good reason to feel left behind.

This new maturity arrived on the back of email, with the Web hot on its heels. As toner sales plummeted, surveys indicated that email had not only overtaken the fax, but possibly even the telephone, as the business communication tool of choice. However, at the same time, it could also lay claim to being the greatest time waster ever introduced into an office with staff spending large chunks of their days reading circulars, forwarding curios, and flirting with their online pals.

Email's speed, and the ease in carbon copying an entire address book, brought new implications to the six degrees of separation. Something with universal appeal, like the infernal dancing baby animation, could be disseminated to millions within a matter of hours, potentially reaching everyone on the Net within days. And, as most journalists were by this stage hooked in, whatever circulated on the Net often found its way into other media formats. Not surprisingly, the fastest-moving chain emails were often hoaxes. One such prank, an address of sensible old-timer advice, supposedly delivered by Kurt Vonnegut to MIT graduates (but actually taken from Mary Schmick's Chicago Tribune column) saturated the Net within a week. "Romeo and Juliet" director, Baz Lurhman, was so taken he put it to music resulting in the cult hit "Sunscreen", which even more incredibly was re-spoofed into a XXXX beer advert. All within six months.

On a more annoying note, almost everyone received virus hoaxes that warned not to open email with certain subject headings. Millions took them seriously, earnestly forwarding them to their entire address books. An email campaign kicked off by Howard Stern propelled "Hank, the ugly drunken dwarf", to the top of People's 100 Most Beautiful People poll as voted on the Net. Meanwhile the Chinese community rallied to push Michelle Kwan into second place. But the biggest coup of all was Matt Drudge's email leaking Bill Clinton's inappropriate affair with Monica Lewinsky, which sent the old world media into the biggest feeding frenzy since the OJ trial. Although it might not have brought down the most powerful man in the world, it showed how in 1998, almost anyone, anywhere could be heard.

## The show must go on

In May 1998, the blossoming media romance with hackers as urban folk heroes turned sour when a consortium of good-fairy hackers, known as the **L0pht**, assured a US Senate Government Affairs Committee that they, or someone less benevolent, could render the Net entirely unusable within half an hour. It wasn't meant as a threat, but a call to arms against the apathy of those who'd designed, sold, and administered the systems. The Pentagon had already been penetrated (by a young Israeli hacker), and though most reported attacks amounted to little more than vandalism, with an increasing number of essential services tapped in, the probability of major disaster veered toward looking possible.

Undeterred, Net commerce continued to break into new territories. **Music**, in particular, looked right at home with the arrival of DIY CD compilation shops and several major artists such as Massive Attack, Willie Nelson and the Beach Boys airing their new releases on the Net in MP3, before unleashing them on CD. However, these exclusive previews weren't always intentional. For instance, Swervedriver's beleaguered "99th Dream" found its way onto Net bootleg almost a year before its official release.

By now, celebrity chat appearances hardly raised an eyebrow. Even major powerbrokers like Clinton and Yeltsin had appeared before an online inquisition. To top it off, in April 1998, Koko, a 300-pound gorilla, fronted up to confess to some 20,000 chatsters that she'd rather be playing with Smokey, her pet kitten.

## The red-light district

Despite the bottomless reserves of free Web space, personal vanity pages and Web diaries took a downturn in 1998. The novelty was passing, a sign perhaps that the Web was growing up. This didn't, however, prevent live Web cameras, better known as **Webcams**, from enjoying a popularity resurgence. But this time around they weren't so much being pointed at lizards, fish, ski slopes or intersections, but at whoever connected them to the Net – a fad which resulted in numerous bizarre excursions in exhibitionism from some very ordinary folk. Leading the fray was the entirely unremarkable Jennifer Ringley, who became a Web household name simply for letting the world see her move about her college room, clothed and, very occasionally, otherwise. She might have only been famous for being famous, but it was fame enough to land her a syndicated newspaper column about showing off and, of course, a tidy packet from the thousands of subscribers who paid real money to access Jennicam.

But this was the tame end of the Net's trade in voyeurism. And these were boom times for pornographers. Research suggested as high as 90 percent of network traffic was consumed by porn images. That's not to suggest that anywhere near 90 percent of users were involved, only that the images consume so much bandwidth. The story in Usenet was even more dire with more than 80 percent of the non-binary traffic hogged by spam and spam cancel messages. Meanwhile, the three top Web search aids, HotBot, Altavista and Yahoo, served click-through banners on suggestive keywords. However you felt about pornography from a moral standpoint, it had definitely become a nuisance.

## The bottleneck

As 1998 progressed, **cable Internet access** became increasingly available, and even affordable in the USA. New subscribers could suddenly jump from download speeds of, at best, 56 Kbps to as high as 10 Mbps. Meanwhile several telcos, such as PacBell and GTE, began rolling out ADSL, another broadband technology capable of megabit access, this time over plain copper telephone wires. However, even at these speeds, users still had to deal with the same old bottleneck. Namely the Internet's backbone, which had been struggling to cope with even the low-speed dial-up traffic.

The power to **upgrade the backbone**, or more correctly backbones, lies in the hands of those who own the major cables and thus effectively control the Internet. It's always seemed inevitable that the global telecommunication superpowers would starve the smaller players out of the market. And the emergence of Internet telephony has forced telcos to look further down the track at the broader scenario where whoever controls the Internet not only controls data, but voice traffic as well. They recognize that their core business could be eroded by satellite and cable companies. To survive, telcos need to compete on the same level, provide an alternative, or join forces with their rivals. At the moment all three seem viable options.

## The dust clears but the fog remains

As we packed up shop for the millennium, fretting over double-digit date blunders, the Internet settled into a consolidation phase. For the most part, what was hot got hotter while the remainder atrophied. Broadband cable, ADSL, and satellite access forged ahead, particularly in the US and Australia. Meanwhile in the UK, British Telecom stooped to an eleventh-hour exploit on its unpopular metered local call system, weaseling deals with local ISPs to enable free access by divvying up its phone bill booty. Surprisingly, instead of torching 10 Downing St for allowing the situation to exist in the first place, browbeaten Brits snapped it up, propelling free access pioneer Freeserve to the top of the ISP pops within months. At the time of writing, the situation is thickening with **budget all-you-can-eat ADSL** and unmetered Internet calls about to hit the UK streets.

Interest in online commerce surged with explosive growth in stock trading, auctions, travel booking, and mail order computers. Big-budget empire builders such as AOL, Amazon, Cisco, Disney, Excite, Microsoft, and Real Networks hit overdrive announcing intertwined strategic mergers and continued swallowing and stomping on smaller talent. Most notably AOL, with little more than a dip into petty cash, wolfed down Netscape. Not, as many assumed, for its revolutionary browser but for the sizable userbase still buzzing its browser's default home page. This, however, wasn't the Netscape of the mid 1990s, but a defeated relic that had lost its way, ceased innovating, and appeared unable to ship products. Its legacy had been passed over to Microsoft, which remained in court squabbling over Internet Explorer, Windows 98, and its success in cornering all but some 5 percent of the operating system market share. Apart from whatever voyeuristic pleasure could be gained from king-hitting computing's tallest poppy, the Department of Justice's case grew increasingly meaningless against the broader backdrop. No matter what the outcome, the computer-wielding public had arrived well before their dinner bell and their problem was not lack of choice, but lack of quality. Even Apple's allegedly foolproof iMac fell way short of a sturdy carriage to traverse the Net, play games, and make life generally more pushbutton computerized.

By this stage the Internet was ready to become a public utility, but both the computing and access provision industry remained rooted within a hobbyist mindset. As PC dealers shamelessly crammed their systems with interfering utilities, ISPs continued to supply inadequate bandwidth, unreliable software and irresponsible advice. Yet no alternative existed, and governments appeared incapable of intelligent input. As the 20th century bit the dirt, you didn't have to be a geek to get on the Net, but it sure didn't hurt.

## The American dream

Doomsday was not televised live as daylight broke across the year 2000. Planes did not crash, Washington was not nuked, and ATMs did not randomly eject crisp dollar bills. Instead, attentions turned to cast fresh aspersions on the ever-inflating **Internet stock bubble**. The new tech stocks were driving the biggest speculative frenzy since Tulipmania. Every grandmother and her cabbie wanted in on the **Dot Com action**. Cisco Systems, a network hardware supplier and hardly a household name, celebrated its tenth birthday by briefly becoming the world's biggest company (in terms of market cap). To add further insult to the old world order, AOL, foster home to twenty million chirpy AOLers, offered its hand to the TIME Warner cross media conglomerate. Meanwhile billionaire playboy Bill Gates, the very essence of the American dream, continued defiantly delivering his own brand of truth, justice and the Microsoft way to the desktops of 19 out of 20 computers. What could possibly go wrong?

Enter US District Judge Thomas Penfield Jackson who declared that Microsoft had maintained its monopoly by anti-competitive means, and that it should sever both physical and corporate ties between its Internet software and Windows. This ruling, he assured, would result in higher quality products due to increased competition. Which raised the question why software standards weren't directly on trial instead. But Microsoft had made few friends outside the fans of Ayn Rand, particularly within the ironically Mac monopolized media. Any public spanking was welcomed, so this was as good as a win. Yet, in reality, it was an unsatisfying outcome for all concerned. Not least for investors, whose tech share portfolios crumbled. And so that was it for the speculative Dot Com start-ups. As the house of Gates fell, so too did the bricks around it. By the time Flash riddled Boo.com folded in May 2000, Dot Com was already a dirty word.

With an appeal pending in the Supreme Court, Microsoft brazenly released **ME**, yet another version of Windows with Internet Explorer inside, and furthermore announced its future applications would be delivered on demand across the Net. What little sympathy remained for Bill and his merry cast of outlaws was almost completely eroded.

## Nobody can stop the music

As wave after wave of email-borne viruses sneezed from Outlook address books, it seemed clear that most office workers lacked basic computer training. Overlooked in the endless blather of mass media hysteria was the simple truth that **Melissa**, **Happy 99**, **I Love you**, and similar Internet worms could only be propagated by the grossly incompetent. It also seemed certain that it would happen again.

But viruses weren't the only source of mischief. A 15-year-old Canadian, going by the name of Mafiaboy, unleashed a bevy of **Denial of Service** attacks temporarily knocking out several high profile Web sites such as Yahoo, Amazon and eTrade. Despite his relatively low level of technical expertise he was able to outwit the FBI for almost three months. Even then it was only his chat room confession that triggered the arrest.

With pirate **MP3 music tracks** hogging the bulk of college network bandwidth, legal action inevitably followed. Napster faced the music against stadium rockers Metallica, and the Recording Industry Association of America sued MP3.com over its ingenious Beam-It service. While the holders of copyright won in the courts of law, back in the real world it was not only business as usual, but the publicity drew millions of new music lovers into the trading loop.

## A brighter tomorrow

Now that the **people's network** has the globe in an irreversible stranglehold, you might assume the wired revolution is as good as over. Perhaps it is, but for those in the dark, the reality can be less comforting. A passable knowledge of the Internet in 1997 was enough to land you a job. Today, in many fields, it's becoming a prerequisite. It's a case of get online or get left behind. But the most worrisome aspect is not the difficulty in getting online, but the time involved in keeping up to date, and its stress on our physical, mental, and social wellbeing.

Still, like it or not, the Net is the closest thing yet to an all-encompassing snapshot of the human race. Never before have our words and actions been so immediately accountable in front of such a far-reaching audience. If we're scammed, we can instantly warn others. If we believe there's a government cover-up, we can expose it through the Net. If we want to be heard, no matter what it is we have to say, we can tell it to the Net. And, in the same way, if we need to know more, or we need to find numbers, we can turn to it for help.

What's most apparent all up, is that humanity looks in pretty okay shape. That's kind of ironic, because it didn't necessarily look that way before. But we've now been able to see that for every extreme there appears to be many more moderates; for every hate group, a thousand peace-makers; and for every conspiracy theory, if not some sensible explanation, then at least a few attentive ears. We've been able to examine the weirdest and the worst the world has to offer and contrast it against a greater global theme. Now that our boundaries are so much easier to explore, the future of not only the Net, but the planet itself, surely looks brighter.

The problem with such rapid improvement is that our expectations grow to meet it. But the Net, even at age thirty-something, is still only in its infancy. So be patient, enjoy it for what it is today, and complain, but not too much. One day you'll look back and get all nostalgic about the times you logged into the world through old copper telephone wires. It's amazing it works at all.

# 21

# Net Language

**B**efore the Internet became a public thoroughfare, it was overrun with academics. The greasy geek types were more likely to be chatting and swapping shareware on the bulletin board networks. Popularizing the Internet brought the two cultures together, along with, more recently, the less digitally versed general public. While the old school types are now in the minority, their culture still kicks on, as witnessed by the continued use of their exclusively online way of expression.

Low transfer speed, poor typing skills, and the need for quick responses were among the pioneers' justifications for keeping things brief. But using Net lingo was also a way of showing you were in the know. These days, it's not so prevalent, though you're sure to encounter acronyms in **IRC** and, to a lesser extent, **Usenet** and **Mailing Lists**. Since IRC is a snappy medium, with line space at a premium, acronyms and the like can be genuinely useful – if they're understood.

Note: nothing will get you on the wrong side of a newsgroup faster than swearing. You can swear freely (almost) in everyday life, so you might think the same should apply online. You're welcome to try, but it probably won't work in your favor. It's not so much that you'll offend someone, it's that you'll be set upon by the pious, who'll furthermore delight in complaining to your ISP. Yet if you reduce your 20th century obscenity to an obvious abbreviation, such as F or F★★★, you'll not hear a word of protest!

# Shorthand: Net acronyms

| | |
|---|---|
| AFAIK | As far as I know |
| AOLer | AOL member (often not a compliment) |
| A/S/L | Age/Sex/Location |
| BOHICA | Bend over here it comes again |
| BBL | Be back later |
| BD or BFD | Big deal |
| BFN or B4N | Bye for now |
| BRB | Be right back |
| BTW | By the way |
| CUL8R or L8R | See you later |
| CYA | See ya |
| F2F (S2S) | Face to face (skin to skin) |
| FWIW | For what it's worth |
| g | Grin |
| GR8 | Great |
| HTH | Hope this helps |
| IM(H)O | In my (humble or honest) opinion |
| IYSWIM | If you see what I mean |
| IAE | In any event |
| IOW | In other words |
| LOL | Laughing out loud |
| MOTD | Message of the day |
| NRN | No reply necessary |
| NW or NFW | No way |
| OIC | Oh I see |
| OTOH | On the other hand |
| POV | Point of view |
| RO(T)FL (MAO) | Roll on the floor laughing (my ass off) |
| RTM or RTFM | Read the manual |
| SOL | Sooner or later |
| TIA | Thanks in advance |

| | |
|---|---|
| TTYL | Talk to you later |
| WRT | With respect to |
| WTH? or WTF? | What the hell? |
| YMMV | Your mileage may vary |

## Smileys and emoticons

Back in the old days, potentially contentious remarks could be tempered by tacking <grins> on the end in much the same way that a dog wags its tail to show it's harmless. But that wasn't enough for the E-generation, whose trademark smiley icon became the 80s peace sign. From the same honed minds that discovered 71077345 inverted spelled Greenpeace's *bête noire*, came the ASCII smiley. This time, instead of turning it upside-down, you had to look at it sideways to see a smiling face. An expression that words, supposedly, fail to convey. Well, at least in such limited space. Inevitably this grew into a whole family of emoticons (emotional icons). The odd smiley might have its use in diffusing barbs but whether you'd want to use any of the others is up to your perception of the line between cute and dorky. The nose is optional:

| | | | |
|---|---|---|---|
| :-) | Smiling | :-X | I'll say nothing |
| :-D | Laughing | :-L~~ | Drooling |
| :-o | Shock | :-P | Sticking out tongue |
| :-( | Frowning | (hmm)Ooo.. :-) | Happy thoughts |
| :'-( | Crying | (hmm)Ooo.. :-( | Sad thoughts |
| ;-) | Winking | 0:-) | Angel |
| X= | Fingers crossed | }:> | Devil |
| : =) | Little Hitler | ( )l | Beer |
| {} | Hugging | :8) | Pig |
| :* | Kissing | \o/ | Hallelujah |
| $-) | Greedy | @}-`—,—- | Rose |
| X-) | I see nothing | 8:)3= | Happy girl |

A few others, mostly Japanese anime–derived, work right way up:

| | | | |
|---|---|---|---|
| @^_^@ | ........................ Blushing | ^_^; | ............................ Sweating |
| *^_^* | .................. Dazzling grin | T_T | ...................................... Crying |

# Emphasis

You could also express actions or emotions by adding commentary within < **these signs** >.

For example:

<flushed> I've just escaped the clutches of frenzied train-spotters
< removes conductor's cap, wipes brow >.

Or by using asterisks to *emphasize* words. Simply *wrap* the appropriate word: Hey everyone look at *me*.

## l33t h4x0r d00dz

When your mouse misleads you into young and impressionable realms you might encounter language that looks like this:
"l00k 4t ME. I'M @n L33t h4x0r dUD3".
("Look at me. I'm an elite hacker dude".)
To translate see: http://www.geocities.com/mnstr_2000/
    Or better still, back-peddle out of there.

## For more

If you come across an abbreviation you don't understand, ask its author. Don't worry about appearing stupid as these expressions aren't exactly common knowledge. Alternatively consult one of the many online references such as:

**Acronym Finder**         http://www.acronymfinder.com
**Emoticon Universe**      http://emoticonuniverse.com
**Jargon and Hacker style**
                           http://www.tuxedo.org/~esr/jargon/html/
**Microsoft lexicon**      http://www.cinepad.com/mslex.htm
**NetLingo**               http://www.netlingo.com
**Slang Zone**             http://www.sabram.com/site/slang.html

# 22

# Glossary

## A

**Access Provider** Company that sells Internet connections. Also called Internet Service Provider (ISP).

**ActiveX** Microsoft concept that allows a program to run inside a Web page.

**ADSL** Asynchronous Digital Subscriber Line. Broadband over the phone line.

**Anonymous FTP server** Remote computer, with a publicly accessible file archive, that accepts "anonymous" as the log-in name and an email address as the password.

**AOL** America Online. Last surviving Online Service. Loved by all.

**ASCII** American Standard Code for Information Interchange. Text format readable by all computers. Also called "plain text".

**Attachment** File included with email or other form of message.

# B

**Backbone**   Set of paths that carry longhaul Net traffic.
**Bandwidth**   Size of the data pipeline. Increase bandwidth and more data can flow at once.
**Baud rate**   Number of times a modem's signal changes per second when transmitting data. Not to be confused with bps.
**Binary file**   Any file that contains more than plain text, such as a program.
**Binary newsgroup**   Usenet group that's specifically meant for posting the above files.
**Binhex**   Method of encoding, used on Macs.
**Bookmarks**   Netscape file used to store Web addresses.
**Boot up**   Start a computer.
**Bounced mail**   Email returned to sender.
**Bps**   Bits per second. The rate that data is transferred between two modems. A bit is the basic unit of data.
**Broadband**   High-speed Internet access.
**Browser**   Web viewing program such as Netscape or Internet Explorer.
**Buffer**   Temporary data storage.

# C

**Cache**   Temporary storage space. Browsers can store copies of the most recently visited Web pages in cache. Called Temporary Internet Files in Internet Explorer.
**Client**   Program that accesses information across a network, such as a Web browser or newsreader.
**Crack**   Break a program's security, integrity, or registration system, or fake a user ID.
**Crash**   When a program or operating system fails to respond or causes other programs to malfunction.
**Cyber**   In IRC, may be short for cybersex, that is the online equivalent of phone sex.

**Cyberspace** Coined by science-fiction writer William Gibson, to describe the virtual world that exists within the marriage of computers, telecommunication networks, and digital media.

# D

**Default** The standard settings.

**Digital signing** Encrypted data appended to a message to identify the sender.

**DNS** Domain Name System. The system that locates the numerical IP address corresponding to a host name.

**Domain** Part of the DNS name that specifies details about the host, such as its location and whether it is part of a commercial (.com), government (.gov), or educational (.edu) entity.

**Download** Retrieve a file from a host computer. Upload means to send one the other way.

**Driver** Small program that acts like a translator between a device and programs that use that device.

**DSL** Digital Subscriber Line. Encompasses all forms including ADSL. Sometimes called xDSL.

# E

**Email** Electronic mail carried on the Net.

**Email address** The unique private Internet address to which your email is sent. Takes the form user@host

# F

**FAQ** Frequently Asked Questions. Document that answers the most commonly asked questions on a particular topic.

**File** Anything stored on a computer, such as a program, image, or document.

**Finger** A program that can return stored data on UNIX users or other information such as weather updates. Often disabled for security reasons.

**Firewall**   Network security system used to restrict external and internal traffic.

**Flame**   Abusive message posted to Usenet.

**Frag**   Network gaming term meaning to destroy or fragment. Came from DOOM.

**FTP**   File Transfer Protocol. Standard method of moving files across the Internet.

# G

**GIF**   Graphic Image File format. Compressed graphics format commonly used in Web pages.

**Gopher**   Defunct menu-based system for retrieving Internet archives, usually organized by subject.

**GUI**   Graphic User Interface. Method of driving software through the use of windows, icons, menus, buttons, and other graphic devices.

# H

**Hacker**   Someone who gets off on breaking through computer security and limitations. A cracker is a criminal hacker.

**Header**   Pre-data part of a packet, containing source and destination addresses, error checking, and other fields. Also the first part of an email or news posting which contains, among other things, the sender's details and time sent.

**Home page**   Either the first page loaded by your browser at start-up, or the main Web document for a particular group, organization, or person.

**Host**   Computer that offers some sort of services to networked users.

**HTML**   HyperText Markup Language. The language used to create Web documents.

**HyperText links**   The "clickable" links or "hot-spots" that interconnect pages on the Web.

# I

**Image map**  A Web image that contains multiple links. Which link you take depends on where you click.

**IMAP**  Internet Message Access Protocol. Standard email access protocol that's superior to POP3 in that you can selectively retrieve messages or parts thereof as well as manage folders on the server.

**Instant Messaging**  Point to point chat such as ICQ.

**Internet**  A co-operatively run global collection of computer networks with a common addressing scheme.

**Internet Explorer**  Microsoft's weapon in the browser wars.

**Internet Favorites**  Internet Explorer folder that stores filed URLs.

**Internet Shortcut**  Microsoft's terminology for a URL.

**IP**  Internet Protocol. The most important protocol upon which the Internet is based. Defines how packets of data get from source to destination.

**IP address**  Every computer connected to the Internet has an IP address (written in dotted numerical notation), which corresponds to its domain name. Domain Name Servers convert one to the other.

**IRC**  Internet Relay Chat. Internet system where you can send text, or audio, to others in real time, like an online version of CB radio.

**ISDN**  Integrated Services Digital Network. International standard for digital communications over telephone lines. Allows data transmission at 64 or 128 Kbps.

**ISP**  Internet Service Provider. Company that sells access to the Internet.

# J

**Java**  Platform-independent programming language designed by Sun Microsystems. http://www.sun.com

**JPG/JPEG**  Graphic file format preferred online because its high compression reduces file size, and thus the time it takes to transfer.

# K

**Kill file**  Newsreader file into which you can enter keywords and email addresses to stop unwanted articles.

# L

**LAN**  Local Area Network. Computer network that spans a relatively small area such as an office.
**Latency**  Length of time it takes data to reach its destination.
**Leased line**  Dedicated telecommunications link between two points.
**Link**  In hypertext, as in a Web page, a link is a reference to another document. When you click on a link in a browser, that document will be retrieved and displayed, played or downloaded depending on its nature.
**Linux**  A freely distributed implementation of the UNIX operating system.
**Log on / Log in**  Connect to a computer network.
**Lycos**  Web search service at: http://www.lycos.com

# M

**MIDI**  Musical Instrument Digital Interface. Standard adopted by the electronic music industry for controlling devices such as soundcards and synthesizers. MIDI files contain synthesizer instructions rather than recorded music.
**MIME**  Multipurpose Internet Mail Extensions. Standard for the transfer of binary email attachments.
**Mirror**  Replica FTP or Web site set up to share traffic.
**Modem**  MOdulator/DEModulator. Device that allows a computer to communicate with another over a standard telephone line, by converting the digital data into analog signals and vice versa.

**MP3**  A compressed music format.
**MPEG/MPG**  A compressed video file format.
**Multithreaded**  Able to process multiple requests at once.

# N

**Name server**  Host that translates domain names into IP addresses.
**The Net**  The Internet.
**Netscape**  Web browser – and the company that produces it, now owned by AOL.
**Newbie**  Newcomer to the Net, discussion, or area.
**Newsgroups**  Usenet message areas, or discussion groups, organized by subject hierarchies.
**NNTP**  Network News Transfer Protocol. Standard for the exchange of Usenet articles across the Internet.
**Node**  Any device connected to a network.

# P

**Packet**  Unit of data. In data transfer, information is broken into packets, which then travel independently through the Net. An Internet packet contains the source and destination addresses, an identifier, and the data segment.
**Packet loss**  Failure to transfer units of data between network nodes. A high percentage makes transfer slow or impossible.
**Patch**  Temporary or interim add-on to fix or upgrade software.
**Phreaker**  Hacker of telephone systems.
**Ping**  Echo-like trace that tests if a host is available.
**Platform**  Computer operating system, such as Mac OS, Windows, or Linux.
**Plug-in**  Program that fits into another.
**POP3**  Post Office Protocol. Email protocol that allows you to pick up your mail from anywhere on the Net, even if you're connected through someone else's account.

**POPs**  Points of Presence. An ISP's range of local dial-in points.
**Portal**  Web site that specializes in leading you to others.
**Post**  To send a public message to a Usenet newsgroup.
**PPP**  Point to Point Protocol. Allows your computer to join the Internet via a modem. Each time you log in, you're allocated either a temporary or static IP address.
**Protocol**  Agreed way for two network devices to talk to each other.
**Proxy server**  Sits between a client, such as a Web browser, and a real server. Most often used to improve performance by delivering stored pages like browser cache and to filter out undesirable material.

# R

**RealAudio**  A standard for streaming compressed audio over the Internet. See: http://www.real.com
**Robot**  Program that automates Net tasks such as collating search engine databases or automatically responding in IRC. Also called a Bot.

# S

**Search engine**  Database of Web page extracts that can be queried to find reference to something on the Net.
**Server**  Computer that makes services available on a network.
**Signature file**  Personal footer that can be attached automatically to email and Usenet postings.
**SMTP**  Simple Mail Transfer Protocol. Internet protocol for transporting mail.
**Spam**  Online equivalent of junk mail. Used as both noun and verb.
**Streaming**  Delivered in real time instead of waiting for the whole file to arrive, eg RealAudio.
**Stuffit**  Common Macintosh file compression format and program.

**Surf**   Skip from page to page around the Web by following links.

# T

**TCP/IP**   Transmission Control Protocol/Internet Protocol. The protocols that drive the Internet.

**Telco**   Telephone company.

**Telnet**   Internet protocol that allows you to log on to a remote computer and act as a dumb terminal.

**Temporary Internet Files**   Internet Explorer's cache.

**Trojan (horse)**   Program that hides its true intention.

**Troll**   Prank newsgroup posting intended to invoke an irate response.

# U

**UNIX**   Operating system used by most ISPs and colleges. So long as you stick to graphic interfaces, you'll never notice it.

**URL**   Uniform Resource Locator. Formal name for a Web address.

**Usenet**   User's Network. A collection of networks and computer systems that exchange messages, organized by subject into newsgroups.

**UUencode**   Method of encoding binary files into text so that they can be attached to mail or posted to Usenet. They must be UUdecoded to convert them back. Most mail and news programs do it automatically.

# V

**Vaporware**   Rumored or announced, but non-existent, software or hardware. Often used as a competitive marketing ploy.

# W

**WAP**   Wireless Application Protocol. Internet standard for cellular phones.

**Warez**   Software, usually pirated.

**The Web**   The World Wide Web or WWW. Graphic and text documents published on the Internet that are interconnected through clickable "hypertext" links. A Web page is a single document. A Web site is a collection of related documents.

**Web authoring**   Designing and publishing Web pages using HTML.

**World Wide Web**   See Web, above.

**WYSIWYG**   What You See Is What You Get. What you type is the way it comes out.

# Y

**Yahoo**   The Web's most popular directory at:
http://www.yahoo.com

# Z

**Zip**   PC file compression format that creates files with the extension .zip using WinZip software. Commonly used to reduce file size for transfer or storage on floppy disks.

## Still confused . . .

Then try:

| | |
|---|---|
| **PC Webopedia** | http://www.webopedia.com |
| **What is?** | http://www.whatis.com |
| **Netlingo** | http://www.netlingo.com |

# 23

# Internet
# Service
# Providers

The following directory lists some major Internet Service
Providers (ISPs) in Britain, North America, Australia and
New Zealand. It's by no means complete and inclusion
shouldn't be taken as an endorsement. We've selected the larger, established providers with multiple dial-in access points, as
these are the most versatile. Still, if you only access from
home, it's possible you might get a better deal from a smaller,
local operator.

Your first priority is to find a provider with **local call
access**, preferably without paying a higher tariff for the convenience. If our list doesn't help, ask around locally, or sign
up temporarily, get online, and consult one of these **Net
directories**:

http://www.thelist.com (global)
http://www.cynosure.com.au/isp/ (Australia)
http://www.internet-magazine.com/resource/(UK)
http://www.net4nowt.com (UK)
http://www.ispcheck.com (USA)
http://www.isps.com (USA)

Unfortunately, these lists aren't so comprehensive either. Nor do they offer advice. For something more subjective, read your local **computer/Internet publications**; in the UK, for example, Internet magazine (http://www.internet-magazine.com) runs monthly performance charts. If you're still having problems, once online, try posting to the newsgroup: **alt.internet.services**

## What to ask

It's important to pick the right ISP. You want a reliable, fast connection; good customer support; and a company who'll stay in the game, so you won't need to change account or (worse) email address. The best approach is to **ask around, read magazine reviews, and see what others recommend**. If someone swears by a provider, and they seem to know what they're talking about, give it a go. That's about the best research you can do.

So if you know someone who's hooked up, ask: Is it fast and reliable? Does it ever get so slow you feel like giving up? Is it ever difficult collecting or sending mail? Do you often strike a busy tone when dialing in? What's its support like? Have you ever been overcharged?

If you're not in that boat, and have to do your own research, look for answers to the following questions – maybe by calling a few of the Freecall numbers listed in the sections following and asking for their information packs and access software. It might seem laborious but it's not as painful as being stuck with poor access.

## Broadband or modem?

The leap in speed between modem and broadband, such as ADSL, cable, apartment networks and satellite, can be astonishing. If broadband is offered in your area check it out, especially if it's reasonably priced. If you're lucky enough to have a selection of broadband options, weigh up their limitations before pouncing. The most notable issues are:

- Cable and apartment networks have to share bandwidth between neighbors, which can result in bottlenecks during peak hours.
- Satellite access comes either one-way or bi-directional. If you're offered the former you'll still need to uplink through a modem. Although it's fast, the packets have to travel long distances through space, which increases latency making it unsuitable for gaming.
- ADSL, cable, and satellite are normally asynchronous services, meaning that they'll download much faster than upload. So if you intend to run a server or share large files, make sure you understand what you're buying.

Still, pricing is likely to be the biggest determinant, in which regard they can be appraised like any other ISP.

## Free ISPs

Internet access provision is a costly business to run so you might wonder how anyone could afford to give it away. The trick is to earn the revenue from someone else. In the UK, where free Internet access has become the norm, it's quite simple – they strike up a deal with your telco and take a cut of your phone bill. This scam can only exist because of the UK's archaic metered local call system. So the longer you stay online, the more you pay. On top of this, they normally fleece by the minute for support.

If this preposterous scenario isn't insult enough, hapless Brits are now facing an intimidating and complicated array of new unmetered options. Shame about all the strings attached. You can read about them here:

http://www.unmetered.org.uk
http://www.net4nowt.com
http://www.ispreview.co.uk

Where local phone calls are unmetered or free such as in the US, Canada and Australia, the only way to turn a profit is to charge, or take commissions from, advertisers and market data hounds. To exchange your privacy for Internet access, scan the lists at:

http://www.emailaddresses.com/email_internet.htm (World)
http://www.aus3isp.com (AUS)

## Costs

If you do have to pay a fee, you'll need to break it down to see that there are no hidden charges. Consider the following:

### Can you access for the price of a local call?

Remember while you're online with a modem you're also on the phone.

### Is there a free trial?

If you can trial a service without having to install any special software you've little to lose bar the email address if you decide not to proceed.

### If not, is there a start-up cost?

You'll lose that money if you switch after the first month.

### So what's the price structure?

A no limitations, all you can eat account is preferable for moderate to high users. That way you'll know your bill in advance and you won't have to keep watching the clock. Otherwise you could be up for all sorts of permutations usually based around a monthly minimum, followed by usage charges.

### Is there a download limit?

Some, mainly broadband, ISPs charge a flat fee, with a megabyte transfer restriction. Once you hit the ceiling, you're billed extra per megabyte. Avoid this plan like the plague.

## Is it cheaper during off-peak?

Dropping rates over the weekends and nights might sound like a good deal, but with everyone scrambling online at once, you'll face busy lines and sluggish networks.

# The basics

## Do they offer free phone support? What are the hours?

Free phone support until the mid-evenings is standard fare. But a few ISPs, most notably the free UK outfits, charge by the minute for their pleasure. Chances are you will strike problems, you will be on the phone to them, and you won't want to wait until Monday morning. Factor that into your calculations.

## Will you get one or more POP3 email addresses?

A recent trend amongst cheapskate providers is to issue a Webmail account in lieu of a proper POP3 address. This is rarely a satisfactory alternative. Sure, you can collect Webmail from any computer, but you can do the same with POP3 through free services like **Mail2Web** (http://www.mail2web.com). You'd even be better off with a free third party Webmail account (p.118) – one you won't lose if you switch providers. But a POP3 account is preferable, or even better, multiple POP3 addresses. Then you can keep separate addresses for different types of mail, and dish out an address or two to family and friends.

## Is your name available?

You always have the option to choose the first part of your email address. You might like to use your first name or nickname. This will then be attached to the provider's host name. Check if your name's available and what the host name would be. The trouble with bigger providers is that most common names will already be taken. You really don't want an address like: John3434@aol.com

## Does it run a Usenet server? If so, which groups does it carry?

Usenet has more than 60,000 groups and it's still growing. That's 95 percent more than you'll ever want to look at in your lifetime. Most providers carry only a portion, but it's still usually over 15,000. The first ones to be axed are often foreign language, country specific, provider specific, and the adult (alt.sex and alt.binaries) series. If you particularly want certain groups, your provider can usually add them, but it may have a policy against certain material. If it says no to Usenet, keep shopping.

## Does it throw in some free Web space?

Most ISPs include a few megabytes of storage free so you can publish your own Web page. In general, if you go over that megabyte limit there'll be an excess charge. Again like Webmail, you might be better off with one of the free Webspace providers (p.254), so you don't lose your home page if you switch. That said, if the ISP offers a page free of pop-up banners or adverts with an attractive address it might be worth considering. Don't make it a decider though.

## Do it have or offer national or global roaming and how is it charged?

If you travel a lot it's handy to know you can still get connected, though if it comes at a high price it may not be worth it. See "On the Road" (p.260) for more details.

## Does it go on about its content?

Your priority is to get fast reliable Internet access. Forget about local content such as news and chat rooms. There's more than enough on the greater Net.

## Apart from Internet access, what else does it offer?

While your first priority should be to get fast reliable Internet access, see what else you can get with the deal, either as part of the bundle or as an added extra.

# Is it fast and reliable?

## How long has it been in business, who owns the company, and how many subscribers does it have?

It helps to know with whom you're dealing. Big operators may offer certain advantages such as national and even global dial-up points, security, guaranteed access, stability, and close proximity to the high-speed backbone. However, they can be slow to upgrade because of high overheads and may have dim support staff. Small, younger providers can be more flexible, have newer equipment, more in-tune staff, cheaper rates, and faster access, but conversely may lack the capital to make future critical upgrades. There aren't any rules; it's a new industry and all a bit of a long-term gamble.

## Which backbones do you connect to, and at what speed?

Backbones are the high-speed longhaul connections that carry Internet traffic between ISPs and around the globe. A good ISP should tell you which backbone it uses and how big its connections are – or even provide a map of its backbone links around the world. Be suspicious of any ISP that can't answer this question. Better ISPs connect to more than one ISP – a practice called multi-homing. This means they're not bound to one route and can thus choose the fastest connection per request.
For more about backbones including the current state of traffic, see: http://www.cybergeography.org and http://www.mids.org/weather/

## What is its maximum user to modem ratio?

The lower this ratio, the less chance you'll strike a busy tone when you call. As a yardstick, anything over 10:1 should start sounding warning bells that they're under-equipped.

## Can it support your modem type and speed?

Modems like talking to their own kind. When modems aren't happy with each other, they connect at a slower rate.

It's not much use if your 56K X2 modem can only connect at 33.6 Kbps. Ask what connection speeds they support. If it's incompatible, or lower than your modem's top speed, look elsewhere.

## Getting started

### Can they supply you with a sheet of clear setup instructions for your system?

If you're running Windows 98+/NT/2000, an iMac or a Mac running OS 8.5, you already have the software, you only need the configuration settings and a little guidance filling them out. Unless you're running an older system, or hooking up broadband, avoid any provider that insists you have to install their special connection software. Nothing will muck up your system faster than meddlesome ISP-ware. Assure them that as soon as you get online you intend to download the latest version of Internet Explorer. If they have a problem with that, take a hike.

# INTERNATIONAL ISPs

Most ISPs operate in only one country (or the US and Canada). For truly international access, if you plan to use the Net on your travels (see "On The Road" – p.260), consider one of the following. Most charge extra outside your local area.

| Provider | Web address | Points of Presence |
|---|---|---|
| AOL | http://www.aol.com | Worldwide |
| AT&T Business | http://www.ibm.net | Worldwide |
| CompuServe | http://www.compuserve.com | Worldwide |
| EUNet Traveller | http://traveller.eu.net | Europe, roaming |
| Microsoft Network | http://www.msn.com | UK, US, Japan |

# NORTH AMERICA

| Provider<br>Web address | Telephone number<br>Points of Presence |
|---|---|
| @Home (Cable) | See Web page |
| http://www.home.com | USA, Canada, Netherlands, Australia |
| AT&T Canada | 1-888-655-7671 |
| http://www.attcanada.ca | Canada |
| AT&T WorldNet (Cable) | 1 800 967 5363 |
| http://www.att.net | USA |
| Bell Atlantic (DSL) | 1 800 422 3555 |
| http://www.bellatlantic.net | USA |
| Concentric Networks (DSL) | 1 800 939 4262 |
| http://www.concentric.net | USA, Canada |
| EarthLink (DSL) | 1 800 EARTH LINK |
| http://www.earthlink.com | USA, Canada |
| Flashcom (DSL) | 1 877 FLASHCOM |
| http://www.flashcom.com | USA |
| GTE Internet (DSL) | 1 888 GTE NET1 |
| http://www.gte.net | USA |
| iStar | 1 888 GO ISTAR |
| http://www.istar.ca | Canada |
| NetZero (Free) | 1 818 879 7250 |
| http://www.netzero.com | USA |
| Prodigy (DSL) | 1 800 213 0992 |
| http://www.prodigy.com | USA |

# BRITAIN

| Provider | Telephone number | Web Address |
| --- | --- | --- |
| BT Internet | 0800 800 001 | http://www.btinternet.com |
| CIX | 020 8255 5050 | http://www.cix.net.uk |
| Demon Internet | 020 8371 1234 | http://www.demon.net |
| Direct Connection | 0800 072 0000 | http://www.dircon.net |
| Easynet | 020 7681 4444 | http://www.easynet.co.uk |
| Freeserve★ | 0870 901 6000 | http://www.freeserve.com |
| Gemsoft | 0114 275 7070 | http://www.gemsoft.net |
| LineOne★ | 0906 302 0100 | http://www.lineone.net |
| Netcom | 0870 5668008 | http://www.netcom.net.uk |
| NTL Internet★ | 0800 183 1234 | http://www.ntl.com |
| Screaming.Net★ | 0800 376 5262 | http://www.screaming.net |
| UUNet (Pipex Dial) | 0500 474 739 | http://www.uk.uu.net |
| Virgin Net★ | 0500 558 844 | http://www.virgin.net |

★ Free or unmetered service.

# AUSTRALIA

| Provider | Telephone number | Web address |
| --- | --- | --- |
| AAPT | 138 888 | http://www.smartchat.net.au |
| AT&T | 1300 307 005 | http://www.attbusiness.net |
| Austar ★ | 132 432 | http://www.austar.com.au |
| Connect | 1800 818 262 | http://www.connect.com.au |
| Dingo Blue | 1300 551 455 | http://www.dingoblue.com.au |
| Internet Primus | 1300 303 081 | http://www.primus.com.au |
| One.Net | 1300 303 312 | http://www.one.net.au |

**Optus Internet★** ...... 1300 301 325 ... http://www.optusnet.com.au

**Ozemail** ....................... 132 884 ........ http://www.ozemail.com.au

**Telstra Big Pond★** ... 1800 804 282 ... http://www.bigpond.com.au

★ Offers broadband services.

# NEW ZEALAND

| Provider | Telephone number | Web address |
| --- | --- | --- |
| **Clear Net** ................ | 0508 888 800 ........ | http://www.clear.net.nz |
| **Telecom XTRA** ..... | 0800 22 55 98 .......... | http://www.xtra.co.nz |
| **Voyager** .................... | 0800 869 243 ...... | http://www.voyager.co.nz |

# 24

# 51 things to do with this book

You're on the Net, so where now? Has it all been worth the effort? Here, in no particular order, are 51 ways to idle away your online time. Just key in the Web address or go to the page in this book for instructions.

1.  **Look yourself up on the Web**
    http://www.google.com

2.  **Re-ignite an old flame**
    See p.178

3.  **Deactivate an alien implant**
    See p.378

4.  **Get fresh with the US President**
    http://www.whitehouse.gov

5. **Go undercover**
   See p.120 & p.193

6. **Dig up dirt on a movie star**
   See p.324

7. **Flirt with a stranger**
   See p.188

8. **Land a cushy job**
   See p.318

9. **Cast a voodoo spell**
   http://www.vudutuu.com

10. **Join a kooky cult**
    See p.400 and p.432

11. **Kick butt**
    See p.232

12. **Tune in to foreign radio**
    See p.391

13. **Work from the Bahamas**
    See p.260

14. **Rekindle your childhood interests**
    See p.129 and p.163

15. **Make your first billion**
    See p.356

16. **Get fanatical about football**
    See p.412

17. **Relocate to Mars**
    http://www.marsshop.com

18. **Confirm you're mad**
http://www.mentalhealth.com

19. **Plot an exotic adventure**
See p.422

20. **Cast no doubt on your ancestry**
See p.384

21. **Become a whiz with nuclear arms**
See p.406

22. **Cheat your way through college**
See p.396

23. **Stock up on frilly bras**
See p.321

24. **Keep up with your hometown gossip**
See p.373

25. **Stare into deep space**
See p.409

26. **Cook up a treat**
See p.331

27. **Toilet-train your cat**
See p.437

28. **Secretly watch sport at work**
See p.412

29. **Nab your crushed one**
http://www.secretadmirer.com

30. **Never lose an argument**
See p.129 and p.163

31. **Track down a killer novel**
See p.305

32. **Build your own computer**
See p.315

33. **Seek legal advice**
See p.354

34. **Obey the Interplanetary Council**
See p.432

35. **Eavesdrop on a drug bust**
http://www.policescanner.com

36. **Clone a companion**
http://www.clonaid.com

37. **Start your own magazine**
See p.239

38. **Sort out your weeds**
See p.346

39. **Show off your baby snaps**
See p.111 and p.303

40. **Consult a mad scientist**
http://www.madsci.org

41. **Become a minister of the Universal Life Church**
See p.404

42. **Indulge in hypochondria**
http://www.diagnosticdoc.com

43. **Learn how to be cool**
http://www.geocities.com/SunsetStrip/4160/big.html

44. **Torment a teen idol**
    See p.327

45. **Start an argument**
    See p.124 and p.129

46. **Sit in on a live gig**
    http://www.liveconcerts.com

47. **Master your own music compilation CD**
    See p.365

48. **Disappear with the Foreign Legion**
    http://www.specialoperations.com

49. **Strike up a bargain**
    See p.201

50. **Email a smoochy tune**
    See p.112

51. **Admit you now have a problem**
    http://www.internetaddiction.com

*Got a favorite site or activity on the Net?*
*Then let us know by email at:*
*angus@easynet.co.uk*

# Index

# Feedback

This guide has already helped more than 3 million people online since 1995, many of whom have written back with suggestions. I'm grateful for this feedback as it makes the job of keeping it up to date and useful so much easier.

You're now holding the sixth edition. That means it's been written six times. And each time it needs a major overhaul. That's how much the Internet changes each year. Sites disappear, addresses change, and things that are hot suddenly go cold. Under these conditions it's nearly impossible to be entirely accurate. So if you find errors, I'd like to know.

Being such a popular book means it's spawned many imitators, which you'll no doubt see on the shelves alongside it. Please compare this guide to those, and if you feel they do a better job, then write to me and tell me where I've gone wrong. I will read your mail and respect your advice.

If you feel we've cheated you out of your money, you can get even by giving this book a scathing review at one of the online bookstores (see p.305).

Angus Kennedy:
angus@easynet.co.uk

# Rough Guides
## on the Web

### www.travel.roughguides.com

We keep getting bigger and better! The Rough Guide to Travel Online
now covers more than 14,000 searchable locations. You're just a click
away from access to the most in-depth travel content, weekly
destination features, online reservation services, and an outspoken
community of fellow travelers. Whether you're looking for ideas for
your next holiday or you know exactly where you're going, join us online.

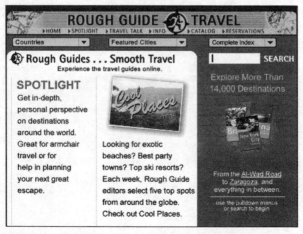

You can also find us on Yahoo!® Travel (http://travel.yahoo.com) and
Microsoft Expedia® UK (http://www.expediauk.com).

# Stay in touch with us!

ROUGHNEWS is Rough Guides' free newsletter.
In four issues a year we give you news, travel issues, music reviews, readers' letters and the latest dispatches from authors on the road.

I would like to receive ROUGHNEWS: please put me on your free mailing list.

NAME . . . . . . . . . . . . . . . . . . . . . . . . . . . . . . . . . . . . . . . . . . . . . . . . . . . . . . .

ADDRESS . . . . . . . . . . . . . . . . . . . . . . . . . . . . . . . . . . . . . . . . . . . . . . . . . . . . . . .

Please clip or photocopy and send to: Rough Guides, 62-70 Shorts Gardens, London WC2H 9AH, England

or Rough Guides, 375 Hudson Street, New York, NY 10014, USA.

# ROUGH GUIDES: Travel

# ROUGH GUIDES: Mini Guides, Travel Specials and Phrasebooks

**MINI GUIDES**

Antigua
Bangkok
Barbados
Big Island of Hawaii
Boston
Brussels
Budapest
Dublin
Edinburgh
Florence
Honolulu
Lisbon
London Restaurants
Madrid
Maui
Melbourne
New Orleans
St Lucia

Seattle
Sydney
Tokyo
Toronto

**TRAVEL SPECIALS**

First-Time Asia
First-Time Europe
More Women Travel

**PHRASEBOOKS**

Czech
Dutch
Egyptian Arabic
European
French

German
Greek
Hindi & Urdu
Hungarian
Indonesian
Italian
Japanese
Mandarin Chinese
Mexican Spanish
Polish
Portuguese
Russian
Spanish
Swahili
Thai
Turkish
Vietnamese

AVAILABLE AT ALL GOOD BOOKSHOPS

# ROUGH GUIDES:
# Reference and Music CDs

**REFERENCE**
Classical Music
Classical:
  100 Essential CDs
Drum'n'bass
House Music

World Music:
  100 Essential CDs
English Football
European Football
Internet
Millennium

**ROUGH GUIDE
MUSIC CDs**
Music of the Andes
Australian
  Aboriginal
Brazilian Music
Cajun & Zydeco
Classic Jazz
Music of Colombia
Cuban Music
Eastern Europe
Music of Egypt
English Roots
  Music
Flamenco
India & Pakistan
Irish Music
Music of Japan
Kenya & Tanzania
Native American
North African
Music of Portugal

Jazz
Music USA
Opera
Opera:
  100 Essential CDs
Reggae
Rock
Rock:
  100 Essential CDs
Techno
World Music

Reggae
Salsa
Scottish Music
South African
  Music
Music of Spain
Tango
Tex-Mex
West African Music
World Music
World Music Vol 2
Music of Zimbabwe

AVAILABLE AT ALL GOOD BOOKSHOPS